Global Borderlands

SERIES EDITORS:
IGNACIO MARTINEZ, LESLIE WATERS, SAMUEL BRUNK

MEXICAN AMERICANS IN WEST TEXAS

THE BORDERLANDS OF THE EDWARDS PLATEAU AND THE TRANS-PECOS

ARNOLDO DE LEÓN

TEXAS TECH UNIVERSITY PRESS

This book is typeset in EB Garamond. The paper used in this book meets the minimum requirements of ANSI/NISO Z39.48-1992 (R1997). ♾

Designed by Hannah Gaskamp
Cover designed by Hannah Gaskamp

Library of Congress Cataloging-in-Publication Data

Names: De León, Arnoldo, 1945– author. Title: Mexican Americans in West Texas: The Borderlands of the Edwards Plateau and the Trans-Pecos / Arnoldo De León. Other titles: Borderlands of the Edwards Plateau and the Trans-Pecos | Global Borderlands.
Description: Lubbock, Texas: Texas Tech University Press, [2023] | Series: Global Borderlands | Includes bibliographical references and index. | Summary: "A synthesis of published accounts on the history of Mexican Americans in the Edwards Plateau and the Trans-Pecos region of Texas"—Provided by publisher.
Identifiers: LCCN 2023016812 (print) | LCCN 2023016813 (ebook) |
ISBN 978-1-68283-189-2 (cloth) | ISBN 978-1-68283-190-8 (ebook)
Subjects: LCSH: Mexican Americans—Texas, West—History. | Mexican-American Border Region—History. | Texas, West—History.
Classification: LCC E184.M5 D397 2023 (print) |
LCC E184.M5 (ebook) | DDC 973.046872073—dc23/eng/20230414
LC record available at https://lccn.loc.gov/2023016812
LC ebook record available at https://lccn.loc.gov/2023016813

Printed in the United States of America

23 24 25 26 27 28 29 30 31 / 9 8 7 6 5 4 3 2 1

Texas Tech University Press
Box 41037
Lubbock, Texas 79409-1037 USA
800.832.4042
ttup@ttu.edu
www.ttupress.org

To the staff at the West Texas Collection, Angelo State University,
especially Shannon Sturm and Erin Johnson

CONTENTS

PREFACE

DESCRIPTION OF PLACE

This overview of Mexican Americans in West Texas gives primary attention to a borderlands area spanning the counties of the Edwards Plateau and the Trans-Pecos region. For the sake of convenience, I have taken the liberty to demarcate the Edwards Plateau as extending from just past the Hill Country counties of Mason, Gillespie, Kerr, and Bandera, ranging from there to approximately the Pecos River but also embracing the conterminous subregion that geographers correctly identify as the Permian Basin. I honor the conventional definition of the Trans-Pecos region, treating it as beginning at the Pecos River and heading west to Hudspeth County, the farthest reach of this study.[1] I omitted El Paso County for several reasons. First, the county and the city of El Paso have their own historians so that coverage of Tejanos there, while still in need of further investigation, has not been bypassed. Second, scholarly publications on El Paso so preponderate over coverage given to the Edwards Plateau and Trans-Pecos regions that incorporating their contents would have meant distracting—and diverting attention—from the focus of my research: to wit, those counties that have been neglected and merit their own histories. Last, I perceived a number of features separating El Paso County from the Edwards Plateau and Trans-Pecos: time delineations, the different economic and political paths El Paso took, and even the makeup of its population (El Paso has always been predominantly Hispanic).

TIME PERIODS

Regarding timelines specific to this region, I discern Tejano history (the history of Mexican Americans in Texas) to have unfolded in spans of about twenty years, at least after 1880. In the period up to 1880, pioneers from Mexico crossed the

Edwards Plateau and Trans-Pecos Counties

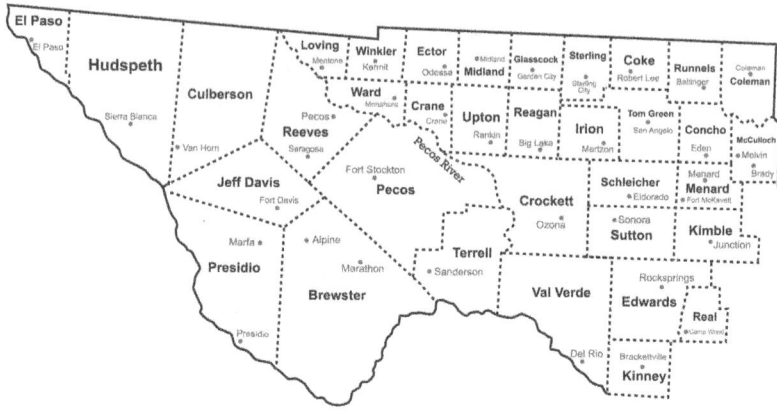

El Paso
El Paso
Hudspeth
Culberson
Sierra Blanca
Reeves
Van Horn
Saragosa
Jeff Davis
Fort Davis
Marfa
Presidio
Brewster
Presidio
Alpine
Marathon
Loving
Mentone
Winkler
Kermit
Ward
Monahans
Pecos
Fort Stockton
Pecos
Ector
Odessa
Crane
Crane
Midland
Midland
Glasscock
Garden City
Sterling
Sterling City
Coke
Robert Lee
Runnels
Ballinger
Coleman
Coleman
Upton
Rankin
Reagan
Big Lake
Irion
Mertzon
Tom Green
San Angelo
Concho
Eden
McCulloch
Melvin
Brady
Crockett
Ozona
Schleicher
Eldorado
Sonora
Sutton
Menard
Menard
Fort McKavett
Kimble
Junction
Terrell
Sanderson
Val Verde
Del Rio
Rocksprings
Edwards
Camp Wood
Real
Brackettville
Kinney

Map drawn for the author courtesy of: Alexis Scott

Rio Grande and founded small settlements in the lower Big Bend and, following the arrival of Anglo Americans (and joining them in the building of military stations during the 1850s and after the Civil War), became co-agents in community building and in bringing political and economic stabilization to what was then the domain of Indigenous peoples.

During the last two decades of the nineteenth century, the region entered a modern age, kindling an influx of new Anglo settlers, causing the creation and organization of new counties, stimulating the growth of towns (and the birth of new ones, among them Alpine, Marfa, Marathon, Odessa, and Sonora), and prompting developers to modernize the West Texas infrastructure. These transformational forces acted to overturn gains made in earlier years and to debilitate the Tejanos' previous standing in West Texas society. Despite the circumstances, ethnic Mexicans during the early years of the twentieth century continued consolidating communities and securing for themselves a permanent place in the West Texas realm.

Entering the twentieth century, West Texas made advances that furthered regional progress. Economically, it saw the expansion of the sheep and goat industries and, in the Big Bend area, the expansion of quicksilver mining. Demographically, West Texas became increasingly Anglo dominant. Frontier towns such as San Angelo and Del Rio eased into modernity and places like

Alpine and Fort Stockton stabilized, as did Midland and Odessa. With the "whitening" of West Texas came an escalation in the capricious treatment of Mexicans, manifest in two major cases of lynching and in retribution taken for raids upon Texas settlements during the Mexican Revolution of 1910. Notwithstanding their minority status and increased Anglo control over them, Mexicans established a measure of regularity in their lives by working in whatever capacity sustained life and practicing old means of survival—or devising new ones—that reinforced efforts at community perseverance. Cognizant of Anglo society's disdain for them, individuals and communities still stepped forward to demonstrate allegiance to country during World War I.

Between 1920 and 1945, West Texas retained its dependence on ranching but embraced new ventures, among them dry-land farming and, more conspicuously, the petroleum industry. Persistent in-migration from the United States and Europe continued giving Anglo Americans a population edge over Mexicans arriving from Mexico or parts of the Texas interior. The Great Depression of the 1930s brought disruption to the region, affecting Mexican-descent inhabitants with threats of repatriation and deportation. World War II (1941–1945) similarly imposed on Tejano communities for men to volunteer for service or make themselves available for the draft. Ironically, the depression era helped Americanize young men recruited for work in New Deal programs such as the Civilian Conservation Corps (CCC) while World War II rallied Mexican American communities in West Texas (as it did elsewhere) to the cause of democracy and freedom. Overall, West Texas *colonias mexicanas* during the 1920–1945 era became settings where residents identified culturally with both their American and Mexican heritages. Speaking for some communities during this period were US-shaped organizations such as the League of United Latin American Citizens (LULAC).

Past World War II and into the 1960s, the West Texas region made greater advances than ever. It survived the great drought of the 1950s to remain a center for cattle and sheep raising and, in some sections, a hub for irrigated farming. A lucrative oil business stimulated the mercantile, banking, manufacturing, and service sectors. People gave way and acceded to and indeed encouraged some of the newer developments spreading across the nation. Like other sections of the state, West Texas acquiesced to the transformation occurring in race relations during the 1960s, retreating from the harsher practices of Jim Crow. Tejanos, for their part, negotiated their way through changing currents, savoring, as did other

West Texans, the postwar culture. West Texas Tejano communities expanded, invigorated now by both Mexican American arrivals and transnationals from Mexico. In the years of the 1960s, Mexican Americans launched new fronts in the battle for political equality.

Since the 1970s, and certainly into the twenty-first century, West Texas has made headway matching developments elsewhere in the state. For all intents and purposes, it has kept pace with urbanization and with the sophistication of the larger metropolises. Once detached from the rest of the country, West Texas in modern times is in step nationally with prevailing cultural trends and political currents. For Mexican Americans in West Texas, the era encouraged greater political participation, expressed in latter decades of the twentieth century through militancy and more recently through coalition politics. Persistent immigration accompanied by natural reproduction transformed West Texas into a borderland populated increasingly by ethnic Mexicans. Change and proactive measures taken for the right to be coparticipants in West Texas society produced visible successes, manifested in the presence of women and men in political posts (ranging from justices of the peace to city mayors), high-level managerial positions in business, and important offices in the field of education.

WEST TEXAS AND BORDERLANDS HISTORIOGRAPHY

How Mexican Americans forged a place of their own in West Texas over time closely resembled the manner in which other Mexicans crossed the international border and successfully established similar borderlands communities, in both Texas and different parts of the nation. The processes undergone in such implantations are informed in the historiography of borderlands and regional studies and, mindful that West Texas was its own borderlands, I apply in this addition to borderlands literature those interpretive insights and approaches in highlighting the course of community building in West Texas.[2] Such perspectives constitute tenets of the scholarship on "Tejano history," and this monograph is a complement to that field.[3]

In underscoring the many ways in which West Texas Tejano community establishment resembled the course of borderlands community founding elsewhere, I give attention to processes such as in-migration, implantation, adaptation, cultural interaction, identity formation, and stability. Transnational forces (of both a push and pull nature) certainly lay behind settler movements north from Mexico and remained as causes in migrants' decisions to occupy West

Texas. Behind initial trailblazing that led to community building in West Texas was Mexico's efforts during the 1830s to explore and claim lands north of the long-standing settlement of La Junta de los Ríos (modern-day Ojinaga). Episodes such as the Mexican Revolution and factors such as poverty drove desperate people to cross the international border and seek a new start in Texas. Resulting from these transnational incursions was, as in the case of other borderlands zones, the creation of a mixed American and Mexican preserve. The hand that Mexicans had in shaping West Texas is evident in enduring architectural housing patterns, methods of stock raising, farm work techniques, and cultural persistence.

In borderlands studies, areas such as West Texas become zones of cultural interaction wherein people of different backgrounds (be they race or place of origin) at various historical moments work peacefully for the common cause of securing community stability and erecting needed social, economic, and political institutions. Accommodation between Mexicans and Anglos—who arrived in the Big Bend in the years before the Civil War to shape it in a form resembling the rest of the American empire—was the order of the day until the 1880s as both people cooperated to fend off hostile forces, namely Indian attacks. The era of accommodation before the 1880s involved political alliances, economic ties among landholders, and interethnic marriages, although coexistence persisted in particular spots, such as in the volatile Big Bend, into the early twentieth century. There in hamlets such as Lajitas and Hot Springs, alliances of convenience remained as Mexicans relied on special skills Anglos possessed (perhaps as teachers or health providers) while the Anglo minority depended on Mexicans for protection against Mexican revolutionaries.

Typical of other borderlands, the Edwards Plateau and Trans-Pecos region became grounds where—at times almost simultaneous with accommodation—the main actors engaged in contentious encounters. Mexicans in sporadic cases threatened harm upon Anglo Americans, such as in frontier days of the late nineteenth century: in 1882, for instance, they prepared to drive out Anglo Americans from Murphyville (Alpine). Then, during the years of the Mexican Revolution (1910–1920), they launched counterattacks against Anglo atrocities such as were committed in Porvenir (January 1918). They made up part of the retribution party that attacked the Neville Ranch (March 1918). But it is generally Anglo Americans whom borderlands studies often find perpetrating acts of violence against Mexicans: variously, in the form of lynching, terror campaigns, or pathological attacks to control and marginalize them. Anglo contempt for

Mexicans was further manifest in subtle, yet harmful, ways, such as in institutionalized acts of discrimination and stigmatization.

Accommodation and conflict could not help but shape the identity of Mexicans in West Texas, much as these processes do in other borderlands. On the one hand, accommodation permitted people space, autonomy, and occasion to continue carrying on old customs and traditions. On the other hand, pernicious acts of violence and malicious expressions of hostility towards them disposed Mexicans to resist Anglo ways. Within Mexican enclaves, therefore, the Spanish language remained entrenched, the faithful attended churches of their own (whether Catholic or Protestant), and celebrations of both secular and religious nature remained as commemorated in Mexico. Such Mexican identity was to be found in analogous borderlands.

At the same time, the dominant culture weighed on all, imposing on *lo mexicano* and reconstructing identity. "*Lo Americano*," of course, encroached on Mexicans early on, but the syncretism of cultures hastened as mainstream Anglo life penetrated the barrios and *colonias* or Mexican themselves absorbed the ethos of the larger society in recognition of the need to adjust and conform. Hybridity produced in the Edwards Plateau and Trans-Pecos individuals proficient as English speakers (actually bilingual) able to move effectively between Mexican and American settings, consumers accepting of American tastes (including foods, fashion, and music), and community leaders preferring to use LULAC instead of ad hoc clubs (as they had earlier) for purposes of obtaining political entitlements.

Scholars note that while culture is refashioned, either by historical forces or by individual or group intent, inhabitants in borderlands communities nonetheless prioritize national identity over loyalty to their own ethnicity. A sense of belonging to an environment that was indisputably "American," residence there for years, and interaction with mainstream institutions all tended to dilute Tejano West Texans' connection to the old country and shift allegiance to the United States. While immigrants crossing the Rio Grande after the Mexican Revolution years might have remained patriotically "Mexican," and while into modern times, Mexican-descent people celebrate Diez y Seis de Septiembre and Cinco de Mayo, there is no question that almost all unconditionally owed allegiance to the United States. Many would be the occasions in which Mexicans in the Edwards Plateau and Trans-Pecos would overtly display this fidelity to country, if not in Fourth of July celebrations, then certainly during wars, including World War I, World War II, Vietnam, and more recently Middle East conflicts.

In studying the borderlands, historians acknowledge regions to have their own dynamics, their singularities producing divergent results for inhabitants. Here in this work, I finalize each chapter by illustrating how historical experiences in the West Texas borderlands varied to some degree from those of the South Texas borderlands. Several forces specific to each region caused historical variation. Military garrisons guarded the western frontier until the 1880s while no similar fortifications protected the trans-Nueces. The settlement of the West Texas region came later than it did in South Texas and town-building, undertaken mainly after the Civil War, developed haltingly into the twentieth century. Parts of West Texas, most prominently the lower Big Bend, even resembled a frontier, at least until around 1920. West Texas remained true to ranching—raising cattle, sheep, and goats until the early 1900s—while South Texas banked its economic future on cotton. Until after World War II, West Texas remained lightly populated, with Anglos in many counties holding a demographic edge over Mexican-descent inhabitants; the opposite held true for South Texas, where Mexicans predominated.

Further affecting divergent experiences in the two borderlands was physical environment. West Texas is range country marked by aridity and a harsh topography that alternates between brush lands, plateaus, desert terrain, and rugged mountain ranges. Comparatively, South Texas is farmland, favored with fecund soils and generous rainfall. West Texas expansiveness, and by extension its spaciousness and remoteness, set it apart from the more compact concentration of settlements common in South Texas.

Borderlands scholars have as well been cognizant that bonding to a geographic region influences self-perceptions. Tejanos found in West Texas's aura of the US West a sense of cultural affinity, belonging, and meaning. Like their Anglo neighbors, Mexican Americans over time came to consider themselves as "West Texans." Their experience fostered the sentiment that they had their own history and instilled upon them an awareness that being a West Texan was to be somehow distinguishable from Mexican Americans living in South Texas and elsewhere. There is, of course, no significant departure in experiences, yet Mexican Americans in West Texas proudly proclaim themselves to be "*de wes' Texas.*"

WEST TEXAS IN REGIONAL PERSPECTIVE

Borderlands studies, of course, do not restrict themselves to particular places such as the Rio Grande corridor. A growing body of scholarship demonstrates

that people from Mexico and areas once considered by old histories as "the borderlands" (that is, pre-1848 Spain-Mexico possessions) have migrated interstate
to found rural (and urban) communities in other parts of the country.[4] The
processes associated with community formation in areas such as West Texas—
among them implantation, accommodation, Anglo racism, identity modifica-
tion, persistence, and stability—also shaped the histories of what became socially
and culturally vibrant regional homelands in almost all American states.[5]

TERMINOLOGY

Regarding labels, I use several to reference people of Mexican heritage. I incline
towards "Mexicans," "Tejanos," and "Mexicanos" (Spanish for Mexicans) to
identify Mexican-origin or Mexican-descent subjects (whether native or foreign born) who have lived in Texas since the seventeenth century. I turn to
"Texas-Mexicans" and "Mexican Americans" once getting past 1845, the year in
which West Texas became part of the Lone Star State (although I posit "Mexican
Americans" to have possessed citizenship). The word "Chicano" I restrict mainly
to the 1960s–1970s era when some segments of the Mexican American population adopted the term as an expression of ethnic pride connecting them (as
Mexican Americans) to their Mexican (including their pre-Columbian) background. The terms "Hispanic" and "Latino" appear in the book once the discussion gets past the decade of the 1970s—it was then that the two labels entered
the national discourse to designate people of Spanish Mexican descent. The
applications of "Anglos" and "Anglo Americans" identify people in the larger
population who socially and popularly are regarded as "white."

ACKNOWLEDGMENTS

Many were the professionals who helped me as I researched this overview of Mexican Americans in the West Texas borderlands. At the Porter Henderson Library at Angelo State University, personnel in the Circulation Unit ensured that I acquired essential books and articles through interlibrary loan. I am especially indebted to the staff members at the West Texas Collection (WTC) at Angelo State University, namely Shannon Sturm and Erin Johnson, who cheerfully aided me in my every call for assistance, whether it was for materials in the WTC's closed stacks or for help in negotiating my away around pertinent websites.

MEXICAN AMERICANS IN WEST TEXAS

CHAPTER 1

ENTRADAS, ACCOMMODATION, AND IMPLANTATION TO 1880

ENTRADAS

Until about the early decades of the seventeenth century, the area of what is today the Edwards Plateau and the Trans-Pecos remained the province of Indigenous groups. European nations found little of attraction in the region; since the late sixteenth century the interests of Spaniards, the main colonizers in what would become the US West, had been on what is modern-day New Mexico.[1]

Then, in 1629, Jumano Indians, natives to the Big Bend region, traveled to New Mexico to ask the priests assigned there for continued religious teaching, having been visited, they said, by a Christian figure they called the "Lady in Blue." History knows the Lady in Blue as María de Jesús de Ágreda, a Spanish nun who by miraculous bilocation voyaged to what is now New Mexico and western Texas to spread the gospel among the Indians. Responding to the Jumanos' appeals, Catholic missionaries trekked to western Texas in 1629 and then again in 1632 and introduced Christian doctrine to potential converts. Due to other pressing issues the Spanish crown faced in overseeing its New World empire, the Church for decades suspended work in West Texas.[2]

Attention to western Texas resumed in 1683 when a man named Juan Sabeata, speaking for the Jumanos, appeared in the El Paso area asking for religious education for his people at La Junta de los Ríos (La Junta)—the junction of the Río Conchos and the Rio Grande. Missionaries responded to Sabeata's

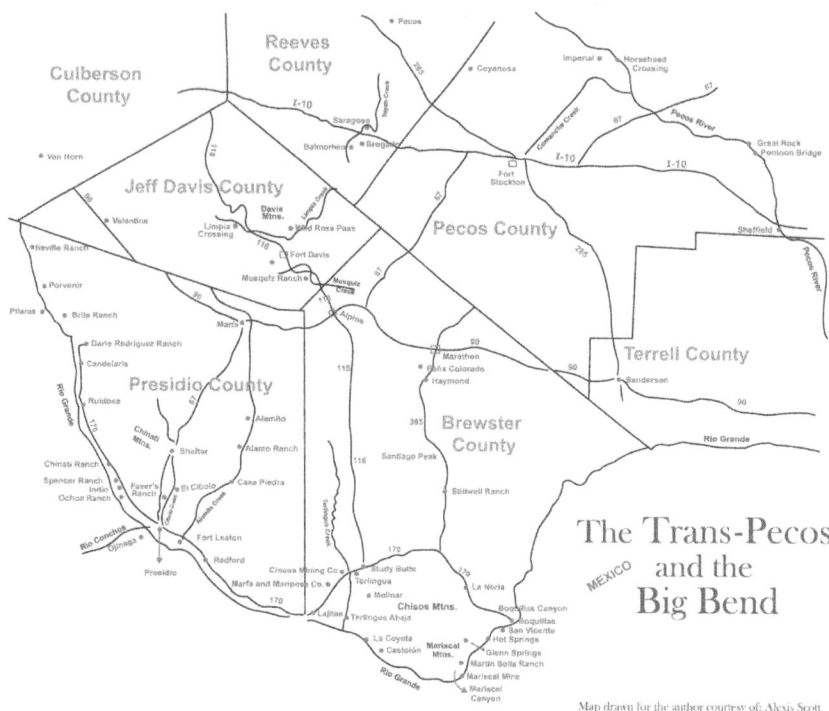

Map drawn for the author courtesy of: Alexis Scott

appeals, traveling there and remaining among the Jumanos for an extended time. Meanwhile, Spanish authorities dispatched a military force to greater West Texas, entrusting it with searching for pearls, enlightening Indian peoples on the proper behavior towards the friars proselyting among them, and with seeking possibilities for trade opportunities. Explorations took the troops throughout parts of West Texas, and ultimately expeditionary leaders made recommendations to royal authorities for the occupation of those lands. But concerns over French activity in eastern Texas took precedence over the settlement of the western hinterlands. The Spaniards would return to La Junta in the early 1770s.[3]

It was in 1773 that New Spain located a presidio at a point on the Rio Grande at La Junta de los Ríos. Its assignment was to establish Spanish sovereignty by laying claim to this far-off land and to guard the frontier against hostile agents. At the same time, it was to protect the friars working among the local Indian population, resident civilians, and pioneers starting up farms and ranches in the surrounding lands. The settlement grew into a community to the point that over time it spread across the Rio Grande into today's Texas.[4]

Like other people on the hinterland, the *pobladores* (settlers) at La Junta coped with adversities endemic to frontier living. They faced off against dreaded diseases such as smallpox and cholera. They worked around conditions caused by primitive sanitation practices while enduring food shortages, inadequate housing, and inattention from bureaucrats in the interior.[5] Many of the colonists, however, had brought with them a familiarity with the travail that attended frontier living. They countered the uninviting nature of the hinterlands with survival lessons passed on to them by their mestizo forebears, most of whom were veterans of colonization initiatives in distant lands.

The settlers' aim most times was simple perseverance. Sheltering loved ones took priority and they improvised at lodging. As important as providing refuge was gaining access to water. The transplanted colonists had enough knowledge of frontier living, however, to settle near water sources, certainly the Rio Grande. Further, the soil had to be tilled, but many possessed ample proficiency to raise corn and other vegetables. Colonists went about digging the necessary canals to irrigate fields. They not only knew farming but also ways to transform the wilderness into lands useful for horse and cattle raising. For religion, they depended on the friars based at the local mission to serve them at key times in the life cycle: baptisms, weddings, and death.[6]

Although Spanish officials tended to neglect struggling communities such as that at La Junta, they accepted—either officially or informally—villager excursions into West Texas. Squatter settlements, therefore, took root in the expanse of the Big Bend, but some sprouted as far north as today's Pecos, Texas, where local Indian groups, probably the Jumanos, already engaged in livestock raising. Further enticing *pobladores* northward from La Junta towards the Texas wilderness were the abundance of wild game and the prospects of buffalo-hide trade with itinerant bands of Jumanos. In the process of exploration and efforts at claiming lands, Mexican-origin people mapped parts of West Texas and named numerous landmarks therein.[7] Such locations, waterways, and geographic formations testifying to Spanish activity in West Texas include the founding of Pilares (1775) and Presidio (1770s) and the naming of the Concho River, the Pecos River, Alamito Creek, Cíbolo Creek, and Santa Elena Canyon, among other sites.[8]

The colony at La Junta de los Ríos proved lasting, even as the government of newly independent Mexico in 1821 supplanted Spain's long stay there.[9] Historians have differed in estimating the size of the population in the settlement during the late 1840s and 1850s (one places the number at 800, but another at not more than 2,000) and in describing frontier conditions the locals encountered. One historian notes that in the late 1840s, "Presidio del Norte, La Junta, was a straggling, sunbaked village," but another writer believes that during the late 1840s and continuing into the 1850s, life circumstances for the people of La Junta might have improved somewhat due to the village's location on the Chihuahua Trail. The commerce on the Chihuahua Trail moved along three roads, one of which extended from the trail's origins at Indianola/Matagorda Bay on the Texas Gulf Coast, headed westward, then dropped down around the modern-day Fort Stockton area, to Alamito Creek towards Presidio and the Rio Grande before ending in Chihuahua. The flow of goods through La Junta probably brought betterment for the community.[10]

Whatever conditions the people of La Junta faced, they remained resilient, so much so that to distinguish between the locality on the Mexican side of the Rio Grande and the one on the Texas bank, the community of La Junta de los Ríos was renamed in 1865: that which was part of Mexico came to be designated as Ojinaga and that on the Texas side as Presidio, Texas. Ojinaga received its name to honor Manuel Ojinaga.[11]

OCCUPATION AND WITHDRAWAL, 1830S TO 1865

Like their Spanish predecessors, officials in the state of Chihuahua acceded to the crossing of people from Mexico over the Rio Grande. The first presence of Mexicans on the Texas side before that section of West Texas became part of the Republic of Texas (1836–1845) occurred in January 1832 when Mexican officials in Presidio del Norte granted Lt. Col. José Ygnacio Ronquillo title to a tract of land embracing a huge section of modern-day Presidio County. Immediately, Ronquillo moved his family into his new possession, settling on Cíbolo Creek on a site they named El Cíbolo located three miles north of present-day Presidio, Texas. There the family lived for almost a year. They farmed and ranched until Ronquillo's military service forced his return to Mexico. Apparently determining that his career as a serviceman took priority over his bid at colonization, Ronquillo sold the land to one Hypolito Acosta. For whatever reason, the property changed hands once more in May 1833 when Juana Pedraza acquired the grant from Acosta. The 21-year-old Pedraza, who subsequently relocated to Chihuahua, later married Ben Leaton, a former freighter and trader on the Chihuahua Trail who would make a name for himself during the 1840s for the baronial estate he built in the Big Bend.[12] Almost at the same time that the Ronquillo grant was exchanging hands, Juan Bustillos acquired land upon which during the decade he established a garrison-like complex (El Fortín de San José) southeast of Presidio. Bustillos then sold the property in August 1848 (by then the United States had gained ownership to that part of North America as per the Treaty of Guadalupe Hidalgo of February 1848) to Ben Leaton.[13]

As settlers from Mexico headed north into the Big Bend country at mid-century, a few Anglos from east of the 100th meridian (and Europe) also entered the region to found their own ranching operations there. How did Mexicans in the territory get along with the newcomers when racial conflict between Mexicans and Anglos was rampant in other parts of the state, such as South Texas?

Not much is known about this issue as it concerns the West Texas setting. Certainly, both groups perceived the need for mutual cooperation within an unfriendly environment where life-giving water sources and fertile grazing lands called for adaptation and where Indians had to be repelled. One form of accommodation between the two peoples was manifest in the assent given to the practice (common on borderlands) of interracial mixing. Needing to live peacefully and wishing to have stability in their own lives, Anglo men in West Texas during that period took Mexican women as either wives or mistresses. Mexican society, for its part, had long accepted Mexican women entering into domestic arrangements with outsiders (Spaniards, other Europeans, and Americans). Since Hispanic patriarchy condoned such relations, Mexican men on the frontier might have been willing to accept Anglos as allies, welcoming them as partners coping with the dangers around them.[14]

As indicated above, Juana Pedraza—whose own titleship to land in modern-day Presidio County went back to the 1830s—lived during the late 1840s at the huge baronial estate of her common-law husband Ben Leaton, with whom she had three children. When her partner died in 1851, she married another Anglo, named Edward Hall.[15] Also reflecting accommodation between Anglos and Mexicans was the marriage of Francisca Ramírez and Milton Faver. The couple had wed in Meoque, Mexico, during the early 1840s (Faver was working in Meoque at that time) and Francisca accompanied her husband around the year 1857 to a site twenty-five miles north of the Rio Grande near Cíbolo Creek where the ex-freighter founded a landed manor like Leaton's. There Francisca raised her son Juan and lived on the family's property until the 1880s.[16]

Actually, both Leaton and Faver immigrated into the Big Bend from Mexico and not the United States. But even those with US (or European) roots readily attuned themselves to local circumstance. According to one historian, "The first American settlers at Presidio during the 1850s accumulated property and established themselves as traders, farmers, and freighters."[17] In this transnational region, ranchers from Mexico found Texas entrepreneurs willing trade partners, selling livestock to Milton Faver, for example. *Vaqueros* regularly crossed into the Big Bend to work ranch lands, as they did for Faver who of necessity required cowhands to handle his cattle herds.[18]

Beyond the Big Bend

During the 1850s while pioneers coming from both Mexico and the US sought a new start in the Big Bend, the US laid tangible claim to the greater region of West Texas by stringing together a line of military garrisons stretching from just west of the 100th meridian to today's faraway El Paso. In quick succession, US troops built and fortified Fort McKavett (1852, in modern-day Menard County), Fort Clark (1852, in modern-day Kinney County), Fort Davis (1854, in modern-day Jeff Davis County), Fort Lancaster (1855, in modern-day Crockett County), Camp Hudson (1857, in modern-day Val Verde County), Fort Quitman (1858, in modern-day Hudspeth County), and Fort Stockton (1859, in modern-day Pecos County). Civilians arrived contemporaneous with the soldiers, for the posts necessarily depended on a citizen workforce to execute a variety of supplementary duties essential to the military mission. The security that the forts offered encouraged settlements nearby the garrisons so that by the end of the 1850s civilians (both Mexicans and Anglos) had clustered in the circumference of Fort Davis and Fort Stockton (the village of Comanche) as well as that of Fort Quitman (Bosque Carmelo).[19]

US expansion of the 1850s sparked further Mexican migration into West Texas; the new pioneers headed into area outside the Big Bend country. Community builders during the 1850s included Manuel Músquiz, Gregorio Carrasco, and Darío Rodríguez. Most prominent of these pathfinders was Músquiz, a rancher fleeing political turmoil in Northern Mexico. In 1855, he established his headquarters at Músquiz Canyon, near Fort Davis (constructed one year earlier to protect travelers from Indian attacks), and the ranchstead soon became home for some twenty people, including family members and workers.

His success as a rancher became such that he is generally credited as among the early developers of the cattle industry in West Texas. He built up his livestock by rounding up cattle in the area around Presidio del Norte and driving them to his ranch. His success lay in part on a ready market for beef at neighboring Fort Davis as well as on the help he got from family members and a crew of loyal ranch hands. Left unprotected from Indian attacks on his family and on his herds when Fort Davis closed with the outbreak of the Civil War, Músquiz and his villagers decided, in the summer of 1861, to leave their holdings and seek refuge in the old country.[20]

Also finding success as a rancher in West Texas by the 1850s was Gregorio Carrasco, another immigrant from Mexico, who established himself and his family at Wild Rose Pass, some ten miles east of Fort Davis, in modern-day Jeff Davis County. According to the 1860 federal census for Presidio County, the value of Carrasco's holdings stood at $2,100. He ranked as the wealthiest settler at the hamlet.[21]

Then, Mexican immigrants settled into what may be considered squatter communities, such as the one at La Limpia (in modern-day Jeff Davis County). Mexicans arrived there in the early 1850s when the Butterfield Overland Daily Mail Stage Company established a stage station on that site and then in the latter half of the decade when the US government built Fort Davis. The villagers apparently made their living raising crops off the area's fertile farmlands, workings at the garrison, and taking advantage of La Limpia's location along both the Butterfield Overland Daily Mail Company and the San Antonio-El Paso Mail line. They serviced the fort as laborers, servants, teamsters, cowhands overseeing the army's livestock, teamsters, and guides. Wives and daughters found employment as laundresses, seamstresses, and housekeepers.[22]

The Civil War halted the population currents—from both Mexico and the US—that during the 1850s had produced the above listed pioneer settlements. The war also affected military policy in the state. With Texas joining the Confederacy, the federal government closed all frontier installations. Defense of the settlements now fell to the Southern and Texas governments, both of which wrestled with funds to protect the region. Predictably, West Texas became exposed to constant Indian raids as well as to attacks by desperadoes, some of them deserters from the Confederate ranks. The turmoil left settlers with little choice but to abandon their besieged communities, including ones that had sprouted aside military garrisons. Mexican settlers either retreated to Mexico or weathered the disorder in places like La Junta while Anglos headed eastward toward the more established communities of pre-Civil War Texas. As both groups of people departed, the frontier was left depopulated west of the line from Gainesville to Uvalde.[23]

REOCCUPATION

Indians, especially the Apaches, had entrenched themselves in the Big Bend area during the four years of the Civil War and following the end of the fighting in 1865 continued to lord over much of the Trans-Pecos region.[24] To restore control over the hundreds of miles in western Texas, the federal government starting in 1867 re-garrisoned the forts it had located there in the 1850s while at the same time constructing new ones.[25]

Into the 1870s, however, the West Texas frontier continued to be violence prone. The forts struggled mightily to counter the Indians' hit-and-run strategy. The Apaches and other Indians swooped down upon the posts, the settlements growing about Fort Stockton and Fort Davis, the villages in the lower border along the Rio Grande, and emerging ranches in the open countryside—even ones near some of the forts (like Fort Concho)—to steal cattle and horses. The hostiles regularly attacked stagecoaches, mail lines, and wagon trains heading west to El Paso and beyond. They struck freight wagons on the Chihuahua Trail passing through Fort Stockton and moving south to Presidio. Apaches raided cattle herds being driven from the interior to provide beef for the troops at military stations. Many in West Texas fell victim during these many strikes, among them local ranch herders, stage drivers, freighters, trail hands, mail riders, and travelers.[26]

Outlaws of sundry types added to the turmoil wreaked by the Indians, taking advantage of the vast and weakly protected domain. Like the Indians, Anglo and Mexican marauders plundered ranches and made assaults on cattle drives passing through West Texas as well as on the laden freight wagons moving down the Chihuahua Trail.[27]

MIGRATION

It is generally agreed that the post-1865 pioneering wave by Euro-Americans and Mexicans into the region west of the 100th meridian began in 1867 with the stationing of federal troops therein. Historian Glen Ely explains that the reoccupation of the several forts brought a degree of stability to West Texas, stimulated the region's economy, and sparked the growth of civilian communities around these fortifications.[28]

As much was true for the most part, but a few pioneers began migration into the region immediately after the Civil War ended. Anglo Americans pushed into the Concho Country to found ranches and farms as early as 1864, and movement by others from the US and Europe followed soon after. Then, in December 1867, the federal government designated a site near the junction of the North and South Concho Rivers for what came to be called Fort Concho. In short order, enterprising men launched business operations conducive to the area's commercial growth, among them Ben Ficklin, who established (1868–1869) a station for the San Antonio-El Paso Mail line, a transcontinental mail route in place since the early 1850s. From these early incursions into West Texas grew San Angelo, sprouting across the Concho River.[29]

The return of the military to the old site of Fort Davis near Limpia Creek and Wild Rose Pass in June 1867 similarly enticed civilians to the area. Arriving settlers established themselves adjacent to the post. They provided it with needed goods and supplies, including lumber, beef, and vegetables. The hamlet took on the garrison's name: Fort Davis.[30]

Civilian migration also progressed towards modern-day Pecos County, more specifically into Fort Stockton (July 1867). Work would be found there for ambitious entrepreneurs managing stage stations, hotels, and general stores as well as for common laborers who could help build the fort and fill other work demands. Families arrived in the area to engage in ranching or otherwise to support the garrison's mission, equipping it with needed materials and provisioning it with required food products.[31]

Just as the return of the military enticed people from different parts of the world westward into the Edwards Plateau and Trans-Pecos regions, so did it attract people from south of the Rio Grande, many of them emigrating from the state of Chihuahua.[32] As migration northward resumed, the gravitational pull was into some of the older areas settled before the Civil War as well as into newer West Texas vicinities.

Among older villages repopulated was Presidio del Norte (part of La Junta, but by then in modern Presidio County) which had been settled with both Spain's and Mexico's authorization long before the Big Bend became part of Texas. With greater certainty for protection from hostile forces, ethnic Mexicans at the same time reoccupied communities they had inhabited next to military installations before 1861. These included Fort Davis (Jeff Davis County), Fort Stockton (Pecos County), and Fort Quitman (Hudspeth County).

Mexicans returning to Fort Davis wrested a livelihood by meeting the requirements of the fort as an installation as well as by serving the needs of Army personnel. According to the 1870 US census, 47 percent of the civilian workforce was Mexican. The next decennial US census (1880) identified as Mexican 57 percent of the total civilian workforce.[33]

Mexicans also trekked to old Fort Stockton. As with other West Texas garrisons being reinstated, Fort Stockton (as of July 1867) required common laborers for the task of rebuilding, and those who answered demand came from the La Junta–Ojinaga area and from San Antonio, Texas. The fort's auspicious location about one-half mile north of Comanche Creek and near Leon Springs complemented the fort's bid for workers (both Anglos and Mexicans) who settled at a budding hamlet named St. Gall (1868). The movement was such that in 1881, St. Gall changed its name to Fort Stockton. Meanwhile, people from the border areas and Mexico arrived in carts drawn by oxen, burros, and horses to work new farms and ranches in the countryside of the future Pecos County.[34]

Most famous of the newcomers to Fort Stockton was the Torres family of San Antonio, there to leave a mark during the 1870s through the 1880s. Cesario Torres (46 years old), his brothers Bernardo (42) and Juan (60), and a relative named Félix Garza (one source identifies Garza as being brother-in-law to Cesario, as Garza's sister was Cesario's wife), arrived as homesteaders in 1869 having acquired acreage from the Texas government through the use of scrip and claiming it on the basis of preemption or squatters' rights.[35] Cesario Torres located his Seven-D Ranch (a farm and ranch venture) some four miles northeast of growing Fort Stockton; Bernardo's farm was situated about seven miles to the southeast of the town; and Félix Garza homesteaded to the village's southeast. Ever the entrepreneurs, the Torres family launched another farm operation at Pontoon Bridge on the west side of the Pecos River.[36]

Postwar Mexican migration hardly confined itself to the old Big Bend settlements nor, for that matter, to reopened Fort Davis and Fort Stockton. The march also advanced into newer areas of West Texas, such as today's Val Verde County. Sometime during the Civil War, ranchers James Taylor and his wife Paula Losoya Taylor (accompanied by her sister María del Refugio Losoya), had traveled from their home in Uvalde, Texas, towards what would become the city of Del Rio. The Taylors had learned, from travelers who passed through that part of the border, of fertile farmlands that could be gainfully irrigated with the waters of the local San Felipe Creek (the creek flowed through the middle of what sometime later became the city of Del Rio). Upon sojourning to the area to inspect it firsthand, the Taylors determined reports of the soil's productive potential to be credible. Armed with land granted them by the Texas government, they moved to San Felipe Creek sometime during the early 1860s with some of their business partners and farmhands. The Taylors founded a hacienda and, with their associates—who had resourcefully acquired land for their own cultivation—contracted an irrigation company during the 1870s to channel the waters of the San Felipe to the expanding fields. Learning of calls for workhands, people from today's Piedras Negras and other parts of Mexico crossed the Rio Grande to help dig the canal and perform labor at the farms under cultivation by the Americans. The immigrants built sheltering on the east side of San Felipe Creek in a tract of town that would become the "San Felipe barrio."[37]

Postbellum movements also occurred into Edwards Plateau counties bordering the Hill Country west of San Antonio, such as Edwards, Kimble, and Menard Counties. Among early Hispanic pioneers into Edwards County was a man named Sánchez (of "Spanish descent") whom history places as of 1867 in the area of the Nueces River headwaters. He established himself in Barksdale, erecting there a small picket house constructed of cedar wood that was abundant in the area. At some point during his residence in the county Indians killed Sánchez, but the threat of hostility did not deter his family from staying; they remained in the Barksdale area for some years after.[38] Another family of long standing in the eastern part of the Edwards Plateau was that of Melitón Morales. In the year 1874, Morales arrived in present-day Kimble County, having left Duval County in South Texas with 2,000 sheep, 200 Spanish goats, and some horses. He selected for his ranch a site at Viejo Creek in northern Kimble County close to the Menard County line. There at Bear Creek, as Viejo Creek came to be known later, Morales in 1881 built a rock house which today remains a testament to the early Mexican pioneering in Kimble County. Morales died in 1924 and was buried in the cemetery at his son Manuel's ranch, located at the corner of Kimble, Menard, and Schleicher Counties.[39] Who first blazed a trail into Menard County is difficult to ascertain, but Catholic Church records in the town of Menard indicate a Spanish-surnamed child born on July 6, 1868, and baptized on March 12, 1872. By the 1870s, Mexican-origin people in the county were applying for naturalization.[40]

Mexicans during this time also began penetrating areas in the northeastern section of the Edwards Plateau, among them part of today's Tom Green County. Into the Concho Country area entered people from San Antonio, Mexico, and New Mexico, all anticipating work possibilities on the farms and ranches that first appeared in 1864 and expanded briskly thereafter. The establishment of Fort Concho in 1867 lured other Mexicans in search of similar prospects. Newcomers settled on the rural lands they worked, but others made their home in the developing villages of Benficklin and San Angelo.[41]

Mexicans also made their way to new sites spread along the border, such as El Polvo in Presidio County. The locale had earlier (sources provide different dates for its origins, either 1683 or 1715) served as a Spanish mission for Indigenous groups, but under a contracting effort undertaken in the late 1860s, Texas officials recruited colonizers from La Junta to reoccupy what as of 1773 had been a presidial site. The colonization program called for each family to be compensated with 160 acres of land for farming and for raising cattle and goats, and to be given entitlement to American rights and privileges. Enticed by the offer, prominent men from Ojinaga, led by Secundino Luján, sojourned about sixteen miles downriver from Presidio to the future site of San José del Polvo, clearing the land for farming and colonization. Sometime in 1871 and 1872, they relocated to their new home with their families: indeed, San José del Polvo (Polvo, or modern-day Redford) is generally considered to have been founded in 1871.[42]

Also blazed in Presidio County was land along the Alamito Creek. John Davis arrived there in 1870, accompanied by a number of Mexican workers and their families, to establish a hamlet that took the name of "Alamito." Immediately, community members built the structures necessary for frontier living, among them a small adobe home, a corral for the livestock, and, as time passed, a small chapel for possible visits from priests. The community made its living off wild game, vegetables that were cultivated (which Davis then sold at Fort Stockton), and livestock that grazed freely on the surrounding range.[43]

In 1874, Victoriano Hernández homesteaded along the same Alamito Creek (some ten miles south of Alamito village). Along with his family and workers, in what came to be called Alamo Ranch, Hernández built his home headquarters and through determined work by his family and the laborers who had accompanied them established the foundation for a rural village that would persist for years after.[44]

Population estimates made by scholars show a rapid increase in the West Texas population between 1860, when the first federal census of the region (then sparsely settled) was taken, and the one enumerated in the year 1880. During the decades following the Civil War, as the area west of the 100th longitude began transitioning away from its wilderness state, an upsurge in demographic growth occurred. The Mexican population, for one, more than doubled: it grew from 3,257 people in 1860 to 7,383 in 1880. But the number of Anglos also swelled: from 625 in 1860 to 3,542 in 1880. Mexicans outnumbered whites by two to one as of 1880, but Anglos would level out the disparity by 1900.[45]

ANGLO PERCEPTIONS OF MEXICANS

Fortunate for Hispanic *pobladores* in the years between 1865 and 1880 was avoiding the kind of Anglo racism that Mexicans in other parts of the state confronted. Certainly, Anglos brought in racist attitudes toward people of Spanish Mexican origin as they entered West Texas after the Civil War, but the circumstances of the period mitigated bigotry. To begin with, association between the two peoples was not always in close quarters where contact was immediate and sustained. People (both Mexicans and Anglos) resided in places, such as ranches and farms, or insulated spaces such as in urban villages, where encounter was not so direct as to incite overt xenophobia.

Furthermore, it was not to Anglo advantage to subscribe to a code of social order such as the one entrenched in their home territory. Frontier survival necessitated interdependence. Anglos could ill afford to alienate (as they did later) a people whose cooperation they felt essential to fighting Indians, to adapting to ecological surroundings, or to converting a wilderness land into fertile fields or into productive cattle or sheep ranges. Anglo men, many of whom reached the frontier as single individuals, sought female companionship and satisfied their longing in the love that Mexican women granted them.

Demographics also acted to curb any racist distaste Anglos harbored toward Mexicans. While true that Mexicans outnumbered Anglos, West Texas was a vast region, different from trans-Nueces Texas between 1865 and 1880 where Mexicans dominated in a more confined area and seemed threatening to Anglos then in the process of "redeeming" that geographic zone for civilized society. West Texas during that epoch was not a place pressing for the suppression and domination of a menacing people. Murders, vigilante acts, and episodes of lynch law against Mexicans were not then as flagrant as they later came to be.

Those who did express racist attitudes toward Mexicans were generally persons traversing the region or servicemen stationed there. Nathaniel Taylor, a newspaperman passing through Texas in the late 1870s, had little of a complimentary nature to say of Mexicans in San Angelo, Texas. He found the men (both Anglos and Mexicans) in the village of some 100 people to be of despicable character, many of them criminals. The town during the 1870s contained few white women; Taylor judged the Mexican women he saw to be sinners, many of them prostitutes who met the carnal needs of the Buffalo Soldiers stationed at Fort Concho.[46] As to physiognomy, military staff stationed in West Texas posts hardly thought the Mexican population around them as being worthy of the classification "white people." Two surgeons in particular, temporarily assigned at Fort Stockton in 1875, regarded the local Mexicans as "a cross between the Spaniard and Indian, which seems to have deteriorated both races."[47]

Outsiders disparaged Mexicans further by smearing them with contemptuous terms, among them the epithet "greaser." The designation was known to Anglos long before their post-1865 encroachment into the region, as manifest in the word's application by Waterman L. Ormsby, a correspondent for the *New York Herald*. Making his way through West Texas in September 1858 on his way to San Francisco on the Overland Mail Company stage, Ormsby unabashedly referred to the mule handlers hired around the Concho River as "greasy Mexicans" and to those recruited around the Pecos River as "'greasers,' as they are commonly called here."[48] Burr G. Duval, part of an expedition undertaken in late 1879 by several railroad companies intending to examine mineral resources around Presidio, Texas, recorded on the trail at Brackettville (Kinney County) to have acquired "fodder from a 'greaser.'" Duval did not think much of the local population in the village, describing it as "a mixture of greasers, Americans, negroes, and dogs." Needing water as his party continued its travels, he arrived at a sheepherders' camp where "Mr. Greaser," as he put it, met his request with consummate politeness.[49]

ACCOMMODATION

Mexicans and Anglos converged on lightly populated West Texas perceiving the region as grounds open to boundless opportunities for material uplifting. But how were the two to get along? Was interaction going to be amiable or antagonistic? Certainly, mutual distrust existed in light of their respective backgrounds, culture, and "race."

The historical moment dictated responses. First, threats such as those from Indians and bandits had to be fended off. More immediately, there existed the "errand" to transform the frontier into a land of bustling towns and cities, one of functioning ranches and farms, all interconnected through an efficient system of infrastructure. These imperatives produced in the period before 1880 an era of "peaceful coexistence" between Mexicans and Anglos.[50]

For a period after the Civil War, a degree of harmony existed in the borderlands between Mexicans and Anglos, displayed in accommodation, cooperation, and sociability. Racial mixing between white men and Mexican women, which had reflected a state of goodwill between the two peoples before the Civil War, persisted past 1865 as an indication of continued friendship. Such relationships seemed crucial for taming the frontier.[51] Accordingly, Anglo men in areas such as the Big Bend, without the option of forging ties with women of their own "kind," entered into marriage partnerships with local Mexican women. In Presidio, some writers maintain, such marriages were with "the most prominent Mexican families."[52] In truth, of course, few Mexican families of well-to-do standing lived in the Edwards Plateau and Trans-Pecos during that period, for in contrast to pre-Civil War South Texas, no Tejano landed elite had ever pioneered West Texas. Ordinarily, Anglo men married women belonging to poor frontier families.[53]

For the most part, these interethnic unions were more than ones of convenience. White men did find Mexican women attractive and desirable, and thus acceptable as marital companions. Anglos in the Fort Davis community during the late 1860s thought of local señoritas as sensuous and seductive. One researcher found that as of 1880, "no fewer than half of married Anglo males in Fort Davis had wives of Mexican ancestry," among them officers in command positions.[54]

Presidio and Fort Davis were not the only settings in West Texas where cross-cultural pairings took place, although such couplings appear to have been more common around military bases such as Fort Davis, Fort Stockton, and Fort Concho. At Fort Stockton, E. W. Bates, district and county clerk and former Army officer, in 1879 married Elvina Torres, eldest daughter of Bernardo Torres (of the Fort Stockton Torres family).[55] In the emerging town of San Angelo, next to Fort Concho, Mexican American Catalina Wuertemburg, daughter of Ramona Wuertemburg (Mexican) and Philip J. Wuertemberg (German), in 1872 married W. S. Veck, a successful San Angelo businessman.[56]

POLITICS

Both Anglos and Mexicans perceived benefits in forging such kinds of social ties. Broader possibilities lay beyond companionship, love, and family togetherness. For an aspiring class of Mexican landowners and entrepreneurs emerging out of opportunities granted by an abundant frontier, there was the expectation that partnerships of convenience could beget political rewards. After all, the political structure in a wide-open land necessitated a network of administrators and officials to oversee governmental affairs as well as a stable and functional economic infrastructure capable of meeting the market demands of the military, budding villages, and arriving settlers.[57]

The political front thus summoned Mexicans who aspired to civic engagement. The postwar era seemed an opportune time for them. The 1870s, in particular, urged accords as counties in the Big Bend and the Concho Country were being created, organized, and populated. Organized during the 1870s were Menard (1871), Kinney (1874), Presidio (1875), Pecos (1875), Tom Green (1875), Kimble (1876), McCulloch (1876), and Concho (1879).

Presidio County, when organized in 1875, stood among those county units receptive to an Anglo-Mexican political coalition. Until 1871, the county had taken in the broader Trans-Pecos frontier, extending west to El Paso County, both of which had been created by the legislature in 1850. That same year, the state detached Presidio County from El Paso County and further split it to create Pecos County. When Presidio County was formed four years later, Mexicans were among those filling public posts. County commissioners' court officers following the first special term (August 1875) of the Presidio County court included Juan José Acosta as justice of the peace (Precinct 5) and Jorge Acosta as constable (also Precinct 5). Throughout the years between 1875 to the early 1880s, Spanish-surnamed individuals in Presidio County were a fixture as justices of the peace and jurors. Further, the homes of Mexican Americans often acted as polling sites.[58]

In Pecos County, Mexicans were present politically since the county's creation in 1871. Among those engaged in its early politics, and that of Fort Stockton, was the previously mentioned Torres family. Cesario, who spoke Spanish and English, was among those in a three-man commission selected to establish the new county unit. In an election held at Fort Stockton in November 1872, Cesario won a seat as Justice of the Peace, Precinct 2, and Hipólito Carrasco, a local rancher, to the same position for Precinct 4. In a special election held following the county's organization in 1875, Cesario remained Justice of the Peace, Precinct 2, and Carrasco Justice of the Peace, Precinct 4. In 1876, when county officials established newer precincts, Cesario Torres continued as representative of Precinct 2 and would officiate in the Pecos County commissioners' court from 1875 until 1886 (Precinct 2).[59] Cesario's brother Bernardo, meantime, also became an involved agent in county politics until he passed away in 1882. It was he who headed the first grand jury in June 1875, reporting as foreman that lawbreaking in the county had subsided and that a state of peace and order prevailed.[60] Félix Garza, the Torres family member related by marriage, also made politics a personal commitment. The record shows him to have been a constable and justice of the peace in Pecos County during the mid-1870s. Other Mexicans during the county's formative era of the 1870s also gained appointments from the county commission to political positions such as precinct constable.[61]

Mexicans were similarly involved in the early politics of the Concho Country. The most prominent figure in Tom Green County during the 1870s came to be Pablo Alderette, a native of New Mexico who had arrived about 1869 or 1870 with his family via San Antonio. Alderette acquired land upon arriving in the Concho Country and summarily created for himself a niche in local politics. When Tom Green County was first organized (1875), Alderette gained an appointment in the county commission (July 1875); he served as a justice of the peace in his precinct at the same time.[62]

But Pablo was by no means the sole figure of Mexican descent involved in Tom Green County political circles during the last half of the 1870s. Guillermo Alderette, Pablo's son, served as part of the first grand jury in 1875. The district court that year selected other Tejanos for service in grand and petit juries, assigned some to constable duties, and chose Mexican residences as polling places.[63] When Tom Green County held its first election in 1876, part of the Mexican population in the villages of Benficklin and Santa Angela went to the polls.[64]

CLASS

Rancheros

In their quest to bring order to the frontier, Anglos needed assistance not only from Mexican Americans serving competently in political posts but also from those possessing business acumen. Essential to the general welfare were developing a serviceable road network, founding agricultural concerns and managing them gainfully, carrying out the business of freighting, and seeing to the growth of town commerce. By forging an accommodation with Anglos, Mexicans acted as co-agents in the economic advancement of the Edwards Plateau and Trans-Pecos frontiers.

Open tracts of land in Presidio County appealed to resolute entrepreneurs with a disposition to take up ranching. One successful *ranchero* was Victoriano Hernández, founder of the Alamo Ranch. His holdings included a large adobe brick house encompassing several large rooms and a patio for casual respite and festivity. To construct it he brought in building supplies from across the border and to furnish it imported necessary household articles and accessories. Other assets at the ranch testified to Hernández's successful operation, among them sheds for storing ranch equipment, herds of animal stock, and numerous fruit trees.[65]

Perhaps as successful as Victoriano Hernández in Presidio County was Darío Rodríguez, who in 1870 founded a sheep ranch (jointly with his father-in-law William Russell) in the western section of the county, north of present-day Candelaria. Rodríguez might have been among the wealthiest individuals in Presidio County, for the federal census of 1880 estimated his personal worth to have been $20,000.[66]

Presidio County as of the 1870s was predominantly Mexican in population (as it is today) so not surprisingly other *rancheros*, perhaps homesteading (like Victoriano and Darío) by claiming squatters' rights, were Mexicans. Dutifully registering their livestock marks in the county during the 1870s were men from El Polvo, among them Secundino Luján, Mateo Carrasco, José Bustillos, and Juan José Acosta. Several beyond El Polvo pursued livestock raising as a means of self-improvement, for during the 1870s they also registered their brands at Fort Stockton.[67] The same was the case at Fort Davis, then the county seat of Presidio County.[68]

In Tom Green County, Pablo Alderette—who as noted earlier was much engaged in the politics of early San Angelo—began ranch operations immediately after arriving in the Concho Country. Like others homesteading in West Texas after the Civil War, Alderette settled on unclaimed land, situating his ranch-farm operation on the North Concho River. During the next few years he expanded upon his landholdings so that his estate, which included animal herds, ranch and farming equipment, and various personal assets, was estimated in 1880 at a $6,000 value. His son Guillermo prospered as well during the era by ranching and farming with his father, but also by running a freighting concern and speculating in local business enterprises. Into the 1880s, Guillermo did well financially in San Angelo until he was killed in 1891.[69]

Farmers

Even as the open range in West Texas steered many towards ranching, some Mexicans pursued farming. Indeed, judging from extant scholarship, entrepreneurs choosing to make their living off rural economics preferred farm agriculture to equine and bovine interests. What would account for that selection?

Several factors discouraged Mexican entrepreneurs from going into ranching. First, a rancho legacy did not exist in West Texas as it did in South Texas. The West Texas region had never been one of land grants bestowed upon people of merit by Spain or Mexico. No discernible vestiges of a once robust livestock range lingered, therefore. Moreover, ranching did not emerge as a potentially lucrative enterprise in West Texas areas, such as the Big Bend, until the 1880s.[70]

But more general factors deterred Mexican prospective farmers from embracing ranching as a vocation. Purchasing land to get started strained people's lean finances. Even if land were acquired through homesteading or squatting, the undertaking required stretches large enough to accommodate livestock. Capital was necessary to acquire herds, purchase riding equipment, build ranch structures (such as houses, barns, and corrals), and support the crew of *vaqueros*.

Farming was comparatively easier to take on. For those committed to the venture, lands could be acquired through the doctrine of squatters' rights. Squatter acquisitions were invariably small, but the land served its purpose: that of raising foodstuffs (vegetables and grains) for families. Additionally, as did some of these small farming operations, land could be expanded to raise goats and sheep, if not a few cattle and horses. Agriculture, even on an expanded scale, did not demand the kind of capital assets ranching required. Landowners could always rely on their family's labor. Work equipment could be of home construction and adapted to the intent of the job. Farmers Secundino Luján, Victoriano Hernández, Darío Rodríguez, and others were able to make their farms a going concern on austere budgets.

Among the most notable of these Mexican farming pioneers during the 1870s were members of the Torres family (respectively, Cesario, Bernardo, Juan, and the relative Félix Garza) of the Fort Stockton, Pecos County, area. The clan displayed enterprise and industry, relying on both the family unit and a dependable work crew to transform their new lands—through calculated planning—into money-making enterprises. They built acequias (irrigation ditches) soon after their arrival at Fort Stockton in efforts to funnel needed water over one-and-a-half miles from the local Comanche Springs to their three respective 160-acre farms. Continuing into the mid-1870s, Cesario's work hands tapped further into Comanche Springs, digging irrigation ditches to the Seven-D Ranch so as to harvest vegetables for the farm owner's family and his laborers.[71]

At the Pontoon Bridge settlement, Torres and his villagers turned to the west bank of the Pecos for water to irrigate their patches of corn and vegetables. The family profited from the farm's location, as it took advantage of passing traffic, selling its goods to teamsters, itinerants, and the military.[72] The brothers also capitalized on the Texas Legislature Act of 1875, a measure aimed at promoting the building of canals and ditches for purposes of irrigation and water travel. That year, the state chartered the Torres Irrigation and Manufacturing Company and the Garza Irrigation and Manufacturing Company, and the family at once set out to build an irrigation canal to feed water to the Pontoon Bridge farm.[73] Their workers routed water southward from the west bank of the Pecos River at a point above Pontoon Bridge and directed it downstream to an area past the Crossing. With this feat accomplished, Cesario Torres by 1878 had 600 acres under cultivation at his Pontoon village. He had some fifty Mexican families working there, most making do for shelter, living in rough-hewn huts.[74]

Immense was the amount of land the Torres family received under the Texas Legislature Act of 1875. The decree pledged to compensate landowners across the state with acreage in return for building canal waterways for local farmers. According to the specific deal the Torres Irrigation and Manufacturing Company and the Garza Irrigation and Manufacturing Company made with the state, "for each mile of irrigation canal they completed at the Pecos, the [state government] would grant them [the Torres family] four or more sections of adjoining land, assuming the waterway attained at last three miles in length."[75] For digging other irrigation canals and ditches around the Fort Stockton area (and ensuring they functioned efficiently), the state further rewarded the family with thirty-seven sections of land in what later (1885) became Val Verde County.[76]

Most prosperous of the family members was Cesario, whose wealth by 1870 amounted to $4,000 in personal value and $1,000 in real estate. He then obtained some 16,000 acres as compensation for his part in the construction of canals and ditches in the Fort Stockton area as per the specifications of the state-chartered irrigation program. His lands by the late 1870s stocked herds of horses, mules, cattle, and hogs.[77] Not left behind was Bernardo, who in his own right helped advance the tempo of progress underway in Pecos County during the 1870s. His success was such in the years after his arrival at Fort Stockton that when he died in 1882, he bequeathed to his family personal and real property totaling some $8,700.[78]

Several others besides the Torres family sought out a livelihood in soil cultivation in Pecos County. Farming was sufficiently prominent that the Pecos County census of 1870 made note of *rancheros* who doubled as farmers by harvesting vegetables and fruits. So did the 1880 census recognize this duality, categorizing several *rancheros* as "farmers," all of them born in Mexico.[79] In northern Presidio County, in the surroundings about Fort Davis, Fabricio Granado prospered at his 160-acre holding during the 1870s. Granado kept improving his land, raising livestock as well, to the extent that the 1880 census listed his farm's worth at $1,300. A number of other Mexicans in the area contributed to the advancement of local agriculture.[80]

Among those active in crop production was colonizer Secundino Luján, who had settled at Polvo sometime in 1871 and 1872. Upon arriving at the new site, Luján and the accompanying colonizer families started working their lands, preparing ditches necessary to water the fields and raising livestock. Then in 1876, the Texas government granted the settlers American citizenship—officially recognizing title to their lands—and helped enhance their farm cultivation by approving a plan to construct a six-mile-long irrigation canal that tapped into the Rio Grande. The project, which took three years to complete, was overseen by "The Presidio Irrigation Company," which the settlers organized and the state government chartered. Luján's own success as a farmer came to be widely recognized at Polvo, so much that he served as a precinct commissioner for Presidio County.[81]

In Val Verde County, Paula Losoya Taylor and her husband continued managing their Del Rio hacienda profitably into the 1870s. They irrigated their vegetable garden and fruit trees from the waters they channeled from the San Felipe and effectively used their workforce, composed mainly of farmhands arriving from Northern Mexico, to maintain the estate in good working order. Following James Taylor's death on April 4, 1876, Señora Losoya (who was bilingual) added more property so that by the 1880s she had enlarged her holdings to about 3,000 acres. Careful attention to her irrigated vegetable garden and fruit trees and her entrepreneurial success earned her deserved recognition and respect, and during the last decades of the century, her place of residence became a sort of center for Del Rio's business and social communities.[82]

Businesspeople

Besides ranchers and farmers, the entrepreneurial class included men steadfast in testing opportunities in the realm of commerce. In the years following the Civil War, when Anglo freighters did not offer much competition, nor had the railroad entered West Texas, Mexicans filled the void for moving cargo across the region. Wagon masters could be from West Texas, but the larger outfits had their headquarters in San Antonio or El Paso. Wherever their base, headmasters either contracted directly with the government or with private business companies or negotiated with both for the lease of their wagon trains. Mexican freight wagons did much of the hauling when in 1867 the government contracted with freighting companies to ferry military supplies, as well as loads of meats and foodstuffs, between San Antonio and frontier posts and camps then being established across West Texas.[83]

Mexican-owned (or managed) freight wagons regularly traversing West Texas also attended to frontier communities. Actually, several of these freight companies were owned by operators from San Antonio or El Paso—such as the Valdez brothers, the Miguel brothers, Anastacio Gonzales, and several others—but the wagons made stops at various points, providing villages with needed supplies, food provisions, and various essentials.[84] Freighters moving along the Chihuahua Trail on their way to important trading centers in Mexico also made stops on the way, serving settlements such as those in the Big Bend. One such freighter was Seferino Calderón, who during the late 1860s moved goods through Presidio, Texas, on trains of ten to twenty wagons.[85]

The Proletarian Class

For a fact, the fruits of accommodation—ones that opened political and business opportunities to men such as members of the Torres family and to women like Paula Losoya—reached only a relatively small element within Mexican-descent communities in West Texas. Immigrants from Mexico, the US, Europe, and different parts of the world set out for the West Texas frontier hoping to find improvement on the kind of life they left behind, and while some achieved a measure of advancement, most seldom fulfilled their hoped-for wishes. For Mexicans the prospects for upward mobility rested mainly on performing dirty work and marginal in nature. During the period from about 1865 to 1880, the mass of working men depended for family survival on jobs largely categorized as general and unspecified.[86]

Renewed government campaigns after 1867 to regarrison old forts or build new ones were contingent on the presence of a laboring class willing and able to discharge a miscellany of arduous duties. Immigrant Mexicans arriving from the Presidio-Ojinaga area and from Northern Mexico, joined by Mexican Americans from the interior of Texas, met part of the demand. Mexican freight crews from San Antonio, for example, were behind the delivery of essential construction materials to garrisons like Fort Concho and Fort Davis then being built or reoccupied.[87]

On site, Mexicans helped resuscitate some of the posts. Skilled Mexican adobe makers at Fort Stockton finished the garrison's offices, barracks, and outbuildings. Artisans and carpenters contributed their own skills; others aided restoration functions as wood haulers. Mexicans performed a similar variety of work at Fort Davis. There, adobe craftsmen from Presidio del Norte were brought in to complete base quarters. Mexicans further carried out sundry tasks such as spreading dirt on the roofs of fort structures to guard against fire hazards.[88]

Mexican workers once having assisted with the construction or reconstruction of the several posts remained to support the US military mission. At the village of Fort Davis, according to the 1880 census, Mexicans bolstered fort operations as wood haulers, herders, gardeners, teamsters, cooks, domestic servants, laborers, laundresses, and more.[89] Around Fort Stockton, Mexicans likewise supplemented military duties as skilled blacksmiths and brick masons or as common laborers doing grounds keeping.[90]

Growing towns needed laborers as much as did the forts. Presidio, Fort Davis, San Angelo, Fort Stockton, Del Rio, and other emerging villages summoned people with special skills or, for that matter, anyone disposed to perform hard manual labor. Mexicans largely filled the demand, working in an array of jobs that included blacksmiths, masons, tailors, butchers, cooks, shoemakers, and a range of unskilled and general work.[91] The wide frontier spaces of West Texas presented Mexicans with a further work option, that of buffalo hunting. Mexicans living in the San Angelo area, for one, turned during the mid-1870s to the plains of the Concho Country in pursuit of buffalo skinning to help satisfy the national demand for bison hides.[92]

An expanding rural economy throughout West Texas opened more work prospects. But farm and ranch labor seldom produced stability for it was usually of transient type, requiring Mexicans to migrate from one part of the region to the other.[93] Yet even in their temporary stays, Mexicans added to the larger society's quality of life. In garden plots, farmhands working in the Concho Country during the 1860s and 1870, for example, raised food products that provisioned the troops at Fort Concho. They also supplied fodder for the fort's animals with prairie hay and grass harvested around the area.[94] From Fort Stockton to border villages like Polvo and Del Rio, it was Mexican laborers advancing the farming economy, carrying out such rigorous tasks as digging ditches, mostly using pick and shovel.[95]

Mexican laborers aided the development of West Texas ranching as much as they did the farming sector. Some worked cattle, as they did in the Marathon area during the late 1870s. More generally, they worked as sheepherders, for the sheep industry appears to have expanded into West Texas earlier than did cattle ranching. In San Angelo—a major sheep ranching center during the 1870s— Mexican *pastores* constituted the workforce that guarded and tended sheep flocks on surrounding ranches.[96]

Mexicans were behind the conveying of cargo across West Texas, commonly in charge of the mules pulling the many freight trains. Teamsters came from the large pool of the working class, but their skills were of such demand that they made up the several military and civilian crews of the many wagon trains that during the 1870s used the trail cut by the San Antonio-El Paso Mail line.[97] One contemporary declared of their overall prowess: "As drivers, Mexicans were more effective than Americans. The Mexicans would pick out their mule teams at night, no matter how dark, and took no more time to hitch at night than if it was day."[98] Francis Corbett Taylor, of the San Angelo area, integrated his stage line (which during the 1870s ran through the Concho Mail Station at Benficklin) using Mexicans from San Antonio.[99]

SURVIVAL TECHNIQUES
Home Building

Residence in an area still very much a frontier in the immediate years after the Civil War required an intuitive knack for improvisation and demanded resourceful creativity at every level of life. Most Mexican pioneers arrived in the borderlands with not much more than the bare essentials, always aware of having to start anew amid primitive conditions. Generally, they brought with them only their clothing, some home necessities, and whatever personal effects they could load on a wagon/cart or mount on a horse. Furthermore, the Big Bend, and West Texas for that matter, lay far removed from supply depots.

Imperative to Mexicans in confronting the dire circumstances before them was devising tactical means to overcome them. Most pressing was protecting the family from the elements and roaming animal predators. They turned to primitive alternatives, as did Torres family workers at Pontoon Bridge in 1870. They took refuge in dugouts, living, as one contemporary put it, "in underground holes." Families in the camp improvised as best as possible but with questionable avail. Covering the trenches with tree limbs hardly kept out the rain or deterred varmints, and the excavation obviously offered no privacy nor ample space for cooking and sleeping.[100] But this was the fate of many who, in their desire to start new lives in West Texas, made do with almost nothing.

More commonly, Mexican colonizers, since their earliest days in the Big Bend, adopted the housing plan employed by the Indigenous peoples. The Jumanos, for one, had long relied on the pithouse *jacal* (so called because the Indians constructed the dwellings so as to be partially underground). For building materials, the Indians borrowed from local flora, vegetation, and other natural resources. Mexicans turned to the same ecological components for their version of the *jacal*, building it so that its presence during the latter decades of the nineteenth century stretched from the eastern line of the West Texas region to faraway El Paso.[101] Immigrants from Mexico entering West Texas also turned to adobe lodging if the *jacal* did not serve them as needed or they found it impractical for the moment. The Jumanos had used this type of living quarters alongside the *jacal*, as had the Spanish *pobladores* in their first *entradas* into the Big Bend.

Adobe was almost unsurpassed in utilitarian qualities out on the West Texas realm. As a nonconductor, it made for comfortable living, permitting habitations to be warm in the winter and cool in the summer. Furthermore, adobe could be fabricated, as was the *jacal*, from components available in local surroundings. Mexicans adept at adobe production concocted the brick by turning to dirt, straw, grass, or mud, and even animal manure (such as that of goats raised around the house yard) if available. They would then either mix the elements manually or mash them with their feet. To advance the process, the workmen would then place the adobe components in wet pits for a period of time, probably several days, in order for the mixture to reach a certain texture. Once the concoction had attained the required condition, adobe makers placed the mud in wooden molds, exposing it to the sun to dry. Inexpensive and requiring only basic skills, adobe came to be a feature of housing throughout West Texas Hispanic communities in the nineteenth century.[102]

Not surprisingly, Anglo Americans copied the adobe model. They appreciated the material's functional capacities and its hardy composition and applied the merits of adobe brick to their own permanent structures: public buildings, schools, and houses. As noted earlier, many of the military installations contained adobe architectural features. Such utility could be traced to the 1850s when the government had initially established the line of forts in West Texas, and its application continued after the Civil War. So much reliance on adobe construction had been part of the rebuilding at Fort Davis after its reoccupation in 1867 that "by the mid-1880s it had more than sixty adobe and stone structures."[103] The same could be said of Fort Stockton, the garrison. The aforementioned Burr G. Duval, traveling to Presidio County in 1879 to study mineral properties there, noted: "The post at Stockton is built entirely of 'adobe.' Officers' quarters and all."[104]

As well, Anglo Americans accepted the practicality and usefulness of adobe in establishing the mail stations, remote stopping points, and various outposts they built in the 1850s. "The stage stands of adobe [during the pre-Civil War period] were all built of the same plan," writes one historian, "the walls of the corrals (twelve or fifteen feet high and two to three feet thick) constructed of adobe brick."[105] Building homes of adobe seemed as sensible to Anglos as it did to Mexicans. Nathaniel Taylor, the newspaperman passing through Fort Stockton in the late 1870s, found housing at Fort Stockton to be of adobe substance. Another traveler through the same town in 1879 observed of local farmhands: "[Mexicans] and whites alike lived in mud huts roofed with long grass covered with dirt several inches deep."[106]

As Anglos went about the task of urban settlement after the Civil War, adobe remained a chosen material for town expansion. When Anglo settlers founded Fort Stockton, they made the courthouse of adobe and the building, later used as a "Mexican school," still stood almost a century later.[107] At Fort Davis, city planners also turned to adobe. Teacher Mattie Anderson arrived in the town in 1883, finding that "A new adobe school house of two rooms awaited me."[108] So was the city jail an adobe building, the main section of the edifice described by one historian as "a square, adobe structure."[109]

Tilling the Fields

Mexicans in West Texas fortunate to own land struggled against formidable odds. The soil, the weather, and the consumer market were not always cooperative. Farming was more often than not a hardscrabble proposition.

To work the fields, farmers had to utilize the most basic resources. Lacking much capital to acquire the necessary implements, equipment, and agricultural tools to work the earth in an effective manner, Mexicans fell back on old practices. They depended on techniques (practical, although somewhat crude) their ancestors had long applied in tilling fertile lands, as did farmers in Presidio County who continued the use of the wooden plow, pulled by oxen teams.[110] In 1870, at the Torres family's Pontoon Bridge farm settlement, impoverished pioneers worked the land using "the ancient plow, consisting of a long beam at one end of which is a pointed stick—secured at an acute angle."[111] Anglo outsiders looked askance at such methods, openly disparaging the people using them and the tools they employed. Nathaniel Taylor (the previously mentioned journalist passing through West Texas in the late 1870s) thought the practice primitive, noting of farming at La Junta de los Ríos: "These people cultivate the ground precisely as the first inhabitants of the world did. They merely scratch the surface with a wooden plow, and sometimes they work whole fields with no other instrument than a hand-hoe. Fortunately the soil is a soft, sandy loam, very docile even to their poor implements."[112]

Despite such denigration, Mexican creativity, inventiveness, and capability as applied to soil tillaging produced positive results in some sections of West Texas. Helped by irrigation, farmers in Pecos County did well during the latter years of the 1870s. One newspaper report for November–December 1880 observed of canal-watered farms in the county: "At present, with the Mexican mode of cultivation, these lands are successfully producing corn, wheat, oats, barley, beans and all kinds of garden vegetables."[113]

Irrigating farmlands also required Mexican farmers in West Texas to contrive ways of transporting water effectively over distance. Water was available from sources like the San Felipe Creek, Comanche Springs, the Pecos River, the Rio Grande, and various other underground bodies, but how to move it where needed? Mexicans accomplished the task sans proper equipment, tools, dynamite, and the technical know-how to dig, break rock, and then channel the water along a proper course. Highly successful in developing workable strategies was the Torres family of Fort Stockton.

To funnel water to their several vegetable and grain fields, the family trusted the brawn, mechanical skills, and tool-making abilities of the laborers who had accompanied them from San Antonio. The workforce did much of the excavating at Fort Stockton using wooden shovels individuals brought with them or ones they crafted locally for that purpose.[114] Not much is known about how the Torres workers in 1870 dug the channel that effectively conducted waters from the west side of the Pecos to their farmlands on Pontoon Bridge. Presumably, they relied on tools as rudimentary as the ones used back at Fort Stockton.[115]

More incredible—considering the primitive work equipment utilized to perform such an engineering achievement—was the master project that the Torres Irrigation and Manufacturing Company and the Garza Irrigation and Manufacturing Company (under the charter the state granted them through the Legislature Act of 1875) completed five years later: moving water southward from the Pecos to the Torres farm site some distance away. The feat required a rock barrier wall (dam) to be constructed at the ditch's starting point, near what was the Great Rock, a massive geological formation thousands of years old. Using antiquated means, not much more than reliable manual tools such as shovels, pickaxes, chisels, and sledgehammers, Torres workers obtained from the Great Rock the boulders intended to block the Pecos current and direct the water into a canal. The Mexican laborers heaved wagonloads of huge, heavy rocks into the Pecos, channeling the water to the Torres farm and past it.[116]

Comparable to the Torres Company's achievement were other canal-digging ventures undertaken in south Presidio County during the 1870s. Almost as astounding as the challenge at Pecos was the construction of a six-mile-long canal at Polvo by the Presidio Irrigation Company, a body corporate that the state legislature chartered in 1876, membership consisting of Secundino Luján and associates. The Polvo operation required the colonists to open a gap through a rock mass near the Rio Grande. Having to do so without the explosives needed to dig the tunnel, the villagers relied on basic intuition. Following directions given them by Secundino Luján on how to find components to create dynamite, they acquired fertilizer from a bat cave, made use of ashes remaining from burned mesquite, and added the ingredients to sulfur brought in from Chihuahua City. After more than three years of toiling steadfastly, Polvo residents effected their purpose.[117]

The canals dredged in the early 1870s at places where the Rio Conchos entered the Rio Grande astonished the historian John Ernest Gregg, who wrote:

The ingenuity by the Mexicans [on both sides of the border] in this work was remarkable. The mouth of the ditch was of necessity some distance upstream from the land to be irrigated. So the ditches were run benches of land higher than those on which the land to be irrigated lay. A small brush or rock dam was constructed so that it extended at an angle out into the river stream. This directed the water into the mouth of the ditch. While it is true that a rise in the river would wash out such a dam, it could be cheaply and easily replaced. The early gravity ditches were constructed without the aid of surveying instruments. A point would be selected from which to begin the construction of the ditch, and the water would be allowed to flow into the mouth of the ditch and the proper fall would be secured by digging in such a way that the water would continue to flow. These early people seemed to have a sense of knowing where the proper leads would run.[118]

Remarkable and creative were other tactics Mexicans utilized to facilitate daily work tasks. In shelling ear corn, Mexicans in Pecos County crafted a device comprised of a rectangular frame—secured above ground by posts on all sides—equipped with a netted seven-by-nine-foot leather sheet stretched and attached to the poles. The workers loaded the canvas with the ear corn in a step intended to separate the kernels from the cob. They would then thresh the heap; the shelled corn would drop onto a wide cloth spread out on the ground. Crew members grasped this blanket, loaded with the fallen seeds, and tossed it upon a wagon. The wind helped filter out the chaff and fragments of the cobs that had remained with the kernels. The corn was then stored for future use.[119]

To provide for livestock (likely belonging to Anglo ranchers), Pecos County Mexicans during the 1860s and 1870s employed time-tested methods in gathering the abundance of grama grass native to areas such as those surrounding Fort Stockton. They sallied to the local fields on wagon carts and with hand scythes hacked at the grass, bundled it up, and by employing the fiber stripped from the leaves of the surrounding Spanish Dagger, tied up the harvest. They then piled the load on their carts, withdrawing with essential feed for the ranch/farm work animals.[120]

IMPLANTATION: THE ENCLAVES

Whatever their point of origin, the immigrants' destination was towards sites offering a favorable chance for life improvement. In most cases, opportunity lay in the countryside where Anglo entrepreneurs, but also Mexican women such as Paula Losoya and men and families with financial means or enterprise (like the Torres family), were opening new lands for farming and ranching. Movement at the same time occurred into some of the urban villages sprouting after the Civil War. As they pushed into either rural or urban settings, Mexicans gravitated, whether by choice or observance to social custom, toward space separate from an Anglo presence. At these micro-levels, cultural implantation occurred.

Settlement in San Felipe del Rio was in or near the estate that the husband-and-wife team of James and Paula Losoya Taylor, along with their associates, had founded. The farming community grew briskly during the 1860s and 1870s from the sale of farm products and animal feed to Fort Clark (in Brackettville) and to people moving along the road connecting San Antonio and El Paso. According to the 1870 census, the population for San Felipe (then in the county of Kinney) consisted of 159 total people, of whom thirty-nine had English names, the remainder being Mexicans, most of these of foreign birth. The site became distinct enough by the 1880s that it was then known as the town's "Mexican" enclave. Residents themselves called the settlement San Felipe.[121]

Little is known of how residential formation took root in the more scattered rural areas of West Texas. People might simply have agreed to live in a designated spot as transient workers (with an owner's consent) on a farm or ranch for the sake of survival. In one irrigated farm in Pecos County in the late 1870s, for instance, Mexicans lived as tenants, providing for themselves working the fields but then surrendering to the farmer a portion of the vegetable crops they harvested. The farm proprietor provided them with food but probably not much more. Presumably, the migrants lived in dwellings of their own making in a part of the farm away from the Anglo owner's property.[122]

In urban areas, the immigrants (and locals) likewise settled in distinct, and separate, cultural zones. In San Angelo, Mexican arrivals during the late 1860s lodged along the Concho River across from Fort Concho, some of them excavating into the riverbanks to carve out caves for housing. When in 1870 Bart DeWitt arrived from San Antonio to found the town of Santa Angela (called Santa Angela between 1870 and 1883), Mexicans acquired house lots from the developer along today's Concho, Twohig, and Beauregard Avenues—the streets north of the fort. During the late 1870s, as Santa Angela grew, Anglos bought land parcels a distance from the area Mexicans occupied, leaving a residential concentration that soon developed into the Mexican side of town.[123]

At Fort Stockton, the movement was into the confines of the community of St. Gall, but also onto the outlying areas beyond the newly reoccupied garrison. Pecos County in the postwar era remained open country so that newcomers such as the Torres family had established their farms and ranches both to the northeast (Cesario Torres's Seven-D Ranch) and to the southeast (Bernardo's and Félix Garza's farms) of the budding village which in 1881 had its name changed to Fort Stockton. Around the Fort Stockton environs, according to the 1870 census, lived some 400 residents. Many of these persons were undoubtedly Mexican workers who came to build their homes in the southern edge of the town, for over the years that section emerged as a visible Mexican barrio.[124]

At Fort Davis, concentration based on race or ethnicity did not take root immediately for several reasons. The fort stood in a remote area where soldiers, both white and African American, intermarried with Mexican women, making such divisions problematic. Further, no sizable white group existed to enforce segregationist rules practiced elsewhere in Texas. A Mexican quarter initially formed close to the garrison, but as the town proper developed, movement was to the east of the community's business center into a settlement that people began calling Chihuahuita ("Little Chihuahua").[125]

In ethnic pockets, whether they were urban locales or spontaneous spots sprouting out on ranch and farm grounds, Mexicans went about building community and establishing order, regularity, and stability. In those quarters, people remained connected to time-honored cultural conventions, including those governing family relations. Old beliefs lingered, such as in the efficacy of folk medicine. *Curanderas/os* treated the sick in the absence of a doctor's care. Folklore, in the form of tales, stories, and ballads, acted to explain superstitions, to teach children the rules of appropriate behavior, and to make sense of the mysteries of nature.

Spiritually, Mexicans persisted in their fidelity to Catholicism. In the immediate years after the Civil War, however, Mexican communities received not much more than superficial attention from the organized church whose administrative center lay in the more developed sections of the state.[126] Fort Stockton did see a Catholic church structure established as early as 1872 when arriving settlers (Anglos included) raised an adobe church on a spot on Comanche Creek. Parishioners replaced it in 1877 with what came to be known as St. Joseph Catholic Church. Whether a priest was permanently assigned to the town is unknown.[127]

It could have been that itinerant missionaries administered to Catholics at Fort Stockton, just as they did to other communities in West Texas. The first Catholic priest to arrive at Fort Davis in 1872, for example, found "no chapel, no rectory, really no place to lay his head." Until 1876, "saddle-bag priests" from San Antonio attended to the faithful in town and to those living in ranches. It was then that the parish of St. Joseph was organized and the first rectory built in 1877. Presumably, it was the rectory that acted in place of a church building, for one historian notes that: "The local Catholic Church (at Fort Davis, in the 1870s) served as a social and cultural center." Priests at Fort Davis, appointed to longer terms toward the latter years of the decade, saw also to the spiritual care of people in the outer countryside.[128] In Del Rio, meanwhile, Oblates of Mary Immaculate priests from Brackettville and Eagle Pass attended to local Catholics. But then in 1885, the Oblate fathers negotiated a loan to purchase property and a building where Mass could be celebrated. Ten years later, the Church elevated the mission's status, converting it to the Parish of Sacred Heart.[129]

Given that the Church's social structure in West Texas was in an embryonic stage, Mexican believers perforce created ways, informal ones to be sure, to address their religious needs. Perhaps a person's home or an agreed-upon community site acted as a gathering place to worship on Sundays or on other holy days. Certainly, they welcomed the arrival of visiting priests who then "blessed" marriages and baptisms. Families and friends mindful of their commitments to the sacraments might then have engaged in cheerful get-togethers to celebrate the solemn occasions.

Mexican Protestants were not much unlike Catholics when it came to practicing their faith on the frontier. In Del Rio's barrio of San Felipe, Mexican Baptists met in people's homes where fellow believers from surrounding barrios joined them. Toward the end of the century, however, church trustees purchased land for what came to be the Primera Iglesia Bautista Mexicana de San Felipe. The Methodists, on the other hand, founded El Principe de Paz Methodist Church in 1878 upon purchasing property along the San Felipe Creek. They held services under a tent until 1917 when they built a wooden frame structure.[130]

In Mexican spaces, especially ones in town settlements, frontier people sought—as they did with religion—to maintain a cultural environment familiar and assuring to all. Leaders organized self-help groups to assist those in difficult situations. Concerned parents looked to the future, schooling the young as best circumstances allowed, perhaps at home. A desire to salute the old country, as well as to provide diversion, prompted patriotic immigrants to take leadership roles in observing the *fiestas patrias* that celebrated Mexico's national holidays.

In such segmented zones, Mexicans also engaged in local politics, at times voluntarily but more generally when being drawn in by a rancher, businessman, or public official wielding influence or having authority over them. For some Anglos in West Texas, Mexicans represented a political resource available for personal use. Anglos wishing to get Mexicans to vote their way relied on several expedients. Those with disposable income could "buy" assumed constituents. Farmers and ranchers might make their workers enticing promises to sway their vote. Other Anglos could use power, accrued through wealth or social connections, to dictate to Mexicans how their ballots should be cast.

In the Concho Country, Francis Corbett Taylor, owner of a mail stage station at Benficklin, in January 1875 exercised his will over local Mexicans, among them those working in neighboring ranches and farms, as well as those whom he employed on his stage line, to get Benficklin voted as county seat—over competing Santa Angela, next to Fort Concho—of the newly organized Tom Green County. He persuaded enough Mexicans to vote his way that Benficklin indeed became the administrative center for the county, at least until a flood in 1882 destroyed the village and made Santa Angela the new county headquarters.[131]

Using Mexicans for political gain was evident in other parts of West Texas, certainly along the border area. In 1872, for instance, an Anglo candidate from Ysleta (in El Paso County) campaigning for a West Texas congressional district journeyed east to Fort Davis (then in Presidio County) and there met with Mose Kelley, a Presidio businessman well acquainted with political machinations in the Big Bend. The two men agreed on a stratagem on how to "obtain" votes in Presidio, Texas, on behalf of the Yselta office seeker. On the day of the election, Kelley was in Presidio and invited potential voters, including those from Ojinaga, to attend a festival to be held in Presidio that night. The guests were promised whiskey and other enticements. Amid the celebration and Kelley's speech-making (presumably in Spanish), the revelers were asked if they would vote for the Ysleta congressional candidate. If they answered yes, Kelley filled out the ballots marking them in favor of the campaigner from Ysleta.[132]

While Anglos saw gains to be made from such intrigues, Mexicans also found some opportunity in them. To the more scheming or selfish of collaborators, returns of the practice involved a night of frolic and wild abandon. If Mexicans looked upon elections as meaningless, without benefit to the masses, why not

simply enjoy a night of merriment at the *gringos'* expense? More noble participants viewed the custom of voting the Mexicans as an approved, or convenient,
manner to elect some of their own. After all, they succeeded in electing fellow
Mexicans to represent them in positions in Presidio, Pecos, and Tom Green
Counties. Others perceived the maneuvering as allowing them to engage the
political system.

A COMPARISON

At points in time, the history of people with a shared national origin tends
towards similarity, even when geographic setting might cause diversity. Thus did
the history of Tejanos in West Texas in the era between the years after the Civil
War to circa 1880 appear to resemble the history of Tejanos elsewhere in the state.

In both West Texas and South Texas, where Tejanos during that period were
concentrated, an immigrant cultural milieu shaped life orientation. Heritage
gave the two borderlands regions a Hispanic flavor as *pobladores* retained a strong
cultural connection, and perhaps an allegiance, to the motherland. In both
areas, a Mexican demographic majority throughout the nineteenth century acted
upon events, occurrences, and conditions. Attitudes about social structuring
affected life similarly in both sections. The broader Anglo population—whether
it was in South Texas or West Texas—reflexively regarded Mexicans as outsiders.
Rank-and-file Anglo-Texans, thus, overlooked Tejano claims to land holdings.
Whites moved confidently in asserting racial dominance, certain of having political support from the power structure in Austin and beyond.

While Tejanos seemed to have faced similar circumstances extending into
around 1880, in point of fact particular settings, timeframes, and incidents
across the state produced varying experiences. Colonists entering West Texas
(either from Mexico or from the interior of Texas) during the 1850s and in the
years after the Civil War encountered obstacles that those immigrating into
South Texas, and those already present, did not. Thinly settled (and scattered
at that) communities to help ease the frontier transition and to assist in survival
made adaptation to West Texas somewhat challenging. In contrast, adjustment
to South Texas—where villas or towns, some of them existing since the colonial
era (such as San Antonio) greeted new arrivals—was less trying.

Further differentiating the histories of Tejanos was the time during which
both Anglos and Mexican settled the respective southern and western regions.
Mexicans and Anglos streamed into West Texas almost simultaneously after

the 1850s. Following this, the two peoples worked peacefully to stabilize the frontier and acted to mitigate violence. Contrarily, Anglos trekked into South Texas to find it already occupied by land grantees and claimed by settled Mexican communities. To displace the inhabitants, they launched armed assaults on them stoked often by the racist contempt they harbored toward Mexicans.

The difference between the two sections seemingly gave Tejano West Texans an edge on opportunity. Historical currents in West Texas allowed civic-minded Mexicans to join the political system, as indeed some did, winning local elections. The situations even drew common folks into politics: homes functioned as voting stations and ordinary individuals became prospective jurors. The historical moment also opened room for those with business acumen, as in the case of men who dominated the vital freighting trade. Pioneers who saw their calling in tilling the soil or working livestock in West Texas found prospects as homesteaders and squatters, some of them aided—such as the Torres family and the members of the Presidio Irrigation Company—by the state government.

If the West Texas borderlands during the period between 1865 and 1880 offered enterprising Mexicans some possibility of gaining a niche in the mainstream, such fortuity did not visit the many clustered in the mass of unspecialized workers. Together, however, Mexicans succeeded in securing cultural space in West Texas, for they left there the stamp of their homeland, as well as a legacy of fortitude, tenacity, and perseverance. Into the last decades of the century and beyond, old pioneers and new immigrants would reinforce that culture and those values, shoring up old communities while founding new ones.

CHAPTER 2

DIMINISHING FORTUNES, COMMUNITY BUILDING, AND PERMANENCE, 1880-1900

INCORPORATION

During the last two decades of the nineteenth century, turmoil and disorder persisted in West Texas even as the region shed its frontier moorings. Into the 1890s, the wide range (most often policed by an underfunded constabulary) acted as a magnet for unscrupulous men, including shady businessmen, horse thieves, cattle rustlers, gunmen, and an assortment of other criminal types dodging the law. Miscreants committed outrages of every kind, including cold-blooded killings, lynchings, and vigilante executions, some of them organized attacks on towns and rural villages. Racist Anglos and hateful Mexicans holding grudges against each other—and prepared to reciprocate vengefully—made the region even more volatile.[1]

Simultaneously, countervailing forces prodded the Edwards Plateau and Trans-Pecos towards a new age that attached them to the broader national network. Certainly, the displacement of some of the Indian nations aided the onward thrust. The Apache war chief Victorio, who made West Texas his people's hunting grounds, met defeat in August 1880 near Van Horn (Culberson County) at the Battle of Rattlesnake Springs when Buffalo Soldiers of the 10th Cavalry chased him into Mexico. There Victorio encountered firm resistance from Mexican troops and on October 15, 1880, the Chihuahua state militia overpowered his forces, killing him and all his followers. In 1881, Texas Rangers patrolling Culberson County delivered a final defeat to his surviving band. With the Indians pacified, the US government implemented a policy of decommissioning the several West Texas garrisons so that by the end of the 1880s, all forts in West Texas had been deactivated.[2] Capitalist development followed, as did modern technological advances. In the process, the region entered a new historical period.

Another factor that pushed West Texas into the modern age was advances in the region's infrastructure. The Texas and Pacific railroad made its way to the emerging town of Pecos in Reeves County (created in 1883 from Pecos County) while almost at the same time in 1882 the Galveston, Harrisburg, and San Antonio railroad reached Alpine; at Sierra Blanca they linked up with the Southern Pacific. The nexus integrated West Texas into transnational commerce and brought it close to the more advanced sections of the state, to large urban metropolises in the nation, and to busy export shipping centers across the US.[3] Concurrently, the railroad opened the region to new communications means, accelerating efforts to extend the telegraph lines that had been strung by the Army during the 1870s.[4]

Further responsible for extracting West Texas from links to post–Civil War conditions was the migration of people from different sections of the state, varying parts of the country, and Europe and Mexico. Newcomers went in search of a fresh start or, in the case of a few, in want of health cures. Ranchers and farmers looked upon West Texas with high expectations, perceiving the land as one open to improved living. Whoever it was, whether immigrants from Mexico or those from Europe, newcomers found the region, especially the Trans-Pecos, as almost inviting settlement.[5]

Population growth had been gradual after the Civil War but escalated between 1880 and 1900. While it is impossible to calculate exactly the population increases for this era, historians have made estimates offering a general sketch of demographic trends therein. According to one analysis, in 1880 approximately 7,838 inhabitants of Mexican origin lived in West Texas; their numbers increased to 23,350 by 1900. By contrast, the Anglo population stood at 3,542 in 1880 and rose to 22,072 in 1900.[6] Through the 1880s and 1890s, the Mexican-origin population (both native- and foreign-born, many of the latter with origins in Chihuahua) exceeded the Anglo population in certain areas of the region. They constituted the majority of inhabitants in counties such as Presidio, Pecos, and Val Verde as well as some towns, among them Presidio, Fort Stockton, and Fort Davis.[7]

Rapid enough was the overall influx into the Edwards Plateau and the Trans-Pecos that Austin officials between 1880 and 1900 created and organized new counties therein. Added to those organized in the 1870s were Runnels (1880), Edwards (1883), Reeves (1884), Val Verde (1885), Midland (1885), Winkler (1887), Jeff Davis (1887), Brewster (1887), Coke (1889), Irion (1889), Sutton (1890), Ector (1891), Crockett (1891), Sterling (1891), Ward (1892), and Glasscock (1893).[8]

Urban expansion accompanied the organization of these counties, as older towns grew and new ones emerged. San Angelo, Del Rio, Presidio, Fort Davis, Fort Stockton, and other settlements that owed their origins to the post–Civil War era progressed to become permanent and thriving urban centers years later. Fort Stockton, the town, expanded from the village that had surrounded the vacated fort of the same name and soon emerged as excellent grounds for sheep and cattle raising.[9] New communities sprouted along the tracks of the iron rail, some of them as railroad stations and others as convenient water stops, among them Odessa for the Texas and Pacific Railway, and then Marathon (1882), Alpine (1882), and Marfa (1883) for the Galveston, Harrisburg, and San Antonio Railway.[10] Arriving ranchers and sheepmen founded villages like Ballinger, Menard, Sonora, Eldorado, Eden, Mertzon, and more.[11]

IMPLANTATION

Newcomer families stimulated economic activity in the region by investing work and time in enterprises they judged to have potential for profit, among them cattle ranching.[12] Prompting expectations for high gain on the free range were different types of grasses indigenous to the Trans-Pecos area, such as tobosa, grama, and bluestem. But ranchmen by the 1880s carelessly exploited the grazing lands, depleting available natural resources for their animals. To add to the troubles, during that decade they dealt with the "big dry-up," a calamity brought on by a devastating drought that killed thousands of their livestock. Despite bank foreclosures and other obstacles, ranchers succeeded in making ranching a viable economic concern in West Texas by the late nineteenth century.[13]

Ranchers also made sheep raising investment-worthy. The industry traced its origins in West Texas to the 1870s and ascended in the region during the following decades with the adoption of innovative means to warehouse wool and with the implementation of new approaches to market it. The world of sheep raising enticed entrepreneurs with such profits that by the 1880s the state counted close to seven million sheep. The hub of sheep production became the Edwards Plateau (namely the ranching counties of Edwards, Real, Val Verde, Kimble, Sutton, Crockett, Menard, Schleicher, McCulloch, Concho, and Tom Green) and of the lower Pecos River country, among them Terrell.[14]

Mining further spurred economic expansion in West Texas during the era. The center of this early activity was in the Big Bend, the region in West Texas most removed from the modernization trends unfolding throughout the Edwards Plateau and the Trans-Pecos during those decades. An early locus of operation was at Boquillas, Texas, in extreme southeastern Brewster County. During the early 1880s, silver and lead mining began in Boquillas, Coahuila, just across the Rio Grande. Aiming to take advantage of this emerging business, the Consolidated Kansas City Smelting and Refining Company hung a cable tram stretching from Boquillas across the Rio Grande to Boquillas, Texas (a length of about a quarter-mile) from which receiving point local mine representatives shipped the ore via freight wagons to railroad lines such as the one that passed through Marathon.[15]

Almost at the same time that the Consolidated Kansas City Smelting and Refining Company began processing silver in Boquillas, John W. Spencer, W. R. Shafter, and other investors initiated exploration for silver ore in the Chinati Mountains in Presidio County. Lacking the resources for major exploration, they leased part of their acreage in 1882 to the Presidio Mining Company, a partnership of mining speculators from San Francisco. The new owners by the mid-1880s found valuable silver deposits and soon a small village that came to be called Shafter grew up in proximity to the mine. Eventually, Spencer and his fellow investors sold their interests to the San Francisco firm, which continued operations at Shafter into the early decades of the twentieth century.[16]

Also during the 1880s, American mining companies undertook a determined effort in the Big Bend to exploit cinnabar, the mineral derived from quicksilver, or mercury.[17] According to a well-documented account, a man named Juan Acosta in 1884 found mercury and took it to a merchant named Ignatz Kleinman for testing. The two then sold their claim to a California business, but that entity soon abandoned the search after finding little of the ore substance.[18] Despite uncertainties, prospecting companies during the 1890s maintained enthusiasm for discovering large quantities of the element, for at that time it was considered to be a reliable detonator for combat weapons (later, quicksilver would be found useful as a medium for conducting electricity, as a substance effective in dental treatment, and as a source for enhancing pesticide toxicity). In 1896, investors from Texas and California, believing that further prospecting for the ore was worth pursuing, organized themselves under the name of the Marfa and Mariposa Mining Company, concentrating operations around a farming village called Terlingua, located some three miles from the Rio Grande. The company profited handsomely until it closed in 1910.[19]

Meanwhile, during the 1890s, Martín Solis, a ranch owner in the Boquillas, Texas, and the Mariscal Mountain areas where he ran livestock, discovered what proved to be new deposits of cinnabar right there in Mariscal Mountain.[20] Anglos deciding to seek financial gain by investing in the Mariscal Mine faced too many difficulties (among them a lack of essential equipment and natural resources for keeping the mine functioning, not to mention its location far from processing sites) to sustain operations. Consequently, they closed the mine in 1908 when the price of mercury fluctuated, but the mine reopened during World War I when demand for quicksilver mounted.[21]

LABOR

Mexicans both native- and foreign-born struggled constantly against daunting circumstances to earn a livelihood. Disadvantaging them was the control Anglo Americans held over the region's economy. Furthermore, because Mexicans were Spanish-dominant, they lacked the facility to negotiate for better opportunities. Also, few had the requisite know-how to infiltrate the skilled or semi-skilled sectors of the economy. Last, the social reality of the region deterred ambition as Anglos viewed Mexicans as foreigners undeserving of American privileges.

Sheepherders
Left for them to take were jobs as common laborers, often those deemed to be "Mexican work." With towns still in the early stages of growth (and few jobs obtainable there), most Mexicans almost by default worked the region's range lands.[22] Their greater concentration seems to have been on work with sheep, judging from the content of the literature attentive to this period: it focuses on the work of *pastores* instead of *vaqueros*. But other reasons may explain this clustering. For one thing, cattle ranching was not readily available to Tejanos as

a work option throughout the region. Livestock raising came somewhat late to the Big Bend, for instance, and even then, ranching as an enterprise did not take root there until the mid-1880s.[23] Further, the economic woes that West Texas cattlemen experienced during this time made work with cattle less available to Mexicans.

Sheep ranches in Edwards Plateau and Trans-Pecos counties relied almost exclusively on Mexican labor. Ranchers trusted the Mexicans for their knowledge of sheep husbandry and knew of the *pastores'* reputation for dependability and endurance. The job required the *pastores* to be on the range year around, spending their days alone in the field, tending to as many as 1,500 to 2,000 head of sheep. They stood vigilant over their flocks, shielding them from coyotes, panthers, bobcats, and snakes, meanwhile sheltering them from storms and inclement weather.[24]

For such prolonged stays, *pastores* set up makeshift camps to serve as a home site, a storehouse, and a sanctuary against the elements. Their company might have been a dog or two. Their main defense against predators was a slingshot; the weapon also permitted them to bunch the sheep tightly, move them around the grazing lands, and otherwise manage them as necessary. For their work and dedication, they earned hardly adequate wages. In Val Verde County in the 1890s, sheepmen paid them about $10 a month, much less than what Anglo cowhands netted for the same length of time.[25]

Pastores improvised their meals, falling back on ancestors-old methods adaptable to outdoor survival. Primary staples included dried meat, beans, and coffee. The shepherd slow-cooked *frijoles* (Mexican beans) as had his predecessors: starting in the evening, he allowed the beans to simmer in a tightly sealed pot through the night. Upon leaving early in the day to tend sheep, the herder fueled the fire, assured that the meal would be ready by evening. Using tallow for lard, the *pastor* embellished his fare with a mix of dry meat or salt pork, seasoning the beans with onions and garlic. Cornbread, if flour was available, could be baked in a frying pan.[26]

Respite from this life of isolation came from periodic visits by a "rustler," a type of foreman who dropped by the campsite to replenish the herder's supplies, food, coffee, and water if no water holes existed nearby. It was the rustler's job to inform *pastores* when to fold camp and move to better grazing locations.[27] After months of being properly shepherded, the sheep were moved to a designated area on the ranch premises for the lambing cycle in March and April and the yearly shearing in May and June. These phases of sheepherding constituted a time of reprieve from the drudgery of the *pastor*'s job.[28]

As with sheepherding, shearing on West Texas ranches fell largely to Mexican hands. The shearers, called *tasinques* (clippers or shearers) in Spanish, applied routines and work rhythms learned in Mexico. They trekked to the job site, wherever the location, on wagons—as they did to Terrell County—carrying with them the equipment and supplies used on the job, often accompanied by family. While the men went about their tasks, family members helped out as needed: women prepared the cooking and young boys assisted in the shearing routine by gathering clipped wool. The day ended around the campfire with family sharing a meal (likely of mutton), relaxing, exchanging stories, singing, and preparing for the morrow. The pay in Terrell County in the last decades of the nineteenth century stood at about 1.5 cents per sheep shorn.[29]

Freighters

Transporting agricultural products, ranch supplies, household goods, and other living essentials across the West Texas countryside required experienced crews able to handle mule- or horse-drawn wagons. Ever present in Mexican communities were those who possessed the adeptness to carry out such formidable and often perilous missions.[30]

RACE AND PREJUDICE

The strides whites made in population advances during the ending decades of the nineteenth century helped perpetuate harmful racial attitudes that Anglos harbored in their movement into West Texas after the Civil War. Racist feelings by then had seemingly become so ingrained that they could not be muted. Compared to earlier times, local Anglos expressed their bigotry without much restraint, as did people in the vicinity of San Angelo on the eve of the twentieth century. A correspondent from the *Chattanooga Times* reported Mexicans there as being "chiefly Aztecs, with a sprinkling of Spanish and Negro," some of them "dark to the point of blackness." Mechanically, Mexicans lacked imagination and creativity, the journalist maintained. In working what little pieces of property they might possess, Mexicans used tools "the same as those of ancient Egypt. A crooked mesquite stick, hardened at the larger end by fire and slightly sharpened, serves for a plow." The many racial attitudes upon which he elaborated extensively in his discourse, he assured readers, derived from discussions with prominent citizens of San Angelo and surrounding areas.[31] In neighboring Coke County, whites shared a similar mindset. A community member there asserted brazenly that whites would be "a happy people [if] Negroes or Mexicans" did not live locally.[32]

In addition to considering Mexicans a racially degraded and technologically unenlightened people, Anglos attributed to Mexicans dispositions that mirrored ones exhibited by fellow whites in the US West. The Mexican temperament was such, some Anglos believed, that inflicting harm or injury upon others was of second nature to them. Bob Kennon, a cowhand speaking of the Mexican *vaqueros* working alongside him at a ranch site west of San Angelo in the 1890s, commented, ". . . often the Mexican riders got into fights. When sober they were fine, but when they got drunk, they'd fight almost anything—horses, saddles and gear, money, or *señoritas*. They were quick on the draw and had red-hot tempers."[33]

Mexicans were attributed with a lust for blood, a trait conspicuously manifest, according to a county clerk in McCulloch County (organized 1876), in the case of a "Mexican greaser" who in 1886 brutally killed a local policeman. The penalty for the transgression was death for local Mexicans—many implicated in the crime by their connection to other Mexicans who routinely engaged in disruptive behavior, gambling, drinking, and disorderly conduct—if they did not leave the area forthwith. The episode came to the attention of the Mexican consul in San Antonio who called for an investigation into the state of local affairs. The county clerk, however, assured the consul that Mexicans need not fear the threat—they were safe to work in the county. The episode in the end seems to have passed without any guarantees made to protect the small community in McCulloch County.[34]

In May 1891, the *San Antonio Express* reported a story so implausible that it would have held no credibility if the alleged offender had not been Mexican. The facts surrounding this "diabolical murder" (as the *Express* branded it) had a Mexican man in Del Rio hacking his lover to pieces with a hatchet after a night's tryst. Following the sadistic act, the Mexican used the blood of his victim to smear the wall ("in Mexican language"): "fresh beef for sale." The murderer then took flight to Mexico, according to the news article.[35]

The wanton perceptions Anglos held toward alleged Mexican inferiority, backwardness, and cruelty rose to be of general acceptance and did not exclude those in influential positions such as Judge Roy Bean, "the Law West of the

Pecos," whose prejudices encapsulated the view that no law prohibited the killing of a Mexican.[36] Bean was not alone in such devaluations of Mexican life, as others viewed killing Mexicans as being of no significant consequence. One Texas sheepman expressed Anglo sentiments when reporting on an instance during which cowmen encountered a Mexican corpse on the road: the men dismissed the body as if it were no one's duty to bury it.[37]

Unsurprisingly, the attitudes Anglos held toward Mexicans and the actions they took in divulging their feelings led Mexicans to reciprocate, at times taking out individual action against their supposed enemy or, in some cases, in collective encounters that came to be interpreted by the white community as race wars or race riots. One of these violent episodes occurred in Murphyville (modern-day Alpine) in April 1886. Smoldering distrust seemingly lay behind race relations there. As Anglos slowly moved into the area with the building of the Galveston, Harrisburg, and San Antonio Railway, Mexicans, according to one newspaper report, had responded by "moving in there secretly in considerable numbers, and have sought to drive out the whites and run the place." The contempt towards Anglos produced on April 18 an attack by Mexicans on the town's Cattle Exchange Saloon where Anglos tended to gather. The raid on the tavern turned out to be a bloody affair, according to newspaper accounts, as the Anglos (in retreat) fired back at the attackers, inflicting casualties upon them while the Mexicans seriously injured one of the patrons. After the "riot," as the episode came to be called, Anglos launched an effort to force all Mexicans from the town and its surroundings.[38]

The resentment Tejanos harbored toward whites also provoked them into taking group action against their perceived nemeses. Potential settings for such clashes would have been Mexican festive occasions, such as *fandangos*, where Anglo males might join the merrymakers. Mexican revelers would hardly have looked kindly upon the interlopers, suspecting them of casting romantic eyes upon the Mexican women present. At one *fandango* held in Valentine (Jeff Davis County) in November 1894, simmering jealously and indignation produced a "fatal fight between Mexicans and Americans" (as one newspaper reported it), resulting in the death of one unfortunate bystander.[39]

Racial tensions could further lead to feuding, as indeed occurred in Del Rio in May 1884. The origins of one family dispute are convoluted, but they may have had their beginnings in domestic difficulties between Jones Griner and his Mexican wife. Somehow, this private affair led Indalicia Rivera (father of Griner's wife) in December 1880 to kill Samuel Griner (brother of Jones).

Tied to the Rivera family by friendship was a man named Albino Pérez Jr. who, since December 1883, when one Thomas Leakey had killed his father in a barroom brawl, sought vengeance upon whites for Albino Sr.'s death (although seemingly the Griners had no connection to the death of Albino Sr.). Albino Jr. had a reputation as a brigand and was under indictment for murder in Val Verde County. Somehow, the grudge the Riveras harbored against the Griners and the hate that Albino Pérez Jr. preserved towards the (unknown) white perpetrators responsible for the murder of his father merged to abet community-wide antipathy between Mexicans and Anglos in Del Rio. The state of tension by the spring of 1884 had reached a point where some of the locals felt that a secret society in the community intended to inflict violence upon Mexican residents, and that police protection for them was nonexistent. Rioting broke out following a raid, led by Albino Pérez Jr. himself, early in May 1884, upon a local dance hall where Henry Griner and friends were indulging in festivities. According to Anglo sources, the well-armed band of attackers apparently had only Henry Griner as their target but fired indiscriminately on the crowd, killing Griner and wounding two women.

The affray inflamed the white population of the city, which felt sure the assault on Griner had been plotted earlier as the Mexican patrons had left the dance hall (supposedly on cue) moments before the attack. Each camp now vowed reprisal upon the other, promising the destruction of Del Rio. Whites actually burned down some of the community's dwellings, including a dance house owned by Albino Pérez Jr., while the Mexicans threatened to set fire to the town. One citizen opined that Henry Griner's death had kindled animosities of long standing between the two peoples. But others noted that those rallying behind Pérez were unsavory characters and, in fact, a group of citizens within the Tejano community was calling for racial peace. In the end, cavalry soldiers brought order to the border community, although distrust scarcely vanished. A dreadful fear of vengeance lingered among some members of the Mexican working class who now considered leaving for safety in Mexico. The Mexican minister in Washington asked the State Department for an investigation of the conflict, but civil officials assured representatives in DC that all citizens in Del Rio were secure under the protection of local authority.[40]

Aside from family antagonisms, feuds surfaced as manifestations of the persistent distrust and suspicion each race held towards the other. One such racial fracas erupted in Presidio County at the Four Sixes Ranch in July 1897 due to long-standing antipathy between the Anglo and Mexican sheepherders at the ranch. According to accounts, animosity renewed in May during the Cinco de Mayo (the Fifth of May, a Mexican national holiday) celebration. Drunken cowboys crashed the feast, shooting indiscriminately at dancers, injuring one Mexican. Some weeks following the May incident, someone set fire to the Anglo sleeping quarters, with suspicion falling upon the *pastores*. The white cowboys swore death to the perpetrators, but the ranch owner dealt with the disorder by firing the sheepherders (and replacing them with a new crew). Feuding between the fired Mexicans and the cowboys persisted, as apparently the former now stirred trouble between the newly hired sheepherders and the cowboys, who had warned the troublemakers of death if they neared the ranch. Tensions mounted and shooting broke out in late July, resulting in injuries to two cowboys and one Mexican. The ranch owner, Floyd Jones, apparently took charge of the matter and settled it locally.[41]

Beliefs that Mexicans were troublemakers, violence-prone, inherently inferior, and even nonhuman justified Anglo use of extralegal means to preserve the racial status quo. Whites considered vigilante action and lynching as acceptable measures for meting out justice against accused Mexican lawbreakers. Still, such cases in West Texas never reached the degree of sadism found in the eastern sections of the state, where public burnings of victims came to be ritualistic.

But lynching was cruel in whatever form the mob carried it out, and the practice was not absent in western Texas. Around Fort Davis in December 1883, whites took the law into their own hands, intercepting a deputy sheriff escorting to town a group of four Mexicans accused of killing a man named Domingo Polomo. The armed group accosted the law officer, wrested the prisoners from his command, and lynched them. Residents a few days later informed the *San Antonio Express*, following the hanging of another Mexican (accused of murder near Fort Davis): "The lawlessness prevailing in this neighborhood is unprecedented. It is to be hoped a few more lynchings and hangings will have a tendency to restore the county to its usual quiet."[42]

Lynch law arrived in Shafter in 1890. When authorities arrested a Mexican creating mischief around the site, some white miners seized the prisoner—who had been chained to a tree—and mortally shot him. With tensions rising, the Mexican community warned all whites (whom they believed to be involved in the killing) to leave the area. Then, on a Sunday while Mexicans frolicked at a *baile* (dance) in the Mexican section of the settlement, racial friction erupted as overly excited revelers commenced gunplay. White policemen responded to the disturbance, but the Mexicans warded them off. The lawmen returned to the scene with reinforcements, only this time to face deadly shooting. The confrontation persisted through the night until whites, who included miners and Texas Rangers, prevailed over the Mexicans. A force of Texas Rangers stationed in Presidio County subsequently helped bring peace to the village and protection to the white mine workers.[43]

Certain to expect lynch law would be Mexicans accused of the rape of a white woman. Such was the misfortune that struck a Mexican in the early 1890s whom citizens in Junction City (Kimble County) believed responsible for such a racially forbidden violation—in this case, upon a rancher's wife. According to one contemporary who heard the call for "Give him Lynch law!" and "Hang him like a dog!": "Had he been a Texan, it would probably have fared very differently with him from the first; but it is difficult to convince these people that a Mexican is a human being. He seems to be the Texans' natural enemy; he is treated like a dog, or perhaps, not so well."[44] In another case of lynching in West Texas, three unidentified individuals in February 1891 detained a man named Jesús Salceda and at the town of Knickerbocker (just west of San Angelo) lynched him from a live oak tree, causes for the act unknown.[45]

DIMINISHING FORTUNES

The historical record encompassing the ending decades of the nineteenth century does not show Mexican Americans to have made political improvement on the benchmark they had set before 1880. Fading noticeably from the scene after 1880 were the likes of the Torres brothers of Pecos County, Secundino Luján of Presidio County, and Pablo Alderette of Tom Green County.

What explains these diminishing fortunes for the Mexican American population as a whole? For one thing, demographic disproportions that earlier had facilitated racial accommodation and cooperation were now less disparate. By 1880, the white population had surged to a point that instilled among Anglos the confidence to be self-dependent.[46] Such an edge gave whites the leverage to deal with any possible disruption (imagined or real) to the social order. Employers might fire their workers for whatever reason, some of them genuine (like filing for office against an Anglo) and others fabricated. Men of influence drummed up charges against Mexican "troublemakers" (perhaps for labor organizing). Police officials had a free hand to arrest Mexicans on suspicion of "loitering" if they found them intruding into the "Anglo part of town." In Alpine, whites during the 1890s (and far into the twentieth century) could use "discretion" to keep "impertinent" Mexicans at bay.[47] With such a power advantage on the Anglo side, the earlier need to coexist receded, as evidenced by one variable: the downturn in the number of interracial marriages. Even in places such as Fort Davis where prior to the early 1880s as high as 20 percent of marriages involved Anglo men and Mexican women, the pattern of cross-cultural marriage arrangements declined. Cases of such older connections now seemed restricted to the Big Bend area, where the number of Anglo males still exceeded that of white females.[48]

Mexican American men of social and economic position had taken proactive stances after the Civil War when the political system accommodated them, but Anglo-American ascendance now curbed political advances, diminished opportunities in government positions, and made control of Mexicans easier. Politically powerful individuals preyed on those most vulnerable to threats, harassment, violence, or job loss. Pecos County Judge O. W. Williams recalled that in the 1890s men such as Fort Stockton Sheriff A. J. Royal could depend "upon the Mexican voters which he can cajole or bulldoze into voting for him."[49] Businessmen and bureaucrats allied themselves with unprincipled politicos to employ the post–Civil War stratagem of identifying potential voters, organizing a feast for them on the eve of the scheduled election, committing them to vote for a selected candidate, and finally escorting them to the polling site.[50]

Along the border, Anglos exercised their own creative methods in efforts to maintain mastery over the Mexican majority. In the 1892 Presidio County election, candidate for sheriff Den Knight herded cattle across the river to feed hungry villagers, and on the day of the election had grateful male voters cross into Presidio town to cast their vote in his favor. In the lower Big Bend area (and throughout West Texas, in fact) at that time, no need existed to prove citizenship, so Anglo candidates on election day simply marked ballots for themselves and instructed the voters to carry the doctored ballot to the polling place and drop it in the designated box.[51]

Should Mexicans attempt to circumvent existing practices or exercise some degree of independence, Anglos stood prepared to neutralize them. In July 1886, several Mexican Americans sought to participate in the Tom Green County democratic convention, but delegates prevented them with a resolution that read "that no party be allowed to vote in this convention who cannot speak the US language." According to a newspaper account, Anglos present endorsed the resolution cheerfully, and the sergeant-at-arms then ushered the Mexicans out of the convention hall.[52]

Still, into the mid-1880s a small circle of men within the Mexican community managed to keep or to gain political office. In Pecos County, Mexicans continued scoring a few victories in some county commission posts: in 1880 Cesario Torres again won election (he was a member of the commission from 1875 to 1886), and Rosario Ureta received an appointment to that government unit in 1891.[53] When in 1883 officials established the Presidio County commissioners' court, Secundino Luján won election as commissioner of Precinct 3.[54]

In places where they enjoyed a numerical majority and Anglo influence was weak, Mexicans were sure to be political actors. In Presidio County, for one, Mexicans consistently served as election officers, at times supervising the election polls at their homes. Some gained positions as county clerks, as did Desiderio Alarcón in the 1890s.[55] In towns such as Fort Davis, where Mexicans and Mexican immigrants constituted the majority population in the 1880s, Mexicans performed jury duty.[56] Other Mexicans worked as constables or as police officers, as did Cleto Herredia, a deputy sheriff in Pecos County in 1880.[57]

COMMUNITY BUILDING

Amidst social denigration, economic disadvantage, and political handicaps, Mexicans (like compatriots who had paved their way into West Texas earlier) continued upon the task of persevering, both in places where they already lived and/or in areas where they hoped to start anew. They undertook such life struggles on lands almost entirely belonging to Anglos; unlike South Texas, Mexicans were neither living in nor trekking into old land grants once given to their forebears by Spain or Mexico and then lost to newcomer Americans. In these Anglo-owned (or claimed) spaces of Anglo hegemony, Mexicans sank roots and forged ahead, striving to establish orderly lives while carrying on old traditions and customs.

Various were the ways in which Mexicans adjusted to harsh frontier settings. In isolated rural areas, where sometimes only simple hope for social improvement greeted them, newcomers made do with whatever the local environment availed them. When the Trinidad and Jesusa (Farías) family from the Central Texas town of San Marcos arrived at Fort McKavett (Menard County) in the early 1880s to work in area ranches, they sheltered in some of the stone buildings abandoned by the soldiers when the fort closed in 1883. They depended on the San Sabá River for water and on the wildlife in the area for food. Life was a bit more stable northeast of Fort McKavett, where at the (Gus) Noyes Ranch (McCulloch County), families of *vaqueros*, with origins in San Antonio, Texas, located in 1886.[58]

In more settled locales, Mexican adaptation followed paths such as taken in Ozona (Crockett County). In the last decades of the nineteenth century, settlers from places like Del Rio and Sonora began moving into the town. Upon arrival, the Mexicans made space in a section of town where they built *jacales* and adobe homes. They went about relying on wild game and home gardens for sustenance and found water to be fetched from a local windmill. They turned to jobs available in the area, working as sheepherders, ranch hands, and adobe builders. For the most part, they made do without schooling or religious services, although occasionally a priest visited the Ozona community to baptize the young and marry couples.[59]

Adjustment in town sites called for accommodating to changing trends. In San Angelo, movement and growth was no longer into the lots near downtown where Mexicans had settled initially with the coming of Fort Concho. As the town grew in the mid-1880s, Anglo newcomers began displacing Mexicans from their old lots, forcing them to find new settlement quarters. Mexicans moved southward away from the downtown district so that by the late 1890s, a Mexican enclave had sprouted along a strip of land situated between the southern edge of the business center and the Concho River. A second Mexican enclave in the meantime emerged with the arrival in 1888 of the Gulf, Colorado & Santa Fe Railway, which built its depot in the northern section of the city. Mexican railroad men found it convenient to walk to work from their homes in the new barrio, which came to be called "Santa Fe."[60]

At Fort Davis, Mexican-descent residents still considered Chihuahuita an agreeable place for residence. Even if the town had been one where Anglos, African Americans, and ethnic Mexicans had interacted quietly since the earliest days of the fort's founding, residents observed the unspoken rule that Mexicans should live apart from Anglos. More logically, Mexicans themselves preferred staying in a cultural environment that was genuinely "theirs."[61]

In April 1882, the Southern Pacific Railroad reached a camp area in West Texas that, as mentioned earlier, grew into Murphyville. Mexicans made up part of the railroad's crew, and to be near their menfolk, families in that day would travel along with them and camp close to the worksite in makeshift shelters. These earliest of pioneers settled along Alpine Creek, on the south side of the railroad, and as history would have it, became the founders of modern-day Alpine (the town's name was changed in 1888).[62]

The coming of the Galveston, Harrisburg and San Antonio Railway in 1883 sparked growth in Del Rio's overall population and simultaneously expanded old Mexican settlements and gave rise to new ones. The San Felipe barrio, traceable to the founding of the Taylor/Losoya estate in the 1860s, grew with new immigration from Mexico, so much so that local Anglos quickly came to regard it as "the Mexican portion of the town." The railroad's presence then created a new barrio in the northwestern section of Del Rio as Mexican track workers and their families clustered in the vicinity of the railroad station. This neighborhood soon came to be known as "Chihuahua."[63]

Entrenchment in settled rural communities followed adjustment patterns akin to ones in urban settings, as occurred in Big Bend villages such as San José del Polvo in Presidio County. Newcomer settlers augmented the existing population at Polvo, turning to farming as had the several other families already there. By the mid-1880s, the expanding settlement had reached a point where the colonists felt a requirement for educational facilities. They hired Desiderio Alarcón from Presidio, Texas, a young man who had received his schooling in Mexico, to teach in a newly constructed one-room building.[64]

The small community of La Coyota in Brewster County remained a fruitful farming settlement as it had been since its founding in the 1860s. Villagers, who occupied about a dozen dwellings in the 1890s, cultivated beans, squash, corn, and other vegetables for their own consumption but in the years ahead began selling their goods to men working the nascent mines at Terlingua.[65]

DIASPORA

Mexican-origin people entering West Texas borderlands during the last decades of the nineteenth century did not always aim for starts in established communities. A pioneering spirit, and the instinct to survive, urged them to ferret out more auspicious places for commencing afresh. Oftentimes, they chose sparsely populated grounds, but ones close to water sources, perhaps a natural spring or the Rio Grande. They settled there assuming preemption would ultimately earn them entitlement to their claims. For their existence, they raised vegetable crops and domestic animals such as goats. In what remained to many a frontier setting, neighboring Anglos were at times inclined to recognize the legitimacy of the Mexicans' presence, depending upon them for farm goods and small animal stock.[66]

Among new communities established was Brogado, founded in 1880 in Reeves County. The settlement proved durable, attracting the attention of the Catholic Church which on a regular schedule dispatched clergymen to minister to the faithful there. The most famous of these priests was named Father Brogado, and sometime during the late nineteenth century locals honored the priest by naming their community after him. The increasing number of people in the village in time required schooling the young, so by the late 1890s a public school operated in Brogado.[67]

Also settled in Reeves County was Saragosa. Some fifteen families in 1880 arrived in the Toyah Creek area intending to make their new life as farmers. The colonists subsequently relocated to present-day Saragosa (four miles east of their original location on Toyah Creek). As the community grew with the arrival of additional people, leaders considered plans for local education, and by 1899 their efforts had materialized in the form of two functioning schools with an enrollment of twenty-nine students.[68]

Domenicio (or Dionisio) Mata, who in 1884 had located with his family to 160 acres at a point in Presidio County called "Punta de la Agua," moved in the late 1890s to a site on Alamito Creek which soon took the name of Casa Piedra (Spanish for the rock house he built). The community flourished to an extent that by the end of the century, in excess of fifty farm families made up the population at Casa Piedra. Locals found the land ideal for farming and so lived off ample supplies of corn, beans, and hay, while at the same time raising cotton.[69]

Sometime around the last decades of the nineteenth century, a community sprouted along land belonging to Estéban Ochoa, the grandson of Ben Leaton and Juana Pedraza. Ochoa established his ranch along the Rio Grande, about ten miles northwest of Presidio, Texas. By the early twentieth century, Ochoa, Texas, grew to host some seventy-five families and had by then a school open for session.[70] During the late 1890s, Shafter, the laboring village that had sprouted with the arrival of the Presidio Mining Company, expanded. Foreign-born common laborers joined the local Mexican population to stabilize the community, and it persisted until its decline after World War II.[71]

The diaspora of the latter years of the nineteenth century led ethnic Mexicans into the lower Big Bend region of Brewster County, there to found more new communities. During the 1890s, Alberto Molinar and Antonio Franco brought

Mexican families to a spot along Terlingua Creek (after mining started in the Terlingua District in the early 1900s, the settlement came to be called "Terlingua Abaja"). A general store owned by Cipriano and Guadalupe Hernández became the social center for the site, which persisted into the twentieth century.[72] From the original Terlingua village of the 1880s sprung the small hamlet of Molinar in the late 1890s. The Molinar family, its founders, thought the new place to which they relocated had good farming prospects, and they soon engaged in subsistence agriculture and in the small-scale raising of goats and farm animals.[73]

Boquillas, Texas, originated during the late 1880s from efforts by Mexican-descent farmers in the Big Bend to furnish farm goods in demand by the miners and their families working the mines across the Rio Grande in Boquillas, Coahuila, Mexico.[74] A recent arrival who would establish stability in southeastern Brewster County was Martín Solis. With his sons during the 1890s, Solis acquired ranch land in the areas around Boquillas, Texas, and in Mariscal Mountain. Together, the family continued to expand its holdings by obtaining more rich spreads for livestock grazing.[75]

The village of San Vicente (five miles southwest of Boquillas) also owed its early beginnings, as did other settlements in the lower Big Bend, to planning by enterprising colonizers. Inez Sánchez and about eighteen families, some of whom had been working the mines at Boquillas del Carmen in Mexico (Chihuahua), crossed into Texas in 1895 to try their luck in the area's farmlands. Improvising, the colonists constructed lodgings—that is, *jacales* and adobes—relying on surrounding flora. As did their neighbors on both sides of the Rio Grande, the villagers harvested beans, squash, corn, and melons, raising enough products to provide not only for themselves but for the mining communities across the river. San Vicente remained the home almost exclusively of the founding families until newcomers began augmenting it in the early 1900s.[76]

In what became Val Verde County, the Torres family of Fort Stockton founded the small village of Eagle's Nest. Using land certificates that the family's companies (Torres Irrigation and Manufacturing Company and the Garza Irrigation and Manufacturing Company) had received from the state under provisions of the Texas Legislature Act of 1875, Bernardo Torres acquired property at an area (the future Val Verde County) locally known as Eagle's Nest. When Bernardo died in 1882, the land (some thirty-seven sections) passed to Cesario, who then sent his son Jesús Pablo Torres to ensure the ranch land's development.

From this venture grew the town of Eagle's Nest (which became Langtry, later made famous by Judge Roy Bean).[77]

With the exceptions of villages clustered along the lower Big Bend belt, among them La Coyota, Boquillas, Terlingua, Molinar, and San Vicente, Tejano communities in West Texas borderlands tended to be separated from each other by remote distances, as was the case with most established settlements. Principal towns such as San Angelo, Del Rio, Fort Stockton, and Alpine were in fact situated in different counties (invariably, these urban sites served as the county seat). Rural villages (such as El Polvo, Saragosa, Brogado, Casa Piedra, and Langtry), mining camps, farms, and ranches also lay broadly diffused throughout the region. Far from each other though these places were situated, Hispanic communities fared well culturally. Newcomers implanted old ways, customs, and traditions wherever they settled throughout West Texas and succeeded in maintaining a cultural ethos almost unchanged. Even without interaction and interplay among dispersed communities, an imported ethnic culture endured, as did social unity.

HOME BUILDING

In the latter decades of the nineteenth century (as well as beyond), West Texas Mexicans continued building and utilizing the kinds of shelter that Indigenous peoples and their own ancestors from Mexico had long adopted as practical and utilitarian. *Jacales* and adobes both persisted as the most realistic means of home protection for folks with little financial means. Culturally, each linked the *pobladores* with a past rooted in the motherland.

Considering adobe's acknowledged superiority over *jacales*, Mexicans preferred it for home living; indeed, West Texas Mexicans of better means, in the nineteenth century and later, favored adobe dwellings. Continuing past practices, adobe homebuilders used local trees to form the house's skeleton. Adobe bricks would then be stacked horizontally in rows along the side sections. The walls would be plastered and sealed to protect against the elements. Large corner pillars braced long planking that framed the roofing. On this crude layout the roofer carefully arranged small tree branches and spread dirt upon them to waterproof the interior. Flat roofs, with a slight slope—a feature imported from Spain—usually characterized West Texas adobe homes. Tenants made do with an earthen floor.[78]

Adobe manufacturing had disadvantages, however. It called for some knowledge of, and experience in, concocting it. Further, the job was time-consuming.

Also, adobe home construction required a greater application of labor than did *jacal* making. The *jacal*, consequently, was more common in West Texas Mexican American communities during the nineteenth century. Several reasons explain that prevalence. *Jacales* could be made cheaply and constructed promptly if the necessary building materials were at hand. A lone individual could assemble a *jacal*, but certainly, the whole family and even a community could assist in the venture. The *jacal* could also be considered as temporary shelter if inhabitants thought their stay in an area was to be brief. According to the circumstances, they could abandon the structure and build a new one at the next site.

Typically, *jacales* consisted of one room, although people could always add quarters. The surrounding landscape supplied materials. From local trees came the vertical columns (dug into the ground) placed at the house corners. Sotol branches or maguey stalks stitched together by slim swaths of wood or of narrow bands of rawhide made do as walls. Sticks, stones, or assorted debris also served as reliable elements for siding. Mud would then be plastered to finish the work.

For the *jacal*'s roofing, Tejanos used the branches of cottonwoods, willows, or other trees as rafters. Plant substances that could include ocotillo, maguey, or yucca, as well as straw, grass, or brush placed on the stalks, served as covering. Adobe would be applied above this base to ensure that the *jacal* be rain resistant. A small degree of slant allowed water to drift off. The floor remained the bare earth, although inhabitants often stomped the ground down hard and smoothed it out. Because the *pobladores* brought with them only the most essential household fixtures, furnishings such as bedding, chairs, and tables had to be crafted out of materials fetched from around the setting's environs.[79]

CLASS

By the last two decades of the nineteenth century, the class order tenuously existing within some Tejano communities faced erosion. Receding was the element that once had constituted the small upper crust of Mexican American society. Several factors caused this fragmentation. By the 1880s, Anglos had solidified their authority over Mexicans, dislodged them from influential political posts, supplanted businesspeople from earlier forms of livelihood (such as in the business of freighting), and dispossessed many who had acquired land either through scrip or squatters' claims.

Gone were ranchers such as Pablo Alderette of San Angelo and, most prominently, the Torres brothers who had been such a success at farming around Fort

Stockton. The siblings now had to deal with the new demographics and racial realities of the 1880s but also, more personally, with misfortune. During 1882, financial problems began haunting Cesario. When Bernardo, his brother and partner in the Torres Irrigation and Manufacturing Company, died that year, commitments the Torres Company had made to the state were to be fulfilled, namely that of maintaining the upkeep of the canals the company was building in Pecos County. Adding to his problems, Cesario alone was now responsible for settling the bonds the two brothers had posted with the county attesting to the trustworthiness of friends who served as county officials. Short of assets, Cesario informed the County Court—at which time he was serving as commissioner for Precinct 2—that he had to default. His difficulties forced him into selling his Seven-D Ranch in 1886. At the same time, he resigned his membership in the court and soon after led his family out of Fort Stockton to his hometown of San Antonio.[80]

The fate of the Torres clan perhaps mirrored that of others in West Texas who had once seen their destiny in farming and not in ranching. The record does not show the startup of new farming operations akin to those established by individuals such as Fabricio Granado, Secundino Luján, Darío Rodríguez, and Victoriano Hernández. Mexicans now gathered in farming villages such as in Brogado and Saragosa in Reeves County, Casa Piedra in Presidio County, and Terlingua, Molinar, Boquillas, and San Vicente in Brewster County.

The circumstances of the new era, however, did not totally dismantle the old class formation. While in the period before 1880 farming appeared to have attracted Mexicans more than had animal husbandry, in the later decades of the nineteenth century, as ranching became associated with West Texas economics, Mexicans of enterprise actively took up (or continued earlier) ranch ventures. Those fortunate enough to possess grazing land and livestock came to constitute a small but discernible element that stood just above the commoners. These stockmen, most of whom were to be found in the Big Bend region of West Texas, tended to, according to one historian, "successful ranching operations that compared favorably with those of their Anglo counterparts." These *rancheros* chose to raise longhorn cattle in contrast to Anglo ranchers in the area who favored investing in Herefords.[81]

Mexicans in the Big Bend successful in the ranching industry included Martín Solis (of cinnabar discovery fame) and his sons. During the 1890s, Solis and his family added to their earlier land acquisitions, obtaining more rich spreads for horses and cattle grazing. The clan owed success to their familiarity with livestock, their business acumen, and then during the early twentieth century, to timely opportunities as new mines in the area opened and workers required food products. Other ranchers in the Big Bend belonging to the small class of industrious Tejano ranchers during the 1890s included Félix Domínguez, Federico Billalba, and Félix Gómez.[82]

The historical record also points to a similar core group present in Presidio County. In the area along Alamito Creek lived several settlers who ranched and farmed. Victoriano Hernández worked his Alamo Ranch, while two of his brothers, Félix and Tomás (and their families), lived at Casa Piedra, located some ten miles further from the Alamo Ranch. Down Alamito Creek from where the Hernández family ranched, and extending to the Rio Grande, could be found a few more ranch/farm communities of Mexican colonists.[83]

The setting at Fort Davis seemed more inviting to Mexican American ranching and farming than were other sections of West Texas, excepting the Big Bend Country. As noted in the previous chapter, interethnic marriages between soldiers (both white and African American) and Mexican women had blunted racial distinctions. Consequently, Mexican Americans who had staked claims to lands in the general area after the Civil War now ranched alongside Anglo cowmen who had settled there about the same time. Among these ranchers were Felipe Domínguez as well as José Salcedo and Julián Márquez.[84] A successful rancher who traced his beginnings to the 1870s and now thrived was Fabricio Granado and his family of ten. By the 1880s, the family claimed some 160 acres of land and assets that included a wagon and numerous livestock. One researcher found their holdings to be assessed at greater than $1,300, making "them the second-wealthiest Hispanic household in town."[85]

Resolute cattlemen, perhaps not with the same extensive holdings as those in Fort Davis, were also to be found in Pecos County. Among these were immigrants Isidoro González, who homesteaded northeast of Fort Stockton (and booked his brand on August 9, 1890) and Pablo Primera, who registered his livestock mark on September 17, 1892.[86]

BUSINESS

Distinguished also by class standing from the mostly poor of the Tejano community were businesspeople. Included alongside those succeeding as entrepreneurs into the last decades of the nineteenth century was Paula Losoya, credited with having founded Del Rio in Val Verde County. Widowed in 1876, Losoya had been adding property to her farming enterprise so that by the early 1880s her workforce tended to some three thousand acres. Paula had her large estate of corn plants, fruit trees, sugar canes, and vines watered through acequias connected to San Felipe Creek. Her financial success allowed her to enhance business life in Del Rio (she started a candy factory) and to engage in charitable work in the area. She donated monies to the Catholic Church along the border region as well as to initiatives underway to create a sound schooling system in Del Rio.[87]

Another successful businessperson was Tula Borunda Gutiérrez, founder (1887), owner, and manager of the Borunda Café in Marfa. The restaurant would go on to enjoy several decades of successful operation; it earned a reputation as a significant eating landmark in Marfa and West Texas.[88]

HERITAGE

As did their counterparts in other sections of the state, Tejanos in West Texas lived culturally in two worlds. Most continued to practice traditions and habits they had brought with them from Mexico (it might be assumed that few at that time would have had the years in the US for much acculturation). Almost all spoke Spanish as their primary language, observed traditional customs in family relations, abided by established religious teachings, honored holy days in the Catholic calendar, practiced longstanding folkways, retained beliefs in folklore, preferred foods common in their native land, celebrated some of the national holidays of Mexico, kept up leisure forms (such as promenades) that linked them to the old country (and even to Spain), and struggled through life relying on tried and true survival mechanisms.

Lo Mexicano

Affairs in Mexico attracted some in the community holding interests in their old country's politics. Catarino Garza, the ex-journalist from southern Texas who in the early 1890s was leading a rebellion against President Porfirio Díaz of Mexico, enticed nationalistic West Texas Tejanos into involvement in Mexico's affairs, at least according to reports from suspicious Anglos. From South Texas, Garza and his followers denounced the dictator for policies that stifled political freedoms in Mexico, thwarted common people's efforts to acquire their own lands, and shamelessly allowed foreign countries unfettered access to the country's natural resources—and even to its economic system—leaving Mexico vulnerable to colonial exploitation.

Accounts of the Garza movement spread into West Texas, and as per stories emanating from the region, had excited elements within Texas-Mexican communities. Garza supporters, some Anglos believed, worked out of Ojinaga, Mexico, and crossed into Texas soliciting support for their cause.[89] News columns reported West Texas Anglos believing Garza followers to be active around the San Angelo, Del Rio, and Marathon environs. A Spanish-language newspaper named *El Chinaco*—managed from South Texas by one of Garza's revolutionary supporters—did exist briefly in San Angelo to editorialize against the Mexican government. Hearsay around town had it that Mexican ranch hands were responding positively to recruitment overtures from Garza agents and clandestinely collecting firearms and preparing to join Garza's army. Even after Garza had by February 1892 left for Key West, Florida, to escape US authorities and Texas Rangers bent on arresting him for violating the neutrality laws, reports in July 1892 revealed that supporters in Del Rio had published a revolutionary tract, the manifesto possibly hinting at the westward spread of the Garza movement. Much of the alarm in the end turned out be exaggerated, as scholarship does not indicate the Garza revolution to have made much headway in West Texas. However, the circulation of such talk does indicate that some within Mexican communities in West Texas remained attentive to political happenings in Mexico.[90]

Aside from politics, connections to Mexico were evident in manners, personal comportment, and courtesy granted to certain members of the community. Observed, for instance, was the tradition of extending proper respect to those of social standing. While the overwhelming number of West Texas Tejanos lived in poverty, there seemed always to be a few in the community slightly above the mass; people acknowledged their class and rendered them proper recognition. Such consideration was evident in San Angelo, where local residents during the 1880s and 1890s extended deserved respect to the city's Mexican founding families.[91] The same probably existed in small Big Bend villages where according to one account, there lived in the last two decades of the nineteenth century "families of proud and aristocratic lineage settled in Presidio, Polvo, Ruidosa, Candelaria, El Indio, Casa Piedra, and Shafter."[92] If such a class ever existed (it may have been more imagined than real) with the immigrants' arrival in those farming settlements, the entire community would have extended due regard and deference.

As they arrived in West Texas, immigrants closely abided by long-standing concepts and traditions concerning family structure and family relations. A patriarchal model with deep roots in Iberian Spain prescribed subservient roles for women. Culture dictated that women be exemplary wives and mothers as well as efficient homemakers. Women, regardless of marital status, were to adhere to strict moral standards and behave in decent ways. Righteous behavior for women meant attending Catholic services or engaging in practical church work. To wives fell the task of teaching the young proper rules of behavior and certainly of perpetuating established cultural conventions. Mothers were to make the necessary arrangements with friends or fellow community residents to have their infants properly baptized or to have their children receive the sacraments the Church required. By taking such steps, women became active agents in the formation of community kinship networks that consisted of *padrinos* and *madrinas* (godfathers and godmothers respectively) and consequently of *compadres* and *comadres* (godparenthood). The role of midwifery was strictly one of women (called *parteras*) and in many cases so was that of *curanderas* (women folk healers).[93]

La Iglesia

Towards the latter decades of the nineteenth century, the Catholic Church sought to increase its reach into West Texas, and in so doing to address the religious needs of ethnic Mexicans. However, the Church at that time still lacked the preparation to adequately serve its parishioners. It was short the required number of priests necessary for assignment to the vast region and it had yet to build the physical structures for holding services. Thus, people passed through weeks, perhaps months or even years, without Mass, the sacraments, and observances that the Church generally provided to worshippers in more settled areas of the state.

Some fortunate communities, however, did benefit from dedicated Church efforts to meet the demands of believers. In 1880, Father Mathurin Pairier arrived in San Angelo and was soon conducting church services out of an adobe church located in today's downtown area. Mexicans constituted the greater portion of the parishioners, since few Anglo-American Catholics had yet arrived in the Concho Country.[94]

At Fort Davis in the early 1880s, a Catholic priest (whether assigned there or serving on itinerant status is unknown) reportedly instructed a small group of Mexican children on the catechism.[95] In Alpine, the Catholic Church seemingly felt well enough established by the latter nineteenth century that it ran a Catholic school. In 1899, this Catholic facility sponsored a small instructional unit consisting of the primary grades. Teaching was in Spanish.[96]

At Fort Stockton's St. Joseph Catholic Church, meanwhile, services were conducted periodically by priests sojourning from different parts of West Texas.[97] Between 1884 and 1904, Oblate of Mary Immaculate missionaries from Eagle Pass traveled to Brackettville (Kinney County) to minister to the mission there. One source told of several children on December 19, 1898, receiving Holy Communion, fourteen of them Mexican Americans.[98]

In the rural areas, Mexicans attempted to abide by Catholic traditions and doctrine as circumstances allowed. It was the chapel that Victoriano Hernández built in 1889 at his Alamo Ranch (in honor of a grandchild he lost during a bandit raid) that served his family and the members of the ranch's labor force. The little chapel became the setting for weddings, baptisms, and other ceremonies needing consecration.[99]

How Mexican American Protestants during this era dealt with neglect from the different Protestant denominations is difficult to determine. It may have been that, as with the Catholic Church's reliance on itinerant priests, Protestant ministers traveled throughout West Texas to fill the void of absent preachers. If so, it was probably Anglos who ministered to the worshippers. Some of these clergymen had to have been bilingual. S. G. Kilgore, for one, in 1891 served as pastor of the Mexican Methodist Church at Marfa.[100]

Folklore

As was the case with other ethnic Mexicans in the nineteenth century, Mexicans in West Texas borderlands used folklore as a medium for passing on beliefs, life understandings, and worldviews. Such has been the way other poor and illiterate people have dealt with events that required explanation, elucidation, rationalization, and the like. In the realm of life struggles, folklore acted as yet another means that helped in daily survival.[101]

As a life function, folklore tied people to old roots, historical periods or occurrences, and an identifiable past. It gave common folks continuity and validated the world of their forebears. Some of the themes, settings, and personalities that characterized the folklore of the late nineteenth century, for instance, harked back to a time in the mid-century when West Texas (more particularly the Big Bend area) belonged to Mexico and Native Americans such as the Apache and Comanche had the run of the place. In one such folkloric account, settlers in the Mexican state of Chihuahua allied themselves with the Comanche against the rampaging Apache who from around modern-day Fort Davis were attacking La

Junta de los Ríos. In a momentous showdown, the Apache killed the Comanche leader Bajo el Sol, "the bravest Indian chief in the Big Bend."[102] A related account involved the Apache warrior Güero Carranza who grew up around the Davis Mountains. According to Natividad Luján, a raconteur whose recollections of nineteenth-century Big Bend folklore historians penned for posterity, during the 1850s Güero pillaged on both sides of Rio Grande, singling out the Americans—who had set up fortifications downriver from Presidio del Norte—for particularly vicious strikes. When they captured him, the Americans gave Güero to the Mexicans, who summarily executed him for his crimes as a robber and killer.[103]

Mexican American folklore in the last decades of the century spoke of an understanding, benevolent, and protective God battling satanic evil. According to the legend of "The Devil's Grotto," God had once shown care for settlers living on the Rio Grande at a location that later became known as La Junta de los Ríos. Indigenous natives (among them the Jumanos) there were enjoying a rich harvest, plentiful rain, and an abundance of food for animals to graze. But then a wicked Satan visited the area, inflicting wrath upon its inhabitants, causing crop failure, livestock fatalities, community disorder, and birth abnormalities. To the rescue came Spanish missionaries wishing to convert the area's people. One priest who had been assigned to parishioners at La Junta used a wooden cross to drive the devil into a crevice at El Cerrito de la Santa Cruz, a mountain located down the river from modern-day Ojinaga. He then instructed the locals to build a shrine (with a cross placed above it) at the cave's opening to contain the evil Satan. Subsequently, the residents of the river village enjoyed good health and abundant crops and lived unafraid of their nemesis.[104]

Folkloric tales addressed matters of romance, often touching on the theme of tragic love. One particular instance had as its time period those years of mid-century when US soldiers left due to the Civil War and the Apache resumed their attacks on the unguarded region. On the edge of Fort Davis, at the barrio called Chihuahuita, lived a young woman named Dolores who was promised to marry a local sheepherder named José. The husband-to-be left the village regularly to tend to his flock of sheep grazing far away in the mountains. To express their love, the sweethearts would signal the other with a campfire visible to each from miles away. But on the day before the wedding, José was killed by Apaches at his mountain camp. After that, Dolores—driven by the force of love—would weekly (on Thursdays) travel up the mountain and light a fire so as to spiritually connect with José and affirm her undying love for him. When

Dolores died, people buried her at the mountain base (the peak subsequently came to be named "Dolores Mountain") in a small cemetery located there.[105]

Through folkloric tales, members of West Texas Mexican American communities learned of the causes, or the events behind, the origins, structuring, and naming of the region's distinct geological landscaping, places, and historic spots. Among those who absorbed such ancient tales and passed them on to curious whites was the aforementioned Natividad Luján. Santiago Peak (in the Santiago Mountains, southwest of Marathon), Luján related, was named after Santiago, his uncle. Santiago, who lived in Presidio del Norte, would lead counterattacks on the Apache following the Indians' repeated attacks on Presidio. On one of those campaigns (seemingly in the mid-nineteenth century) Santiago and his men caught up with the raiders, and in a fateful encounter he was killed. His comrades from Presidio who buried him then named the peak: Santiago.[106]

Further explaining topographical forms was the previously mentioned folktale of "The Devil's Grotto." The story not only spoke of a beneficent God who had once protected the settlement of La Junta but also explained to fellow Mexican Americans in the Presidio, Texas, area the presence of a cave in the Mountain of the Holy Cross (El Cerrito de la Santa Cruz). In an effort to protect himself from the cross-carrying priest, the devil retreated to a grotto across the Rio Grande. Thus did folklore explain to the people of Presidio how that unique geological formation (the cave) in El Cerrito de la Santa Cruz came to be.[107]

Las Fiestas Patrias

In semiautonomous communities, Mexican American leaders established *mutualistas* (benevolent societies) to help fellow barrio dwellers confronting emergency situations, among them sickness, death, and unemployment. In San Angelo in the 1880s and 1890s, for example, residents founded the Sociedad Fraternal Union México Texana, with its stated purpose of caring for neighbors during critical times.[108]

Fraternal societies took on other barrio obligations, such as overseeing the observation of Mexico's patriotic days. Throughout many Texas communities, ethnic Mexicans, many of them still retaining nationalistic feelings toward the motherland, commemorated the Diez y Seis de Septiembre (Sixteenth of September, Mexican Independence Day) and the Cinco de Mayo (Fifth of May, the day in which Mexico's military in 1862 defeated a French army landing at Puebla with designs on conquering Mexico and incorporating it into France's larger empire). They remembered those monumental dates through what are generally called the *fiestas patrias* (patriotic feasts) celebrations.

Specifically responsible for ensuring the memorialization of the two historic episodes was the *comisión honorífica* (honorary commission). A community's *comisión honorífica* (organized either informally or by request of Mexico's government) would appoint a *junta patriótica* (a civic group) and charged it with carrying out the production of the *fiestas patrias'* annual festivities. By the 1880s, San Angelo's Hispanic community already had a functioning *junta patriótica*, and on September 14–16, 1888, through individual donations (cost for the entire event was around $56) successfully organized the year's public tribute.[109]

Towards the latter half of the 1890s, San Angelo's Sociedad Fraternal Unión Mexico Texana yearly took up the role of staging and financing the fiestas (presumably selected to do so by the *junta patriótica*). The *sociedad* held the formal functions at its own hall, or alternately at Pickwick Hall, a civic building in town.[110]

Fun and frolic made up much of these San Angelo fiestas during the 1890s. Patriotic speeches delivered in Spanish, a parade, a barbeque, band music, and a dance collectively became part of the annual remembrance. The acknowledged ties to Mexico were evident among a cross section of celebrants, including pioneers who had first settled in San Angelo some twenty or thirty years before and who still commanded the approbation of the entire Hispanic community. Also prominent in their participation were some of the Hispanic women who had intermarried leading Anglo men in the town. Not surprisingly, Mrs. James B. Keating (Jesusita Alderette) in 1894 opened her home for a dance to salute that year's Diez y Seis commemoration.[111]

Diversion for the Spanish-speaking could also embrace intellectual and cultural presentations as exemplified by the San Angelo community in 1896. In that year, the Mexican Dramatic Company, consisting of amateur actors in town, staged a comedic production called "In the Hilt of the Sword." The *San Angelo Standard* reported the show, performed entirely in Spanish, to have been well received by audience members, among them some of the town's leading families. The newspaper praised the director and complimented the actors for their costume wear.[112]

Lo Americano

While seldom disassociating themselves from the mother culture, Tejanos trended towards a bicultural identity. They understood that cultural modifications constituted a practical course to take for coping in an Anglo-dominated milieu. A stubborn reluctance to change would arrest advancement in a land that promised new hope. Thus they adjusted, dispatching their children to the local school (usually the "Mexican school"), joining neighboring Anglos in celebrating the country's national holidays (e.g., the Fourth of July), and, despite their political downturn, attempting to retain some measure of engagement in local politics.

That parents enrolled children in school programs where available attested to the belief that familiarity with the American system was essential to social and material survival and life improvement. At Fort Davis, families sent young ones to study at the local school, which in some years during the 1880s had Hispanic tutors. The 1880 census for Presidio County listed a man named Juan Ordean, identified as being from Mexico and teaching in town. Also in the early 1880s, Jesús Albando held classes for Mexican boys at what was described as "a small school north of town [Fort Davis]."[113] In 1883, Mattie B. Anderson took over part of the teaching duties at Fort Davis: she found her first-day class had some seventy-five or so children enrolled, several of them Mexicans having no command of the English language.[114] By the latter years of the 1880s, Fort Davis (after 1887 the county seat of Jeff Davis County) had formally established a school specifically intended to teach Mexican children.[115]

During the 1880s, Presidio County expanded its educational system to serve outlying areas such as Marfa, Polvo, and Presidio and in the 1890s to Shafter and Ruidosa. The presence of these schools presumably derived from Mexican parents' demands for local education, for these were predominantly Hispanic villages. By no means was the education of Mexican children in the county superlative, however. School trustees seldom appropriated enough funds for classroom needs. Thus, teachers were underpaid and forced to teach in most unfavorable circumstances, doing without essential equipment and resources such as books, desks, and other classroom necessities.[116]

In Del Rio during the 1880s, the Mexican American community undertook its own initiatives to have appropriate instruction provided to local youths. In the San Felipe barrio, the enclave in the city situated east of San Felipe Creek (as opposed to the Chihuahua barrio, west of San Felipe Creek), the call for a local school led county officials to build during the decade a public school administered by the San Felipe Common School District.[117] On the west side of San Felipe Creek, meantime, Mexican families demanded schooling of the quality the city offered to its Anglo students. Finally, in the 1890s, the Del Rio Independent

School District (DRISD) built a new grade school that accommodated both Mexican and Anglo students.[118]

In San Angelo during the 1880s and 1890s, a few Mexican American children attended the city's school system, but on a segregated basis. As of the mid-1890s, the scholastic population at the "Mexican school" numbered about sixty, therein receiving instruction from Anglo teachers.[119] To ensure some level of education, Hispanic residents of San Angelo in the 1880s established—as was done in other communities in Texas—an *escuelita*. The *escuelitas* were private barrio facilities organized and financed by town folks wishing youngsters to preserve their Mexican culture, including language. From what little is known of the San Angelo *escuelita*, it provided instruction in English, and learning exercises were patterned after ones in American schools. The teacher must have applied a bilingual format, however, translating from Spanish to English, since most of the students were native Spanish speakers.[120]

Acceptance of life as "Americans" was manifest further in continued Mexican American efforts at political participation, even after they faced a political downslide after the 1880s. In San Angelo, for instance, Mexicans retained membership in the Tom Green County Democratic Club, notwithstanding the rejection by the Democrats at their convention in 1886.[121]

A COMPARISON

Historical currents in West Texas between 1880 and 1900 moved the region in a direction divergent from that in which South Texas, if not other sections of the state, headed. What happened in the western borderlands thus configured the history of West Texas Tejanos, making their encounter a variation of that felt by ethnic Mexicans in the eastern portion of the state. Admittedly, much connected Tejanos whether they lived in South Texas or West Texas. In both places, they came from Mexico and thus transplanted the same cultural accouterments. In the social, economic, and political order of the Anglo hierarchy in either setting, Mexicans confronted forces that obstructed material ambitions.

Nonetheless, the peculiarities of West Texas, among them its spaciousness, geography, and aridity, weighed on Mexican Americans therein and set life on a trajectory divergent from that shaped by South Texas' own particularities. So too did the disparate pace of Tejano settlement and implantation. As late as 1880, municipalities such as San Angelo, Del Rio, Fort Stockton, and Fort Davis remained in the early stages of development and in no way possessed the cultural ambience characteristic of some of the old South Texas urban sites that traced their beginnings to the eighteenth century, among them San Antonio and Laredo (as well as many small villages and ranches below the Nueces River). South Texas settlements, furthermore, emitted a cultural aura and assurance absent in the West Texas expanse. Buttressing a further semblance of cultural security in the southern pocket of the state was demography. As of the 1880s and 1890s, the numerical command Tejanos had over Anglos in South Texas reinforced culture. On the other hand, a flood of incoming whites into West Texas after 1880 transformed the region into one of Anglo cultural and institutional dominance.

An ongoing Anglo quest for redemption and domination of West Texas also shaped the life experience of Tejanos therein. Although by the latter two decades of the nineteenth century West Texas was headed towards modernization, it remained tolerant of a Wild West culture that unsettled Mexican American communities. For some Anglos, vanquishing West Texas called for quelling elements perceived as menacing to civilized society. Unlike South Texas, which had been largely brought under submission through violent acts by the 1870s, West Texas in the last decades of the century remained a terrain condoning murders, vigilante acts, and lynch law against threatening elements, such as Mexicans.[122]

Then, demographic imbalances respective to the two regions produced differing political outcomes for Tejanos. With their population numbers failing to keep pace with increases among Anglos, Tejanos in West Texas lost their earlier political edge. Their hampered state hardly allowed them the needed political clout to extract concessions from influential Anglo officials or from political machines, which were largely absent from West Texas anyway. While political decline after 1880 became the fate of Mexicans in the Edwards Plateau and Trans-Pecos region, South Texas Tejanos engaged in brisk political activity, due in part to their numerical advantage, growth in new settlements needing political operatives, an urban environment that gave impetus to organization and the growth of political machines and even to a nominal slump in violence.[123]

Declining fortunes, however, did not spell the passing of a Mexican American presence in West Texas. People continued entering the area from Mexico as well as from different sections of the state. They would stabilize existing communities, reinforce culture, and, more broadly, aid in advancing a region they considered home.

CHAPTER 3

CHANGE, CHALLENGES, AND COHESION, 1900-1920

During the early decades of the 1900s, the course of history advanced the changes West Texas had experienced during the later decades of the nineteenth century. The ranching economy remained relatively stable, as indicated by a newspaper report in 1908 boasting that at least one part of West Texas, specifically Pecos County, was "the Cowman's Paradise."[1] Particularly profiting from cattle raising between 1900 and 1920 were Big Bend ranchers. They prospered for a number of reasons, not the least of which was demand for grass-fed cattle—such as that produced in that section of West Texas. Cattle owners engaged in "cow-calf" breeding: that is, they raised calves (able to produce leaner meat) for national consumption. Ranchers shipped the cattle to Midwest feeders who, upon fattening the beeves in feedlots, delivered them to the slaughterhouse for profit. But ranchers throughout West Texas also made good during this period by benefiting from innovative crossbreeding practices and by profiting from World War I demands by the federal government for beef to feed people both at home and abroad.[2] In their quest for bigger returns, however, West Texas ranchers continued as they had since the 1880s to overrun the range with too much livestock. Overgrazing arrested the cattle industry, but ranchers dealt with the problem in subsequent decades by turning to managed breeding and other control techniques.[3]

Advances in sheep and goat production kept in step with progress realized in range cattle management. Numerous developments engineered growth. First, sheep and goat ranchers introduced the wire-mesh (or "woof-proof") fence to guard against predators. Arranged into six-by-six-inch squares and held securely with wire knitted around each joint, these wire-mesh barricades, while not completely replacing the role of Mexican sheepherders, allowed ranchers to scientifically engineer their stock for improved breeding and permitted them, moreover, to control conditions that yielded a better quality of wool and mohair. Second, livestock owners organized the Wool Growers Central Storage Company of San Angelo in 1908. For years, ranchers—without facilities to hold wool and mohair until the fibers' value increased—sold the crop at whatever price buyers offered them. The Wool Growers Central Storage Company sought to overcome this drawback. Ranchers built warehouses throughout the state and by using the Wool Growers Central Storage Company as a buy, store, and sell exchange, they successfully came to command more attractive bids for their wool and mohair commodities. A last measure aiding in the advancement of the sheep and goat business in Texas was the creation of the Texas Sheep and Goat Raisers Association in Del Rio (1915). Ranchers had as their intent establishing a means for generating research that focused on livestock afflictions and remedies for plagues such as bluetongue, sore mouth, and stomach worms. They succeeded in doing as much from the association's headquarters in San Angelo.[4] By the late 1910s, the sheep and goat industry had gained stability and in subsequent decades would become a mainstay of West Texas economics.

Advanced as well between 1900 and 1920 was the modernization of the region's infrastructure. The iron rail that traversed the vast expanse beyond the 100th meridian was upgraded, helping to tie West Texas to outside commercial hubs, among them thriving centers like San Antonio and El Paso. Improvements in country roads simultaneously integrated remote and isolated places, among them those in the Big Bend, into the state's larger commercial structure. Expansion of communication networks, such as the telephone, further served to uplift the region.

The forces of modernization acted to detach West Texas settlements from their nineteenth-century frontier moorings. Communities such as Fort Davis, Marathon, Alpine, Marfa, and Odessa benefited from the new order and emerged as viable cores of economic activity. Visibly affected by the historical currents of the day were the larger towns such as Del Rio, San Angelo, and Fort Stockton. These urban posts became distribution centers furnishing outlying communities with articles of clothing, shoes, dry goods, luxuries, and necessities like furniture, range equipment, carriages, and more. The railroads thrust several communities throughout West Texas into new roles (and profits) as they became departure points for cattle and sheep transferred to rangelands elsewhere or sent to feedlots in the Midwest.[5] Towns also served as diffusion stations for silver, lead, zinc, mercury, and other ores brought in by wagon to the railhead.

As the region became more established, it beckoned outsiders to settle therein. According to findings from census research, the total population within the Edwards Plateau and Trans-Pecos regions increased from about 46,000 persons in 1900 to about 253,000 by 1930. Most trekking west came from the US joined by others from European nations so that while in 1900 this Euro-American element constituted only 50 percent of the entire population in the western region, by 1930 it totaled 80 percent of inhabitants.[6]

Mexican Americans now occupied a distinct minority position. There occurred during the Mexican Revolution (1910–1920) a transnational influx of refugees, exiles, and defeated soldiers with families into West Texas, especially into the Big Bend, the closest area to Ojinaga where units of the federal army and rebel forces clashed. Some of these expatriates passing through Presidio moved into interior sections of Texas, but the majority remained in Big Bend settlements, working at local ranches, the mines, and the railroad, in the process augmenting existing Tejano communities. Still, the number of new arrivals dispersing throughout West Texas did not offset the greater gains made by Anglos, so that Tejanos in general faced even more setbacks than ones experienced between 1880 and 1900. Deterring West Texas Mexicans' efforts toward material advances now were demographic shortcomings.[7]

Diverging somewhat from currents unfolding across the broader West Texas borderlands were developments in the Big Bend. Despite its success in advancing cattle breeding, the region—unlike the rest of West Texas after the 1890s— did not entirely break with the past. Until the early 1920s, it remained frontier country. In comparison to other parts of West Texas, furthermore, settlements along the Rio Grande such as those in Presidio and Brewster Counties retained pre-1900 demographic ratios; Mexican Americans continued to dominate there. Also, the Big Bend became, during the first two decades of twentieth century, the center point of a mining boom. Moreover, while the Big Bend region attracted a good degree of turmoil due to the Mexican Revolution, the interior sections of West Texas such as those around Alpine, Fort Stockton, Del Rio, San Angelo, and Odessa escaped it.[8]

LABOR

Several factors kept West Texas Tejanos from securing the types of jobs most propitious for material uplifting. Generally, Anglo workmen received priority in job openings. Stereotypical perceptions routed Mexicans towards the lowest levels of the labor force. Farmers during this time, for instance, accepted the idea that Mexicans were physically framed for farm work: short and lithe to grub brush and pick cotton. Then, many of the occupations allowed to Mexicans tended to be of temporary or seasonal nature.[9] Facing few job prospects, Mexicans took whatever positions Anglo society permitted them, most of the sort condescendingly branded as "Mexican work."

Vaqueros

Men of the range managed to find work on the many ranches scattered throughout West Texas. As a workforce, these *vaqueros* might have come from the ranks of experienced riders fleeing the revolution in Mexico as well as horsemen who had worked old Tejano-owned spreads, such as ones belonging to Big Bend *rancheros* like Martín Solis and Federico Billalba, or Anglo ranch operations founded in the late nineteenth century.[10] In border ranches, they either formed a small group working on the ranchstead the year round or lived there to respond in the spring and fall to the greater workforce required for the seasonal round-ups throughout the area.[11] In rural villages such as Porvenir, indeed, Mexican horsemen migrated as necessary to work surrounding ranches.[12]

But *vaqueros* might also have been men (with their families) entering the eastern sections of the Edwards Plateau to labor on emerging ranches in counties such as Edwards, Real, and Menard. When Manuel Aguero Sr. crossed into Texas from Sabinas, Coahuila, sometime around 1910 to 1915, he took a job in Edwards County at the Mamie Powers ranch located west of Barkdsale. There he lived with his family for the next twenty-five years.[13] Some families from Central Texas seeking to start anew in West Texas obtained employment in Menard County; Melitón Morales, the Kimble County *ranchero* whose family ranchlands reached into Menard County, hired some of them at Fort McKavett.[14]

Actually, ranch work involved a miscellany of tasks not directly associated with the range but essential to the local mission. Dwellings and outlying structures had to be erected, so that Anglo landowners, as in the case of the Alpine area, often turned to town residents knowledgeable at adobe making for such jobs. In addition to helping establish physical structures on ranches, Mexicans engaged—invariably with only pick and shovel—in the construction of surface tanks essential for watering cattle out on the range. Men adept at working with concrete partnered in the making of the cement tanks that ranchers also depended upon for watering their animals.[15]

Sheepherders and Sheepshearers

In ranchlands, Mexicans dealt more with sheep than they did with bovine and equine stock. Ranchers had always valued the Mexicans' skills at handling woollybacks, certainly since sheep raising had come to be a profitable enterprise. In turn, sheepherding and sheepshearing offered a steady opportunity for families countering grinding poverty.[16]

Sheepshearers still worked the range abiding by holdover practices and labor understanding of frontier days. Shearing teams relied on the *capitán* (contractor) to negotiate agreements with ranchers and depended upon him to provide the essentials for executing work tasks. Generally, the *capitán* contracted for money enough to cover payment for each sheep sheared, his own profit, the expense for maintaining equipment (wagons and mules), an allocation for a hired cocinero (cook), and, of course, wages for crew members. Once he had negotiated for the job, the *capitán* had the responsibility of taking (generally in buggies and wagons) his crew to the shearing site (usually at the ranch barn and adjoining holding pens) where an entire flock awaited. To him fell the responsibility of supervising the *tasinques* and a supporting cast of *laneros, empacadores, amarradores,* and *corraleros.*[17]

The skilled team then went to work. The *tasinques* (shearers) cut through thick wool with hand clippers (as mechanical means had not yet been introduced), relying on dexterity of hand motion, finger agility, and overall strength in operating the blades. As the *tasinque* finished the fleecing, the *lanero* (one who works with *lana*, or wool) gathered up the clippings and carried them to a spot convenient for the *empacador* (the packer). This phase in the shearing sequence called for the packer to stuff the wool, using his feet to compress the fiber into a heavy burlap sack. An *amarrador* would then sew the bag at the top for later grading. Rounding out the pool of workers were the *corraleros* (from the word corral, or pen). They managed the pens holding sheep awaiting shearing, ran the unshorn sheep to the shearing pit, then herded the sheared sheep into another corral. Sheepshearing duties started at sunup and continued until sundown.[18]

Farm Workers

Field work continued as a further means for survival during the early decades of the twentieth century as some landowners in West Texas began clearing land to make way for farm cultivation. The family of Apolonio Esparza moved from Fort Stockton to Imperial, Texas (Pecos County), during the early 1910s to work for local Anglos wishing to convert their lands from brush to fertile farm fields. Apparently, the Esparza clan during that era was part of the migration of people into Imperial, many as well coming to clear lands and then dig the needed canal ways to water the crops.[19]

Midland lands were in similar need of clearance. Mexicans by the 1910s arrived at area ranches (such as one belonging to Andy Fasken) to engage in grubbing (*el desenraiz*)—that is, ridding grounds of weeds, invasive grasses, and brush using hand tools such as a mattock/pickaxe. Some families contracted to work as many as 500 to 600 acres that local owners wished to turn into cotton fields or range lands.[20]

Similarly, migrants from Mexico and other parts of Texas began trekking in new numbers into farms sprouting in the Edwards Plateau, such as ones in McCulloch County, which lured them by the prospects of work in farms around communities like Brady. The ingress into McCulloch County escalated during the early 1900s as families came in covered wagons to engage—as had those entering Imperial and Midland—in grubbing and cotton picking. Some were able to make arrangements to work as tenants; others, like the Juan and Isabel Pérez family from Jiménez, Mexico, even purchased land (shortly after their arrival) around what was the budding village of Melvin.[21]

In the Big Bend, no real migration was necessary as the local population supplied the workforce to chop weeds and pick cotton when some (Anglo) ranchers commenced experimenting with cotton farming. Mexicans also worked new acreage opened up to the harvesting of edible crops such as wheat, corn, and a variety of foodstuffs.[22]

Candelilla

Nature produced candelilla plants in quantity throughout the Big Bend, and investors in the early twentieth century soon engaged in efforts to turn the source—useful for producing various wax products such as candles, wax sealer, properties for water proofing, and more—into a possible profit-making venture.[23] Naturally, the operation in its entirely required laborers, and Mexicans became the source for

doing the work of extracting the shrub from the soil, processing it, and then hauling the wax to market. The plant grew wild in the mountains and other isolated
spots of the Big Bend, but it was not so secluded that Mexicans could not gain
access it. Workers would take burros up the mountains, camp out (while going
about the grueling task of pulling the candelilla, bundling up their crop, and loading their cargo on the burros), and then come down the trail with their harvest.[24]

"Wax production required people with experience, proper skills, and a reputation for reliability to do the craft," writes one historian, and Mexicans answered
the call, handling the manufacturing in places like Glenn Springs.[25] Processing
the candelilla involved scrupulous attention. Workers soaked the shrub in a *pila*
(vat) full of boiling water mixed with sulfuric acid. Under the intense heat, the
wax would float to the top of the water while the plant remains dropped to the
bottom of the pila. Workers would then skim the waxy layer off and transfer it to
a tub for more boiling; when finally permitted to cool, the extract would solidify.
Workers would then store the wax in containers for delivery to a terminus beyond
the Big Bend.[26] Demand for candelilla declined after World War I and so ended
this line of work for Mexicans.[27]

Guayule

Also attractive to investors for a period between 1900 and 1920 was the exploitation of the guayule plant, a natural producer of rubber. Because rubber came
to be in great demand during World War I, the harvesting of guayule became
during the 1910s another opportunity, along with candelilla work, for Mexican
Americans. It was they who contracted to harvest the shrub, gather it, pack it,
and transport it via mule teams to the factory in Marathon.

Factory production of guayule demanded similar diligent attention as that
for candelilla. Mexican plant operatives oversaw the lengthy process, one that
encompassed crushing the shrubs by steel rollers, running them through a pebble
mill for grinding, separating the fiber material from rubber particles, and at the
end of the cycle salvaging the pure rubber. By 1920, the guayule industry had run
its course, and so did another outlet for Mexican workers in the Big Bend expire.[28]

Mining

The surge in silver, zinc/lead, and mercury mining offered Tejanos still one more
avenue toward sustenance, especially for those living in (or moving to) the Big
Bend. However, the boom in silver, lead, and zinc did not extend beyond 1920.

Silver mining remained an outlet—as it had since the 1880s—at Boquillas (Texas) and at Shafter where the Presidio Mining Company operated. In the early twentieth century, the American Smelter and Refining Company (ASARCO) took over operations in Boquillas, methodically ferrying silver and lead to the village via an aerial tramway from mines in Mexico. Tejano residents of Boquillas then treated it at a locally built processing plant; Mexican teamsters residing in the areas then transported the ores to the nearest railroad line running through the Big Bend. But the work in Boquillas (Texas) lasted only until around 1919 when most of the mines in and around Boquillas, Mexico, closed.[29] At the Presidio Mining Company in the Chinati Mountains (Presidio County) during the 1910s, some 300 men from around Shafter worked the deep tunnels of the company's silver mines. By the 1920s, however, activity declined around the town amid uncertainties in the value of silver.[30] By 1920, the business revolving around lead and zinc, transported from Mexico into La Noria (in extreme southeastern Brewster County) via a cable tram for shipment to Marathon, ended.[31]

Quicksilver mining, which had produced attractive profits in the lower Big Bend country during the 1890s, reached its peak during the years between circa 1900 and 1920. Several quicksilver mining companies established themselves in the Terlingua area, or what was commonly referred to during that time as the Terlingua District; most notable were the Marfa and Mariposa Mining Company (1896–1910) and the Chisos Mining Company (1914–1930s).[32] Other companies active in quicksilver mining in the Terlingua region were ones excavating at Study Butte. Then, around 1919 in the southeastern edge of Brewster County close to the Rio Grande, the Mariscal Mine opened operations in the general area where Martín Solis had discovered quicksilver in the 1890s.[33]

The Chisos Mining Company proved to be the most successful of all ventures in the lower Big Bend. Its origins went back to 1903 when Howard E. Perry of Maine legally incorporated it; mining activity led in 1914 to the discovery of a vast deposit of cinnabar ore on his Terlingua property, and business boomed. The company then entered an era of unrivaled prosperity. The nation's involvement in World War I produced an increased demand for quicksilver, and some of the mines that had closed production in the Terlingua District for a time now reopened to compete with Chisos Mining. But none could rival Perry's Company—fortunate to be located in part of the Terlingua District richest in quicksilver ore—so that by the end of the 1910s it had become the largest producer of the element in the entire country.[34]

Mexicans, most of them from the mining state of Chihuahua, Mexico, constituted almost the entire labor force at the quicksilver mines. Some 1,000 to
1,500 miners, according to historical accounts, worked the Marfa and Mariposa
Mining Company at least until 1910 when the mine closed down after exhaust-
ing the mercury deposits.[35] An equal number of laborers, some 1,000 to 1,500,
worked at the Chisos Mine.[36]

Miners worked under horrendous conditions. Most labored deep underground amid blasting and poor lighting.[37] At the Presidio Mining Company,
where Mexicans dug some 100 miles of tunnel, workers used hand drilling (at
least until the 1910s when the company introduced air-driven drills) in order
to plant the explosives necessary to find the silver ore. The drilling required
toughness of arms and dexterity of hands. A miner by himself of necessity had
to grip the spike in one hand while forcefully sledgehammering it with the other.
Often working in narrow crevices, miners risked injuring hands with an errant
swing. Working in couples hardly minimized danger: miners holding the metal
pin while another hammered it faced the danger of having their arm, hand, or
fingers smashed by a missed strike. Next came placing explosives in the drilled
opening in order to break the rock for further prospecting. Workers postponed
blasting until the end of their workday, for the dust and gas had to clear before
another shift arrived to do the job of policing the rubble.[38]

Workers at the Marfa and Mariposa Mining Company dealt with equally
brutal and dangerous conditions. After chipping the ore manually in the pits,
there then followed the hazardous and wicked task of carrying the ore, carefully
bundled on backpacks, up ladders. Workers on the surface then emptied the
cinnabar ore onto a cart designed to transport it to an aerial tramway. The tram
car next conveyed the cargo towards the crusher situated some one-half mile distance. Once mashed, the ore went to the company's furnace where the mercury
was heated to 360 degrees Celsius to render it to liquid. Furnaces such as those
used at the Marfa and Mariposa Mining Company and other quicksilver companies were patterned after the Scott Furnace (named after Robert Scott, who
developed it in California). Physically, the structure consisted of a brick (usually
locally made) exterior and an interior of special fire brick (of necessity, this brick
material came from other parts of the country, among them St. Louis).[39]

As did silver miners worldwide, Mexican workers at the Presidio Mining
Company ominously faced the risk of disease affliction, most commonly the
evil scourge of consumption. Throughout the day, Mexican miners inhaled the

quartz dust that collected in the tunnel bowels due to improper ventilation and to crude drilling methods that scattered powder indiscriminately. The irritating conditions attacked arbitrarily, but older workers, invariably heads of families, seemed the most vulnerable. Victims suffered from uncontrollable coughing, scarred lung tissue resistant to treatment, and the banes of pneumonia and tuberculosis. Contemporaries witnessed numerous deaths at Shafter attributable to the dreaded consumption.[40]

Historians have yet to come to some agreement as to disorders that afflicted Mexican workers in the quicksilver mines. Elsewhere, such as in the quicksilver mines of California, miners encountered what is called "chronic mercurialism." Generally referred to as "salivation," the sickness, one scholar elucidates, induced muscle atrophy, as well as "convulsions, numbness of the mouth and limbs, loss of teeth, constriction of the visual field, and speech difficulties." According to one researcher, salivation was less of a factor at the Chisos mine; most maladies resulted from accidents.[41]

Typical workdays at the mines spanned long hours and rotated around day-and-night turns. At the Presidio Mining Company, "working morning, evenings, and graveyard shifts" was customary. The same schedule was in place at the Marfa and Mariposa Mining and the Chisos Mining Company.[42]

The mining companies treated their workers like serfs. All hands toiled for barely livable wages under terms dictated by the mining companies. Pay at the Presidio Mining Company in Shafter stood at $1.25 a day, at the Marfa and Mariposa Mining Company from $1.00 to $1.50 a day, and at the Chisos Mining Company from 90 cents to $1 a day (less efficient workers, among them younger and older men, did not receive as much).[43] Laborers then had to spend their earnings at the company store. At the Marfa and Mariposa Mining Company, purchasing policy mandated workers spend their wages—made out to them with a punch-out check—at the company's mercantile, stocked with food, clothes, and supplies. At the Chisos Mining Company, miners followed more or less the same procedure, obligated to acquire food, merchandise, and other needs at the company post.[44]

Circumstances compelled miners to shelter themselves and their families in improvised structures (and on land owned by the mining companies). Workers at the Chisos Mining Company relied on tents, lean-tos, or simple huts built of mud brick or improvised from scavenged materials such as old canvases, rags, and tree products. These dwelling served as the only accommodations for most, although some workers did manage to construct more comfortable adobe houses.[45]

Freighting

Freighting was less hazardous than working the mines but not any more profitable; teamsters barely earned a livable wage. But the work represented an avenue to survival, and Mexican yeomen dominated the traffic of transporting extracted minerals overland to railheads outside the immediate region. From the Shafter silver mine Mexican freighters handling wagons pulled by large teams of burros hauled the silver ore to the railroad station at Marfa. Such was similarly the case at Boquillas, where Mexicans operating some 200 to 300 wagons during peak periods moved silver to Marathon; from there the wagons returned to the village with provisions and materials brought into Marathon from San Antonio by railroad.[46] As Mexican workers from across the Rio Grande brought lead and zinc into La Noria during the 1910s, Texas-Mexican teamsters took the elements to the Marathon railroad station from whence it was shipped to the smelter in El Paso by train.[47]

As for quicksilver, Mexican waggoners driving pack mules carried the wrought-iron flasks (the containers into which the quicksilver was poured from the condenser) from both the Marfa and Mariposa Mining Company and the Chisos Mining Company to rail points at Marfa, Alpine, or Marathon; on the return trip to Terlingua teamsters brought loads of merchandise, mail, and sundry supplies needed at the mines, as well as people heading to the site on business. From the railheads, the trains moved the flasks to places as far away as St. Louis.[48]

Wagon drivers plodded over primitive roads. Trains heading out of the Terlingua District trudged to Marfa—a distance of some 100 miles that took ten to fourteen days to complete—on what have been described as "dry and badly eroded paths."[49] But the managers at the Marfa and Mariposa Mining Company and the Chisos Mining Company trusted the freighters carrying the flasks of quicksilver north. By most accounts, the Mexican workforce that constituted the bulk of the transportation business in the Big Bend area exhibited expertise and prowess on the trail.[50]

With teams consisting of from eight to twelve Spanish mules, drivers hired by managers of the Chisos mining district fulfilled assignments with assuredness and dependability. They handled their mules with the expert use of the rawhide whip and the skillful orchestration of the several reins. Carrying out their mission satisfactorily required adjusting to life away from the comforts of home. On the open trail, crew members improvised at times of breakdown or during other mishaps. From wood and rawhide the teamsters could effectively repair their wagons and gear without stalling to wait for manufactured parts. Distances between points required meals to be cooked by a campfire and sleeping to be kept close to the train. Protection at night might be nothing more than a canvas cover impervious to rain and other elements. Straw hats and garments able to repel the heat, dust, rain, wind gusts, and other weather conditions served tolerably during the workday.[51]

Railroads

In places where not enough white labor existed to meet the demand for railroad work, companies of necessity turned to Mexican Americans. Historians have not conducted the required research that reconstructs the role Tejanos played in the upkeep of railroad lines stretching across West Texas between 1900 and 1920, although Mexicans must have been present at every phase of railroad operations. In Sanderson, Texas, for one, Mexican Americans constituted almost the entire crew at the roundhouse in the early 1900s. At that facility, Mexican American inspectors checked the steam locomotives as they arrived for their scheduled examination, carefully studying parts for possible problems. If repairs were in order, it was Mexican mechanics who attended to machine malfunctions.[52]

Work Alternatives

Another employment alternative for basic survival was wood hauling. Men from the La Coyota community (and other Big Bend villages in the Terlingua District) provided the timber that mining companies needed to heat up the furnaces. This line of work lasted only for some four to five years during the peak days of mining in the Big Bend as demand soon depleted the amount of cottonwood trees growing locally as well as the supply of mesquite that grew throughout the lower Big Bend. Further, modernization made wood hauling passé. After about 1911, operations such as the Chisos Mining Company replaced wood with coal to fuel the furnaces.[53]

In the eastern sections of the Edwards Plateau, pioneers found work in the new cedar industry rising in Real County. They labored alongside Anglos employed by the Uvalde Cedar Company cutting firewood, posts, and telephone poles. Many of the Mexicans settled in the budding village of Camp Wood, then emerging as a result of cedar production in the area.[54]

Women at Work

While Mexican American women complied with prescribed roles as housewives and mothers, necessity impelled many to work. At home, some women took in washing and ironing to supplement the family budget. Others knitted, crocheted, or made quilts from cloth scraps, then sold their finished merchandise to whomever could afford the purchase. Outdoors, West Texas wives living in farm villages cared for the household's vegetable gardens or saw to the well-being of the family's goats, chickens, and livestock when husbands left on business or migrated to a work site. Doña Matilde Piña of Pecos County could fulfill men's work, able to "plow, handle a team of mules, thresh wheat, pick and husk corn, and grind it." Doña Agustina Terrazas of Fort Stockton, when necessary, took charge of her husband's freight operation, hauling wheat from Chihuahua to San Antonio.[55]

Work Ethic

Despite circumstances under which they worked—laboring on the range or/ and farm fields from sunup until sundown, risking injury and disease in mine tunnels, and, as in the case of freighters, surviving under difficult outdoor conditions—Mexicans carried out their job duties responsibly and with care. Ranchers employed sheepshearers because they had faith in the Mexicans' sense of service and mastery of their occupation. Managers during the 1910s hired Mexicans to work in candelilla manufacturing, trusting their crews to methodically take the shrub through the intricate steps required to transform the candelilla into wax. Mine owners relied on Mexicans because of the resoluteness workers applied to their jobs. At the Terlingua silver mines, observed Charles A. Hawley, the accountant at the Chisos Mining Company store, Mexicans toiled for two weeks in day shifts, then rotated to two weeks at night turns. They got time off only every alternate Sunday on account of the shift change. One or two of the miners, he observed, had been on the job for six or seven years and never missed work. The two miners' diligence was "remarkable," he proclaimed.[56]

Those who commissioned freighters for service could be confident that the loading, transporting, and delivery of goods would be performed with steadfastness and assurance. According to one historian, around Terlingua and Marfa, the freighters were considered "an elite group within the Mexican community."[57]

MANAGING WEST TEXAS MEXICANS

Although the frontier era gave way to trends that the twentieth century ushered in, West Texas remained encumbered by problems associated with an Old
West age. A still underdeveloped network of infrastructure made travel difficult.
Obstacles to finding (and financing) dedicated police personnel hindered the
enforcement of law and order. Remoteness delayed the pace of modernization as
was underway in other parts of the state. Finally, suspicion, distrust, and xenophobia towards the region's Mexican-origin population persisted, even as Anglo
society casually considered Mexicans as docile, obedient, and nonthreatening.

Old attitudes toward Mexicans prevailed in the long-standing custom of
discouraging racial mixing in social settings. Charles Hawley, traveling from
Alpine to Terlingua to assume his job at the Chisos Mining Company, witnessed
a case of discrimination on the route. It moved him to comment on the "unfair
and unreasonable race prejudice and discrimination" that dictated etiquette at
the dinner table. The episode involved José Herrera, the expert driver taking
Hawley's party to the border. When the group stopped for a meal at a half-
way station, the Texas-born Herrera had to eat separately from the passengers.
Hawley, the outsider, was informed that in Texas, Mexicans did not take meals
at the same table with white folks.[58]

Actually, Hawley was not without his own jaundiced view of Mexicans.
He thought villagers (mainly miners) at Terlingua, most of them illiterate and
wholly dependent on white people (like himself) for their material well-being and
survival, to be "poorly fit to compete with the white race." Hawley elaborated:
"Under the guidance and supervision of white men, Mexicans become capable
and efficient workmen, and dependable operators of machines, but they possess
little originality with this field." Such were the condescending attitudes of mine
administrators toward a people who made incredible profits for the company.[59]

Race prejudice diminished the value of Mexicans as human beings. Robert
Cartledge, who oversaw the Chisos Mining Company in Terlingua for
Howard E. Perry, reported that the Spanish influenza, the deadly pandemic of
the late 1910s that took thousands of lives in the US, had caused much distress in
the broader Terlingua mining area. As to Chisos, Cartledge informed Perry: "I
lost two good men, possibly three. I just don't recall. This didn't count Mexicans.
Don't know how many of them died."[60] Some Anglos entertained the belief that
predators too devalued Mexicans, even as corpses: myth held that coyotes would
not devour Mexican bodies.[61]

Residual beliefs in segregation perpetuated residential restriction and led to social exclusion in most public places, just as it had been during the nineteenth century. Passing through Del Rio on his way to Terlingua, Hawley observed: "Most of the Mexicans were employed by the white people but were not permitted to live in the same neighborhood with them."[62] In Fort Stockton during the early years of the twentieth century, the commissioners' court certified an already established situation: the south side of the city was predominantly Mexican, but the court now officially designated the farming community situated on the north side of town as "Little Mexico" (which the Spanish-speaking residents informally called "Nuevo Mexico").[63] At the Glenn Springs ranch in southeast Brewster County, the small Anglo settlement during the 1910s stood on the east side, while the west side went by the name of "Mexican Glenn Springs."[64] In Alpine, Mexicans were concentrated in the city's south side, just as they had been since the town's founding in the 1880s.[65]

In point of fact, circumstances could well interrupt the development of segregation. The practice was almost nonexistent in Fort Davis and in Presidio during the early decades of the century, for example. In the case of Fort Davis, historical particularities going back to the 1870s and 1880s explained the lack of forced segregation.[66] In Presidio race separation was minimal, since the Anglo population in the town was relatively small.[67]

School segregation aligned with residential configurations. When Fort Stockton formally established its Independent School System in 1917, it kept old school boundaries that separated Anglo from Mexican children. In configuring districts, council members used the same borders demarcating the city; children living south of Division Street attended the school in town while those in "Nuevo Mexico" went to the school in that barrio. But two years later, the board of trustees ended the school in "Nuevo Mexico" and integrated the children with those attending the segregated school in Fort Stockton proper.[68]

At Fort Davis, even as residential segregation was not enforced by rule, Anglo school administrators had always made provisions for separate education. Since the late 1890s, all students, regardless of ethnicity, could attend the adobe South Fort Davis "Mexican" School. Then in the early 1900s, Jeff Davis County school trustees declared that state "separate but equal" laws applicable to African Americans extended to Mexican children. As a result of the proclamation, Mexicans were to attend the South Fort Davis "Mexican" School, which as of 1902 had been considered unsafe (due to weather damage and vandalism) for Anglo students. The school was located some distance away from the pre-dominately Hispanic section of town, but in 1905, the school board built a one-room "Mexican" school in Chihuahua and pronounced the old South Fort Davis School defunct.[69]

The town of Alpine by the early 1900s had its own school for Mexicans, which during the late 1910s took on the name of Francisco E. Madero Ward School. In the community, people came to know it as La Escuela de Don Clemente, report-edly as it had been financed by a local merchant named Clemente J. Uranga, who believed a school for Mexicans necessary as the city did not fund one.[70] Similar separatist patterns existed elsewhere in West Texas. Big Bend towns like Marathon and Marfa subscribed to the same custom: the "Mexican school," as such schools were designated during that epoch, addressed Tejanitos' educational needs.[71]

The practice of segregating Mexicans from white students was most pro-nounced in the larger cities of West Texas, among them Del Rio, where two school districts existed: the Del Rio Independent School District served Mexican children living in the barrio of Chihuahua (but segregated them from Anglos students) while the San Felipe Consolidated School District (SFCSD) attended to students in San Felipe.[72] San Angelo formed its Independent School District in 1903, keeping nineteenth-century segregationist norms. School officials sought to accommodate children living in the two barrios then emerging in the city, one to the north and the other to the south of the downtown district. But they vacillated in decisions to establish permanent sites; not until the 1920s did the school district finance the building of a school in the north side barrio and the other in the south barrio.[73]

As to religion and worship, the Catholics generally sought to maintain differ-ent churches for Anglos and Mexicans, but in places such as in San Angelo and Fort Stockton with only one church edifice present, priests practiced discreet protocol during services. In San Angelo, Mexicans sat on one side of the church during Mass and Anglos on the other, while in Fort Stockton, Anglos occupied the front pews and Mexicans sat behind them. More visible segregation in Fort Stockton occurred in 1918 when the presiding priest raised the necessary funds to finance a chapel for the Anglo Catholics in town. The priest argued the sepa-ration was necessary because of language differences. But Mexicans who recalled those days insist it was due to racial prejudice.[74]

Social conventions dictated that separation also be practiced at the local graveyard. Marathon, a town with a population of about 600 in 1914, had its segregated *campo santo*. But in those frightening days of the late 1910s during the Spanish influence contagion, families (as well as others in West Texas) buried loved ones hurriedly and indiscriminately.[75]

THE MEXICAN REVOLUTION

Transnational forces impacted the West Texas borderlands during the period from circa 1911 to the late 1910s—the years of the Mexican Revolution. Adherents of both political camps in Mexico crossed into Texas in efforts to gain an edge on their adversaries. Rustlers moved cattle over the Rio Grande and sold the beeves to speculators in the cattle trade (as well as to other opportunists, among them law officials) and acquired arms and ammunitions with profits gained. Mounted marauders splashed across the river to pillage stores, steal horses, and otherwise acquire supplies needed for their cause. Bandits representing one or another revolutionary faction looted and plundered along the border almost at will. People fleeing into Texas to escape the tumult in their country aided and abetted the revolutionaries. The president of the Chisos Mining Company in 1911 informed military authorities in Texas that "about 40% of the Mexicans in our camp were born between San Carlos and Ojinaga in Mexico (where there is fighting which we can often hear) and their sympathies are naturally with the *Insurrectos*."[76]

Indeed, many Tejanos sympathized with the rebels, actively lending them support. Accord for revolution against Mexico had been manifest in Del Rio's Mexican-descent community early on when the Partido Liberal Mexicano (PLM) followers of Ricardo Flores Magón (the exiled radical idealist from Mexico) had established in town a cell calling for the overthrow of Porfirio Díaz. In 1908, the United States Consul (Luther T. Ellsworth) assigned to Ciudad Porfirio Díaz (Piedras Negras) reported on June 26, 1908, an attack, originating from San Felipe, the predominantly Mexican section of Del Rio, upon the military garrison at La Voca (Villa Acuña) by supposed *magonistas*. Ellsworth and Collector of Customs Robert W. Dove investigated the incursion and found that the PLM operated out of the San Felipe *colonia* (where the Party had followers) and that given the evidence gathered, "many of the attackers had crossed the border with weapons from Del Rio." They found further that the newspaper *El Liberal* published anti-Díaz addresses out of San Felipe and that editors at the same time actively networked with the PLM. Such propaganda and activities, they ascertained, appealed to many ethnic Mexicans around the Del Rio area.

Obviously, such sympathy would lead to support for the revolution when it broke out in 1910.[77]

Then, in the Big Bend after the fighting started, locals driven by personal reasons—immigrants identifying with the old country or with family members or friends in the fighting—crossed into Mexico to contribute to the revolution. Other border residents rendered assistance to the rebel insurrectionists by engaging in contraband, smuggling to them arms and munitions through trails in secluded Big Bend areas, or by giving them a hand at stealing Texas livestock. There were those who furthered the revolutionary cause by conducting fundraising campaigns throughout West Texas. Self-aggrandizers became profiteers and acted as middle men, shipping weapons from the Texas interior to border crossers awaiting them to transfer the cache across the Rio Grande.[78]

Anglos looked distrustfully upon Big Bend Tejanos thought complicit as brigands in the border turmoil. According to lawman E. E. Townsend, "A Mexican's word in those days did not mean much. Too many Mexicans had participated in cattle rustling operations and given the region its bad reputation, and law abiding citizens had very little respect for them."[79] Among those treating Mexicans disrespectfully were soldiers stationed at border camps. In the Big Bend, servicemen used their authority almost arbitrarily in conducting searches among local residents. Soldiers, such as ones posted in Terlingua (briefly in 1915) to guard the Chisos Mining Company, abused them verbally and physically and stole their meager possessions, generally degrading Mexicans as being savages who did not deserve to live in Texas.[80]

All the region of West Texas felt the stress of the border turmoil, although communities closest to the Rio Grande experienced the worst of the troubles. Civilian officials and federal troops responsible for patrolling the vast and isolated area found it beyond their means to keep order and defend the populace.[81] The most serious threats to border residents occurred between 1916 and 1918. On May 5, 1916, bandits from Mexico raided the Brewster County villages of Glenn Springs and Boquillas with the aim of acquiring goods stocked at their respective company stores, of stealing money believed kept by the candelilla wax factory in Glenn Springs or held by the mining company at Boquillas, and of taking goods from among residents in both communities.[82]

The manner in which the Mexican population there was directly affected by these raids is left unclear. In Glenn Springs, about sixty men worked the wax (candelilla) factory, some of them native-born Tejanos but others being newcomers fleeing the turmoil in Mexico. Surely, they and their families (living in segregated "Mexican Glenn Springs") must have been terrified by the attacks and the damage done to their homes and property, but such aspects of the raids are omitted in scholarly accounts that focus on the fate of the "Americans" locally, on military efforts undertaken to punish the raiders, and on suspicion that grew against all border Mexicans. Dread most certainly intensified as Anglo Americans in the Glenn Springs area raised the specter of local Mexicans being involved in the attack. According to accusations, Mexicans must have known of its planning, covered it up, and then participated in it. Anglos shortly rounded up Mexicans for questioning and afterwards obliged Mexican Americans to carry documentation (in the form of letters of recommendation from Anglos) that vouched for their good character and attested to their gainful employment in the area and its vicinity.[83]

Across the broader Big Bend, the raids deepened antagonistic feelings toward Mexicans prevalent among Anglos. Some within the region's white population equipped themselves to guard against "foreigners." In Alpine, Anglos imagined a general Tejano uprising. Summarily, town officials placed a 9 p.m. curfew upon local Mexican residents.[84]

Raids in the proportion of those that hit Glenn Springs and Boquillas subsided along the Big Bend for the remainder of the year and into a good portion of 1917. But then on Christmas day in 1917, some forty-plus invaders attacked the Brite Ranch located on the upper Big Bend area in Presidio County. Luring them were the ranch's abundant livestock herds (especially horses) and its general merchandise store (which included a post office) that stocked an enticing selection of food, dry goods, and range gear. The small community of fifty to seventy inhabitants included a majority Tejano population of ranch employees but also some Anglo-American residents, among them the family of T. T. Van Neill, the ranch foreman, and a few Anglo guests. The bandits laid siege to the ranch for some five hours, then showed no mercy to the hostages. They killed three people (two of them Mexicans), seized money from a cash box, rustled part of the livestock, and otherwise took clothing and supplies as needed.[85]

Reprisals ensued. An Anglo posse and a detail of US soldiers crossed into Mexico the day following the raid. They skirmished with the raiders near Pilares, Chihuahua, located a few miles downriver from Porvenir, Texas, and successfully retrieved part of the booty.[86] As for Texas-Mexicans, Anglo citizens of the Big Bend responded, according to one prominent scholar, by assembling "a vigilance committee to register and disarm the Mexican population of Brewster, Presidio, Jeff Davis, Culberson, and Hudspeth counties. Suspicious Mexicans were to be watched and their activities reported to the committee."[87] More ominously, Anglos and Texas Rangers resolved on exacting vengeance on Mexicans not solely for the Brite Ranch incident but also for the deaths of Anglos and Rangers allegedly killed by the Mexican rebels during the revolution. Whites intended also to clean out pockets of Mexican bandits on the Texas side, such as ones at Porvenir, a rural community in northwest Presidio County, which Anglos suspected to be a hideaway for accomplices helping to plan bandit attacks on Texas soil. In reality, Porvenir was a small Mexican village (some sources estimate the population to have been about 140; the 1910 census counted 105 families) inhabited mainly by native-born Tejanos and refugees from the war-torn country surviving as small farmers, goat herders, and cattle raisers. The community had taken root in land owned by two Mexican American property owners who sympathized with the émigrés.[88]

On January 28, 1918, around midnight, a combined force of Texas Rangers, area ranchers, and military men descended on Porvenir, awakening the sleeping villagers and taking them outside their homes into freezing weather. The Rangers and members of the civilian posse then searched the village for weapons, picked and marched some fifteen males (boys and old men) some distance away from their dwellings (while their families cried and begged for the Lord's mercy), and killed their hostages cold-bloodedly. Survivors deserted Porvenir as they hurried off to Mexico, carrying with them their murdered loved ones in order to give them a proper burial.[89] Historian Glenn Justice writes of what followed elsewhere along the border:

> ... word of the massacre spread panic among the Mexican population of the upper Big Bend. Fearing the Rangers were coming to wipe them out, hundreds of Mexicans living near Candelaria on the Texas side bolted across the Rio Grande to Mexico, some taking only their families, hurriedly leaving their possessions and livestock behind.[90]

Almost all accounts of the massacre confirm that those killed by the Rangers were not involved in the Brite Ranch attack.[91]

On March 25, 1918, raiders from Mexico waded across the Rio Grande to attack the Ed Neville Ranch, a large landholding in northwest Presidio County stretching for several miles parallel to the Rio Grande and almost abutting Porvenir six miles downriver. According to Army reports, many of the raiders (some fifty of them) were related to victims killed at Porvenir two months earlier and now sought vengeance. They left tangible signs of their fury, terrorizing and killing the rancher's son and murdering and mutilating the Mexican cook, a woman named Rosa Castillo, who lived on the ranch with her husband and three children. Fortunate in escaping the attack were Mexican workers who commuted weekly to the Neville Ranch from Porvenir and Pilares but had left for Mexico in the aftermath of the Porvenir massacre.[92] Federal troops the next day followed the raiders into Pilares, Chihuahua (across from Pilares, Texas) and engaged and killed several Mexican riflemen posted there. Upon confiscating horses and personal possessions taken from the Neville Ranch, they set the small village aflame.[93]

Raiding persisted for the rest of the decade along the border despite the presence of US troops there. Exposed to the raids on ranches, villages, and stores was everyone living in West Texas borderlands, although more imperiled were people in settlements near the Rio Grande where ethnic Mexicans predominated. Peace for the border arrived when the revolution began winding down towards the later 1910s.[94]

ANTONIO RODRÍGUEZ AND LEÓN MARTÍNEZ

While the violence committed against Mexicans in West Texas during the period between 1900 and 1920 never matched the greater atrocities committed against Tejanos in South Texas during those same years, ingrained attitudes towards Mexicans as being troublemakers, foreigners, and low-class beings still swayed Anglos in responding to actions threatening the white racial order. Such attitudes in part explain how whites during the 1910s reacted to the foul deeds allegedly committed by Antonio Rodríguez in Rocksprings (Edwards County) in November 1910 and by León Martínez in Pecos (Reeves County) in 1911.

On November 2, 1910, Antonio Rodríguez drifted into a ranch in Rocksprings and, according to his version of events, asked Mrs. Lemuel Henderson (the rancher's wife) for food; when repulsed he angrily killed her. The crime breached racial codes in places such as Rocksprings where whites could hardly countenance impudence from Mexicans; indeed, Anglo Americans expected gratitude and deference towards them as Mexicans in Rocksprings and around Edwards County depended on the goodwill of local sheep ranchers who provided Mexicans work and otherwise contributed to their stay in the areas. At a nearby ranch on November 3, law authorities caught up with Rodríguez—a man in his mid-twenties, with roots in Mexico (perhaps Las Vacas, or modern-day Ciudad Acuña)—arrested him, and incarcerated him.

Outraged by the forbidden offense (that of a Mexican killing a white person, and a woman at that) a mob of white men on November 4, 1910, converged on the city jail, broke into the cell holding the prisoner, and dragged him to a nearby hill, where a fire awaited him; in a gruesome act of vindictiveness, the perpetrators tortured Rodríguez before burning him alive. There followed international protests, as rioters in Mexico denounced Americans—albeit with no particular effect on those involved, as no Anglos were charged with the crime.[95]

Some months later (July 1911), fifteen-year-old León Martínez allegedly killed a 26-year-old schoolteacher named Emma Brown and was subsequently executed according to law. But because of the particulars that surrounded the case, historian Nicholas Villanueva asserts, Martínez's hanging amounted to no more than a "legal lynching."[96]

Martínez worked at a general store in Saragosa, Texas, a rural community near Pecos, Texas (both in Reeves County). Witnesses testified to having observed Martínez and Miss Brown engage in what seemed romantic talk at the store on the Saturday morning of July 22, 1911; the two purportedly agreed to a tryst outside of town that afternoon. But when on the following morning Brown was found dead on a road some two miles outside Saragosa, suspicion turned to Martínez. A number of citizens tracked him down and came upon him that afternoon as he relaxed at a watermelon patch on the outskirts of town—seemingly unsuspecting of the future that awaited him.[97]

At this point, Martínez became a casualty of racial antipathies Anglos held toward Mexicans. The loose crowd of angry whites quickly seized him and threatened extra-legal justice upon him should the Mexican not admit that he had killed the teacher. But Martínez pled innocence. The sheriff then arrived on the scene and carried Martínez off to the Pecos jail, only to face a posse collecting outside and calling for the suspect's life. The sheriff at this point gave Martínez a choice: confirm the allegations or be surrendered to the determined vigilantes. At dawn on July 23, Martínez signed a confession iterating what his accusers alleged he had done.[98]

Martínez remained in police custody but for the next several days became the target of various malicious accusations: citizens and the local press depicted him as a no-good foreigner and a sex fiend as well as a radical. His father allegedly was a follower of Ricardo Flores Magón, the anarchist from Mexico, and concerns of threatening revolutionary ideas entering West Texas with refugees reinforced old prejudices toward all Mexicans. A Pecos jury on July 28, 1919, tried Martínez and found him guilty the next day, solely on the basis of his forced confession.[99]

Although he was condemned to hang on September 1, 1911, angry citizens demanded he be dispatched forthwith. Martínez's attorneys (subsequent to the guilty verdict) moved to file an appeal, but an irate Anglo mob threatened them with harm, effectively impeding them from moving forward. The Texas Criminal Court of Appeals reviewed the Pecos case in November (1911) and rejected a new trial. León Martínez was executed on May 11, 1914, in Pecos, maintaining his innocence at the scaffold.[100]

RACIAL COEXISTENCE

Despite the state of race relations throughout the West Texas region, instances of neighborliness, understanding, cooperation, and interracial bonding prevailed. Certainly, the changing demography of West Texas led to a reduced number of cross-ethnic marriages. Still, unions between Anglo men and Mexican women occurred, especially in the Big Bend. Several noticeable cases may be cited. Howell W. McGuirk, a customs agent, married Josefa Navarro in Lajitas in 1903, and the couple cooperatively worked until the mid-1910s trying to improve conditions for the local Mexican American community. In Presidio County, Gus Elmendorf wed Julia López of Fort Davis in 1904, and the couple was blessed with seven children. Sam Robert Miller Jr. married Leonor Durán of Fort Davis in 1907; they had fifteen children.[101]

In remote areas, most noticeably the Big Bend, close attachment and dependability developed between some Anglos and the communities in which they lived; such individuals provided services conducive to the moral, intellectual, and physical standing of Mexican residents. Howell W. McGuirk (mentioned above) during his time in Lajitas from about 1899 to 1917 designated a small portion of his land for church services, funded a church structure, and helped support a school. In 1917, he sold out to Thomas V. Skaggs, and Skaggs continued helping Mexican American settlers with church services and schooling. He generously made school supplies to the students available from his own trading post.[102]

When J. O. Langford arrived at Hot Springs in the Big Bend in 1909, he soon became the local schoolteacher at a one-room adobe building in the village of San Vicente (some five miles from where Langford lived). Instructing the Spanish-speaking children proved an enjoyable experience for Langford, as he saw firsthand the eagerness of his pupils to learn not only a foreign language but the various other lessons he taught. The gratification parents expressed toward Langford was equally fulfilling to him.[103]

Langford also doubled as a healer of sorts. With what little he knew of ailments and sicknesses and employing the meager medical supplies he possessed for treatment, he attended to the local Mexicans, including those living in villages across the border unable to acquire professional help. Apparently, Langford succeeded in his trade, for he stated that after a time at Hot Springs he had become "the unofficial doctor in the community."[104]

In turn, Mexicans could look after kindhearted Anglos facing frontier adjustments. Having to build a dwelling for his family and to claim his homestead in Hot Springs, Langford discovered Cleofas Natividad ready to assist him. Cleofas had been living and farming in the area for years but now found himself having to "rent" from Langford, who had bought the land from the state. Cleofas negotiated with his landlord, prudently exchanging his labor for the rent money owed. Cleofas and his family made the 12″ x 4″ x 12″ adobe blocks for Langford's cabin and transported the bricks from their house to the Langford site. Cleofas then helped his neighbor finish the entire home.[105]

Mexicans also came to the rescue of Anglo West Texans threatened by the upheaval of the Mexican Revolution. In 1912, for instance, Cleofas again extended aid to Langford, standing vigil for several nights in an attempt to protect his friend's home from raiders feared ready to cross the border.[106] Additionally, Mexicans would assume harrowing risks in order to provide safety to trusted Anglos. During the Glenn Springs raid in May 1916, C. G. Compton, manager of the village's general store and post office, hurried his daughter to the west side of the settlement (Mexican Glenn Springs) and placed her under the safeguard of a Mexican woman. A local Mexican family prevailed in getting a Mrs. Alice Hart out of harm's way during the raid. They placed her in their wagon and by camouflaging their load successfully passed several search posts on their way to safety in the nearby community of McKinney Springs.[107]

Then, during the Brite Ranch raid when Mrs. Neill (the foreman's wife) made a rush for the telephone at the ranch store, Cresencia Natividad, a Mexican cook, sheltered Neill with her body as the two sprinted toward their destination, defying possible gunfire. Those who witnessed the act came to consider Cresencia the "Heroine of Brite Ranch."[108]

In the time previous to the 1916–1918 troubles (i.e., Glenn Springs to the Brite Ranch raid), Mexicans living along the Presidio County border willingly extended a helping hand to soldiers who passed by the villages policing the region. At Porvenir, locals sold food and farm products to the patrols and even served them homemade dishes. Some felt safe enough to ride into the troopers' camp to purchase luxuries such as coffee and sugar.[109]

ENTRENCHMENT

Several of pre-1900 Hispanic communities in West Texas remained intact as the region crossed into the twentieth century. These included the greater West Texas towns of San Angelo, Del Rio, Fort Stockton, Alpine, Midland, and Odessa.

San Angelo's Hispanic community grew (between 1900 and 1920) as calls for sheepshearers, farmhands, and railroad workers mounted. In reality, the Mexican American population continued being proportionately small compared to the number of Anglos in town, but growth and community entrenchment was nonetheless visible. A part of the downtown barrio retained its place as the center of social vibrancy (Anglos considered it a "village" and called it "Little Mexico"), although the enclave saw a demographic decline as Anglos pushed Mexicans out of the district. Mexicans by then were anyway spanning towards other parts of town where residential restriction were laxer and properties more affordable. The Santa Fe barrio continued to attract Mexicans who worked in the Gulf, Colorado & Santa Fe Railway while a new barrio took form south of San Angelo's central business zone when the Kansas City, Mexico and Orient Railway arrived in the city in 1909. Mexicans called this fledgling barrio "Oriente," as it grew around the Orient depot.[110]

Del Rio's Mexican population also increased during the first two decades of the twentieth century as Mexicans moved into both the Chihuahua barrio (west of San Felipe Creek) and the San Felipe barrio (east of San Felipe Creek). This was due to immigration from Mexico but also to hurried calls by railroad lines for workers.[111]

As Alpine's overall population grew between 1900 and 1920, so did the number of Tejanos in the town's majority Mexican south side. The Mexican American population in that section of the segregated city more than doubled between those two dates: from 649 in 1900 to 1,801 in 1920, constituting about 40 percent of the city's inhabitants throughout that era.[112]

Similarly, growth and endurance marked development in some of the smaller communities in the eastern section of the Edwards Plateau, such as Melvin and Rocksprings. Comparable stability was evident in the ranch village of Knickerbocker (Tom Green County), home since the 1880s to Mexican American families working for sheep rancher Joseph Tweedy. As of 1920, Mexican Americans, most of them sheepherders, ranch hands, and common laborers, made up about one-third (197) of the 545 total population in Knickerbocker, but they retained their cultural traditions into subsequent decades.[113]

More manifest of Tejano permanence in West Texas would be those settlements in the Big Bend area, a part of West Texas that has attracted more than welcome attention from regional historians. In Presidio and Brewster Counties, communities established by Mexican-descent *pobladores* in the nineteenth century persevered or were rekindled, while others emerged from in-migration from Mexico or from Mexican resettlement to new sites. The Mexican-descent population of the old town of Presidio grew substantially, although the settlement remained small in contrast to other West Texas municipalities. In 1910, Presidio had a total population of 278 (Mexicans made up 87 percent of the population), and this figure jumped to 1,401 in 1920 (93 percent of whom were Mexicans).[114]

Polvo (Redford) struggled during the early 1900s but has survived into recent times. As of the 1910s, the town featured a post office and a few general stores that served the small number of residents.[115] Casa Piedra in Presidio County remained home for about fifty families in the early 1900s who relied on harvesting cotton, hay, and vegetables. Lucía Hernández Russell (wife of W. E. Russell, a long-standing member of the community) conducted a one-room school in 1906, and the facility subsequently expanded to a two-room establishment as more people moved into the neighborhood. Then in 1912, Conrado and Natividad Vásquez launched a small business they called the Casa Piedra Mercantile Store. The town soon had its own post office and then in 1930, the Kansas City, Mexico and Orient Railway Company, passing through the settlement, built a depot; Conrado Vásquez became the depot agent.[116]

North of Casa Piedra, the small settlement of Alamito, founded in 1870 by John Davis and Mexican families working for him, contained close to 400 inhabitants as of 1908. A school functioned there, with a student population of fifty-seven children.[117] The small Hispanic community in Ruidosa depended for its livelihood on raising cotton, as did fellow Anglo farmers. Children attended the local school established in 1902.[118]

Porvenir, the scene of the 1918 massacre, traced its origins to the nineteenth century when Tejanos and arrivals from Mexico bought land or began occupying it under the principle of squatters' rights. According to the 1910 census, some 105 families lived in that northwestern Presidio County settlement, making their living as did their neighbors in other border villages. In Porvenir's rough terrain, which some viewed as uninhabitable, locals managed existence by raising goats, pigs, chickens, and cows and by growing vegetables.[119]

Not as fortunate in surviving as had other settlements in Presidio County was Shafter. It continued active as a typical company town during the early decades of the twentieth century as people working at the Presidio Mining Company made it their home. The village declined during the 1920s and 1930s as folks moved away with the falling demand for silver. Although it experienced some revival into the years after World War II, Shafter no longer exists.[120]

In Brewster County, Boquillas remained lively at least until the late 1910s. As noted in the previous chapter, a stimulant for its beginning during the 1880s had been mining activity just opposite on the Rio Grande (at the mining town also called Boquillas). Anglo merchants and farmers on the Texas side with connections in Boquillas, Mexico, provided work for local farm laborers and teamsters. Most jobs for Mexicans in Boquillas, Texas, however, were tied to transnational mining operations; the ore extracted in the silver mines of Northern Mexico was ferried via tram over the Rio Grande for processing by Tejanos. When mining activity ended in the area by the late 1910s, the population in Boquillas decreased.[121]

The community of La Coyota (also in Brewster County) continued as home for the family of Severiano Chavarría. During the early 1900s Severiano's sons Ruperto and Cecilio as well as several other families continued living in La Coyota, working for local Anglo farmers. They supplemented their living by relying on their own small-scale farming operations raising wheat, melons, and various vegetables as well as cutting timber for the local mines and engaging in freighting enterprises.[122]

Other pre-1900 resilient communities included the Martín Solis ranchlands in southeastern Brewster County. Solis and then his sons until about the mid-1910s raised beef and met demand for meat by the mining companies and the mine workers in that area.[123] Tejano ranchers who had established themselves in the region before 1900 also continued their rangeland interest, among them Benito Solis who ranched in the Glenn Springs vicinity, Félix Domínguez at the southeastern foot of the Chisos Mountains, Felix Gómez along the upper Alamo Creek, and Federico Billalba.[124]

Terlingua Abaja persisted as a viable settlement even as it saw outflow as workers around 1903 moved closer to the Chisos Mining Company to settle in what came to be known as Terlingua Arriba. Remaining inhabitants during the early 1900s survived by producing farm products and raising livestock for local consumption as well as for those working in the mines. The village featured a small school (most times administered by local Anglo wives) for the Mexican children.[125]

During the early 1900s, settlements reemerged from abandoned villages while others appeared with the arrival of new ventures entering the lower Big Bend. Among communities resprouting due to changing circumstances was Lajitas. Mexicans from Mexico and neighboring parts of the Big Bend gave new life to Lajitas when Howell W. McGuirk bought acreage in and around the old village in 1899 for farming purposes. Mexicans working for McGuirk supplemented their livelihood by farming on lands along the Rio Grande, laboring at the local mines, and hiring out to freight companies. The town during the early twentieth century was overwhelmingly Mexican (population sixty-four in 1910), excepting for a handful of Anglos, among them McGuirk and a few river guards. A newspaper account in 1902 read: "Lajitas is becoming quite a town. It has one store, a beer saloon, a school house with fifty pupils, and a Custom-house for the sub-district port or entry." When McGuirk sold out to his business partner Thomas V. Skaggs in 1917 the change had little effect on the community's resilience.[126]

Then, Mexican Americans pioneered new settlements during the early twentieth century, some of which remain today. Among these was Candelaria in western Presidio County, founded in 1901 as a farming-ranching community the settlers called Gallina. It flourished from the cotton industry introduced to the area during the 1910s, so that by the second decade of the century it had become home to more than 500 settlers, with a post office, a general store, a church and a school, and even a cotton gin.[127]

Downriver from La Coyota, Cipriano Hernández in 1903 established a grain and vegetable farm in what was then called Santa Elena (the village changed its name to Castolón in 1914). During the last decades of the century, Hernández had earned a livelihood in the Big Bend delivering goods to different parts of the region on wagons he had gradually acquired with savings. Settling down to farming, he now provided needed vegetables for local residents and miners working at Terlingua as well as feed for draft animals.[128]

Villages, furthermore, sprouted out of the mining boom of the early 1900s, Terlingua Arriba among the most conspicuous. When the Chisos Mining Company opened in 1903, local Texas-Mexican labor hands from old Terlingua relocated to the emerging upper site where they were quickly joined by arrivals from Mexico, both groups sinking roots in land near the mine.[129] They called the new home Terlingua Arriba, a necessary designation to distinguish it from the original Terlingua (now referred to as Terlingua Abaja) located some eight miles to the south of the new mining camp. Terlingua Arriba as a Mexican colony did well during the heyday of Chisos Mining's production, but people began leaving it during the 1930s as mining activity in the area ceased.[130]

SURVIVAL STRATEGIES

Having to fend for themselves in a society indifferent to them because of race and other prejudices, Mexicans pursued means crucial to maintaining a semblance of order in the community. They struggled against difficulties through reasoned judgment, workable approaches, cultural traditions, religious faith, and whatever strategies (either old or newly devised) proved effective in countering travail.

Illnesses and various health disorders were common to Mexican barrios and rural settlements in West Texas, just as they were to all communities in the region. But with meager resources to gain access to professional help, Mexicans faced formidable challenges. Among the many menaces that posed health threats to community survival during the early years of the twentieth century was the Spanish flu. The epidemic spread to West Texas beginning in the fall of 1918, discriminating against no one until it weakened in the spring of the next year. Trans-Pecos newspaper accounts reported it ravaging most counties, with Tom Green, Sutton, Brewster, Pecos, Reeves, Jeff Davis, Terrell, and Presidio most commonly named. Towns and rural areas seemed helpless but sought to fend off the pandemic with determined force. Communities sent out urgent calls for volunteers to help the infirm, quarantined neighborhoods (if not entire towns), prohibited public gatherings, suspended church services, closed school doors, converted school buildings and churches into makeshift hospitals, and directed people to wear masks. These attempts took into consideration Mexican sides of towns as well as ranches and farms where Mexicans served as the core labor pool.

At its height, the contagion took a brutal toll on everyone in West Texas but severely afflicted Mexicans. One historian has advanced several explanations for a higher mortality toll among Hispanics: general impoverishment, unsanitary conditions in adobe houses or *jacales* where loved ones huddled in refuge, little or no access to medical aid, and a shortage of nutritious fare that left them especially vulnerable. The onslaught caused the death of entire Mexican American families, of mothers (in one case, a mother left eight children behind), of husbands, or, equally horrifying, of all children, leaving parents childless. To be sure, Anglos experienced the same terror and agony.

As would most people facing a frightening crisis, Mexicans called upon God and the saints for intervention, summoned the powers of the local *curandera/o*, resorted to decades-old survival remedies, or simply counted on the resources of their will to overcome the emergency and to go on living. They abided by cultural traditions, if circumstances allowed them, to give lost ones a decent burial, including clothing them in the best wear they could manage. Mexicans who could afford it ornamented their loved ones' coffins with satin, selecting the colors pink and blue particularly for children. In their grief, many parents could best remember their dead children by naming newborns after the ones they had just lost.

Pressed by the immediacy of the moment, people could only bury their loved ones as the urgency dictated, most times without the customary dignity and decorum expected at the time of interment. Some families buried lost ones in their backyard property. Rural folks were often compelled to lay their dead to rest at the designated ranch, farm, or mining cemetery without the benefit of a proper marker. At Terlingua, no mortician was available to perform funeral rites, and survivors buried the dead in what amounted to crates hastily assembled at the Chisos mining woodshop. Like fellow West Texans, Mexicans bore the dishonor of having their closest relatives interred wantonly in mass graves or bulk trenches, such as happened in Candelaria.[131]

Just as Mexicans found the resolve to confront infirmities and resist distress, so did they muster the skills to cope with what poverty exacted upon them. Preserving and perpetuating a knowledge of adobe making ensured Mexicans a measure of domestic protection. As had their ancestors in the Big Bend region (as well as other parts of West Texas), heads of families continued to rely on individual skill and whatever usable materials nature availed to them for producing adobe. The aforementioned Cleofas Natividad illustrated such prowess as he helped his newcomer neighbor J. O. Langford (and his family) build shelter. Adhering to a proven process, Cleofas gathered mud and grass from the Hot Springs area and added manure deposits from his goat herd. His children then mixed the composition by mashing it with their feet. Thereafter, Cleofas laid out the concoction in ground pits until it reached the appropriate texture. He then removed the compound from the trenches and placed it in wooden molds and allowed it to dry to brick strength. The Langfords lived in their sturdy adobe home until 1913 when they left the region (due to the border troubles).[132]

Others in West Texas placed similar confidence in adobe's merit. Many of the houses in the Fort Stockton barrio, writes one historian, were of this material, most of them unpretentious structures that endured into the post–World War II era. Most, however, lacked amenities, including electricity and plumbing.[133] Helpful as well in providing necessary shelter was the simple but serviceable *jacal*—built still in the old-fashioned way. In Boquillas in the early 1900s, people made such lodging "of sotol and maguey bloom stalks, with ocotillo roofs on which clay was laid about six inches thick."[134] Actually, maguey served as thatching as well as did ocotillo. The Mexicans would use the plant's long stalks as rafters; they then finished up by covering the roof with maguey leaves.[135]

Other kinds of vegetation improved living conditions, among them the lechuguilla plant that grew wild in the Big Bend. Its fiber served functional purposes. Mexicans stripped it from the plant by hand and used the fiber to fabricate bags and cords and to make a variety of household products.[136] Mexicans also engaged in small-scale gardening, growing crops like corn, beans, and squash as a way to further ensure family and community well-being. They located their vegetable plots near homes or available open areas (preferably close to creeks) such as those along the Big Bend region. They depended on recent rains to nourish their plants, either channeling available waters towards the vegetable patch after a rainfall or digging trenches from higher grounds so that the rainwater would flow to their arable plots.[137]

While all types of survival strategies counted in warding off hardship, garden yields often substituted for currency. At Porvenir, for instance, residents during the 1910s used the corn, beans, and various vegetables they harvested to acquire finished products at general stores such as existed at Valentine or the Brite Ranch. Alternately, they traded their garden crops for supplies or goods neighbors possessed.[138] Bartering at Porvenir probably mirrored practices common throughout rural communities in West Texas. As elsewhere, lending personal tools for the use of another man's draft animals was routine. Men at Porvenir exchanged individual skills (e.g., in carpentry, mechanics, or farm labor) for work that friends or relatives could not otherwise do. An agreement with Anglo ranchers to make adobe for large construction projects, build small bridges, or dig canals (to move water) over difficult terrain could mean fruitful compensation for Mexicans with special talents.[139]

Poverty exerted all to rely on improvisation, among them those engaged in the transportation business. Freighters working for the Chisos Mining Company, for instance, came to prefer *huaraches* instead of boots or shoes. But how to acquire such footwear with meager wages? Once tires became commonplace, Big Bend freighters saw practicality in using rubber for their sandals and rejected the old rawhide footwear. The leather still could be used for shoe laces.[140]

Informal family alliances, formed through marriage arrangements, helped in mitigating adversity. In towns such as Fort Stockton, such cultural ties were more likely to involve community members possessing (real or imagined) political standing, social stature, or earned respectability. Developing marital bonds with others of similar social position might lead to an improved livelihood, a feeling of security, and, in an environment where most everyone was impoverished, psychological affirmation of an enhanced status.[141]

INSIDE THE MEXICAN DISTRICT

Life in Mexican *colonias* (Mexican enclaves, or neighborhoods) was hardly ever inert. Wherever Mexicans lived—be it ranches, farms, or towns; whether along the border counties or interior ones such as Tom Green or Pecos; or in places where they constituted either a minority or majority group—they carried on staving off difficulties and striving for life improvement. Persistent poverty, uncertainty, and vexations hardly stifled liveliness inside communities.

Business and Professional People

During the early decades of the twentieth century, some within the Mexican quarter rose, as had others before them, above grim poverty. They included teachers—more than likely schoolmarms—working in the border towns of the Big Bend. In Presidio County, Hispanic educators (most of them Tejanas) taught in village settlements such as Alamo, Loma Pelón, El Indio, and Redford, as well as in mining towns like Shafter.[142] Historical documents do not reveal these teachers' credentials, but in remote places during the early 1900s, those with bilingual abilities and a high school diploma likely substituted for those (mainly Anglos) with Normal School certificates. As indicated above, Lucía Hernández Russell, for one, headed a little school at Casa Piedra in 1906.[143] At Imperial, Apolonio Esparza (whose family had arrived there as farm laborers in the early 1910s) taught at an old school, where in a single room (according to one account) he taught "sixty students of varying ages. The seats were wooden boards on blocks. The bigger children would learn their lessons, then they would in turn teach the younger or slower learners what they had learned."[144] But exceptions existed to this general rule of employment under provisional status. Elena Herrera of Presidio County, as an example, in 1909 earned teacher certification, and expectations were that "Miss Herrera would be a successful teacher of Mexican children in the river country."[145]

Businesspersons ran general stores or small trading shops, mercantile enterprises, or family cafés, having benefited from their own business acumen to meet requests for ethnic merchandise and foods.[146] Among these were María G. (Chata) Sada and her husband Juan. Although Boquillas entered a period of disintegration during the mid-1910s, the couple continued to operate a combination general store, eatery (offering traditional Mexican food), and rooming house (in the form of adobe cabins) that catered to area farm laborers and to visitors, among them (Anglo) law authorities, surveyors, mining personnel, and ranchers who occasionally passed through the once lively mining village.[147] Seferino Madrid, a ranch owner from Lajitas, operated in 1908 a general store at Redford that went by the name of "Las Casas de Madrid." From the border, Madrid regularly conducted business with Marfa, conveying goods there and bringing back supplies. Apparently, Madrid gained a degree of success as a merchant, for in 1920 he helped update education in Redford by financing a new school.[148]

Conrado Vásquez and his father Natividad Vásquez during the early 1910s were well-known mercantile owners around the village of Casa Piedra.[149] In Marathon, Lázaro Ornelas had delivery service at his small store. Customers in surrounding areas mailed household needs to his small store, and on payday Ornelas packed his car with the requested orders, taking with him miscellaneous provisions, supplies, and clothing he hoped to sell upon making his deliveries. Also at Marathon, the Terrazas' Grocery and Drygoods Store came to be a successful going concern, profiting from the freighting business associated with the mining boom of that era.[150] In Fort Stockton, Don Francisco "Chico" Gómez was a familiar figure around the barrio by 1908 for his customer-friendly store and barbershop.[151] Among the most vivid descriptions of merchant life in West Texas is to be found in a 1920 issue of the *San Angelo Standard Times*. Reporting on what it called "Little Mexico," the newspaper noted:

> There are small stores and restaurants. These form the downtown section of "Little Mexico" while on each side not more than a block away in each direction lies the residence district. Business is conducted just as is true in any village and to all intents and purposes it is separate and distinct from the city of San Angelo.[152]

Freight contractors also comprised part of that small but discernible cohort that achieved economic good fortune. Upon them fell the responsibility of scheduling the movement of wagons between points and guaranteeing the load while in transit.[153] Less obliged to the mining companies than workers, freight contractors could negotiate with management on terms agreeable to both. But they owed it to their outfits to commit necessary resources to maintain working efficiency: ASARCO wagons going from Boquillas to Marathon required constant maintenance, for instance, for they were often laden with 10,000-pound shipments.[154] Naturally, business success depended on constant upgrading of assets; to remain competitive, some of the Mexican freight owners invested in Studebaker wagons. These Spanish mule–driven conveyances had a reputation for endurance, capacity to withstand punishment, and ability to carry three to four tons of quicksilver.[155]

Among those who found success in the shipping business at ASARCO's Boquillas silver mine was Ben Gallego, who freighted from distant Alpine.[156] Others constituting this cadre of freight company owners included Francisco Luna and Juan Medina of Marfa. The two men profited when in 1910 the operators of the Presidio Mining Company converted from wood to fuel oil for heating the company furnace. Using both their trucks for twice-daily round trips (from Marfa to Shafter), Luna and Medina guaranteed the mines would have the necessary quantity of oil at hand.[157] Contracting with the Chisos Mining Company were Félix Valenzuela and Paz Molinar. Carrying an 88-pound flask went at a price of one dollar so that Mexican contractors like Molinar and Valenzuela fared well financially. With the profits, Paz and his brothers from nearby Terlingua Abaja expanded on their own homestead, known locally as Rancho Molinar.[158]

But the transportation business in those days of mules and horses was not restricted to the mining industry. There was also guayule to be hauled to market; Pedro Terrazas, for instance, during the early 1900s took the guayule from Terlingua where he lived at that time to the nearest production plant at Marathon.[159] In Del Rio, Serapio Cárdenas, who arrived in town in 1901, acquired stock and wagons so that by 1908 he had established a prosperous hauling business. Pouring back earnings into his company, he became a dominant force in the commerce of freighting by 1915. His hired hands drove Cárdenas's wagons from Del Rio to outlying Anglo ranches, hauling to them fresh supplies from town or bringing back ranch products such as wool.[160] In Terrell County, Pablo Adame operated a countywide business freighting wool and supplies from the rural areas to Dryden and Sanderson.[161]

The entrepreneurial class included ranchers and farmers. Fermin Aguirre Sr. of Val Verde County gained wide prominence raising Rambouillet sheep and Angora goats—reputedly, he had the finest Rambouillet sheep in the county. His flock of thousands was such that every spring and fall he hired large crews to undertake the shearing job on his ranch.[162] Engaged in tilling were Estéban Ochoa and Bartelo García of Presidio County. Ochoa's prosperity owed in part to a gravity ditch he completed in 1917 with the help of unemployed immigrants (some 80 to 120 hands) fleeing the revolution in Mexico. His crew routed water over a sixteen-mile stretch from the Rio Grande to the Ochoa farmlands and to that of fellow farmers in the Indio, Texas, area. That same year, Bartelo García undertook another irrigation project just below the ditch Ochoa had constructed. This conduit capably served a total of 1,500 acres in what was the Haciendita community, including the property García cultivated. Success earned through the application of hard work, foresight, and efficient engineering placed farmers such as Ochoa and García in a tier that along with others of similar accomplishment constituted a middling class.[163]

Among landowners living at Porvenir in the northwestern district of Presidio County was Manuel Flores. As did some of the other residents of that farm community, Flores turned to raising cotton, achieving positive outcomes. To water his cotton, Flores, with the help of local labor and that of his brothers, dug canals stretching from the Rio Grande to his farm acreage. His deeds gave notice to neighbors that ranch land could also be put to farm use and that cotton planting could be pursued as another avenue toward life amelioration.[164]

Also to be found within Tejano communities were denizens engaged in a miscellany of vocations, trades, and crafts that not only rendered them a livable salary but, equally gratifying, bestowed upon them a level of prestige. Devoted to journalism was Amado Gutiérrez of Del Rio. Gutiérrez moved to the city during the 1880s, and during his long stay published several Spanish-language newspapers, first *Concordia*, followed in the 1890s by *El Liberal* and in the 1920s with *La Nueva Era* and *La Razón*.[165] Then there were members of the constabulary—such as deputy sheriffs maintaining law and order along Big Bend counties—who, it would be supposed, drew a reliable salary and received justified admiration for the work they performed.[166] Others with job security and earning deserved esteem due to the notable positions they held were postmasters and postmistresses; among those who worked in this capacity in Redford after 1907 were Irineo Luján (1907), Josepha Madrid (1911), Ramón Valenzuela (1914), A. L. Rede (1917), Lucy Franco (1925), C. J. Alvarado (1927), and others. Similarly considered of some note were postal carriers who delivered the mail between remote spots in the Big Bend, including the mines.[167] Then there was Sebastian DeAnda of Culberson County, who in early 1905 negotiated a contract with the government to carry the weekly mail from Van Horn to Orange, New Mexico, and then back to Van Horn.[168]

Similarly successful as a government employee was Apolonio Esparza of Imperial (Pecos County) who ferried the mail between Buena Vista (also in Pecos County) and Grandfalls, Texas (Ward County), doing so on "a two-seated buggy" that he also utilized as a transportation vehicle, charging only a small passage fee.[169] In the eastern section of the Edwards Plateau, Andrés Rendón rendered a similar service, working from 1905 to 1911 conveying the mail from Brackettville to the post office in Henze (now a ghost town) in Edwards County. On a schedule that had him going from Brackettville to Henze on Friday and returning home on Saturday, Rendón relied on a buggy and horse— the main means of mail carrying in those days— making his trips terribly cold during winters.[170] Looked up to by fellow Mexicanos also were scouts for the federal government: men such as Juan Ochoa of Indio who in 1919 served with the 8th Cavalry.[171] Rounding out membership in that group whose occupations netted them a livable wage were barbers, blacksmiths, ranch foremen, and artisans.[172] One's talent or ingenuity could also win a level of material comfort (or at least tribute). Such was the case of Serapio U. Santos, a refugee of the Mexican Revolution, who settled in Shafter. "Maestro Blacksmith," as he came to be known, invented and built in 1914 a little train capable of towing cars loaded with ore from the mine proper to the mill for processing.[173]

Religion

Mexicans in West Texas rarely experienced neglect from churches and organized religious groups despite the remoteness and isolation of settlements. The Catholic Church, well aware of its commitment to the faithful, minded them either through the use of itinerant priests who periodically traveled to smaller rural communities or through services at the local church in urban areas. Families in the Terlingua mining district, for one, would yearly await the arrival from Alpine or Marfa of a Catholic priest. During the latter's brief visit, devoted Catholics wishing their sins confessed, their marriages validated, and their children baptized received the dutiful attention and blessing of the visiting padre.[174] Believers elsewhere also awaited (and acquired) similar services, as did families of Sonora, Ozona, Eldorado, Fort McKavett, and surrounding rural areas. To these remote places the Immaculate Conception Church in San Angelo directed priests who conducted services at people's homes or in the outdoors.[175]

More stable areas by the early twentieth century had permanent places where people worshipped. Marfa's Catholics attended St. Mary Catholic Church[176] and Mexican Catholics in Alpine went to Our Lady of Peace Catholic Church.[177] In 1919, the nuns of the order Servants of the Sacred Heart of the Poor in Alpine founded a teaching facility known as the School of the Sacred Heart. Because it was in the hands of the sisters, Spanish speakers in town referred to it as La Escuela de las Madres.[178] In Del Rio, the Church considered it necessary to care for the growing population of the San Felipe barrio and in the early twentieth century founded the parish of Our Lady of Guadalupe, then providing a modern brick church for the faithful in 1918.[179] In San Angelo, locals prayed and met religious commitments at the Church of the Sacred Heart until the diocese in 1930 built for them St. Mary's Church in the south side barrio.[180] In nearby Knickerbocker, the faithful in 1908 dedicated Immaculate Conception Church on land earlier donated by local ranchers Elizabeth and Joseph Tweedy.[181]

Parishioners often played prominent roles in plans to help themselves. Catholics, upon arriving in Melvin village during the early years of the twentieth century, held Mass in private homes; priests from nearby Brady led the services. In 1913, dedicated Catholic men in Melvin moved to town a farm building from the nearby Noyes Ranch—church members would over the year remodel, update, and modernize the original structure.[182] In Ozona, a man named Pedro Mata sometime in the early years of the 1900s took it upon himself to erect a meeting place (probably made of adobe) for the faithful, although locals also used the building for social gatherings and even a schoolhouse.[183] Members of St. Joseph Church in Fort Davis succeeded in establishing schooling for the young: they negotiated an agreement in the early 1900s with the parish priest allowing the church edifice to double at times as a school for Mexican children.[184] At Van Horn (Culberson County), the leading force behind the building of the first Catholic church in town was Pete Oñate, who began the organizing efforts around 1910. Some four years later, locals succeeded, through donations they raised, in finishing the first church, a 24-by-54-foot building. Services were conducted by out-of-town pastors, coming in from distant places such as San Elizario.[185] In Redford, worshippers in 1912 undertook the formidable task of constructing San José Catholic Church.[186] The faithful in Marathon physically raised St. Mary's Church in 1908 after acquiring five lots of property and building materials from local Anglo donors. Those with teams and wagons dutifully conveyed the sand and rock needed for the base foundation. Other parishioners fabricated the adobe brick, which a crew of skilled craftsmen then used for the building's walls. Contributions financed the acquisition of the church bell in 1911.[187]

Whether Catholic or Protestant, Mexican believers organized religious clubs and religious associations in their parishes and church districts. In Fort Davis, for instance, men could belong to the Círculo Católico. During the early 1900s, the men's society at St. Joseph Catholic Church in Fort Stockton formed El Círculo Mexicano, although it gradually morphed into the Unión Católica Mutualista.[188]

Not much is known about the Protestant churches in West Texas for this period. In San Angelo, Presbyterians initiated work in 1912, making credible headway in the barrio by 1915 when they founded—behind the leadership of Reverend Narciso Lafuerza, a Spaniard transferred to the town from Cuba, and with the help of Jennie Suter—the First Mexican Presbyterian Church.[189] Responsible for bringing Methodism to Sanderson was Juan Zepeda Sr. and other barrio families. In 1908, Zepeda and supporters banded together to build El Buen Pastor Methodist Church out of adobe, then used their own craftsmanship to make the pews and pulpit.[190] The Methodists in Marfa as of 1914 were under the care and guidance of Marcos de la Garza. In 1918, the Methodist Mission established "El Circuito de Marfa, Texas."[191]

Schooling

Educators of the day posited that Mexican American parents did not value education. Such attitudes contributed to children's deficiency in English, to youngsters' failure to acquire essential knowledge and skills, and, consequently, to students' inability to function adequately in the American mainstream. Some contemporaries further held the view that trying to educate Mexican children would be a disservice to them since schooling would disrupt the simple way of life with which Mexicans were satisfied. Influenced by such thinking, Anglo school board members failed to make Mexican American education a community priority. Where schooling existed, officials crowded students into large classrooms, not uncommonly containing several grades, with one teacher assigned to instructing all at hand. In most cases, students spent two or three years in school learning the English language before being promoted. After that, they attended until about their early teenage years, which was to about the fifth-grade level.[192]

In point of fact, evidence indicates that—notwithstanding the discouragement and obstacles that Mexicans encountered in pursuing an education—parents saw value in school instruction and motivated their youngsters to acquire learning when feasible. In the rural areas, they dispatched children to receive instruction from Anglo landowners or merchants who altruistically gave of themselves for the good of the community. As mentioned earlier, such was the case at Lajitas and San Vicente. At Porvenir, Harry Warren conducted a public school on his ranch property during the latter years of the 1910s, and as of early 1918 some twenty students attended, most of them from established families in the area.[193]

Community activism also pointed to parental desire to have enlightenment reach the barrio. So committed were San Angelo parents to seeing their children obtain wholesome instruction that starting in 1910 (and continuing into the mid-1910s) they implemented a boycott (discussed below) against the city's schools, aimed at achieving equal education with Anglos.[194] Parental pressure on school districts to expand upon schooling accommodations (by either adding annexes to schoolyards or building new structures) further attested to the Mexican community's desire to have children advance in life. The Del Rio school systems (both the Del Rio Independent School District and the San Felipe Consolidated School District), for example, dealt continuously with growth in student enrollment. County commissioners constructed two schools in the San Felipe barrio (the SFCSD) between 1908 and 1910—the first a one-room structure referred to by locals as Escuela Amarilla (due to its yellow paint) and the other as Escuela Calaveras (situated, as it was, close to the enclave's cemetery)—but school board members kept enlarging both edifices to meet rising attendance. Because of overpopulation, some of the parents in San Felipe sent their children to *escuelitas*, although some opted for them because they preferred that their children learn in their native language.[195]

As had their predecessors in the late nineteenth century, families opted for these instructional types as *escuelitas* upheld people's own ethnicity. Teachers (almost always women) might be residents of the barrio who had teaching backgrounds—perhaps acquired as immigrants from Mexico. Despite instruction in Spanish, the curriculum paralleled in many ways the local school district's own program. It included reading and writing, science, mathematics, Mexican history, and other courses intended to inculcate proper morals and ideals.[196]

To teach children in rural areas where public school facilities did not exist (or were not made available to them), Tejanos turned to home instruction. Teaching in those student-friendly surroundings may not have been as structured as it was in *escuelitas* such as those present in San Felipe, but it served the intended purpose. In Melvin during the 1910s, such private schools were present; generally in charge were women from neighboring ranches who taught out of their homes. Once the town built a public school for Mexicans in 1923, Melvin parents chose public over private education.[197]

Other West Texas school districts, similar to the San Felipe Consolidated School District, faced the problem of providing adequate building space for Mexicans. In Marfa, overcrowding in old run-down buildings was such that county officials in 1910 built on the town's south side the Hidalgo Ward, a new two-room elementary school constructed of adobe. By the next year, so many more students had enrolled for attendance that officials assigned a second teacher to the school.[198]

"Mexican schools" were regularly segregated, physically substandard, and often administered by inattentive school boards. The teachers assigned to them ranged widely, from the vicious racist mentor to the dedicated professional. In the latter case were sympathetic persons such as Hallie Stillwell, who relocated from Alpine to Presidio in 1916 to assume the job of teaching Mexican children (almost everyone in Presidio was Mexican). Her sister taught in another border village, about three miles from Presidio.[199] According to one report, good teachers served in the Mexican school at Marfa. Among them were ones who appreciated the poverty of their charges, and on one occasion in 1919, they solicited donations for gifts to be presented to the children at Christmas time (among those contributing were men serving in the Armed Services at Camp Marfa).[200]

There were, certainly, options available to parents who rejected the type of inferior education associated with the public schools. As in the case of Del Rio (and no doubt elsewhere), some West Texas parents opted for *escuelitas*. Others, similarly able to afford private education, turned to quality institutions such as ones that churches administered. In San Angelo during the period between 1900 and 1920, the Catholic Church sponsored at least two private schools: Immaculate Conception Academy (although the school practiced segregation) and St. Joseph's school.[201] Other children in San Angelo attended the Mexican Presbyterian Mission School, founded in 1912. Its curriculum emphasized the learning of English, and to that end the Presbyterian school set up night classes for adolescent boys (and adult males) interested in learning this alternate language.[202]

Self-Help Groups

Self-help societies remained active in Tejano communities as they had through the latter years of the nineteenth century. These *mutualistas* (mutual benefit groups) had purposes akin to those of organizations founded throughout the state and nation by working-class people of different nationalities: such fraternal orders sought to aid members finding themselves in desperate circumstances or facing family emergencies. In Fort Stockton by the early twentieth century, men had formed, in their commitment to the ideal of benevolence, El Club Protectivo Mexicano Independiente.[203] Also in San Angelo during this time were the Sociedad Fraternal Unión México Texana (initially established in the late 1890s) and the Obreros del Universo, formed in 1909 (the Obreros was patterned after the Woodmen of the World). Members found protection in these types of associations upon loss of jobs or the death of loved ones. Also present in San Angelo to assist in community needs during the early 1910s was a Masonic society.[204]

West Texas Mexican communities as a matter of course formed clubs and associations for purposes besides self-help. Some of these barrio organizations had entertainment as their goal. Among them was the Club Atlético Católico of Sanderson, Texas, which brought sports to the local Mexican American population during the early 1900s.[205] At the Chisos Mining Company, organizers assembled a baseball squad—which they aptly called the Miners—offering local mining villages a recess for leisure and relaxation. To complete the team, the players invited company officials to join; the Anglo administrators agreed to play despite the breach of social norms.[206]

Barrio musicians, many of them skilled in their craft as guitar and violin players, formed local combos and played upon request, such as on the occasion of the two-week shift change on Saturday at the Terlingua mining camps.[207] In Marfa, Juan Peréa and Cruz Martínez by 1919 had made their ensemble, La Música de Peréa, one of the most popular around.[208] Those having an interest in theater founded drama clubs. In Sanderson there existed in those early twentieth-century days such a troupe under the instruction of a Margarita Gonzales. Consisting mainly of young people, the troupe presented plays, some of which contained elaborate plots.[209]

Then there were organizations that addressed particular community issues. In 1911, some Hispanic women in Marfa responded to the town's newly organized Anti-Saloon League's invitation for attendance. Seemingly enough showed interest in the league that Mexican American speakers addressed its members in Spanish.[210] Furthermore, some barrio clubs acted to realize community solidarity. In San Angelo, people in 1906 started the Club Latino Americano to promote social discussion and meet the need for local celebration and entertainment.[211]

Leisure

Within enclaves, Mexicans engaged—often with genuine zest—in various favorite leisure pastimes. Sheer inventiveness offered some diversions, as in the case Charles Hawley witnessed in Terlingua. On Sundays, Hawley reported, some of the miners would take aim at goats they tied to a post on top of a hill. From their angle, they fired a .30-30 Winchester rifle (paying a certain price per round discharged) at a luckless animal brought in for the purpose. The competitors delighted in seeing the frightened victim dodging the many bullets, for the goat might not fall on the first hit. The game persisted until the goat was either dispatched or mortally wounded, and whoever successfully killed the helpless creature took it home. The contest involved shooting one goat after the next and lasted throughout the afternoon.[212]

More organized affairs included community functions, family receptions, and private galas. Some events were open to all in the community. As one spectator observed in astonishment upon witnessing Mexican Americans in Terlingua coming together:

> Men, women, children, the young and the old, miners, foremen, freight-ers, all classes and all groups entered into the festivity in the most com-plete abandon. We American people cannot do that. We are somehow restrained by our consciousness of differences in position, wealth, occu-pation, politics, religion, social status, etc. Complete freedom in social intercourse is difficult, often impossible.[213]

On the other hand, occasions could be exclusive and required conformity to family and community propriety. In Fort Stockton, for instance, residents came together at the Terrazas Hall to host more "proper" social balls. The hall served for years as a place ideal for wedding receptions and family gatherings.[214]

Barrio Violence

Certainly, segregated Mexican communities had a side other than that wherein people worked hard for a living, strived for individual, family, and community uplifting, and pursued satisfying leisure activities. Internecine violence and var-ious sorts of criminal activity unquestionably dogged the barrio just as they did other communities in West Texas regardless of race. Acts of Mexicans criminally abusing other Mexicans occurred, and some are recorded in county histories and the available scholarship.[215] But published sources for this time do not identify any particular cases on a sensational scale. For the most part, unlawful activity and wrongdoing within enclaves did not necessarily imperil Mexican American community wholesomeness during the early decades of the twentieth century.

An exception might be made of the town of San Angelo, where incidents involving Mexicans assailing Mexicans appear disproportionate to what hap-pened in other Tejano settlements of West Texas. Perhaps the phenomenon was an extension of the violence that was part of the village's nineteenth-century frontier history. Whatever the cause, the period between 1900 and 1920, judging from the city's newspaper reports, was a time of recurrent entanglements among Mexicans. The Mexican business district (today part of San Angelo's down-town) then accommodating a motley array of bars, restaurants, and *tienditas* (mom-and-pop stores), was the scene of some rather serious clashes. In that city space, men engaged in rows that involved brawls, stabbings, and even killings.

Further to the south of this downtown district, in the emerging enclave called Oriente, at least two murders took place during the 1910s.[216]

LO MEXICANO

Mexican Americans during the early twentieth century observed customs and traditions earlier brought transnationally to West Texas by their parents and grandparents and then later by newcomers. The unprecedented number of people entering West Texas fleeing the Mexican Revolution or searching for work opportunities across the border reinforced the connection that long-time settlers in the region shared with the old country. People honored familiar conventions, behaviors, and lifeways. The old practices created stability in life, normalized people's existence, bred social cohesiveness, and buttressed group spirit and community fortitude. Heritage, attitude, and identity acted as bulwarks against community disintegration and a shield against a perceived alien world.

Mexican Americans still placed faith in traditional curative methods. Because of poverty, they turned to time-tested home remedies (*remedios caseros*) or to local *curanderas* and *curanderos* whom they believed to be gifted with extraordinary skill and healing capacities. Treatment came at little or no expense (often no charges were demanded). Historically, folk healing had its roots in old Mexico. Curanderos learned their craft by working alongside older curanderos who had gained their knowledge through on-the-job training, oral instruction, and years of practice. While unlicensed, the practitioners nonetheless adeptly diagnosed patient ailments, then prescribed the appropriate and necessary treatment for cure. They considered nature a "pharmacy"; in many places, most especially in the terrain of the Big Bend district, the herbs and plants they needed grew wild and abundantly. Commonly, backyard gardens of curative herbs and other plants supplemented what the natural surroundings rendered to the healers. No particular social status was attached to being a *curandera/o*; in fact, most were common laborers such as sheepherders, *vaqueros*, farmhands, freighters, and the like who possessed no distinction due to literacy, class, profession, or official accreditation.[217]

Mexican and Catholic tradition informed rituals to be heeded at the time of a person's death. Loved ones attended to the departed at a private home, likely the deceased's. Preparations for burial began immediately; ideally the funeral would take place within twenty-four hours. Poverty dictated improvisation: those in charge of preparing the body placed it on a table, bound the feet, and then, to ensure that the mouth remained closed, wrapped cloth strips or bandages from under the chin to the top of the skull. Women decorated the room and coffin as means allowed, perhaps taking crepe paper and cutting it into flowers. In the evening, people observed a wake (*velorio*) lasting all night; the women remained close to the body and the men congregated outside. By then, relatives and friends had dug the grave; after Mass the next day, they laid the person to rest.[218]

Among time-honored cultural conventions upholding life in the Hispanic community was the Spanish Mexican ritual institution of *compadrazgo* (co-parenthood). Marriages, baptisms, first communions, and other Catholic occasions necessitated sponsors (*padrinos* and *madrinas*). By engaging in these Catholic rites, individuals formally bonded as *compadres*. Such connections produced spiritual and kinship alliances in the Mexican enclave.[219]

As to marriage traditions, Mexicans abided by them with respect, formality, and reverence. The protocol followed in the case of Eva Camúñez, scion of one of the founding Hispanic families in San Angelo, is instructive. Camúñez informed an interviewer:

[In 1909] Juan Flores came to act on behalf of the [suitor's] father when they asked for my mother's hand in marriage. Back in those days they would bring a letter [to the bride's family]; a certain grace/decision period would be worked out; the groom's representatives would leave with an understanding to return at the end of the grace period.[220]

Elsewhere in West Texas, Mexicans maintained a similar courtliness. When Catarino Gonzales and Leonor Olivas of Fort Davis wished to be married in 1912, Mr. and Mrs. Genaro and Anna Gonzales (Catarino's parents) went to Leonor's house one Sunday in June, visited with Alejandro and Concepción Olivas (Leonor's father and mother), and left with them a letter (which spoke to their son's good character) asking for their daughter's betrothment. The Gonzales returned the subsequent Sunday and, after a brief visit, received the letter from the Olivas consenting to Leonor's marriage to Catarino. Another visit the following week between the young couple's respective parents addressed the important preparations to be made for the wedding. By custom, Catarino was to bear the cost of the ceremony. Then, Catarino (in a gesture signifying his standing as a good provider) was to favor the Olivas with groceries and supplies. He was to complete his responsibilities by purchasing a wedding dress and ring for the bride, a duty he fulfilled.[221] Similar custom and solemnity was followed in Alpine when 18-year-old Francisco Sánchez and 14-year-old Francisca Gallegos married in 1915.[222]

In Boquillas, Mexicans abided by the same decorum. The courtship period, according to J. O. Langford who lived there in the early 1910s, was brief, and chaperones kept vigil on the bride and groom. When ready to petition for consent to marry, the suitor asked two friends to join him in the protocol of calling on the bride's father. Upon receiving the father's approval for the union, the bride-groom extended funds to the man; the money paid for the wedding dress and other accessories the bride needed for the nuptial event as well as for groceries to last the groom's future in-laws' family until such time as the parties agreed on the wedding date, usually some two weeks. A few days later, the young man returned, accompanied again by his two escorts, this time to ask the bride to marry him. Following the wedding and a feast, the husband would take his wife to the family home; there his father welcomed the newlyweds with six-gun shots. The couple remained there for a day but then moved in with the bride's parents. Custom required that they stay there, perhaps for three months, after which they left to pursue their own beginnings.[223]

Feasts following marriage ceremonies could be grand affairs, and while poor people at that time had few resources for extravagant display, celebrations could extend throughout the wedding day and beyond it. Most parents probably were unable to amass money sufficient to arrange something as grand as a ranch hand named Juan prepared at the Fenley Ranch in south Terrell County in 1902. To celebrate his daughter Pancha's marriage to a man named Pedro Fuentes (apparently a worker in a neighboring ranch), Juan killed four calves for the barbecue (which Juan presumably acquired from Fenley, who presented them as a gift). According to reports, families from as far as twenty miles away descended on Juan's place at the Fenley Ranch to celebrate the occasion, which featured music and dancing over the course of three days.[224] Undoubtedly, some degree of distress fell upon those within Mexican American communities unable to afford indulgences similar to Juan's.

The birth of children could be communicated to the community by different means. Langford recorded one particular way heeded in Boquillas. There, fathers announced births with gun shots: one round declared the child as a girl, while two heralded a boy. The man then informed his other children of the new arrival; the kids welcomed the baby with much glee.[225]

As to more common and less ritualistic-bound observances, such as the staging of the fiestas of Cinco de Mayo and the Diez y Seis de Septiembre, Mexicans marked them with old-time fare and proceedings. Responsible for ensuring their celebration during the first decades of the 1900s was the standing *comisión honorífica*. As per practice, the *comisión* designated a *junta patriótica* for the task; it in turn relied on local fraternal societies, barrio clubs, or volunteers for coordinating the event. In Fort Stockton, during the early years of the twentieth century El Club Protector Mexicano Independiente took charge of these patriotic galas.[226] In Brady, the local paper announced, Samuel Breceno, the president of the local patriotic society, was to oversee the 1911 Diez y Seis event scheduled for commemoration at the Colton Ranch, hosted by Señora Delfina Florez who lived there.[227]

At most celebrations, processions of floats and buggies paraded through the barrio while horse races and games of horseshoes, tennis, basketball, and baseball rounded off other segments of the program. Patriotic themes interspersed the open setting: depictions of Mexico's heroes and flags (both Mexican and American) supplemented with flowers, streamers, and assorted decorations fitting the occasion blanketed the scene. Standard features of these fiestas were demonstrations from a public platform or pavilion: orations, declamations, dramatic performances, and other public expressions inspired by the moment. Speakers could be anyone, from acknowledged leaders in the community to ordinary folks. Hawley wrote about one of the functions he attended in Terlingua: "I . . . was much surprised when several illiterate miners, mounting a rude platform, each delivered short, patriotic addresses full of feeling for and devotion to the mother country." Wherever in West Texas communities might hold the *fiestas patrias* celebrations, revelers visited *puestos* (food booths) vending ethnic delicacies such as tamales, enchiladas, tacos, cabrito, and buñuelos.[228]

Folks from the countryside descended on the town to join fellow merrymakers there. Such was the case in Sanderson, where ranch and farm work slackened (ostensibly with the courtesy of landowners) at the time of the fiesta. At the scene (perhaps in someone's back yard or on a vacant lot) attendees found great excitement in planned contests, such as climbing a greased post to retrieve a dollar bill placed atop the pillar. Not infrequently, revelers remained overnight in town to enjoy dances that lasted until dawn.[229]

Wherever Mexicans lived in the United States, and by extension West Texas, they welcomed the impending approach of Christmas Day with the Mexican (and Christian) tradition of *las posadas* (the inns). At Sanderson, residents organized themselves into groups and as in past times reenacted Mary and Joseph's quest for lodging in Bethlehem. Participants marched from one barrio house to another appealing for a place to rest, only to be rejected. Not until Christmas Eve did someone open the door to the petitioners. On the next day, people engaged in much enthusiastic activity, celebrating with the exchange of gifts and the making of tamales. Town folks then held a fiesta and dance honoring the occasion on which the Kings brought presents to the infant Jesus.[230]

Celebrated with reverence but equal merriment were religious holidays. In Sanderson, residents commemorated San Juan's Day and St. James Day, the latter with such diversions as horse races and rodeos. A contest popular in town was the *hombre con pollo* (man with a chicken) game, in which several horse riders chased down Main Street a man with a chicken clutched under his arm. The object was to steal the bird from the fleeing player; no doubt all participants and spectators considered the pursuit as harmless fun.[231] During the 1930s, and presumably before then, the Mexican American community of Melvin, Texas, also amused itself with the same game—although it was carried out during the secular Cinco de Mayo festivities.[232]

Maintained as part of Mexican American culture in West Texas was the art of remembering and narrating historical moments through the medium of the *corrido*. These ballads had a long and popular tradition in Mexico, and immigrants disseminated them throughout the United States. Not surprisingly, they were to be found in West Texas, although many of them have now been lost to time. Examples of early twentieth-century *corridos* in the Big Bend are two salvaged by Professor Elton Miles of Sul Ross State University in Alpine.

Corridos told of incidents witnessed by the composer or remembered by contemporaries and then performed by the balladeer soon after the event took place. Subjects of the story were real, not fictitious, characters, invariably members of the working class; if Anglos entered the plot, they did so tangentially. In the Big Bend, the settings were often rural spaces (perhaps Anglo ranches and farms where much of the population was concentrated in the early twentieth century) although they could also be urban enclaves. The singer spoke to an audience of fellow Mexican Americans probably gathered at a private occasion, perhaps a house party, a family get-together, the campfire, or the local cantina (saloon).

Corridos recounted ordinary happenings, as in the tragic killing in "El Corrido de Antonio Casas." The episode occurred in 1908 at a cantina in the

Alpine barrio, apparently a result of a personal dispute between patrons. The senseless crime, the narrator tells the listener, brought unmeasured grief and an unpredictable future for the murdered Antonio Casas' widow and family.[233]

Some jobs carried potential danger and risk, certainly for those living in the countryside. Working with livestock, for instance, involved adventure, bravado, and daring, but also the potential of injury or death. "El Corrido de José Martínez" told of a rider killed at a ranch near Casa Piedra in 1915 when thrown off a horse despite his horsemanship, fearlessness, and experience as a bronco buster.[234]

HOME IN AMERICA

The historical sociologist Paul Wright asserts that loyalty to old ways in the barrio arrested Mexican American advancement. Isolationism, whether it was forced, voluntary, or an unintended consequence of life, had its downside. Living on the periphery meant not gaining literacy (schools during that time were still not a fixture in many enclaves). Lacking full command of the English language inhibited Spanish speakers' ability to stay abreast of world (and even local) news, and to acquire pertinent information issued by municipal authorities. Separated from the mainstream, Mexicans missed chances to learn how to navigate their way in an Anglo universe. Without proper networking skills, they could hardly negotiate with Anglos who might share common interests, such as in the sports field (most likely baseball). But, Wright acknowledges, Mexicans saw little value in accepting Anglo ways, as whites would still consider them as "Mexicans."[235]

Actually, barrio life was not unchanging. Segments within the Hispanic population of West Texas balanced the love they harbored for their immigrant/ Mexican heritage with respect and appreciation for the values, ideals, and principles the United States represented. Assimilation pressures weighed on all. Strands of group and personal commitment to the American example and even trust in the American promise, thus, coexisted congruently with "*lo mexicano.*" Building upon their acquaintance (traceable to the nineteenth century) with facets of the outside Anglo world, Mexicans carried on participating in American patriotic celebrations, using the political system for community amelioration and, on occasion, confronting management to improve the workplace environment.

Several factors accounted for the consideration and allegiance given to America, the land most counted as their home. Many were citizens, having been born in Texas. Immigrants who came to West Texas in the nineteenth century now instinctively recognized the US as their native country. More recent arrivals felt grateful for the employment they found in the region, for while meager, it improved upon what they had left behind in Mexico.

The American way of life could not but influence their sentimentality. Daily, whether directly or vicariously, they interacted with the cultural world of Anglo Americans, be it with *el patrón* on the job, with teachers at the Mexican school, or even with political operatives. Such contacts influenced people's feelings toward the nation of their residence, converting them into genuine patriots or at least sympathetic to the standards America symbolized.

Then came World War I, which tested people's sense of loyalty. Throughout parts of Texas, judging from the extant scholarship, divisions occurred within Mexican American society. On the one hand, elements within the broader Tejano community viewed the war as not one of their own. Why side with people (Anglos) who did not consider them true Americans, hurled epithets freely at them, and consigned them to the lowest grades of physical labor?[236] In Big Bend towns such as Alpine and Fort Davis, the immigrant connection to Mexico and to events experienced firsthand swayed many towards impartiality: large numbers had fled the turmoil of the Mexican Revolution and were not eager to become involved in yet another fight. Others had taken the Pershing Expedition (March 1916) into Mexico personally, viewing it as an encroachment on their country's sovereignty. Still others sided with Mexico in the neutral position it took towards the war.[237] Conversely, other young men from several West Texas areas honored their obligations and dutifully served on the front lines.[238] As well, many of civilian status identified with the war's aims. Community support for draft calls and assistance to the war effort through the purchase of war bonds quite certainly helped shape group outlooks.

Residence in the United States, exposure to US cultural behavior, and sincere feelings of allegiance to the country during times of crisis (such as World War I) inspired Mexican Americans to demonstrate their patriotic spirit publicly— as did villagers at the Terlingua quicksilver mines. There, workers and their families enthusiastically celebrated holidays such as the Fourth of July. Despite paltry earnings, it was their practice to acquire—via orders through the company store—ribbons and various decorative items in an effort to give the entire mining complex a festive appearance. Revelers neglected no post, window, porch, or open spot to artistically fasten American national symbols in red, white, and blue. The office, the workshop, the mine entrance, and house gardens became scenes of genuine emotional expression. But the people did not for the moment betray their cultural links to Mexico. As a reaffirmation of their heritage, the Mexicans in the camp interspersed July Fourth fixings with emblems featuring Mexico's national colors of red, white, and green.[239]

Political Engagement

An understanding of American politics, acquired through experience during the nineteenth century and enhanced in the new century by contact with Americanizing elements, permitted Mexicans to engage the political system through several channels. It was most manifest in the role they assumed as voters in the entrenched practice of political bossism.

Nineteenth-century bossism persisted as a practice into the 1900s. In 1902, the *Alpine Avalanche* noted its presence, reporting that Anglos were calling upon Mexicans in the area to declare their intention to naturalize and then were compelling them to vote as instructed.[240] But Mexican voters could find the system accommodating for self or community purposes. In Alpine in 1900, for example, Mexicans were to have the opportunity to decide whether the sale and consumption of alcohol would be allowed within city limits. An element among political leaders in the town promised them liquor and barbecue on election day to ensure the town voted dry. Seemingly, Mexicans saw prospects in possible bootlegging—should the vote go in favor of prohibition—and they thus followed instructions. But part of the white population saw machination in display and in 1906 attempted to disfranchise the Mexicans throughout all of Brewster County by applying the rule being administered elsewhere in the state: the White Man's Primary. The measure called upon potential voters to attest that they were "a white person and a Democrat," an assertion almost impossible for Mexicans to validate.[241]

Mexicans had options other than boss opportunism to engage in political practice, among them compromising with influential Anglos in exchange for patronage appointments. In those parts of West Texas where the number of Mexicans and white people was almost equal, or where Mexicans constituted a preponderance of the local population, it was convenient for Anglo politicos to use intermediaries in the barrio to help maintain their political fortification. Such was the case in Fort Stockton, where the politically powerful Rooneys (a family of landowners, merchants, and officeholders) entered into arrangements with some of the more "prominent" barrio Tejanos, allowing them positions such as store clerks in Rooney family businesses or granting them law enforcement duties. The Rooneys profited from the impression they were helping uplift the working poor and, of course, from the Mexican vote upon which they partly depended for maintaining control of city and county government. Patronage, at the same time, allowed Mexicans—through benefits dispensed by the bosses—to make inroads, however slight, into the very system aimed at disfranchising them.[242]

Acquaintance with the political system also permitted Mexicans to take action for possible community uplift beyond what established structures such as bossism or patronage enabled. In 1910, for instance, Mexicans in San Angelo opted for confrontational measures in an effort to achieve improved educational opportunities. As Americans (most of the protestors claimed to be American citizens), parents of school-age children felt they had the right to challenge unequal educational opportunity, substandard school facilities, and especially the entrenched system of racial segregation in San Angelo. The movement was in the grand American political tradition of exercising the freedom to protest and of using the rights of speech, petition, and assembly.

The effort to rectify the discriminatory state of affairs unfolded in a course of action seemingly formulated in the spring of 1910. When a census taker for the federal government visited the barrio in April, parents refused to disclose students' names; their intent was to force the school system to terminate segregation, as the allocation of funds to school districts depended on student attendance. Then, the community formed a four-member committee and hired a law firm, tasking both with presenting their grievances before the school board.

On June 7, 1910, the committee with legal representation went directly to the board and submitted to it a written request to end separate schooling. But board members were unmoved and rejected the petition. Exercising their right to peaceful assembly, community members held a hall meeting (some 300 attended, as reported by the town's newspaper) about ten days later. Speakers there urged parents not to be discouraged, emphasizing the people's right to protest under the law. Attendees left agreeing to implement a boycott of schools, which they did on September 19, 1910, with the start of the school year.

In the end, the boycott did not yield desired results. It lasted until about the middle of the 1910s when parents gave in to reality and returned their children to the Mexican school in the south side barrio. But students had not lacked for education; during the boycott some attended the city's Immaculate Conception Academy and the Mexican Presbyterian Mission School.[243]

Labor Activity

Aside from political engagement, Mexicans acted on other fronts, among them the labor field, confident they possessed the legitimacy to tackle the American foundational order. How did Mexican workers come to believe they had the right to challenge management? Two schools of thought on Mexican American historiography seek to explain early twentieth-century Tejano response to labor exploitation. One traces the source of resistance to Mexico's trade union tradition. The other sees Mexican workers confident in their citizenship status challenging conditions they faced directly on the job. With such self-assurance, Mexican American workingmen in South Texas joined unions such as the Texas State Federation of Labor. On cotton fields, pickers at times simply walked off.[244]

In West Texas, Mexicans faced unique obstacles to work protest. There was an abundance of laborers in the region, almost all of them poor, who took jobs at barely survival wages lest they face starvation. Whether it was mines, farms, or ranches, people had little flexibility to change occupations and thus stayed in the company village or rural settlement fearing eviction for contemplating labor organizing. As in many other places throughout the state during that time, moreover, labor agitators were susceptible to dire consequences.[245]

Still, a sense of having the right to make demands of management produced encounters between Mexican laborers and their employers. At least some of those in the Terlingua mining district dared take such a step in 1910. But the effort ended in disappointment: the call for an increase in wages led to the death of three protestors at the hands of a mine owner. In 1912, men at the Chisos Mining Company requested Sundays off (from their seven-day schedule) but management rebuffed them; the owner asserted that suspending work meant shutting down the furnace and that the interruption would produce several days of deferred work until the furnace heated up properly. Later that year, some of the more daring Chisos miners launched an effort to organize fellow workers, but many crew members balked, not wanting to chance losing their jobs. Upon learning of the plot, management arrested the principals and drove them from Terlingua.[246]

A COMPARISON

On first impression, ethnic Mexicans throughout Texas during the first two decades of the twentieth century appear to have lived similar histories. Whether settled east or west of the 100th meridian, political, social, and economic obstacles largely impeded Tejano efforts at life improvement. Mainstream society blocked Mexican American political participation, employing numerous mechanisms, including the newly adopted rule of the White Man's Primary deterring non-white people (among them Mexicans) from voting. Segregation for Mexicans continued as a way of life into the new century: Anglos still enforced conventions precluding social mixing in public (if not private) spaces. A path up the economic ladder seemed remote given the jobs—of an unspecialized and uncategorized nature—whites thought apt for Mexicans. Violence could well visit Tejanos if they committed heinous crimes against white people (and especially against white women—as was the case for León Martínez), threatened the status quo with revolutionary ideas, or otherwise raised the ire of white men.

In point of fact, experiences were hardly uniform across the state, with South Texas and West Texas serving as examples of contrast. Several factors effected regional divergence, and thus variation in Texas-Mexican experiences—among them ecology. West Texas is an arid expanse of rugged terrain, with much brush, scrub, and wild grass. South Texas, on the other hand, tends rather to be a place of fair rainfall and of flat earth lands with fertile black soils.[247]

Economics further acted to differentiate West Texas from South Texas. The physiographic nature of West Texas dictated a way of life conducive to livestock herding, sheepshearing, mining (in the lower Big Bend district), and the harvesting and manufacturing of the region's natural products such as candelilla and guayule. West Texas Tejanos thus sought to find a niche in the labor force as sheepherders, sheepshearers, and *vaqueros*. In contrast, Mexicans in South Texas began clearing pasture land and working the fields, as agriculture there became the primary commercial activity. The farm revolution led to a need for stoop labor, which ethnic Mexicans came to provide. Uneven economic development within urban centers separated the sections as well. West Texas towns, unlike San Antonio, Laredo, and Brownsville in South Texas, did not offer much in the light industries, work in infrastructure upgrades, or openings in privately owned business ventures.

Engendering differences also between West Texas and South Texas was demography. While West Texas Tejanos quickly became a minority in much of the region during the early 1900s, Mexicans retained a majority throughout most of South Texas. Then, immigration from Mexico took place at disparate rates; fewer refugees and exiles ventured into West Texas's ranch country and into its small urban and remotely located communities. Moreover, the class of immigrants entering the two respective regions differed. Well-to-do exiled families fleeing the revolution were more inclined to make their way to South Texas than to West Texas.

A further reason behind deviations between West Texas and South Texas was the Edwards Plateau and Trans-Pecos region's nexus to the US West. Its geography and landforms (encompassing plains, plateaus, and stretches of desert), its semi-arid or dry climate, its natural habitat for distinctive flora and wildlife species, its economics (inclined towards livestock raising), its culture and identity (associated still with a Wild West aura), and other determinants could not help but make West Texas more like the country past El Paso.[248]

What resulted, then, for Texas Mexicans from regional differentiation? For one thing, peculiarities of West Texas moderated the stringent segregationist practices applied so pervasively to Mexicans in the southern section. Scholars argue that prejudice in the Edwards Plateau and Trans-Pecos regions were a reflection of American West customs where racism existed in a milder form than it did in those parts of Texas more closely connected to the US South.[249]

While violence certainly visited Mexican communities during the early 1900s, the West Texas link to the US West appears to have blunted the extreme ferocities that victimized Mexicans in other parts of the state. Violence toward Mexicans in the Edwards Plateau and Trans-Pecos seemed more comparable in character to the less severe outbursts occurring in the rangelands of western America, which by then had moved beyond the application of lynch law.[250] Atrocities against Mexicans in West Texas erupted around 1917 and 1918 during the Mexican Revolution, but only in the attack on Porvenir did the Texas Rangers inflict mass executions comparable to *la matanza*, the indiscriminate slaughter of Mexicans carried out by *los rinches* and assorted ruffians in South Texas.[251] The *rinches* and their reputation as an enforcement constabulary tasked with controlling Mexicans in South Texas do not much occupy the historical memory of West Texans.

Tejano history is hardly monolithic. Too many variables have diversified it, not the least of which would be region. But then again, regions have a way of molding character, culture, consciousness, image, identity and more, regardless of residents' race, nationality, or ethnicity. Thus, just as South Texas singularities produced association with place (some would say "homeland"), so did the land west of the 100th meridian construct Tejano self-perception. Indeed, Mexican Americans living in the region as of the early decades of the twentieth century held themselves up, with some pride, as being West Texans.[252]

CHAPTER 4

YEARS OF
TRANSITION, 1920–1945

An aggregate of historical forces transitioned the West Texas region of the 1900 to 1920 era to the more modern age of the 1920s and unto the World War II years. Improvements to the region's infrastructure, especially the road network, increasingly integrated rural sections into the greater West Texas orbit. Experimentations in dry-land farming, underway by the 1910s, proved effective by the 1920s and after in parts of the Edwards Plateau and Trans-Pecos. Some farmers attempted water-well drilling, doing so with some success, although field irrigation did not become an effective means for crop cultivation until the 1940s. Crop diversification proved successful. Along border communities during the mid-1920s, local farmers added cotton raising to traditional harvesting of onions, cabbages, and melons.[1] Agriculture as an integral component of the economy was accepted in almost all parts of West Texas, including the farm and ranch counties immediately west of the Hill Country, the Big Bend region, and the Permian Basin during the 1920s and 1930s.

As for ranching, cattlemen and sheep and goat raisers took developments from the years 1900 to 1920 and modified and integrated them into contemporary realities. They better designed wire-mesh fences, for instance, to the point that these woven wire barriers became commonplace.[2] Staying apace with the modern age, they embraced the new innovations being introduced in range management, such as controlling for overgrazing. They adopted more successful means of delivering their livestock to market. Ranchmen made breakthroughs during the 1920s in watering cattle and sheep by adopting windmills, digging wells, and improving on field reservoir systems.[3]

Sheep and goat raisers shared in the advances of the day. They used the Texas Sheep and Goat Raisers Association advantageously: the organization became a crucial venue for disseminating to sheep growers the latest knowledge and progress infusing the industry. Early 1900 efforts to feed sheep under more regulated circumstances led to organized commercial feeding by the 1920s. Sheep raisers continued to expand on the warehouse system established earlier; they stored the wool and mohair in warehouses until the opportune time to buy or sell.[4]

Also responsible for leading West Texas into modernity was the rise of the oil industry.[5] Oil exploration arrived in a big way in West Texas after 1923 when that year wildcatters made a major strike in Reagan County. During the early 1930s, the Permian Basin became the focus of oil exploration, and in 1932, the first of several more discoveries in the area was made. This turn of events altered the West Texas region into one that no longer relied mainly on ranching (and some farming), but on oil production as well.[6]

These and other developments produced numerous changes in and shaped West Texas. Discernible was the expansion of midsize cities such as San Angelo, Midland, Odessa, and Del Rio but also the increasing growth of towns like Alpine, Fort Stockton, Sonora, and Pecos. Then, there was the transformation of the Big Bend: the section shed its ties to its frontier past and joined the rest of West Texas in becoming part of the twentieth century. No longer was this area distinct by its connection to the mining boom nor to the border raiding that had accompanied the Mexican Revolution. Intermarriage therein, common since the later nineteenth and early twentieth centuries, now diminished as families from the US and Europe arrived, ending gender disparities.[7]

Despite change, the Edwards Plateau and Trans-Pecos expanse retained a connection to the West Texas of old. Of course, not much could be done about its distinct geography nor about its want of rain. Culturally, it was still livestock country and ranch spreads dotted the terrain extending from the San Angelo–Del Rio line to faraway El Paso County. The section remained largely rural. Long distances separated urban centers, almost all of which had nineteenth-century origins. No town in West Texas grew in population, size, and degree of prosperity comparable to Houston, Dallas, Fort Worth, or even San Antonio and Corpus Christi. In its many features, including Anglo demographic predominance, West Texas remained more closely tied to the US West than it did to that part of state east of the 100th meridian.

MEXICAN LABORERS

As of 1930, Mexicans and Mexican Americans in the West Texas borderlands were inclined to be settled in predominantly livestock counties where they could work cattle and sheep or in counties where they could alternate between ranch and farm labor.[8] But such work, generally seasonal in nature, hardly led to real-life improvement. On ranches, Mexicans had to live with wage differentials; usually Mexicans made less than white cowboys for performing the same tasks. In Sutton County in the early 1920s, monthly pay for Mexican *vaqueros* (not living on ranch premises) often totaled about one-half to two-thirds of what white men received, and the same scale applied to those Mexicanos who boarded at the ranch.[9]

But in the exigency of the times, anything that offered food and shelter tempered hardship. Certainly, there were other chores to be done in West Texas besides working on the range. In the Val Verde County and the Devils River areas, ranchers hired Mexicans to build fences or to mend them when in need of repair.[10] At the Stillwell (Roy and Hallie) Ranch on the lower Big Bend, trans-border migrants during the 1920s carried out needed tasks, earning only whatever wages the struggling ranch owners could muster. Responsibilities included fetching feed for horses, as in the case of one father-and-son team that arrived at the Stillwell Ranch and were soon asked to collect Chino grass (more wholesome as horse feed than hay and oats) from the proximate mountains, an assignment they carried out efficiently, bundling up the crop (perhaps using the leaves of the yucca plant to bind the cargo, as was the practice of the time), mounting it on their burros, hauling it down to the ranch, and expertly stacking the grass in hay mounds.[11] There at the ranch, Mexicans also cleared brush land so that the Stillwells could raise corn, maize, or cane for their household needs or for the upkeep of ranch animals. One man from Mexico named Baltazar—with an instinct for improvisation (as was the case with other Mexicans)—successfully constructed for the Stillwells a reservoir to hold rainwater for cattle; he relied on only his brawn and whatever natural materials he found about the place.[12]

The Sheep Industry
Sheep ranching emerged as a mainstay of the region, more so than it did in other parts of the state and even in the western US.[13] Mexicans came to depend on it as a source of stable employment. For the most part, they served as the backbone of the industry.

In open-range herding, such as that which prevailed in Terrell County as late as the 1920s, *pastores* (as discussed in the previous chapters) abided by centuries-old practices, routines, strategies, and conventions. Out on the range, at times away for weeks from ranch headquarters, *pastores* tended flocks following proven management methods (among them utilizing vocal commands) and abiding by long-standing procedures such as leading sheep to grazing, "nooning them" (giving them rest time), grazing them again, and bedding them nightly. Mexican shepherds still relied on starting campfires with an *eslabón* (a steel piece for igniting fire) and *mecha* (a wick). They continued to honor operations that recognized a hierarchy of workers responsible for various aspects of the trade, from the *mayordomos* overseeing the entire process of raising sheep to the pastor guarding the flocks.[14]

As had been the practice since the nineteenth century, Tejanos during the spring and early summer joined crews, some arriving from Mexico, to work the lambing (March and April) and shearing (May and June) cycles in West Texas. Among sheepshearing crews working West Texas ranches were ones coming into McCulloch County—beginning in the 1920s—from Uvalde, Rock Springs, Del Rio, and Kerrville.[15]

By the 1920s, most West Texas sheep ranchers had adapted to the times by abandoning hand clipping. Sheep owners in Terrell County now equipped their shearing pens with plants rigged with machine clippers, properly attached to the end of a shaft whose maneuverability allowed the shearers to move freely as they went about their work.[16] Mexican *capitanes* by the 1920s themselves adapted to the new developments and applied them to their trade. Relying now on motorized vehicles, *capitanes* equipped both sides of their trucks or wagons with several shearing stations. They could then deploy these rigs to the designated shearing site.[17]

Farm Work
Mexicans turned to labor in cotton fields as another survival alternative, although landowners in the Edwards Plateau and Trans-Pecos region until after World War II (when farmers turned to crop irrigation) still prioritized ranching.[18] Seasonally, Mexicans (both native- and foreign-born) either as individuals, as families, or as part of whole crews took to cotton patches in startup farms and generally around the fall and through the early winter months worked in *el desenraiz* and then picked the cotton harvest.

Cotton cultivation during the season required a large number of field hands to chop weeds as the plants sprouted and then during summers to pick the cotton crop. Of necessity, McCulloch County cotton farmers hired workers from outside the area to perform this labor. During the picking cycle, Mexican American truck owners from Melvin would travel to places such as Del Rio, Eagle Pass, Uvalde, Fort McKavett, and Menard to sign up farmhands willing to become part of the migrant force. These *troqueros* would then transport the recruits to neighboring farms to pick entire cotton fields.[19] Invariably, children followed the crop with family and as a result stayed away from school (even where available) for several months. During the fall session, students started late, having been picking cotton, and in the spring, they dropped out early to resume the seasonal weed-chopping and picking cycle.[20]

As with other types of work, cotton picking hardly yielded adequate wages (around $1 to $1.50 per hundredweight), but cotton farmers refused to, or could not, pay more, whether during prosperous or hard times. In Presidio County during the 1920s when cotton irrigation produced a boom, farmers only offered Mexican cotton pickers about $1 per day.

Survival for Mexicans in some cases required entering into tenancy and share-cropping agreements of small land parcels. While such arrangements in West Texas never got to be institutionalized as they were in Central and South Texas during that time, Mexicans who got caught up in that web of tenancy, as in Presidio County, faced the same outcomes: buying on credit while they planted, picked, and then ginned the cotton. There did exist variation in tenancy patterns, as in cases where Mexican Americans negotiated terms with Anglo landowners willing to compensate them in land for their labor. In Melvin, Anglo farmers contracted with people to clear land, permitting them to plant on that acreage for one or two years.[21]

Farm operators depended on their Mexican labor force not only to provide the cotton picking but also to perform various ancillary tasks essential to a successful harvest. Mexican hands having semipermanent or temporary residence on a farm worked feeding draft animals, keeping farm implements and equipment in ready functioning condition, and handling machinery. At the border town of Castolón, for instance, a man named Alvino Ybarra capably ran a cotton gin for a local farm owner and entrepreneur during the mid-1920s.[22]

The Oil Fields

The oil boom of the 1920s and 1930s offered new means for West Texas Tejanos to obtain a passable livelihood. Available in this industry, however, were only the dirtiest, most exacting and undesirable tasks. When (and if) companies hired Mexican Americans, they relegated them to back-breaking duties—such as ditch digging and pipe laying—and reserved less grueling occupations for white laborers. Company work, furthermore, disrupted family stability. Rail hands in the Midland area, for instance, often left home for long periods as jobs entailed stringing pipelines over routes from Oklahoma to northwestern Texas. Some took their families with them. But this also upset domestic order as sometimes employment required moving to new sites (or new towns) as companies abandoned exhausted oil fields and relocated to new productive ones.[23]

Mining

Recent arrivals and native-born Mexicanos along the lower Big Bend continued to depend on the mercury fields as others had during the high point of quicksilver mining during the first two decades of the twentieth century. Mainly at the Chisos Mining Company and at the Mariscal Mine, they worked as before: amid danger, exploitation, and manipulation by company personnel. The latter mine had closed in 1908, but in response to the World War I demand for quicksilver, a New York–based venture named the Mariscal Mining Company reopened it in 1919.[24]

At the Chisos Mining Company during this period, work remained almost unchanged since the mine's opening. With shirts off to cope with the heat in the underground shafts, Mexicans—some of them teenagers—still labored a six-day week, working nine hours a day to earn $1 for the shift. Company accident records indicate not much improvement over earlier numbers of death or serious injury. Poor lighting, outdated equipment, and disregard of safety precautions in the era of the 1920s and 1930s led to frequent accidents. Fatalities and injuries included broken bones, crushed skulls, severed limbs, burns, and various casualties attributable to infections. Moreover, as a form of control, the Chisos Mining Company retained the policy of requiring employees to trade at the company store.[25]

Conditions at the Mariscal Mine were no different. The resuscitated company relied almost totally on Mexican nationals fleeing the Mexican Revolution and seeking relief across the border. Many came from mining districts (in Mexico) to face conditions at Mariscal as stark as ones they had left behind.[26] In the uncertainty of the circumstances, newcomers took refuge in hastily built *jacales* or in hollowed spaces they carved out in Mariscal Mountain. Over time, some of them found the means to move out of their temporary quarters and build permanent structures. The more imaginative builders utilized rocks and stones strewn around the mine, arranging them artistically so as to give their home exteriors an appealing look.[27]

The immigrants advanced the mining industry at Mariscal by applying vital skills and technical knowledge they brought with them.[28] Using locally fired brick, they helped build a new Scott furnace designed by company engineers. They further laid out a rail line for cars to ferry the mercury, developed a way to raise and lower baskets of the ore from the depths of the mine pits, expanded the company's plans for additional physical space/buildings, and improved the road infrastructure.[29]

There at Mariscal, immigrants worked for six days of the week, alternating in three eight-hour shifts. The furnace remained in operation during the crew's day off as turning it off meant having to let it cool for one month and then wait another month to get the heat back to 360 degrees Celsius, the level required to vaporize mercury. Because of that temperature point, those who worked the oven suffered extreme heat exposure, but such intensity was compulsory to separate the quicksilver from the ore.[30]

The wage rate at the Mariscal Mine resembled the scale for work performed in other regions of the mining industry during the 1920s. For a day's work, management at Mariscal paid veteran miners $1.50 but compensated unskilled miners with less. Muckers, who composed cleanup crews, earned $1.25 per day while general workers drew $1 per day. The company then expected the miners to patronize its commissary. Workers there could choose from an assortment of goods, among them groceries, clothing apparel, and working supplies.[31]

Offering a possible alternative to mining work at Mariscal was the business of freighting. Mariscal's relative isolation required importing provisions and water for the miners and community residents from surrounding sites in the Big Bend region. Materials to keep the mine functioning properly also had to be hauled over long distances. Meeting demand, Mexican freighters lugged in mesquite wood to the Scott furnace, doing so from as far as fifty miles away and over rough terrain. Unfortunately for miners, teamsters, and villagers, work ended at the

Mariscal Mine in 1923 when the owners closed it due to financial problems. The settlers subsequently relocated to Terlingua and other places in West Texas.[32]

Other Unspecified Labor

During the 1920s and into the World War II years, the candelilla industry continued apace along Big Bend lands and so remained a job option for Mexican laborers from the region and Northern Mexico. Mexicans engaged both in the old method of uprooting the plants from area fields and in working production equipment in local processing factories.[33] Mexican crews during the war years also found employment cutting lechuguilla in places where the plant grew abundantly, such as in ranch areas around Dryden (Terrell County).[34]

Because of national rubber shortages, the US government during World War II contracted with Big Bend growers for guayule plants. Mexican laborers then probed the region's terrain combing for the plants, bunching and baling them and preparing them for transportation, usually to California, where factories processed the guayule into rubber.[35]

No job or task was too menial for Mexicans to take. Often lacking English proficiency and literacy, town dwellers throughout West Texas nonetheless managed means to support families. In Alpine, some men commuted to area ranches to assist in a variety of chores, among them constructing water tanks of dirt. Such employment for many required staying on the ranch proper for the week and then returning to Alpine to reunite with loved ones. Others took on work, mostly pick and shovel labor, at Sul Ross State University when building of the college began in the 1920s. Then there were individuals such as Manuel Luján who created their own manner of livelihood. Along with his children, Luján peddled to townspeople wood taken from the mountains in the surrounding Alpine area. He drew water from local wells and, relying on his mules and wagon, carried it directly to those who had ordered delivery.[36]

In several towns, rapid urban development demanded large numbers of manual laborers. In communities such as Midland, Mexicans came to comprise crews behind the prewar drive for modernization. They helped construct the Petroleum Building, the Scharbauer Hotel, and the Turner Mansion. When the government began building the Midland Army Air Field, Mexican workers were among those involved in laying the runways.[37]

Mexican Americans with marketable skills worked as cooks, bakers, artisans and carpenters, painters, and windmill repairmen. Women relied on domestic work such as washing and ironing clothes and cleaning houses while others found employment as dishwashers in cafés and restaurants, as laundry workers, and as stand-ins at sundry low-paid menial jobs.[38]

The Mexican Work Ethic

Certainly, Mexicans toiled dutifully during the 1920s and into the World War II years, attempting to support themselves and those close to them. Yet often was heard the old trope that Mexicans were a "lazy people." Voices rose to counterbalance such views, however, speaking to the Mexicans' strong work ethic. In the Terlingua mining area during the 1930s, as one Anglo interviewee recalled in 1972, everybody worked as a matter of survival. "All Mexican boys had work to do, haul wood, water. After a kid got up to six or seven years old he had to work. Everybody in Terlingua worked, women, children, and all."[39] Mexican sheepherders and shearers came in for well-earned praise. Residents of Terrell County viewed *pastores* with respect and admired the sheepherders' selfless dedication on the open range. Generally, the *amo* (the Anglo ranch owner) touted the Mexicans' attention to sheep flocks they did not even own. Sheep men trusted the shepherds—from the *mayordomo* down the hierarchy to the *ahijador* (lambing boss)—to efficiently execute assigned tasks on the sheep range. Growers counted on sheepshearers, whether native or foreign born, to perform assigned shearing duties expertly. Bosses commended those doing the support work at the shearing site, among them the ones charged with tying and packing the fleece.[40]

Labor Discontent

The pride Mexicans took in their work performance surely did not translate into satisfaction with monetary rewards and with acceptance of difficulties they faced on the job. Indeed, some Tejanos rejected their exploitation. In one case occurring during the mid-1920s in Rowena (Runnels County), for instance, cotton pickers called on farmers to grant them better pay. A local newspaper denounced the "greasers" for audaciously petitioning for a wage of $1.50 a hundred weight at a time when cotton sold at a very low price.[41]

One definite outburst of labor dissatisfaction took place in 1934. It involved sheepshearers in the towns of San Angelo, Sonora, Ozona, Del Rio, and their surroundings who joined the Sheep Shearers' Union of North America (headquartered in Montana). Mexicans struck against what they felt was unjust treatment on the part of both *capitanes* and sheep owners who barely compensated them with adequate wages. But West Texas sheep ranchers mustered powerful forces, including legislators, police authorities, and strikebreakers, to crush the revolt.[42]

SEGREGATION: WEST TEXAS STYLE

Regarding perceptions that Mexicans—socially and otherwise—were not equal to white people, West Texas Anglos continued treating their Mexican neighbors in line with old attitudes and practices. Even in remote areas such as in the mining districts of the Big Bend where Mexicans overwhelmingly outnumbered Anglos, an understanding prevailed during the 1920s and 1930s that Mexicans stood apart from white people. In the Chisos mining area during that period, for example, the sole law administrator there dispensed justice with such an understanding in mind: Robert Cartledge, the justice of the peace representing local authority, dealt firmly with Mexican lawbreakers yet looked the other way when Anglos committed similar transgressions.[43]

City officials, with the acquiescence of Anglo residents, routinely neglected the people of the barrio in the areas of utility services, police protection, and proper schooling. Where towns did show concern for the welfare of the entire community, such as in health matters, attention was given Mexicans as if they were wards or dependents instead of deserving residents. In Pecos County (and Fort Stockton in particular) during the 1930s, for instance, health officials dispensed authorized public assistance to Mexicans but on a segregated arrangement; in administering children's immunizations, county health providers reserved some days and times for Anglos and others for Mexicans.[44]

Segregation as a way of life prevailed in West Texas through the 1920s and into the war years. There were places, however, where segregation existed casually or not at all. Along the border towns, Mexicans as late as the 1930s still constituted a majority, and communities there were more race tolerant. Presidio, for one, did not create a segregated educational system when officials established the town's independent school district in 1929. In fact, the board hired Mexican teachers for grade levels from elementary to high school, an employment practice absent almost everywhere else in West Texas.[45]

But most communities in West Texas abided by segregationist customs of the day. Social understanding discouraged Mexicans from intrusion on white neighborhoods. Jim Crow norms kept Mexicans from mixing with whites in popular settings such as theaters, restaurants, and bars.[46] Signs that read "FOR WHITES ONLY" and "NO MEXICANS ALLOWED" were commonplace until after World War II if not beyond.[47] City and county boards often enforced a restrictive policy for Mexicans' use of the local swimming pools, in some cases strictly prohibiting them from any access. Certain towns, on the other hand, opened their local swimming facilities on Mexican-designated days, presumably on the worry that "dirty Mexicans" would contaminate the waters for Anglos if daily admission were allowed. The practice existed as a constant reminder to Mexicans, both in rural and urban areas, of their subaltern status in a white society.[48]

During the 1920s and 1930s, as Hispanic communities in the region expanded, church officials strategically located new edifices so as to avert racial contact. The Catholic Church often built two churches in towns where the presence of a sizable number of Anglo Catholics justified supporting separate accommodations. In 1930, for instance, the Diocese of Amarillo established St. Mary's Church to serve San Angelo's Spanish-speaking parishioners, although Mexican Americans felt that actually it was an attempt to keep them apart from the Anglos at Sacred Heart Church situated downtown. When the diocese first turned to the needs of Catholics in Eldorado (Schleicher County) in 1925, it had the church built in "Mexico," the town's Mexican quarter. The same segregationist norms pertained to cemeteries: Mexicans were ordinarily interred in an out-of-the-way plot in the community's graveyard. Thus to be found throughout West Texas (actually throughout the state) was the "Mexican cemetery" (or the *campo santo*).[49] In Alpine, Mexicans led by Clemente Uranga (the town's business leader who had in the late 1910s raised the capital for building the school that came to be popularly known as La Escuela de don Clemente) in the latter years of the 1920s established the Mexican Cemetery Association. Through the association, the barrio would be able to maintain upkeep of the segregated Mexican section of the Alpine Cemetery.[50]

School districts during the pre–World War II years similarly embraced segregation. The logic rested on the pedagogical grounds that Mexican children needed preparation in English and exposure to American institutional life before they would attend the upper grades where English acted as the language of instruction.[51] Aside from pedagogical reasoning, segregation seemed justifiable on the widely held belief that Mexicans were biologically inferior and in general should not have close contact with the superior white race. Even in the Big Bend community of Terlingua, where the overwhelming number of school attendees during the 1930s were of Mexican origin, voices could be heard protesting the mixing of the few white students with Mexican children.[52] In Sanderson, where whites and Mexicans comprised an almost equal percentage of the total population, Mexican students were assigned to Lamar Ward.[53] Maintaining that insufficient room existed in Melvin's school to accommodate Mexican students, the local board of trustees in 1923 built a one-room edifice for Mexicans, locating it just two blocks from where the Anglo-American school stood.[54]

Where both Mexican and Anglo students attended the same school institution (perhaps due to the small size of the total student population), policy dictated either different buildings for the two groups or at least their separation in classrooms. In the case of Valentine, Texas, when school officials integrated the system in the late 1930s, Mexican American children from the first three grades were taught in two rooms located in the basement of the Anglo school.[55] In Odessa, Mexican American students during the 1920s also went to Anglo schools (this after the school district in 1923 scuttled a plan for establishing a separate facility), although it is unclear whether the children were taught in separate accommodations within the campus.[56]

As a rule, however, students were assigned to the ubiquitous Mexican school. Such schools lacked modern equipment, basic study materials, and other learning essentials granted Anglo pupils. In Fort Stockton, as one example, Mexican children during the 1920s and 1930s studied amid crowded school conditions while their Anglo peers apprenticed in more comfortable surroundings. Mexican American education in the city was unequal in other ways. Faculty assigned to the Mexican school during the 1920s received lower pay than teachers in the white schools. Moreover, the school board did not heed compulsory attendance policy, reasoning that families needed the children's help in the cotton fields.[57]

The intent of having the primary grades serve as preparation for secondary school instruction naturally dictated segregation early on. But once students advanced to the secondary level, practicality called for integration with Anglos. However, administrators did not much concern themselves with the problem of race control as forces acted to further foil Mexican American attendance. To begin with, many secondary school–aged children had to work. Furthermore, society (and school administrators) tended to discourage Mexican Americans from continuing into the higher grades. Such "discouragement" at times was unspoken. In Midland, one graduate of the Mexican primary school in the city recalled: "[Before World War II], there was no written law, but it was just known you could not attend [past the sixth grade]."[58] Those who chose to continue into the Anglo school then faced constant hazing and harassment from their Anglo classmates; many decided to stop attending. The small number of Tejano students who did go on to junior high and high school did not gravely threaten segregationist conventions; presumably officials, parents, and classmates acquiesced as to their presence.[59]

LA COLONIA MEXICANA

In almost all parts of West Texas, demographic growth expanded barrios beyond earlier physical boundaries. In San Angelo itself during the 1920s and continuing into the World War II years, the south side enclaves stretched in a direction away from downtown, acquiring names reflecting neighborhood conditions and land forms (e.g., Bulto Prieto and La Loma).[60] The San Felipe barrio in Del Rio continued spreading as well.[61] In Alpine, a new Spanish-speaking quarter appeared during the 1930s as a result of people arriving after the Terlingua silver mines closed operations. Locals called it Pueblo Nuevo, as opposed to the original barrio, which understandably took the name of Barrio Viejo.[62]

In these semiautonomous cultural zones, Tejanos sought to establish an ambience that was personally gratifying, helpful to family-raising, and conducive to community order. Sul Ross State University scholar Paul Wright notes that while segregation in Big Bend towns he studied certainly was race-based, it simultaneously stemmed from self-interest. In their own cultural zones—the Mexican district—Mexicans could speak Spanish, abide by religious beliefs passed on by their forebears, and organize their own feast days and celebrate special occasions, all the while avoiding relentless insults from white people. In the barrio, "*lo mexicano*" extended affirmation, comfort, security, and belonging.[63]

Better off Than Most
Although the bulk of Mexican Americans in West Texas continued to be very much a part of a laboring group during the pre–World War II period, there remained a persistent complement of individuals whose social position, more visible in the urban areas, stratified the Mexican American community. Unquestionably, such a socioeconomic group might have understandably gone unnoticed to those who did not delve into life in the barrio. Indeed, one scholar estimates that in 1930, the "middle class [which] included managers, proprietors, sales and clerical works, and professionals" made up about 9 percent of all occupations in the entire state of Texas.[64] While almost imperceptible to

outsiders, both throughout the state and in the Edwards Plateau and Trans-Pecos borderlands, embedded in the barrios was a coterie of folks somewhat better off than most.

Who exactly comprised this budding class in Mexican American communities? Among them were *comerciantes* (merchants), grocers, restauranteurs, saloon keepers, barbers, and an assortment of other vendors meeting the needs for Mexican American goods and services. A case in point would be Santos Garza, who taught himself in both English and Spanish and by doing so attained social prominence as a successful *comerciante*: he is known as the father of San Felipe in Del Rio.[65] Then there was Chata Sada (María G. Sada), who with her husband Juan operated Chata's Store—or Chata's Place—their small trading post in Boquillas.[66] In Alpine, Pedro R. (Pete) Gallego started a Mexican restaurant in the late 1910s and ably turned it into a going concern (under the name of the Green Café) during the next few decades, managing it until he passed away in 1944.[67] Rafael Riojas arrived in Melvin from Sheffield (Pecos County) in 1934 and soon managed a most successful dry goods establishment named The Economy Store. He subsequently became the acknowledged leader and spokesperson on issues of concern to the Mexican American community in Melvin.[68] Overall, *comerciantes* throughout West Texas networked casually but could also do so more formally, as in the case of Del Rio in the 1920s, through commercial associations like the Camara de Comercio Mejicana, a kind of Mexican chamber of trade.[69]

Many more constituted this discernible contingent of businesspeople and professionals. Among them were building contractors and freight haulers (by this time relying on motor vehicles) who developed gainful connections with the broader business sector in West Texas municipalities.[70] Professionals in this sector included ministers and policemen.[71] Where Anglos as a group did not meet the numbers needed to fill roles ordinarily restricted to white people, Mexican Americans served, in such capacities as notaries, postmistresses, mail carriers, and customs service and depot agents. There were, furthermore, Hispanic high school or college graduates who found work as teachers (although school boards generally assigned them to the "Mexican school").[72] At Imperial, Texas, the aforementioned Apolonio Esparza found work instructing barrio children, having taught himself "how to speak, read, and write in English from books and a dictionary."[73] Rounding off membership in this industrious corps were men whose political interest and involvement garnered them ties (as well as influence and respect inside the barrio) to white political circles.[74]

Also positioned slightly above commoners were Mexican Americans who found success in rural pursuits. In Del Rio during the 1930s, José Córdova Martínez launched his own J. C. Martínez Shearing Company and within a brief period had amassed a crew of almost fifty *tasinques* who in their travels lugged two portable machines with them. The company sheared an average of 125,000 woollybacks yearly, working ranch sites from Texas to New Mexico to California.[75]

Then there were those who did well in small-scale ranching and farming. In McCulloch County, Rodolfo Bermea, Guillermo Herrera, and Juan and Anastacio Pérez worked their own lands: Bermea sharecropping in Melvin and nearby Salt Gap, Herrera in Melvin with the help—as was necessary in those days—of his entire family, and the Pérez brothers on their own ranches southeast of Melvin.[76] Daniel Rodríguez of Sanderson during the 1930s raised a flock of chickens and a herd of cattle, Angora goats, and sheep at his small ranch. As side ventures Rodríguez ran a hauling business and engaged in fencing and road construction; to assist in the building of a local highway project during the decade, he leased out his mule teams to the company charged with the operation.[77] In Big Bend areas like at La Coyota, Terlingua Abaja, and Redford, Mexicans worked individual parcels of land during the early 1920s and raised enough products to supply neighbors, miners, and fellow Anglos living close by with various farm staples, including vegetables and melons. They irrigated by turning to nearby creeks and the Rio Grande, resourcefully relying on ditches dug earlier to direct the flow of water towards personal plots that among assorted farm goods also yielded wheat. Farmers around Ruidosa expanded upon their enterprises to engage in cotton raising.[78] Such industriousness elevated this class of yeomen above the rank and file.

In reality, the viability of this heterogeneous corps of entrepreneurs, professionals, and skilled or semi-skilled agents rested on the support it got from fellow compatriots having little social standing of their own and wielding weak purchasing power at that (which then diminished further during the Great Depression). Still, it was understood within the Mexican quarter (i.e., "the Mexican side of town" or "the village across the tracks") that there were those who through dogged determination had risen above the many.

Churches of Their Own

Significant in barrio life were churches of various denominations. The Catholic Church, as indicated in previous chapters, had always endeavored to address the religious needs of parishioners. But during the 1920s and 1930s, it became increasingly responsive to the needs of a growing Mexican American population in West Texas.

In truth, the Catholic commitment to West Texas during the period between the two world wars remained in somewhat of an early (and fluid) stage. It was more active in towns like San Angelo, Fort Stockton, and Del Rio where secular priests or those from orders, such as the Franciscans, took charge of church business and tasks. In Del Rio, the Catholic Church in 1927 added St. Joseph's Parish (in the Chihuahua barrio) to the two existing parishes—Our Lady of Guadalupe Parish (San Felipe) and Sacred Heart Church Parish—because of the increasing number of Catholics in the growing city.[79]

To address the needs of those in distant or remote West Texas areas (and even in sections of town away from the main barrio, such as in San Angelo), the Church established mission stations. During the 1920s, ecclesiastics from the more settled communities performed missionary duty in towns such as Imperial, Brackettville, Eldorado, Mertzon, and Sonora. In Brackettville, Diocesan priests in 1911 had taken over for the Oblates of Mary Immaculate missionaries who had ministered there since 1884; in 1929, however, the Oblates of Mary Immaculate returned to pastor the mission at St. Mary Magdalene Church. As for Big Bend towns and villages, clergymen from Fort Davis as late as the 1930s traveled to those distant places on a regular monthly basis or on holy days. Additionally, Catholic sisters visited some of these isolated towns to dutifully offer children religious instruction.[80]

Protestant churches began making successful inroads in ministering to West Texas Mexican communities during the 1920s and continuing into the 1930s. In San Angelo, the Presbyterian Church (discussed in the previous chapter) continued its work as it had done since the 1910s.[81] Then, during the mid-1920s, the Mexican Baptist Church established itself in the city's south side barrio.[82] In 1927, three families of the Assemblies of God Church undertook action to establish a Pentecostal Church in the same enclave. Their determination grew to the point that church members in 1930 built an adobe house of worship, appending to it during the early World War II years. Over the decades, people would refer to it as the "Stone Church," located at the corner of South Hill and West Avenue Q.[83] Other Protestant churches founded in San Angelo during this period were the Mexican Methodist Church (1938) and La Iglesia Apostólica en la Fe de Cristo Jesús (1944).[84]

In Alpine during the 1920s and into the 1930s, the Mexican Baptist Mission Church pressed forward managing without official leadership; in the absence of a pastor, lay people conducted services. But during the Depression decade, the Alpine Baptists acquired an old restaurant and modified it into a church building. As for the Methodist Church in Alpine, it sent during the 1920s the husband-wife team of Esau Pérez and Febriona Florian Muñoz to minister to the town's Mexican Methodists. The pastor and his wife soon started a school.[85] In Sanderson, Reverend Evaristo Picaso looked after the Mexican Methodists during the late 1920s and into the 1930s. The Reverend and his wife were partially successful in winning converts from among the local Catholic population.[86]

Protestant churches were equally attentive to Tejanos living in eastern Edwards Plateau counties. In Rocksprings at a revival meeting held in 1931, the Baptist Church apprised those in attendance of the mission work being carried out among Mexicans. The missionary to "Latin Americans" noted that following one of his services, some sixteen individuals had been accepted for baptism. José de la Rosa then was appointed as superintendent of the newly formed Sunday school for Mexicans. Soon after, the membership organized a mission and subsequently came together as the Rocksprings Mexican Baptist Church, meeting at the Rocksprings Mexican school.[87] In Brady, the Reverend Antonio Guillén arrived in town in 1925 and promptly embarked upon organizing among the local population, successfully building in 1928 what came to be called the Latin American Methodist Church.[88]

On occasions when barrio Catholics built their own church (financing its construction through fundraisers and donations), they located it in the Mexican section of town, presumably because of a preference to worship in a setting where they interacted with others of a shared culture. Mexican Protestants were predisposed to act similarly. Such decisions made sense since services in the churches were ordinarily held in Spanish.[89]

Regardless of denomination, barrio churches played integral roles in community life. Segregated Catholic churches extended services that paralleled ones offered by Anglo houses of worship on the white side of town. They involved parishioners in various holy day celebrations. In Fort Stockton during the 1930s and 1940s, Mexicans at St. Joseph Church regularly commemorated the feast of Corpus Christi with a grand march through the streets of the barrio. Participants looked upon the event not only as an opportunity to display heartfelt devotion but also as an occasion for freely expressing Mexican American cultural and ethnic pride. Locals in Sanderson during the late 1930s held *las posadas* in the days just before Christmas with the enthusiastic support of the local Catholic Church. Other town churches held *kerméses* (charity bazaars) to raise funds for church needs. Without objection, the Catholic hierarchy approved of and even promoted secular barrio festivities. San Angelo's St. Mary's Church often served as a venue for *fiestas patrias* celebrations.[90]

Protestants, for their part, also situated their church structures in the Mexican district. In the barrio, Spanish-speaking ministers (as opposed to Catholic priests, usually of Anglo or European origin, some of them Spaniards), generally led congregations, among them the Reverend Donato Ruiz who served the Baptists in San Angelo and neighboring counties during the 1920s and 1930s. In addition to ministering to his flock at the barrio church, Ruiz conducted his ministry part time on radio station KGKL (during the 1930s) and periodically held district meetings for the Mexican Baptists.[91]

In churches of their own, Hispanics of necessity took charge of ensuring the church's well-being and seeing to the continuation of its religious services. In Fort Stockton's Catholic church, Spanish-speaking (or bilingual) women attended to parishioners as counselors or spiritual advisors, as teachers of the catechism, and as choir organizers or directors. They fulfilled their assumed duties by working alongside their male counterparts in organizing church fiestas. Mexicanas volunteered for such chores as dusting, cleaning, sweeping, and mopping church premises.[92] Single girls in the city joined church societies, among them the Hijas de María (Daughters of Mary, which existed during the early 1920s), and by so doing devoted themselves to following Christ's example of piety, virtue, and goodness. The society emphasized Christian principles; membership and adherence to its Catholic teachings would hopefully mold girls into exemplary mothers. Duties for the Daughters of Mary included fundraising for the church's upkeep (including wall and altar adornments) and conducting Bible classes for children.[93]

In small-town barrios and remote ranches and farms where the Church (for whatever reason) appeared to overlook them, Mexican Americans developed self-gratifying means for achieving spiritual comfort. Parishioners in Mertzon and Imperial, due to great strain on their meager budgets, raised funds to facilitate scheduled priests' visits; in the latter town, locals built a chapel-like church for visiting clergy.[94] When necessary, people held church rites in private homes. In Ozona, before the city's first Catholic church was built in the mid-1920s, girls would go throughout the barrio ringing bells and announcing the time and place where Sunday services would be observed.[95]

Attending the Neighborhood Schools

Numerous factors discouraged Mexican Americans during the period between 1920 and 1945 (and earlier, of course) from school attendance. These included distaste for the inferior quality of schools designated for their attendance, the entrenched idea among whites that the higher secondary school grades were not for Mexicans, questionable teaching methods, and the need to work in order to supplement the family budget. Overall poverty additionally deterred parents from buying their children proper school clothing or marshaling the money to pay for lunches. The emphasis state educational leaders placed on the exceptionalism of Anglos in Texas history—and, by implication, the failure of Spaniards and Mexicans to bring progress and prosperity to that Far North province before the Texas war for independence of 1836—acted to make student learning unpleasant and curbed enthusiasm for further class attendance.[96]

Despite these many obstacles and encumbrances, Mexican American parents in West Texas encouraged education and dispatched their children to the school campus as circumstances permitted.[97] They took advantage of Anglo sympathy and understanding in places such as those in the Big Bend. Like those who had earlier shown consideration for Mexicans, ranchers and mine owners, sensitive to the schooling needs of their workers' families, turned to locals with teaching proficiency (among them wives of merchants and landowners) to educate Mexican children at villages and hamlets such as Terlingua, Molinar, and the Chinati Ranch.[98]

Anti-intellectualism was hardly (nor had it ever been) an inherent trait of Mexican American culture, as school boards frequently learned from the number of children and adolescents desiring school instruction. Parents in Midland during the 1920s sent so many of their offspring to the Mexican school (established in 1928, later named De Zavala Elementary) that the overflow embarrassed officials who had failed to provide adequate space for all seeking attendance. During the 1930s, Midland board members contended with increased Mexican American registration by adding to the existing structure and erecting temporary quarters.[99] In light of the mounting student enrollment in Marathon, the Hidalgo Ward School, built in 1910, had to be enlarged during the 1920s. Student attendance swelled by the late 1930s to the point that the system had to provide further space to the original structure and even add a second building.[100] Fort Davis similarly saw the need to accommodate its growing student population during those years. In 1924, it built a two-room school for Mexican American children, locating it across from where the Catholic Church then stood. Further expansion occurred to the school during the next decade: the district affixed a new room to it in 1935 and four years later used a New Deal labor grant to amplify the school with six classrooms and a section that served as both an auditorium and a cafeteria.[101]

In Schleicher County, the growing presence of Mexican American families led the Bailey Ranch School District in 1926 to establish a one-room assembly for Mexican children, and during the 1930s, Eldorado expanded its staff at the "Latin American School" to two teachers.[102] In Sonora, educators in 1935 responded to augmentation in the Mexican American population in town by building a Mexican Ward School in the Loma Alta addition, calling it the L. W. Elliott School. To formalize segregation, the school board in 1938 approved a resolution stipulating that Mexican Americans attend the "Mexican school."[103]

In larger towns, inevitable scholastic growth in the barrios forced school boards to undertake new school construction. The San Angelo ISD added two elementary schools for Mexicans during the 1920s, the North Mexican School and the South Mexican School. The two received their official names—respectively, Guadalupe and Sam Houston—in 1936. The Fort Stockton ISD in 1926 acquired a vacated building once used by Catholic priests and converted it into a Mexican elementary school and in 1938 constructed a new Mexican school; it was large enough to house students of all grades.[104]

The two school districts in Del Rio similarly saw need for expansion. Del Rio Independent School District built three elementary schools during the next decade. The San Felipe ISD, with its own school board separate from the DRISD, had to construct new secondary grade schools for Mexicans as students by the 1920s began increasingly to enter junior high school and, by the latter 1930s and World War II years, high school.[105] Bending to the reality of more and more Mexican Americans wishing an education, some districts allowed Mexicans to join Anglo students in white secondary school campuses. Among these were San Angelo, Marfa, and Fort Stockton. The city of Fort Stockton integrated its high school in 1942.[106]

While school attendance fell short of being a positive experience for a majority of children, some who reminisced of those times recall sympathetic teachers who went out of their way to help them with their coursework. In San Angelo, teachers of that period, among them Ruth Rich, Roberta Parks, and Ruth Hillyer, achieved almost legendary status in the south side barrios (at Sam Houston Elementary and, after 1950, Rio Vista Elementary). Favorably remembered teachers in the Madero Ward Elementary School in Alpine from the 1920s and 1930s were Melvin P. Slover and Berta Clark Lassiter.[107]

Many Mexican American students found schooling gratifying and took pride in their achievements. One example was students at the Marfa Ward School who ably participated in the Interscholastic League competition. According to one of the town's histories, Principal Jesse Blackwell acquired permission to form a Spanish-speaking division of the Interscholastic League in 1936 so that Hispanic children would be allowed to use their native language in the league's literary events. The next year, students competed in Marfa with more than 100 of their counterparts from neighboring Fort Stockton, Alpine, Sheffield, Fort Davis, and Redford.[108]

Not to be overlooked as another example of student pride in school achievement and success is a case in point from San Felipe ISD. During the 1920s and 1930s, Mexican American students there received bilingual instruction in the first three grades in order to acclimate them; for the most part, they studied under administrators, teachers, and staff who conducted school business in Spanish. Such a system, whose pedagogical structure would be discouraged today (indeed, the district would be desegregated in 1971), actually proved rewarding to attendees. Mexican American students after 1930 took pride in their high school's football team, their music program, and other culturally friendly Mexican American clubs and societies.[109]

Then there were the school graduates, who through sheer determination and support from parents achieved remarkable success. Eva Camúñez of San Angelo (San Angelo ISD class of 1930), for instance, gained prominence as a generous philanthropist in the last half of the twentieth century. Another story of accomplishment included that of Noé Camúñez, Eva's brother, who graduated in 1934 and became San Angelo's first Hispanic elementary school principal in the early 1950s. Several Mexican Americans finished up at Sul Ross State College in Alpine during the decades immediately preceding World War II, among them members of the Rede and Madrid families of Marfa. Lucy Rede Franco was the first person of Hispanic origin to have attended Sul Ross State College—in 1920. After earning teaching credentials, she found an assignment at Redford.

Others from Presidio County moved to Austin to get their university education and subsequently established productive professional careers.[110] The Melvin Independent School District in the period between 1936 and 1946 employed at least six Mexican American teachers, all of them assigned to the town's Mexican school. Some of them had graduated from Melvin High and gotten their educa-tion at Southwest State Teachers College, now Texas State University.[111]

Aside from encouraging their children's education, parents took assertive action in attempts to ensure quality education in their communities. Such was the case in the San Felipe barrio in Del Rio, where (as noted in the previous chapter) a separate, Mexican-oriented, school system existed under the adminis-tration of the San Felipe Consolidated School District (SFCSD). When starting in February 1928 the rival DRISD attempted a takeover to appropriate land in the SFCSD (wherein a company initiated oil operations, its potential success generating great tax revenue for the DRISD), residents of San Felipe would have none of it; the annexation attempt ignited a determined response. Parents did not wish to forfeit oversight of district school policy nor concede a curriculum they believed to be culturally friendly and enriching to their children. Leading the countermove against the DRISD overtures were Santos Garza, Hernán Cadena, and Andrés Cortinas. Through legal efforts and majority support from San Felipe folks who preferred controlling their own school system, Garza (the prime mover) succeeded in getting the courts to grant the SFCSD independence. In 1929, the SFCSD became the San Felipe Independent School District (SFISD).[112]

Further indicating community commitment to student achievement was parental involvement in West Texas PTAs. When trustees built the Mexican school in Melvin in 1923, Mexican American parents immediately founded La Asociación de Padres y Maestros Latino Americana (LAPTA) in an effort to develop rapport between parents and teachers and to address concerns related to their children.[113] In Fort Stockton, parents in 1929 helped promote student welfare by soliciting donations to provide children with school supplies and milk money. The PTA assisted also by helping to prepare and organize special events, as during Christmas.[114] Mexican American PTA members at the Madero Ward Elementary School in Alpine during the 1920s helped administrators plan and hold school festivals, the most popular being the Halloween Carnival that presented a "Children's Cultural Program."[115] At the Marfa Ward School, Mexican Americans in 1933 organized a PTA, and officers (Mexican Americans) and members worked stridently to promote student progress. The local Mexican

American citizenry took great pride that year in the PTA's activities, in witnessing a best-ever enrollment at the school, and in having about eighteen seventh
graders pass to the city's high school.[116] PTAs could also get involved in legal
battles, as was the case in Del Rio ISD in 1930 when the Latin American PTA
expressed support for a suit against a school board that sought to perpetuate
racial segregation.[117]

Barrio parents dissatisfied with public school instruction (or who preferred
religious teaching) found educational alternatives in Catholic and Protestant
schools. In San Angelo, parents enrolled children at San Pedro Catholic School.
In Fort Stockton, they sent students to Our Lady of Lourdes (1920s), although
for two decades this latter institution faced numerous problems. Struggling
financially and lacking an ability to attract pupils, it closed its doors in 1937.[118]

For those hesitant to dilute ties to their culture, there existed the dependable *escuelita*. In Sanderson during the pre–WWII era, some parents considered
summers an opportune time to enroll their children in basic Spanish reading
and writing courses. Teachers with sound credentials, fondly remembered by
former students, staffed these classes. Among them was Manuelita Gonzales
who, according to one family history, "taught the girls in her Spanish school to
embroider. She also taught poetry (*poesías*) and Mexican patriotic songs. She used
to stage productions in Sanderson for the 16th of September and 5th of May."[119]

Clubs, Fiestas, and Leisure

While Mexican American communities in West Texas towns and rural areas
depended on established institutions for order, stability, and survival, mainstream life did not hinder social and cultural traditions and practices that barrio
dwellers sought to observe as part of their heritage. Perpetuated, for instance,
was the *corrido*. The story-telling medium remained into the Depression era and
the World War II years, although, as noted previously, the tradition gradually
fell victim to change as a younger generation increasingly accustomed to contemporary amenities—among them the written word and the phonograph—lost
interest in oral recitation. But two more *corridos* recovered by Sul Ross State
University Professor Elton Miles point to the tenacity of the art form as it persisted into modern times. Both these ballads display the standard characteristics
of the traditional folk song and its thematic content: of places familiar to the
audience, of adventure, of bravery and heroism, of risk and danger, and, at times,
of human sorrow.

"El Corrido del Rancho Jandred-huan" embodied such components. The time was 1931; the setting: two Anglo livestock ranches located southwest of Alpine; the characters: common, ordinary *vaqueros*; their job: to round up some of the horses at the ranches and tame them for duty. The narrative spoke of a regular work time on the range, but the assignment to the *vaqueros*—to each break five of the broncos (the surliest of the bunch being "El Moro")—tested the men's individual courage. All were skilled riders, fearless at their trade, but any mishap would affect loved ones. The several days of work (the period covered in the *corrido*) ended successfully, with even the recalcitrant "El Moro" being subdued.[120]

The danger of work in the quicksilver mines of the Terlingua District was told in the *corrido* "La Tragedia de los Dos" written around 1943. Spotlighting the hazards poor people faced in struggling to make ends meet, the storyteller movingly described life in the quicksilver tunnels. Two miners jeopardized their lives for the sake of the job, praying that God would see them through the risk, aware of an uncertain reality for family if they should meet disaster. According to the tale, Miguel Hernández and Alonso Vásquez took an unnecessary chance in setting off dynamite, and the miscalculation killed them. Equally victimized by the tragedy were members of the men's immediate households.[121]

Living on as an aspect of ethnic and barrio life in West Texas, and persisting into the decades immediately preceding World War II, was the standard of maintaining Mexican-oriented social, cultural, and recreational clubs. An aggregate of men and women, united by a desire to ensure a semblance of orderly cadence in their Spanish-speaking enclaves, generally took the lead in organizing and maintaining these bodies. Important were self-help societies such as the Sociedad Mutualista (the Mexican Mutual Lodge) formed by prominent members of the Marfa Hispanic community in September 1922. The *sociedad* sought to act as an agency of self-help but, according to one account, it also intended "the social uplift of the Mexican community."[122] In San Angelo during the late 1920s, the Alianza Hispano Americana offered assistance to members who found themselves in financial distress or faced personal or family troubles. Locals called the order the "Emilio Carranza Lodge" in honor of a Mexican pilot killed in an air crash in early 1928.[123] The Woodmen of the World Insurance Company in the years before World War II had an agent named Norberto Ortiz serving the Melvin Mexican population.[124]

Mexican American men and women wishing to improve their community's welfare and standing helped rally neighbors and friends in support of organizations, associations, and clubs with particularized missions. Active during the pre–World War II era in Sanderson (Terrell County) were the Club Atlético Católico and the Club México-Tejano. Clubs such as these in other West Texas communities sponsored social activities like dances, skating rink parties, sports teams, and other entertainment pastimes intended to uplift public spirit.[125] In Marfa, the previously mentioned Sociedad Mutualista not only held club business at its community-friendly hall (built in 1928) but, displaying civic ideals, also hosted various community functions such as dances.[126] Groups like San Angelo's La Unión del Pueblo Latino Americano aimed to encourage increased association among neighbors within congenial social settings.[127]

In some towns, associations like the *junta patriótica* could act—during those times when organizers were not preparing for the *fiestas patrias* celebrations—as a forum for discussing community concerns, addressing local grievances, or simply fostering barrio fellowship. In Melvin during the 1920s and 1930s, the junta's meeting hall at La Plataforma Jiménez served as a place where members organized cultural programs, debated ideas politely and decorously, and honed skills at public speaking.[128]

The *baile*, an obvious expression of ethnicity, tapped the talents of local fiddlers, guitarists, and drummers. Some dances were open by invitation only, perhaps for a wedding, but others called for payment at the door. Ceremonials might be different at the hall (or the platform or pavilion), but invariably were proper and polite. In dances held in Terrell County, the ritual was as follows: "The patrons, on paying, were given various colors of ribbons which were attached to their shirt collars. The band leader then would call out, before each dance set, the color coming up. Dancers wearing ribbons of other colors would retire to the sidelines to await their turn." There were protocols to some of these affairs; girls were often carefully chaperoned.[129] Young people considering themselves too closely supervised by their parents formed San Angelo's Club Recreativo Cuauhtémoc. The club scheduled outings, picnics, and various other entertainment events.[130] Barrio leaders feeling the need for civic clubs saw the virtue of LULAC (the League of United Latin American Citizens), discussed below.

Present in almost all towns of West Texas (and the state) by the 1920s and 1930s were long-standing *juntas patrióticas*, their primary purpose being to organize the *fiestas patrias*. In San Angelo during the 1920s and 1930s, the *juntas* continued to effectively bring the several barrios together in mass celebrations. In 1929, *junta patriótica* leaders saw some 1,000 patriotic spectators assemble to hear discourses from home-grown orators and fiesta promoters. From open-air stands the speakers praised Mexico and the United States for their ideals and values. By the 1930s, the *fiestas patrias* festivities in town were attracting more than 2,000 enthusiasts. Some streets had to be closed, and the expanding lineup of activities now featured a parade, food booths of many sorts, and an honorary visit by the Mexican consul. During World War II, community participants at the fiestas raised money for the war campaign.[131]

Wherever communities observed the fiestas, the turnout was always massive and the excitement robust. The Diez y Seis commemoration in Presidio in 1937 included (as was the case with other border settlements) the participation of the Governor of Chihuahua, who provided the music for the ceremony and invited citizens from neighboring Ojinaga. The celebration that year featured a rodeo, a parade, and a multitude of pastimes.[132] In Melvin, according to one newspaper account in 1938, "hundreds of Mexicans" from neighboring ranches and farms attended the Diez y Seis. The newspaper added: "The observance in Melvin is the largest and most interesting Mexican celebration this side of San Antonio." Like other commemorations, the occasion featured dancers in colorful dresses, speechmaking, programs by students from the rural areas, sports competitions, and more. A queen contest brought to Melvin young ladies from surrounding towns like Junction, Menard, Brady, and Eden to compete with local girls.[133]

Several other opportunities for community festivities presented themselves. There were birthdays to be celebrated, certainly, but also commemorations of holidays such as the Fourth of July. Also observed were religious events, among them holy days, wedding, and baptisms. Some communities held *kerméses* to raise money for the benefit of the parish church.[134]

Enjoyed in Del Rio was the *carrera de cintas* (ribbon race), a sport held in the barrio of Chihuahua during the late 1920s. The scholarship on Tejanos does not reference this game, although apparently it is popular in Latin American countries. As played there, horse riders gallop towards a wire stretched between two poles, on which hang short *cintas* (or belts). With a peg in hand, the contestant attempts, upon reaching the line, to successfully pass a peg through a loop at the belt's end and then dash on. The competition excited people in Del Rio to the point that community spirit prompted families to festoon their homes with brightly colored flowers and beautify them with various ornaments. Promoters of the game organized grand programs that featured festival queens and more.[135]

Almost all communities during the 1920s and 1930s followed sports. Men with a passion for baseball made sure their respective West Texas towns formed a competitive outfit. The Sanderson baseball squad (sponsored by two of the local clubs, the Club Atlético Católico and the Club México-Tejano) competed against teams from Marfa, Alpine, Fort Stockton, and other West Texas Tejano communities. In Fort Stockton, Mexican Americans played for Los Lobos and in Alpine for the Alpine Internationals.[136] On Sundays in San Angelo, people during the 1920s and the Depression era took in the play of Los Osos, Los Dorados, and the Black Tigers. Huge crowds sitting on makeshift stands or car hoods yelled vigorously, urging on their friends, relatives, and star players on the field. Musical ensembles roused spectators to cheer their team to victory. After-game relaxation might include a dance or an appreciation dinner. Other sports popular in San Angelo during the pre–World War II years were boxing, wrestling, and golf.[137]

Disseminating Information

During the 1920s, Mexican American leaders began to use the Spanish-language press as a venue for maintaining contact with literate Hispanic communities and through it informing the public of local news and events transpiring in Mexico. In Del Rio, journalist Amado Gutiérrez continued his newspaper career (started in the city in the 1880s) by publishing *La Nueva Era* and *La Razón*.[138] Juan Rivera and Juan Valdez in 1925 contributed a section titled "Edición Español" to Marfa's *The New Era*. Juan Rivera (presumably the same person as above) in 1928 launched *La Voz de Marfa*, the first Spanish-language newspaper in the Big Bend. It publicized itself as "the mouthpiece for the Mexican population of Marfa and Presidio County."[139]

Accompanying the Spanish-language newspaper as a source of information for a listening audience was radio. Mainstream radio stations during the 1930s reserved scheduling for Spanish-language programing, and some barrio leaders made convenient use of this time. As indicated earlier, the local Baptist minister Donato Ruiz during the 1930s employed this medium to spread the Baptist word in San Angelo and throughout the Concho Country.[140]

Health and Community

Persisting in Mexican communities into the 1920s and the World War II years (and even beyond) was faith in *curanderismo*. As in the past, poor people without the resources for adequate medical help, or living in remote areas of West Texas, called on the local *curandera/o* for treatment of heart ailments, liver and kidney disorders, dysentery, broken bones, cuts, and other ills.[141]

But where possible, Mexicans turned to alternatives other than folk healing. During the 1930s and continuing into the World War II years, Mexicans in the area of the Chinati Ranch relied on Kathryn Casner for medical help. Actually the local teacher at the Chinati School, Casner made no claim to medical knowledge. But as frequently occurs in borderlands settings, where people coexist regardless of race or ethnicity, she gained the trust and confidence of her neighbors as a qualified provider. She felt a responsibility to help the many who fell ill, who could not afford clinical care, and who, in this remote area of the Big Bend, had no access to medical facilities. In due time, through on-the-job training she accrued a measure of skill in treating patients. Having to do without adequate medical supplies, she improvised at treating small ailments such as abrasions and infections, which at times she disinfected with sotol. She tended to emergencies, rushing to the homes of the suffering. If the local midwife (*partera*) was not available, she stepped in as substitute. In isolated West Texas regions, it was "border doctors" such as Kathryn Casner who in addition to *curandera/os* became the primary agents providing relief to the Mexican American population.[142]

A Sub-Economy
In West Texas communities, Mexican Americans devised practical economic strategies in attempts to overcome life hardships. Bartering continued as a sensible mode for dispensing or acquiring what of value or exchange neighbors possessed. Mechanics, carpenters, barbers, and others with specialized skills traded their services in return for family necessities, among them ironing, washing, and sewing.

To stretch lean budgets, Mexicans working for the Chisos Mining Company found avenues to circumvent the local policy that confined them to buying only from the company store. Instead, they and their families turned to mail-order catalogues for better selections and bargains. Others bought from traveling salesmen coming from Alpine and Marfa. To avoid the watchful eye of the Company, these merchants would park at some discreet spot where people could then amble over to make purchases. On the other hand, local farmers—with the tacit consent of the Chisos Mining Company—sold to Big Bend villagers assorted vegetables and *cabrito* (kid goat), goods the company store did not stock.[143]

During the 1920s, Tejanos in a daring breach of local dry laws and national Prohibition engaged in illicit trafficking of liquor. Apparently, the desire for the illegal brew was as intense in the barrios and distant farming and ranching villages of West Texas as it was among the region's Anglo communities.[144] Expectedly, Tejanos—as did other Texans who hatched ways to evade existing laws—devised their own machinations to avoid law enforcement in order to meet demand. Scant research exists on Tejano bootlegging operations in West Texas, but county histories, mainly for Big Bend locations, reveal something about the practices. Among the many who participated in this Tejano clandestine economy were men employed at the Chisos Mining Company. They knew the risks they took, aware that Chisos management expected abstinence from its workforce. Nonetheless, they ventured into the illegal trade in still another effort to deal with life's burdens. Their suppliers—as indeed was the case for consumers throughout West Texas defying cultural and legal proscriptions— were generally shadowy figures from the interior of Mexico using pack trains to carry liquor to the Texas border.[145]

Such transnational operations required intrigue, stealth, and craftiness from all involved. One historian describes how rumrunners from Mexico cleverly disguised the contraband they hauled: "[The *contrabandistas*] carried the tequila, sotol, or mescal in pig bladders or goatskin bags because these containers were not difficult to fasten on pack mules or burros and, in case of accident, were not so easily broken as bottles."[146] Smugglers would then purchase the goods and, utilizing the most opportune passages over the Rio Grande, pirate the intoxicants into the Big Bend. Those who generally transported the bootleg commodity once it made it to Texas soil (which by then would probably have been poured into bottles and jugs) were Mexican and Texas Mexican middle men, teamsters, and guides. Traffickers (many times armed) preferred doing business at night, but if by day took precautions. They relied on *avisadores* (abettors using reflective objects, like mirrors, to warn accomplices some distance away of possible problems on the road) who acted as their eyes and ears. In out-of-the way trails, these *avisadores* colluded in helping the contrabandists avoid the Border Patrolmen (whose border surveillance extended from Presidio to Candelaria to Ruidosa) assigned to look out for pack trains on the move. The dealers then whisked their goods to distant communities such as Valentine and Sanderson, to Alpine, Marathon, Marfa, and to other Big Bend settlements. From there, these intermediaries carried the intoxicants to West Texas oil towns or delivered them to organized distributors who then moved them to locations throughout the United States.[147]

Mexican Americans cashed in on the illegal commerce in ways more personal than just being crew members in pack trains traversing the rough Big Bend countryside. In Fort Stockton, where local option had existed since 1911, natives used relationships with fellow Mexicans living in the Big Bend border areas to smuggle distilled brew from Mexico to town. Once the bootleg commodity had made it into the city limits, those receiving it sold it for personal gain or as a neighborly gesture shared it in turn with friends.[148] In some cases, domestic home brewing was not so much an endeavor to make a quick sale but rather another means to mitigate the harshness of life. In one incident in Casa Piedra in 1930, law authorities confiscated the concoction a family was preparing for sale (presumably clandestinely) on the occasion of the upcoming Fourth of July celebration. One historian wrote kindheartedly of the misfortune: "People needed what solace they could find in those difficult years."[149]

Mexican Americans and Crime

Criminal acts committed by Mexican Americans against fellow compatriots still troubled Mexican communities (both in rural and urban settings) into the pre–World War II years. Certainly, crime did not confine itself to the "Mexican quarter": as studies have shown, the 1920s and 1930s were rowdy and tumultuous times in West Texas settlements due to a range of causes, among them the oil boom of the era, bank robberies, and bootlegging.[150] Indeed, it was a dispute about the banning of alcohol in the Terlingua area that in 1938 caused the death of constable Félix R. Valenzuela. As the story is remembered, a bootlegger from Mexico mortally shot Valenzuela as the peace officer attempted to enforce the Chisos Mining Company dictate requiring worker abstinence.[151]

While the barrios to a degree acted as havens shielding residents from outside lawlessness and thus places where residents might live in relative safety from egregious crime, people were not immune from dreadful offenses committed by troublemakers living within the enclave. Local histories record several cases of a heinous nature, the more sensational ones involving perpetrators killing members of their own family. In one instance, a man named Juan Galindo clubbed his wife to death in Marfa in 1926. In Grandfalls (Ward County) in 1930, Pedro Aguilar, allegedly enraged by jealousy, murdered his in-laws. Close to Marfa in 1933, Geraldo Najar's wife and son killed their husband/father, mutilated the man, and then buried the body in the sands of the Alamito Creek. For their crime, the courts sentenced the two to ninety-nine years in the penitentiary.[152]

TEXAS MEXICANS

Living in the Mexican quarter may have kept people from gaining a working acquaintance with mainstream institutions and learning the skills essential for success in a white man's world,[153] but segregation did not entirely deter inhabitants from knowing what transpired outside their neighborhood's boundaries and thus from familiarizing themselves with some of the ways of the Anglos. In actuality, the barrio was ever in flux, constantly absorbing mainstream viewpoints, assumptions, and tenets. Moreover, Tejanos regularly had contact with the world beyond segregated zones. Aside from association in job settings and classrooms where students studied English and were exposed to the ideal of the American promise, Mexicans made contact with Anglos in churches staffed with Anglo priests and ministers, in the political arena where Anglos made overtures to barrio dwellers during election time, and in a multitude of other domains. Further, Mexicans during the 1920s and 1930s watched English-language movies, saw or read American advertisings, listened to the music of the age, and admired (and wished to adopt) popular fashion styles of the time.[154]

Identity

In actuality, various cultural identities flourished in the barrios. The Mexican quarter continued to host people who faithfully subscribed to traditions and customs that tied them to the mother country. Many in the *colonia* thus barely familiarized themselves with mainstream institutions. But the enclaves simultaneously housed many who embraced Americanization and regarded themselves as full-fledged US citizens. Some Tejanos so immersed themselves in Anglo ways as to dilute their ties to the customs of their ancestors. Increasing in numbers were others in "Little Mexicos" syncretizing cultures, able to move between a world of old traditions and a universe of English-speaking people.

In addition to the impact that contact with Anglos on several fronts had on Mexican American bi-culturation, formal organizations acted to aid ethnic transformation. The Boy Scouts, wherever Hispanic adults helped troops to charter, instilled sound American values in young boys. In Marfa, local organizers established the first chapter of Hispanic Boy Scouts in 1926; they apparently partnered with the Catholic Church, for the club held gatherings at the

Knights of Columbus Hall.[155] In Fort Stockton, community organizers during the mid-1930s also founded a Boy Scout unit. The local Catholic Church sponsored it.[156]

La Crisis

Certainly, Tejanos did not escape the more adverse effects of the 1930s economic slump. They were singled out, for instance, as labor market threats. In towns such as San Angelo, local Anglo workmen complained early during the Depression era that Mexicans took scarce jobs, such as in road surfacing, work that presumably belonged to white men. In 1931, a group of white workers took the menacing step of directing Mexican laborers to leave town.[157] Tejanos working at the Chisos Mining Company dealt with uncertainty of their own during the mid-1930s as the company owner refused to submit to employer labor requirements established by the National Recovery Administration (NRA), a New Deal agency. Rejecting the administration's codes of fair practices, company management shut down temporarily in 1934. The action left miners in limbo for the next two weeks, and then when the mine resumed operations, they continued to face the same severe conditions they had sustained since the company's opening in 1914: bare survival wages, inadequate compensation for overtime, danger in the workplace, and, lamentably, the exploitation of their children.[158]

For some ethnic Mexicans in Texas, anguish over continued life in the United States led to harsh decision-making. This was not so much a concern for Mexicans in West Texas as for those in other parts of the state—or the United States as a whole for that matter—as deportation drives in the region were not as acute. Nonetheless, to be of Mexican background in the Edwards Plateau and Trans-Pecos borderlands meant being considered a societal burden, a position more likely to distress those of foreign birth. Reluctance by local communities to consider Mexican-origin people eligible for relief assistance reinforced a sense of rejection for all. Agencies locally dispensing aid specifically excluded the foreign born and the unnaturalized but tended to lump Mexicans together regardless of their citizenship status.[159] In San Angelo in 1931, one group of noncitizens, stressed by the crisis around them, appealed to the government of Mexico for financial help so they could relocate to their native land. In another case in San Angelo (April 1939), a local group named the San Angelo Committee for Repatriation of Mexicans launched an effort to assist destitute nationals in town to reestablish themselves back home. Seemingly, these immigrants were so impoverished that they were willing to return to Mexico even while leaving behind them US-born family members and precious possessions.[160]

Despite hardship, Mexican Americans made do, crafting new and practical survival tactics. The stark reality of declining sales during the Depression compelled Hispanic commercial establishments, for example, to discard old business methods and adopt innovative entrepreneurial approaches. In Fort Stockton, one merchant survived the downturn by having family members work for practically nothing; only by doing so could he meet customer needs. He further implemented a type of easy-payment plan: patrons would pay at the end of the week with meager job earnings or barter with goods dispensed by the relief office, perhaps trade for flour to make tortillas.[161] But attempting new strategies did not work out for many. When M. R. González of Fort Stockton saw his business decline precipitously, he humbled himself to milk cows in a determined effort to care for his family. As to the general population, survival called for irregular measures, such as in the Fort Stockton region where people turned to surrounding woodlands to hunt small game like jackrabbits and armadillos.[162]

Then, there were those in the Mexican American community who pulled through the Depression with federal assistance. Stories spread widely of Franklin Delano Roosevelt (FDR) and his promise under the New Deal to help the poor. In the Terlingua area, for instance, a personal visit to the Chisos Mining Company by a National Recovery Administration agent made known to the Mexican mining employees and others in the Terlingua District that the government of the Democrats and FDR had "not forgotten the man at the bottom of the economic ladder."[163]

Throughout West Texas, Mexican-descent people placed trust in the various New Deal programs, particularly on Social Security. Among these hopefuls were Chisos Mine workers. According to the mine's general manager: "We now have a good many boys working for us [the Chisos Mining Company] that are underage but who are filing for numbers under the Social Security Act." Such information about the act's provisions no doubt spread throughout Big Bend communities via word of mouth.[164]

Among those profiting from New Deal assistance were Mexican American boys who joined the Civilian Conservation Corps (CCC). Newspapers and county histories reported Mexican American young men from places like San Angelo, Fort Stockton, Fort Davis, Presidio, and Valentine working at the several CCC camps placed throughout West Texas. Recruits from Fort Stockton and

Big Bend towns and settlements helped in the construction of roads for the Big Bend National Park when the federal government assumed restoration oversight of that landmark.[165]

Other New Deal programs, such as the Works Progress Administration (WPA), the Public Works Administration (PWA), and the Reconstruction Finance Corporation (RFC), acted not solely to assist Mexicans in time of dire need but to confirm their faith in the American system and their country's good will. But even in these federal programs, Anglo supervisors followed entrenched social practices and assigned Hispanics to the most arduous, punishing, and backbreaking tasks. Mexicans, therefore, generally toiled as pick-and-shovel hands helping in the grading and paving of local roads, most likely in the Anglo-American side of towns. When the PWA hired crews of Mexicans to provide a sewage system for Fort Stockton (1933), work mainly entailed laying down the pipes and mains needed for the project (which hardly extended into the barrio).[166] The RFC called for similar manual work tasks. When in 1933 it solicited laborers to build a dam in the Pecos Valley, Manuel Rodrigo of Fort Stockton managed to net a deal with the program but only for hauling dirt. Like so many other Mexican Americans having been incorporated into New Deal projects, Rodrigo no doubt considered himself lucky to have received the contract, feeling grateful to the president for the consideration he gave to all Americans regardless of social standing.[167]

Political Engagement

The Americanization of West Texas Mexicans by historical forces attendant to the 1920s and 1930s once more lured Tejanos to the political arena. The downward political slide traceable to the 1880s faded toward the mid-1930s, followed then by a modest upswing in Tejano participation. It was true that Anglo Americans dominated demographically, politically, economically, and otherwise and never relinquished control over politics.[168] Nonetheless, the interest Mexican Americans retained in civic affairs affecting barrio life drew them towards political involvement.

As they had earlier, Anglo leaders continued trying to make dishonest use of the Mexican vote. They could force Mexican men to cast ballots in a designated way (threating them, for instance, with losing their jobs). They might bribe them or pay for their poll tax and tell them for whom to vote. Still common in West Texas was enticing prospects with food and liquor on the day of the election and, with a commitment from the revelers to vote as instructed, piling them up in wagons (as would happen in Alpine during the 1920s) and hauling them to the polls.[169]

Mexicans saw in the dictates of Anglo politicians some assurance of personal and family security. In Terlingua during the 1920s and 1930s, for instance, Tejano miners acceded to boss politics by voting as told but did so with the knowledge that their vote ensured their jobs. Historian Kenneth Baxter Ragsdale quotes a man named H. C. Hernández: "In the old days they used to slip a marked ballot to a guy [a Mexican] and all they would do would just run 'im through a votin' line, and that was that." According to Hernández, the Mexican workers fully understood the process: "That's how they played the game."[170]

In particular circumstances, Mexicans with a sense of political duty counted on local patronage customs to fill vacant offices with fellow Mexicans. In the Big Bend, accords developed between Anglo power brokers and Mexicans when necessity mandated (e.g., due to scarcity of Anglos) led to the appointment of staff to official positions. In gaining positions as policemen, postmistresses, custom service personnel, depot agents, and so on, Tejanos assumed a level of influence that permitted them to assist local Spanish-speaking communities.

In Fort Stockton, Manuel R. González negotiated ties to the town's political establishment by paying the poll tax for some of the local Mexican American voters (many of whom owed González favors) and instructing them to vote for certain office seekers. He then contrived to sway elections in favor of Anglo candidates more likely to help the Tejano community.[171]

Ad hoc committees comprised of civic-minded leaders acting to address barrio issues further illustrate ongoing Tejano efforts to obtain their due rights. In San Angelo, as an example, a delegation of Mexican Americans in 1937 objected openly to the proposed segregation of Mexicans and Anglos at a scheduled performance—to be held at the municipal auditorium—by the Orquesta Típica from Mexico. The barrio representatives complained that designating the balcony for Mexicans displayed overt prejudice, and they brought the case to the attention of Mexican consuls, the leader of the *orquesta*, and the national LULAC office. In the end, the event sponsor agreed to integrate the production.[172]

The Americanization that gained momentum during the 1920s and 1930s produced among Texas Mexicans a broader, more formalized effort to address community problems. This drive to fully coordinate campaigns against issues of inequality had its roots in South Texas where during the 1920s Tejanos created the Order of the Sons of America (as well as two other civic organizations) and then in 1929 the League of United Latin American Citizens (LULAC). LULAC councils quickly sprouted throughout South Texas—led by a cohort whom historians identify as members of the "Mexican American Generation"—and then in quick order in a few West Texas towns. LULAC councils appeared in Del Rio (1930), San Angelo (1931), Marfa (1931), Sonora, Ozona, and Fort Stockton (1936), and probably other places that historians have yet to bring to light.[173] West Texas councils mirrored South Texas chapters in a united purpose: to address educational deficiencies, eliminate discriminatory practices, and remove barriers such as those that impeded Mexicans from jury participation.

The first significant case LULAC litigated in West Texas (1930–1931) had Del Rio as its setting and involved segregation in the public schools. As indicated earlier in this chapter, the town of Del Rio at that time had two school districts, the DRISD and the SFISD (formerly the SFCSD); the latter had opted to stand alone in 1929, preferring segregation. Then, in early 1930, the DRISD School Board won a bond election to build new schools for the system but promising only to add rooms to the existing segregated Mexican school.[174]

Parents in the DRISD resisted the board's plan, for unlike their counterparts in the SFISD, they desired integration in order that their children learn to function adequately in an English-speaking environment as well as to avoid the stigma of mediocrity—that is, not being worthy of opportunities granted Anglos. They hired lawyer John L. Dodson and in the name of Jesús Salvatierra filed suit in March 1930 in State District Court, arguing that segregation based on race violated the equal protection guarantees in the Constitution.[175]

The state LULAC took an interest in Salvatierra, as the case highlighted the deep-seated practice of segregation, one salient element of injustice that had roused civic leaders to action during the 1920s. In April 1930, therefore, San Antonio LULACer M. C. Gonzales entered into collaboration with Dodson, Del Rio LULAC Council 18, and supportive local groups such as church societies, *mutualista* associations, and women's clubs to fight against the DRISD's segregationist designs. That May, the district court found for the plaintiffs and issued an injunction halting plans that perpetuated the status quo.[176]

Challenging the decision, the DRISD turned to the Texas Court of Civil Appeals in San Antonio. To the plaintiffs' disappointment, this tribunal in October 1930 ruled against them, agreeing with DRISD administrators that segregation was not race-based. The court concurred that educational practicality justified the arrangement. First, Mexican American children needed special attention for improving their English-speaking skills; a friendly and understanding Spanish-speaking setting served best for that objective. Second, many students enrolled late (and left early in the spring) due to their work in the cotton fields; the Mexican school (in contrast to the Anglo schools) had a trained staff qualified to ease these latecomers into the semester.[177]

Unwilling to accept the ruling, the state LULAC in early 1931 appealed to the US Supreme Court (SCOTUS).[178] At the local level, Jesús Salvatierra's committee (El Comité Pro-Defensa Escolar de Del Rio) supplied the league with $1,089.54 to finance the hoped-for hearing before the high court.[179] But the SCOTUS declared in November 1931 that it could not take up the case as it fell outside of its field of authority.[180] The school board consequently proceeded to implement plans as intended by the proposed bond election: it built a new high school, expanded the two elementary schools for Anglos, and attached new rooms to the one "Mexican school" (another Mexican school would be added in 1938, as noted above), leaving the segregation of Mexican children in place.[181]

In San Angelo, LULAC Council 27 rallied behind the state LULAC when in 1936 the organization denounced the Social Security Board's decision to have Mexican Americans classify themselves as "Mexicans" instead of "white." Council 27's letter to Washington, DC, officials read:

> We are engaged in educational work designed to make our people conscious of their citizenship rights and obligations and duties. We are not ashamed of our blood heritage; in fact we are justly proud of the blood that courses through our veins. But we want to feel that we are not just a group of "Mexicans" but a vital part of the American people that make up this great nation in which we live.
>
> We cannot do this work effectively if an agency of our government is going to discriminate against us as to a separate class of group. We therefore urge you to revise your form and permit our people to be classified as "WHITE."[182]

In the face of the coordinated response from state LULAC chapters, the Social Security Board retreated and informed government administrators to allow Mexicans to register as "white" under the Social Security program.[183]

Council 27 remained an activist bloc in San Angelo for the remainder of the 1930s and into the World War II years. In 1940, it and other barrio groups, among them Ladies LULAC, confronted (albeit unsuccessfully) the Plaza Theater in the city when management announced the movie house would be segregated. But the chapter did not confine itself to Mexican American causes. It assisted in Red Cross money-raising drives and, as war approached, supported draft calls. In carrying out its local mission, Council 27 abided by the state LULAC policy of trying to uphold pro-American values whenever possible; in those days, the country hesitated to tolerate groups suspiciously engaged in un-American activities.[184]

Actions to deal with entrenched segregation doubtless occurred in other towns in West Texas, although research remains incomplete on such struggles. Little is known of efforts undertaken in towns such as Sonora, Ozona, and Marfa, for instance, where LULAC councils appeared by the 1930s.[185] The opposite is the case for Fort Stockton, where research reveals at least two sustained offensives against standing segregation in town. In 1938, the Fort Stockton school board motioned to proceed with plans for allowing Mexican American children to attend public schools alongside white children, but a public outcry from Anglo citizens pressured the board to reverse course. Then, on the eve of World War II (1940), the board thought it necessary to reaffirm its policy of institutionalized segregation. This time, barrio leaders, with membership in the city's LULAC Council 62, protested strenuously to the Texas State Education Office. Though rebuffed, locals kept state LULAC officials apprised of the district's practice. Bending to the persistence of M. C. Gonzales, National Executive Secretary of LULAC, the State Superintendent of Schools, L. A. Woods, in 1942 intervened in the case and instructed FSISD to undertake integration in the city's high school. Abiding by this order, board members adopted a policy permitting Mexican Americans to enroll in the only high school in town.[186]

Less successful was Council 62 in its goal of integrating the city's swimming pool (built with WPA funds) at Comanche Springs southeast of town. In 1939, Mexican Americans confronted the exclusionist policy, invoking protections as citizens and taxpayers under the US Constitution. But Fort Stockton's white community remained recalcitrant. Problems reached a breaking point in 1943 when Corporal Jesse García, on Army leave and wearing his uniform, sought access to the pool, only to be callously rejected by the supervisor. LULAC Council 62 immediately called on M. C. Gonzales, noting the arbitrary nature of the refusal, as Mexican Americans had helped pay for and maintain the pool and were then fighting for democracy on different theaters of war. As late as 1945, the pool remained for whites only.[187]

WORLD WAR II

The coming of World War II drew West Texas into the national emergency that mobilized the greater population, equipped the country's military forces, and deployed soldiers to the war fronts. Among draftees and volunteers who saw combat in Europe and the Far East were Mexican Americans from the region's several towns, ranches, and farms. The saga of Mexican Americans in war service may never be fully learned, but their participation in the war is maintained in an array of sources, among them the works of scholars,[188] lay historians, and avid county chroniclers. The efforts of public servants assisting in preserving that record is evident further in the construction of public memorials and monuments.

Important to the preservation of Mexican American wartime accounts are the writings of individuals with interest in military history or a desire to ensure that the heroism of their loved ones (those killed in action and those survivors who served with honor) not be forgotten. Of note are accounts of lay historians from Melvin, Texas, the small rural town in McCulloch County. According to their research, the community of some 600 Mexican American inhabitants at mid-century sent numerous young men to the war fronts, among them the sons of some of the earliest Melvin colonizers like the Juan and Anastacio Pérez and the Juan and Genaro Laing families. Anastacio Pérez at one point had five sons fighting in the war.[189]

Among county histories noting servicemen who fought in World War II (and that list the names of Mexican American participants) are those published on Menard County and McCulloch County. A history of Menard County reads: "With a total population of slightly more than forty-five hundred people, Menard County sent more than seven hundred to the aid of the United States in armed service." Of these seven hundred, approximately nine percent had Spanish surnames, and of the twenty-three men from the county who were killed in action, five (perhaps six, as one person had an English surname) were of Mexican descent. In neighboring McCulloch County, according to the *Handbook of McCulloch County History*, sixty-eight total individuals were killed in the nation's two world wars. Of these, eight were of Mexican origin. The book states that the names of those who died in combat are shown on the "the war memorial at the entrance to Memory Lane in Brady."[190]

More specific in preserving the record of sacrifices Mexican American soldiers made in World War II is the information engraved in a public memorial erected in Midland, Texas. Designated the Reyes-Sanchez Plaza World War II Memorial, the park (named after two Midland servicemen killed in action) pays tribute to Midland County Mexican American veterans and the two men who died in the service of freedom. Beginning in the late 1990s, Ciro Sánchez, spokesperson for a group of World War II veterans, led a drive to secure private funding for the proposed landmark; assisting them was the Midland Hispanic Chamber of Commerce, which assumed responsibility for soliciting donations, ensuring the builders accurately abided by the architect's design, and finally seeing the project reach completion. The organizers arranged with Midland city for a donation of land, and through monies collected from private sources and the collaboration of the city, which undertook construction of the site, the Reyes-Sanchez Plaza World War II Memorial was dedicated on Veterans Day, November 11, 2001. The memorial is located at Unity Park (on the corner of Lamesa Road and South Street) in the general vicinity of Midland's prewar barrio. Inscribed on the stone dedication wall are the names of about 123 WWII veterans from Midland's east side, most of whom resided within an area of ten to twelve blocks around Unity Park.[191]

A COMPARISON

The West Texas Mexican experience through various epochs does not seem to be much of a departure from the larger history of Tejanos in the Lone Star State. As this chapter and those preceding it have illustrated, the history of people in West Texas and their counterparts in South Texas (where much of the population then was concentrated) took similar paths. Both in South Texas and West Texas, Mexican-origin people lived and struggled as a subaltern class. In each section, Anglo Americans sought control over them through means that included racial prejudice, physical intimidation, segregation, and an educational curriculum that fell short of preparing students for fair competition in the larger society. Further, the prevalent economic system in both regions relegated Texas Mexicans to low-grade jobs. As did their counterparts in South Texas, West Texas Tejanos endured discriminatory wage practices, often facing dangerous workplace conditions.

Tejano community development in West Texas during the 1920s and 1930s did not deviate markedly from what transpired within segregated South Texas barrios and rural villages. In semiautonomous zones, South Texas Tejanos and West Texas Mexican Americans used Spanish as the primary language of in-group communication, honored traditions and customs their forebears had imported north from Mexico, and kept faith in long-standing beliefs, among them folklore and folk medicine. In both regions, Mexican Americans successfully established churches, business concerns, mutual aid societies, recreational clubs, and, in some cases, schools intended for preserving and enhancing Mexican culture. Celebrated commonly were multiple holy days, Mexican national holidays such as the Diez y Seis and Cinco de Mayo, and special community or family affairs.

Historical change modified life in *colonias*, but it did not drive the two sections in discernibly different directions. Whether in South Texas or West Texas, education produced similar outcomes: literacy and increased Americanization of children. Popular or mainstream culture of the age in like manner affected those absorbing it. New Deal programs, among them Social Security and works projects such as those run by the WPA and CCC, earned the gratitude of Tejanos across the state. Young men profited from CCC experiences by exposure to different environments and seeing new aspects of life; their stay at CCC camps helped sharpen English speaking skills and reinforced citizenship. World War II fostered an equal level of patriotism among Mexican Americans and neither in South Texas nor West Texas did young men generally shirk the call to duty. The changing times of the 1920s and 1930s reinforced the developing class of businesspeople, professionals, and small farmers and ranchers fortunate to purchase or rent land. Continuing acculturation spurred civic-minded leaders to activism on behalf of *la gente* (the people), whether in South Texas or West Texas.

Despite similarities in experience between South and West Texas, forces existed that dichotomized life. Much of South Texas relied on farming. Commercial agriculture thrived therein during this period (1920 to 1945), demanding armies of Tejano cotton pickers for seasonal field labor. By contrast, West Texas continued as livestock country. While some Tejanos obviously engaged in cotton picking in places where farmers experimented with the crop, the struggle for survival in West Texas led Tejanos to ranch work, most often to sheepshearing.

The different economic structure in the two regions might explain brisk labor organizing activity in South Texas as opposed to the relative lack of it in West

Texas. In South Texas, an almost colonial relationship existed between agribusiness and the massive number of migrant field workers who demonstrated worker discontent by joining local unions. Strikes and union organizing also occurred in the urbanscape, in places like Laredo, Corpus Christi, and San Antonio, where workers struck for better workplace conditions during the 1930s.

In West Texas, on the other hand, no particular heritage of labor confrontation and organizing existed. The geography of West Texas, with its isolated ranches and farms and scattered urban areas, made it difficult to coordinate labor organizing campaigns. Little urban industry existed in the towns of the Edwards Plateau and Trans-Pecos regions (exempting El Paso city) to incite factory strikes such as occurred in Laredo and San Antonio during the 1930s. Being beholden to Anglo bosses for scarce job opportunities, some historians note, tended to discourage Mexicans from being confrontational.[192]

Then, the strategies Anglos employed in dealing with Mexicans differed between South Texas and West Texas. In South Texas, Anglos turned to entrenched Jim Crow regimens to control Mexicans socially. In contrast, means of managing Mexicans in West Texas were less stringent, perhaps because of West Texas's likeness to the US West. Every-day segregation in West Texas varied, according to historian Glen Ely, from the legalized and intransigent Jim Crow type found in the US South. As per Ely, segregation developed de facto, more closely resembling the relaxed practices that existed in the western US. The cultural environment of West Texas, distinguishable from that of South Texas more closely connected to the Old South, mitigated race relations friction.[193]

In general, West Texans have historically identified with the US West's pastoral aura, and so have West Texas Tejanos. A Western rural and ranching character and quality, present since early community-building efforts and persisting into the 1920s and 1930s, could not but help Tejanos identify with place. In contrast, South Texas Tejanos were more likely to have been influenced by that region's agricultural and urbanizing context. Locales, having special consideration and attraction for inhabitants, diversify experiences. As much has been the case in Mexican American history.

CHAPTER 5

ACCULTURATION, ADVANCEMENT, AND ACTIVISM, 1945-1970

C ontinuity alongside change characterized the West Texas economy after World War II. Ranchers still raised large herds of cattle, sheep, and goats, counting on ranching as a lucrative investment. In places like Schleicher County, ranchers could rely on cattle only but might mix different stock, adding sheep and goats. According to one appraisal, "the county appears to be a composite of the entire Edwards Plateau."[1]

Success on the cattle range revolved around reliance on long-standing grazing practices, continued manipulation of the grasslands to improve soil nutrition and enhance the quality of feed for stock, and dependable methods for marketing and selling livestock.[2] As for sheep and goat raising, ranchers continued to employ time-honored methods of woollyback management. The use of *pastores* had long ended, but the trusted practice of fencing the range for grazing sheep and goats remained intact. Mexican *tasinques*, as before the war, conducted the shearing, traveling the West Texas circuit under the leadership of the *capitanes* and fleecing the sheep with electric shears.[3]

But the post–World War II years also saw cattle ranchers adopting advances in range management. Rotating the stock around different parts of the ranch gave grass in the undisturbed area time to regenerate. Situating water wells throughout the rangeland allowed cowhands to move herds to new grounds and thus prevent grass from being mercilessly trampled in any given spot. Ranchers turned to recently available conveniences and to modern technological developments that boosted profits. Working the range on horseback became less common; some of the cowboys used motorcycles.[4] Cowhands working on and managing herds in the different pastures communicated with each other via two-way radio. Ranchers and ranch workmen transporting stock to market in the 1960s drove the newer truck models as well as pickups capable of pulling the new line of gooseneck trailers. Aircraft could spray fields to eradicate brush and control diseases that afflicted animals by exterminating parasites such as the screwworm. Electricity now reached many range lands, benefiting ranchers in extracting water from underground sources.[5]

Change similarly entered the sheep and goat industry during the post–WWII era. Ranchers adopted newer scientific methods to the management of their stock and devised new means of marketing their product. They upgraded strategies for carrying their animals to different market centers or packing houses.[6]

But ranching as an entrepreneurial enterprise contended with a wide range of problems during the Cold War years. One predicament was rain scarcity: the drought of the 1950s brought ruin to many livestock ranches in the West Texas region.[7] Overgrazing, traceable to the latter decades of the nineteenth century, continued to diminish the amount of range acreage open for feeding cattle and sheep. By the mid-twentieth century, once-fertile lands in counties such as Pecos and Reeves had been left bereft of native grasses; the consequence of the practice was a range overcome by brush, weeds, and wild vegetation.[8]

Sheep and goat ranchers dealt with specific problems. For one, consumer tastes changed as the preference moved to synthetics instead of wool and mohair products. A decline in the number of sheepshearers added to ranchers' troubles. Mexican Americans, although still constituting the bulk of *tasinque* crews, gradually but surely turned to employment in less strenuous work, part of it to be found in the towns and cities.[9]

Farming in West Texas remained a viable enterprise, especially in the cultivation of cotton, grains, and vegetable produce. But rain deficiency plagued farmers as much as it did ranchers; the solution was in irrigation, a necessity especially for farmers west of Big Lake and Ozona. Thus, throughout the Edwards Plateau and Trans-Pecos countryside, huge electric motors helped to make farming economically profitable.[10]

During the Second World War, the oil industry in West Texas experienced a drop in profits due to losses in trade with foreign countries, government regulation, and a dearth of workforce personnel—many men had been recruited for war service.[11] But once peace returned, the oil boom of the prewar years resumed, primarily in Ector and Midland Counties but also in other counties running parallel to the Pecos River.[12] Pipeline construction, meanwhile, had begun anew in the Permian Basin, facilitating the delivery of oil discovered in new oil fields.[13] So promising was the recovery that by 1952, Ector County had come to be the largest oil-producing county in West Texas.[14]

CULTURE

The transformation of West Texas that occurred in the decades after World War II ended the region's relative partition from the rest of the state and lured it towards the modern age to reflect the patterns of change occurring elsewhere. While still mainly a rural area, discernible urban maturity in some of the more prominent cities such as Midland, Odessa, Del Rio, and San Angelo led them to resemble other similarly sized cities outside the region. Indeed, by the 1960s all four had acquired airport facilities as well as colleges and universities. Up-to-date medical units by then came to be commonplace, as well as shopping plazas. Town dwellers in the Edwards Plateau and Trans-Pecos borderlands sought to stay abreast of the rapid pace of change, maintaining contact with (and absorbing the amenities of) the larger metropolises, making excursions there to patronize grocery chains and large department stores and depending on their hospitals for health needs. Students took advantage of the new progress by attending West Texas universities.[15]

Modern communications, an improved road infrastructure, increased public school attendance, and regular visits to the larger cities all coalesced to disseminate mass culture to much of West Texas. Television, radio, popular magazines, and other media helped circulate the latest trends in music, fashion, and national crazes (including, of course, Beatlemania). The cultural revolution of the 1960s and beyond altered ways of thinking, prying West Texans from long-standing rural outlooks and easing them towards attitudes more attuned to mainstream thought.[16]

TEJANOS IN CHANGING TIMES

A Population Increase

Since the turn of the twentieth century, Mexican Americans had lived as a minority group in West Texas. As of 1950, their status had not changed. The

171

number of Texas Mexicans living in the counties under study (in the Edwards Plateau and Trans-Pecos) stood at just less than 20 percent of the total West Texas population. When their numbers increased after 1970 to reach 128,351 in 1980, they still constituted only 27 percent of the entire population. For the most part, Anglo Americans continued being the majority group as of 1980.[17]

Geographic Dispersal, 1945 to 1980
In the years following World War II, Mexicans lived throughout all sections of West Texas (as had always been the case), but a clustering of population centers was evident by the late 1970s as people now pushed into those counties that were becoming more economically prosperous and rapidly accepting the trappings of modernization. Still enticing to many people of Mexican origin as a worthy site for livelihood was the ranch and farm county of Tom Green in the Concho Valley. The region now offered more promise as farmers opened new acreage to cotton planting. The county seat of San Angelo, at the same time, was transitioning into a mecca for industry, banking, real estate, education, medical treatment, and commerce for surrounding agricultural counties—it even earned the moniker the "Wool Capital of the World."[18]

But a major shift in population movements after World War II was (besides Tom Green) into the counties that were at the center of the West Texas oil boom, among them Reeves and Pecos Counties, but more visibly to Ector and Midland Counties. The two major cities therein, Odessa and Midland (their respective county seats), had prospered from the oil industry and now enticed outsiders, among them Mexican Americans; those possessing white-collar experience and service work skills readily found a niche in the two cities' burgeoning economies.[19] Along the border, Del Rio by the 1960s was assuming amenities characteristic of the larger cities in the state, aided by the presence of a local Air Force base, air traffic (its airport was built in 1964), a growing college campus, and international trade.[20]

In reality, of course, movement also occurred into ranch and farm counties such as Runnels, Concho, McCulloch, and Schleicher.[21] Mexicans also located (or relocated) into smaller towns in ranch counties, among them Sonora and Alpine, most of them county seats.[22] Naturally, the migration into the urbanscape produced population losses in what were predominantly ranch counties, ones that engaged Mexicans handling cattle, sheep, and goats. Work there was always more arduous (presumably less so than in the city) and the droughts of the mid-century probably prompted Mexicans during the 1950s and after the 1960s to search out options in counties experiencing urban expansion, population growth, and economic prosperity.[23]

Trabajadores

In the years following World War II and continuing into 1970, work possibilities for Mexican Americans in West Texas improved, although the bulk of the population still struggled to find ways to wrest a passable livelihood. According to one authority, in 1930 some 90 percent of the Mexican American population in the state of Texas belonged to a proletarian group, and while there was progress over the decades, as of 1970, 60 to 70 percent of the Texas Mexicans were still part of the laboring class.[24] One might assume that the economic standing of Tejanos in West Texas paralleled that of the Mexican American population statewide.

With the number of good paying jobs up to the 1960s still limited to (or withheld from) them, Mexicans in West Texas counted, as itinerant families had for years, on ranch and farm work. On sheep ranches, Mexicans attended to the sheepshearing (*la trasquila*) as they had perennially. From the late 1940s until the 1960s (and beyond for that matter), they applied to their trade practices and routines that harked back to earlier eras. The *capitán*, head of the shearing crew, hired his workforce in early spring for the year (taking into consideration the various work assignments to be executed), extending to his recruits, when necessary, what workers called a *reganche* or *renganche* (in either case, the term referred to a loan, or advance pay, made so that the family would have budget money during the period the *tasinque* was away on the shearing journey), in the meantime contracting jobs with the various ranchers. The team traveled in trucks, old buses, or individual autos, accompanied by a mobile shearing unit (an assembly of shearing plants mounted on a trailer pulled by the more modern "heavy-duty" vehicles of the age). The working platform accommodated several stations, perhaps six on each side of the flatbed. In the immediate postwar years, *tasinques* earned twenty-five cents per sheep clipped. Wages depended on skill level, the more experienced—i.e., those gifted with hand dexterity and agility and known for their work diligence—receiving more money for each fleece.

Work took crews to various West Texas ranch sites, among them those around Rankin, Big Lake, Mertzon, Del Rio, Rocksprings, Sonora, Eldorado, Menard, and Ozona. But demand for *tasinques* many times called for out-of-state excursions, so that crews often left for the US Northwest, to Wyoming, Montana, and

North and South Dakota. Whether it was in-state or out, life for the men on the circuit bordered on the brutal. Hardships involved having to find their own accommodations, which often meant living outdoors. Under more auspicious circumstances, shearers sheltered in barns or sheds. They had to provide their own drinking water, cook their own meals (although this was the job of the *cocinero*), and relieve themselves of bodily waste wherever they could.[25]

Farm workers seasonally travelled throughout West Texas counties clearing fields, chopping weeds, picking cotton, handling farm machinery, and performing any job assigned to them.[26] In counties such as Schleicher, they labored alongside arrivals from Mexico (derisively labeled "wetbacks" by Anglos), poor people willing to do arduous work around farms and ranches for barely livable wages.[27]

In contrast to individuals who performed seasonal ranch or farm labor were those that secured stable employment at various West Texas ranches. Such kinds of labor arrangements were not unknown in Sutton County after World War II. Some of the Mexican Americans of Sonora who during the 1970s provided interviews to the compilers of the book *Sutton County, 1887–1977* spoke of their parents and grandparents having developed long-term associations with Anglo ranch owners, more or less steadily working on the ranch premises for years. The Pedro Galindo family, for one, started to work at the Bryant Hunt ranch when Pedro's father Jesús arrived there in 1919. Pedro joined his father on the ranch in 1926 and continued working for Mr. Hunt until the boss (*patrón*, or *amo*) passed away in the 1970s. Even after relocating to Sonora proper, sometime after World War II, Pedro continued his work at the old *patrón*'s estate.[28]

The oil and gas industry that emerged before World War II and expanded during the postwar era—most prosperously throughout the Permian Basin and those counties spanning both sides of the Pecos River—afforded Mexican Americans further avenues for material amelioration. Most demanding of workers (of native or foreign birth) were the oil lands in Ector and Midland Counties that soon became among the largest oil- and gas-producing fields throughout the entire stretch of West Texas.[29] But as in other work settings after the war, Mexican oil field hands were consigned to the customary "Mexican work": cleaning around the grounds (including the buildings), digging ditches, laying pipelines, doing section work, and, after the 1950s (when teaming became outmoded), truck driving.[30]

On the other hand, some Tejanos in West Texas did obtain jobs customarily reserved for white workers. Such was the case of Santiago L. Rodríguez of

Terrell County who after World War II (until 1954) secured employment with a telephone company. His work entailed fixing the lines out in the countryside when they broke or otherwise malfunctioned.[31]

Town dwellers—many of whom had joined the post–WWII movement of Mexican Americans from the rural areas of the state into the cities—experienced mixed success in finding fruitful work opportunities. In an oil town such as Odessa, with presumably better opportunities than were in the non-oil-producing counties, a great majority of Mexican Americans in the late 1940s still worked as general laborers. Circumstances did not differ greatly in neighboring Midland in the early 1950s. Almost as many Mexican American heads of households there were filling openings in the grade of manual labor, including construction, road maintenance, street cleaning, and trash pickups for the sanitation department.[32]

Generally, Mexican Americans in the urban areas worked as home builders, painters, restaurant and hotel employees, hospital aides, and in miscellaneous capacities within the service sector. Many worked in dry cleaning establishments and in print shops. Naturally, there persisted that group of successful business-people and professionals who made up a segment of the Tejano middle class. Their place and role in communities is discussed below.

PREJUDICE, DISCRIMINATION, AND SEGREGATION

Sometime during the 1950s and early 1960s, racist attitudes towards Mexicans harbored by Anglos began eroding.[33] Until such a time, West Texas remained a place—much as in sections of the US Southwest, if not South Texas—where prejudice, discrimination, and segregation dictated Anglo and Mexican race relations.

The secondary literature that speaks to discrimination against Mexican Americans in West Texas is abundant for the years up to the mid-1950s. From what may be culled from publications treating the late 1940s, racism was as entrenched in those years as it had been before the war against the Axis powers.

Some West Texans, for instance, showed little tolerance for their Mexican American neighbors, dismissing the contributions Mexican Americans had made to the war effort—both on the battlefield and at the home front. According to one such individual complaining from Sonora in 1945, he and his fellow West Texas veterans had not fought to have "ill-smelling Mexicans" mixing with white people at the local theater, nor to have them soon be demanding service at West Texas restaurants, petitioning for entrance to the Anglo schools, and even wanting to integrate municipal swimming pools.[34]

The roadway from Marfa to Austin during the late 1940s, warned an educator from Marfa, was notorious for the refusal of towns along it to provide service to Mexicans. Coaches taking sports teams (that included both Anglo and Mexican athletes) were not permitted at cafés in towns such as Fort Stockton, Ozona, Sonora, and Junction, with the explanation that "we do not serve Mexicans here." School administrators instructed faculty in charge of integrated teams to completely avoid traveling on Highway 290, considering the ugly discrimination along that route.[35]

In an attempt to expose to those in authority the presence of discrimination across the state, lawyer and civil rights activist Alonso Perales of San Antonio published in 1948 a book titled *Are We Good Neighbors?* This compilation of affidavits, letters to federal authorities, newspaper editorials, complaints from common citizens, and other sources of information dealing with West Texas revealed the kinds of blatant discrimination practiced in the region after World War II. Listed as not permitting service to Mexicans at eateries were Alpine, Pecos, Ozona, Brady, Mason, Marathon, McCamey, Midland, and San Angelo. It was common to find signs at cafés (and indeed in other public places) announcing "NO MEXICANS ALLOWED." Most of these towns also barred Mexicans from Anglo hotels, barbershops, libraries, and numerous other public establishments.[36] *Are We Good Neighbors?* singled out Ozona, Brady, Fort Stockton, and Midland as towns engaged in such un-American practices as harrying soldiers, even those wearing their uniforms.[37]

Violent encounters involving race verified the degree of contempt some elements of Anglo society entertained towards Mexicans in West Texas after World War II. Three cases of savage violence are salient due to their cruelty and brutality. One occurred in San Angelo, the other two in Sonora. Certainly, they do not approximate the character of violence found in the eastern section of the state where up to World War II white men publicly lynched, dragged, and burned minorities.[38] But the outrage displayed strikingly informs that in some instances Anglo people in West Texas, even after World War II, were as capable of inflicting horrific acts on Mexicans as were Anglos in eastern sections of Texas.

According to Mexican Americans in San Angelo who lived at that time, racism was manifest in the regular harassment and hazing of Mexicans: some in Anglo gangs even saw it as a "sport" to sally into the barrio and taunt Mexicans. For Mexican Americans, these sorties were part of a habitual Anglo impulse to "go over into Mexican town" and "hunt down greasers." Such menacing episodes reached a tragic end on September 1, 1945 (only a few weeks after the ending of WWII) when according to the city's newspaper, some fifteen Anglo kids ranging in age from sixteen to twenty caught up around 1 a.m. with Benigno Aguirre, a 20-year-old ex-soldier, and two of his friends. The three were returning home from a Latin American club and walking down Chadbourne Street, the main route to the south side barrio. Coming upon the three, the white assailants leapt from their pickup and beat Aguirre senseless (his two companions managed to scurry away). Deputies arriving on the scene carried Aguirre to the hospital where he underwent brain surgery; he remained hospitalized and unconscious for some thirty-two days. The Mexican community responded to the atrocity with consternation and protest, but the case passed inconspicuously following punishment of the perpetrators. As a sign of the times, all except for one (who was fined $125) received probated sentences despite the serious accusation of "assault with intent to murder."[39]

Two years later, prejudice in Sonora led to a beating of one Francisco Ramírez, who on the bus from Fort Stockton to Eagle Pass innocently entered the town's bus stop café for a cup of coffee. Three white racists called him out for his transgression of Jim Crow custom and, according to an editorial in the Sonora paper the Devil's River News (September 10, 1947), overtook him at a draw behind the café where he sought escape from his pursuers and where he was:

> ... given a thorough "treatment" which left him lying in the water in the bottom of the draw, his cheekbone smashed, his lips split, his head cut and bruised, a citizens of the United States, half crazed with fear and in a pitiful condition because he happened to be born in the wrong bed, and because he had accepted in good faith the bus company's information that it had a franchise with the café whereby the café agreed to serve food and drink to ALL bus passengers.[40]

Another episode of pathological violence occurred in the same town of Sonora in March 1953. According to newspaper reports and contemporaries who remembered the episode years after, Anglo citizens of that West Texas town murdered 17-year-old Raúl Arevalo and sadistically mutilated his body for a then almost criminal violation: that of courting a local white girl.[41]

Such manifestations of prejudice and discrimination, whether done peacefully or violently, spoke to the pervasive understanding that Mexicans and

Anglos were not to mix socially. In places where race association under normal circumstances would be almost unavoidable, the dilemma was solved through segregation. At downtown theaters, for instance, social custom dictated that Anglos use the main section whereas Mexicans took their place in the balcony.[42] At the public park and the city's swimming pool, local governments made arrangements designed to avoid commingling, perhaps specifying a parcel of the park (or designating a different park altogether) for Mexicans, or stipulating a certain day for Mexicans at the swimming pool (after which the pool would be drained and refilled for white patrons).[43]

Segregation was most overt, of course, in the layout of residential areas, the barrio into the 1950s and 1960s still denoted (by Anglos) as "Little Mexico."[44] It was understood that the place for Mexicans in town and cities was in their own quarter, and the rule was enforced via long-standing custom, consenting civic policy, and implicit agreements among real estate companies that Anglo neighborhoods should be kept white.

The secondary literature records as much. As men with families from neighboring counties (Pecos, Brewster, and Presidio) as well as from Mexico arrived in Midland after World War II seeking work in the oil fields, they settled as per unwritten rules in "Mexican town," that part northeast of the central city in the neighborhood of the De Zavala School. The proscription acknowledged in Marfa during the 1950s applied to almost all West Texas towns: after dark, Mexicans had no business on the white side of town.[45]

Into the 1960s, the belief held that Tejano children should attend the designated "Mexican school." Plain was educators' adamant rationale for such arrangements. They argued that most of those children did not have a good command of the English language. Professionals also contended that Mexican Americans as a group were slow learners. To give them special attention, they opined, was almost impossible in an integrated environment, and, moreover, to do so only hindered the schooling regimen of the Anglo students. Then, entrenched attitudes on race permitted school boards to reject integration. Separating children according to racial or ethnic categorization remained in place even after *Delgado v. Bastrop* (1948), a case in which Judge Ben H. Rice of the United States District Court, Western District of Texas, ruled that the segregation of Mexican American children violated state law; he further directed that the practice be ended.[46]

School board policy of "free choice" buttressed segregation further. This "freedom" allowed Anglo parents to select the school they preferred for their own children, even when their neighborhoods were in proximity to the barrio. Anglo families naturally chose the facilities on the white side of town, leaving the barrio school for Mexican Americans.[47]

According to one report released by Mexican American civil rights activists in 1949, towns in West Texas practicing segregation of Hispanic children included Del Rio, San Angelo, Pecos, Alpine, Sonora, Ozona, Sanderson, and Marathon.[48] Very much an exemplar of the practice after World War II was the Del Rio Independent School District, with its segregated elementary school campuses. North Heights Elementary north of the railroad tracks was for whites only. Mexican American grammar school children, including those in the residential area north of the tracks, were assigned to the southern campus (a compound of four buildings). Both Mexicans and Anglos attended this latter site but were separated nonetheless: Mexicans were taught at two of the structures, together named West End Elementary, while Anglos went to Central Elementary, actually one of the four buildings on that same southern campus. In 1937, the school district built Garfield Elementary to relieve an overloaded West End Central; its location was just across the street from the Mexican West End Elementary. Only in the high school did Mexicans and Anglos come together for their education.[49]

San Angelo maintained three segregated elementary schools after the WWII, two of them with origins in the 1920s: Guadalupe in the Santa Fe barrio and Sam Houston in the south side barrio. As an increasing number of Mexican people moved into the south side of town past Avenue N, the school board in 1950 created Rio Vista School. Fort Concho and Santa Rita elementary schools served white students.[50] In Midland, the Mexican school (named the De Zavala School), established in 1928 for grammar school children, continued as a segregated institution; in the 1950s, the district built an up-to-date structure for De Zavala children but made no move to lift segregation.[51]

In Pecos, grammar schools functioned in compliance with "custom and tradition": Mexican American children attended Earl Bell and West Pecos Elementary. Then, in 1952 the Pecos ISD implemented a new neighborhood zoning plan that impacted junior high school attendance: barrio students would now be enrolled in the predominantly Mexican East Pecos Junior High while all others—regardless of residence—went to Pecos Junior High. According to one report, the student body at East Pecos Junior High a decade later consisted totally of Mexican Americans.[52]

At Alpine as late as the 1960s, the school district had one grammar school intended for Anglos (Central Elementary School) and another for Mexicans

(Centennial Elementary). These were the same teaching grounds that had serviced the city's grammar school population since the early years of the twentieth century; the railroad tracks still stood as the dividing line between the Anglo side of town and the barrio. As common in other parts of West Texas (if not the entire state), facilities and instruction at Centennial Elementary did not measure up to the more favorable learning environment at the Anglo school.[53]

In smaller towns such as Sonora, Ozona, Brady, and Melvin, school separation by race remained commonplace for several years after World War II.[54] So it was also in Marfa where it was understood implicitly, even as the population was overwhelmingly Mexican, that Hispanic students were to attend Blackwell Elementary School.[55] In Sanderson during the early 1950s, the practice was applied to all elementary grades: segregation in grades two through six was based on "achievement grouping."[56] Segregation, as has been indicated previously, was at times not feasible in areas such as Presidio County, where association between whites and Mexicans had been common for decades.[57]

Despite segregation, there were those in the postwar era—like some who attended Mexican schools before them—who found aspects of their education to have merit. Mexican American students at the L. W. Elliott School in Sonora would go on to take genuine pride in attending "La Elliott," as they came to call it. Besides serving as the town's Mexican school, La Elliott acted as a core center that bestowed upon neighboring residents a feeling of attachment that nurtured social, cultural, and family cohesiveness and crystalized community friendships.[58] The same sense of attachment most probably existed in other "Mexican schools." Mexican Americans who attend Marfa's segregated Blackwell Elementary over the years similarly remembered their experience at the school fondly, recalling their accomplishments as students, bandmembers, and athletes.[59]

RACE RELATIONS IN TRANSITION

Winds of change during the 1960s caused open discrimination and enforced segregation to diminish throughout Texas. Numerous causes contributed to the "demise of Jim Crow for Texas-Mexicans," as one author phrased the transformation of race relations between Anglos and Mexicans. Of note were gradual but successful assaults upon Jim Crow from the 1940s and beyond by Mexican American civil rights organizations, mainly the League of United Latin American Citizens (LULAC) and the American GI Forum (AGIF).[60] Their fervent drive paralleled the African American civil rights crusades of the era, ones that produced the passage of the Civil Rights Act of 1964 and the Voting Rights Act of 1965; by extension, these two acts advantaged Mexican Americans. The 1960s indeed portended change for Tejanos: the liberal temper of that age (which produced Lyndon Johnson's Great Society programs) diluted old prejudices as white society grudgingly accepted Mexican Americans as intellectually competent to occupy professional jobs, hold government positions, and practice responsible citizenship. This retreat from bigoted views of Mexicans led to the diminution of segregationist practices throughout West Texas by the latter years of the decade.[61]

SYNCRETISM

Post–World War II modernization swiftly penetrated segregated urbanscapes (as it did all corners of society, among them rural areas), accelerating biculturation. Mass culture exposed Tejanos via schooling, television, English-language radio, movies, newspapers, and other conduits to modern fashion styles, formal ways of speaking English, standard forms of comportment, the idealized Hollywood role model, and other trends unfolding throughout the nation. Contact with Cold War developments excited Mexican Americans—whether still living in the barrio or by the 1960s (with old real estate restrictions abating) having moved to white neighborhoods—about the grand possibilities available for upward mobility and for joining the political establishment.

Increased Americanization highlighted the long-existing presence of the two ethnic strands that had constituted being "Mexican American." But in the era after World War II, biculturation ascended with increased momentum to compete forcefully with "*lo mexicano*."

The Mexican Strand

La colonia mexicana (that is, the wider community of Mexican-origin people, regardless of where they lived in a town) continued to play home to Mexicans, whether they were bicultural or faithful to the old ways. The barrio remained a familiar universe that reaffirmed social belonging, bolstered self-assurance, and tendered moral support. It offered goods, services, and other cultural amenities not ordinarily obtainable in the segregated white part of town. Meeting consumer tastes were grocery stores that acted as counterparts to the chain stores of the day such as the Piggly Wiggly.[62] These food shops tried to please customers by keeping general merchandise but then adding culturally oriented goods: perhaps food products (tripe and chorizo), spices, curative herbs, Spanish-language magazines, or enticements (such as Mexican candy). Supplementing these grocery marts in the enclave were *panaderías* (Mexican bakeries), *tortillerias*, and eateries/diners/cafés. Additionally in *la colonia* were individually owned rooming houses, barbershops, filling stations/garages, cantinas, and dance halls. In Midland during the 1940s, for instance, one Alvino Rodríguez was proprietor of two dance halls; linking the establishments to Rodríguez's heritage was their names: the Cinco de Mayo and Benito Juárez (the latter venue doubled as a movie theater).[63] Inventive entrepreneurs peddled along barrio streets desirables like tamales, watermelon, *raspas* (snow cones), candy, and ice cream. Adding cultural affirmation to barrio life was the presence of *curanderas* and *parteras*; they cared for residents who relied on them due to faith or impoverishment. Residents substituted alternatives for recreational activities denied them by de facto segregationist rules. Instead of the municipal swimming pool, some resorted to having fun at a local canal or even a ditch. A pasture area in the barrio might make do as a park for family outings like, for instance, an Easter picnic.

Institutions such as churches, by their presence and ongoing work, gave the barrio stability and validation. The Catholic Church continued its commitment to new constructions where needed, in towns such as Ozona, Midland, and Brackettville. In Ozona in 1953, the local congregation built Our Lady of Perpetual Help Catholic Church.[64] Parishioners in Midland successfully replaced the old St. George's Church in 1960 with Our Lady of Guadalupe Church; with the new structure in place, St. George's Church was demolished two years after.[65] In Brackettville, Mexican Catholics in 1965 helped the Church establish a new brick structure on Ann Street.[66] Mass in barrio churches was performed in Spanish, at least the homily (the rest of the service was in Latin). Choirs sang hymns in Spanish. Clubs such as the Catholic Youth Organization (CYO) and committees responsible for fundraising, sponsoring of kermises, holding *posadas*, and organizing *fiestas patrias* events conducted their business mostly in Spanish. A mixing of languages commonly occurred in the conducting of these various church affairs as more and more people became bilingual.

Protestant churches were as much a fixture in barrios as were those of Catholics; the examples provided here may be considered as representative of the Protestant presence in both the large and small towns of West Texas. In Midland, the Methodists and Baptists believed it due time to provide services to the growing number of Mexican American followers. The First United Methodist Church assisted in forming El Calvario Methodist Church in 1956. Three years later, the First Baptist Church began a mission and by 1961 Emmanuel Baptist Church had been organized.[67]

Continuing to provide services in San Angelo during the post–WWII era were the Assembly of God Church and the Latin American Methodist Church. The Church of Christ, active in town as of 1946, built its house of praise at 2510 Ben Ficklin Road. Growth within the Mexican Presbyterian Church in town was such that the membership decided to relocate from its Washington Drive address to 313 West Avenue N.[68] In Del Rio persisted Protestant churches whose origins went back to the late nineteenth century. El Principe de Paz Methodist Church, founded in 1878, thrived so much over the course of almost a century that in 1962 it built a new church structure. As for the Primera Iglesia Bautista Mexicana de San Felipe, it had long outgrown the early one-room adobe dwelling that had served it well over the years; during the 1970s, the *iglesia* relocated to a spacious area where it built a church able to accommodate the congregation's growing numbers.[69]

Protestants in some of the smaller towns in West Texas were similarly active in responding to calls from true believers. In Eldorado, where the First Baptist Church (or missionaries from Sonora) had long preached to the Mexican Baptists (at the Mexican School House), Mexican Americans earned their own place of worship in 1947 when the First Baptist Church built a new church house for the duly recognized Mexican Baptist Mission. Through the 1950s and 1960s, Baptist Mission experienced lively growth: in 1957 it built a parsonage (and added to it later) and in 1970 acquired new properties for future plans such as perhaps building a new church. On October 2, 1976, the Mexican Baptist Mission became a church, now named the Primera Iglesia Bautista.[70] In the equally small town of Sanderson, activity among the Mexican Protestants was as brisk. In July 1955, the local pastor, the Reverend Ramón Navarro, supervised the remodeling of the Latin American Methodist Church.[71] The Latin American Methodist Church, which the Reverend Antonio Guillén started during the 1920s, continued in Brady. As of 1950, Reverend Guillén still presided over the church; it was his second time to have served as pastor.[72]

"*Lo mexicano*" persisted within West Texas Tejano urban and rural communities in numerous firmly embedded practices and cultural expressions. "Mexicanness" was manifest in the popularity of *bailes* wherein guests danced to accordion-led conjunto music, or into the 1950s (and beyond) that of *orquestas*.

This latter ensemble combined Mexican-based *ranchero* music with the professional, big-band sound that some *orquestra* leaders and members of their group had learned while playing with junior high or high school orchestras.[73] Dances might be held at a platform someone had built on their empty property or on one of the barrio's streets, but, when possible, in a hall rented from some willing Anglo entrepreneur. These festive occasions might celebrate a young woman's coming of age (a *quinceañera*), a high school graduation, a wedding, or a special date or anniversary. Ambitious Mexican Americans might stage for-profit dances to meet demand by fellow citizens wishing to socialize with friends, relax after a stressful work schedule, enjoy the featured music, or simply delight in the gala.

Retained in Mexican-origin communities was the respectful custom of christening infants, at least into the 1960s, with customary Spanish names. It does appear, however, that by then older names common among pre–World War II immigrants had lost their appeal. Few newborns were christened Cirildo, Espiridión, Epifanio, Pascual, Jovita, Eulalia, Consuelo, Carlota, or other once favored names.

Segments within the barrio population still trusted self-help societies. In Presidio, locals with patriotic sentiments toward Mexico organized the Comité Auxiliar Mexicano (CAM). The organization's goal was to enhance the rights and freedoms of Mexican-origin residents and to perpetuate the kinship many retained for the motherland.[74] Indeed, patriotic loyalty to Mexico remained intense among those within the *colonia Mexicana* who still felt a patriotic affinity to their land of origin or who at least retained loyalty to the culture of their forebears. Ties between West Texas Hispanic populations and officials in Mexico were evident in the endurance of the *comisiones honoríficas* which into the 1960s coordinated the *fiestas patrias* observations with representatives from Mexico. Obviously, the fiestas were holdovers from the nineteenth century and have persisted even until modern times.

In San Angelo, commemorations of Mexico's national holidays reached their apex in the 1950s and 1960s, due largely to unrelenting efforts by Estanislado Sedeño and compatriots. The Cinco de Mayo and Diez y Seis celebrations, which covered two or three days, were held in what people came to call Sedeño Plaza, a spacious lot extending out from the front of the family home. The festivities at the Plaza on Avenue N featured patriotic speeches, *puestos* (booths) offering an assortment of foods and games, music and dancing, and general socializing and merriment. Expanding the event beyond what other West Texas communities might stage, Sedeño and his committee invited the city to be part of the observations. Each year, a motorcade of people departed from Sedeño Plaza and headed toward City Hall. There, officials greeted the group excitedly, welcoming it with warm speeches and words of support for their continued tribute.[75]

A miscellany of other entertainment activities connected Mexican Americans to the culture and heritage of Mexico. By the postwar period, several West Texas towns featured a theater that catered to a Tejano clientele. This might be a movie house on the edge of the downtown district or an open-air *cine* (such a drive-in might be owned and/or managed by some enterprising Mexican American businessperson) showing the latest films made in Mexico. Films and movie stars of the 1950s and 1960s were popular in West Texas communities and throughout the state of Texas, as they were in Mexico. West Texas Mexicans were eager to view these productions, then part of Mexico's Época de Oro del Cine Mexicano. This Golden Age of Mexican Cinema actually spanned the years from about the mid-1930s to the late 1950s, but the movies associated with it continued circulating (and being viewed) in US cities long past that era. Moviegoers flocked to see the famous film artists of the age: Jorge Negrete, Pedro Infante, María Félix, and comedians Mario Moreno (Cantinflas) and Germán Valdés (Tin Tan).[76]

Mexican Americans further kept abreast of the latest music developments in Mexico. By the 1950s (and in some cases, going back to the 1930s), it was not uncommon in many West Texas towns such as San Angelo, Midland, Odessa, Kermit, and Pecos for radio stations to allot Mexican American announcers daily or weekly spots for entertaining Spanish-speaking listeners, conveying general information to them, and advertising services and consumer products. In Odessa as of 1952, Salvador Guerrero hosted three Spanish-language programs at KRIG: "Madrugada Tejana" (Early Dawn Over Texas), "Merienda Musical" (Musical Luncheon), and "Ritmo Latino" (Latin Rhythm). Delivered thus to homes or car radio listeners during the 1950s and 1960s were songs written and performed in Mexico by José Alfredo Jiménez and Armando Manzanero, among others. Throughout the state, said music was then reinterpreted by Mexican American *charro* groups or by *conjuntos* and played—alongside Texas-Mexican favorites—at lively venues held at local dance halls.[77]

Mexican Americans adjusted American leisure forms to accommodate ethnic (bicultural) preferences. Sunday *béisbol* popular in many West Texas towns, for one, brought afternoon excitement to local fans. Coaches or managers assembled teams from working-class young men or older adults with a passion for the game. Such all-Mexican *equipos* (teams) might play in some sort of organized city league and compete with all-white or all-Black baseball outfits. Functioning as the baseball diamond in that postwar era might be an area cleared for Sunday competition: perhaps a pasture on some rancher's land (used with the owner's permission), a large city lot (acquired with the consent of local officials), or land rented for the contest. In San Angelo by the 1960s, the games were aired live on the local Spanish-language radio station KTXL.

Similarly, Tejano golf enthusiasts established semi-private clubs; seclusion from Anglo competitors let players engage in ethnic joking, mocking, and lampooning fellow teammates, or simply bonding with them. In San Angelo, golfers organized during the 1960s the Pan American Golf Association (PAGA). Members played the game in an area located on the outskirts of town, away from the municipal golf course and the several other private links, such as those of the Country Club. Not all Mexican Americans belonged to the PAGA, so that there were those who opted for play at the city park.

At a more private level, people found amusement in games rooted in old Mexico. Families delighted in playing the popular Mexican version of bingo. At children's parties, parents ensured there would be a piñata stuffed with candy for the young revelers' delight. Adolescents engaged in the game of *canicas* (marbles). Perhaps in one of the players' backyard or some area cleared for the purpose, the competitors sought to win over as many marbles as possible, jealously hoarding their winnings until the next contest with their buddies.

Nothing evidenced more saliently the ties Mexican Americans had to their Mexican heritage than Spanish; its use remained strong wherever in West Texas they resided. In practice, Mexican Americans spoke different variations of the language. Few actually communicated in formal Spanish; only a small percentage of people in the community had received language instruction in Mexico and, except in high schools, practically no facilities existed in West Texas to teach Spanish in its more formal style. The majority of people spoke what grammarians might call "Tex-Mex"—that is, the Hispanicizing of English words and integrating them into Spanish discourse. This method of speaking increased after World War II as the Spanish imported by the pre–World War II immigrants gradually lost its sway and the younger set, now impacted by increased schooling and acculturation, relied on English vocabulary terms they thought favorable to Spanish or found useful as substitutes to Spanish words that succumbed to acculturation.

Also existing in Spanish-speaking settlements was the presence of an argot, a slang called *caló* that was incorporated into the Spanish lexicon and employed by younger men in peer-group dialogue. No one knows with certainty the exact origin or dates of this mode of speaking; some find its source in El Paso, Texas, others in Tucson, Arizona, and others in Los Angeles, California. After World War II and extending into its dilution (probably by the 1970s), this creative version of Spanish involved the invention of new words and wordplay and a unique style of expression or delivery.[78]

The American Strand

Among an expanding element within Tejano society in the post–World War II period stood alongside "*lo español*" (that is, with a Hispanic ethnicity) an increased trend towards acculturation. Not that people during this time jettisoned their long-existing ties to "*lo mexicano*," only that "*lo americano*" assumed a more robust place than in earlier eras. A bicultural/bilingual identity now came to characterize being Mexican in the West Texas borderlands.

Numerous forces accelerated the pace of acculturation, a process in elaboration since the nineteenth century. Obvious would have been the changing times as Mexican Americans adjusted, along with the rest of the US population, to the postwar milieu. As of 1960 according to census data, 86 percent of Tejanos were US born and, by that time, most knew only the United States as their home (and probably the only nation people arriving from Mexico wanted to call their country). It was to the US most owed allegiance unequivocally—as exemplified in their participation in the Korean and Vietnam Wars. The new order of the fifties and sixties, then, was not being rejected, nor did Mexican Americans object to it.[79] Increased schooling after the war and continuing thereafter furthered the process of biculturation. Present by then were institutions, programs, and a flow of events allowing Mexican Americans to improve their educational situation and thereby become more engaged and involved citizens.

Among the institutions of education advancing acculturation were parochial schools. The present scholarship does not reveal much about such learning centers in West Texas towns—if they existed to any extent, they would have resembled San Angelo's St. Mary's Parochial School located on Avenue N, adjacent to St. Mary's Church in the south barrio. When originally founded in the late 1930s, instruction there was under the Sisters of Charity of the Incarnate Word, although with time the parish hired lay teachers. The curriculum combined traditional secular subjects with religious instruction. The student body consisted mainly, if not entirely, of Mexican American children; it would be presumed that it took great sacrifice on the part of some families to afford tuition. The school was successful enough through the 1950s that in 1960 the parish financed a new brick building. The high expense of keeping up St. Mary's Parochial School got to be overwhelming, however, and the parish-financed institution closed its doors in 1970.[80]

School programs financed by government acted as another agent hastening Mexican American integration into West Texas mainstream society. Among those government-sponsored initiatives was the Preschool Instruction Program. Its forerunner was the "Little School of the 400," an educational project initially developed by Felix Tijerina of Houston and funded by the Texas Legislature in 1959. Little is known of the program as it existed in West Texas, although there is evidence that the Little School of the 400 as of 1958 was present in Fort Stockton, where Mrs. Terry Barrera was the teacher.[81] Then there was the federally funded Head Start program, created by Congress in the mid-1960s and administered by many communities across the state.

None of these educational ventures intending to improve literacy and to prepare disadvantaged youths for success during the post–WWII years matched the public schools in influencing Mexican American culture and identity. As throughout the state, Mexican Americans unprecedentedly began going to local (barrio) schools during the 1950s, and their enrollment increased into the 1960s. By then, parents took it for granted that their children should at least acquire a high school diploma. It appeared a greater possibility by mid-century to do so as most high schools were being racially integrated.

Writings on West Texas Mexican Americans make only sporadic references to high school attendance. But it is most certain that the record of high school presence and participation in campus activities in other West Texas towns reflected student experiences similar to those in San Angelo. Student prominence at San Angelo's Central High School during the postwar years was conspicuous on several fronts. In 1958, twenty-three of the 301 Central High School graduates in town were of Mexican descent. The impact of the Mexican American presence at Central that year was such that the student body elected Wilma Figueroa Homecoming Queen. Then, there were the sports standouts. During the 1950s and 1960s, several Mexican American athletes gained distinction at Central for their competitive prowess, namely as basketball and football players. Some went on to continue their careers at the college level.[82]

The student presence in high school by the 1950s was such that it produced an epic chapter in San Angelo's Mexican American history. For some years, it had been a tradition for high school seniors to stage at the Country Club what was casually called the German Dance, a prom to celebrate their upcoming graduation. Made confident by their increased presence in high school (and the election of Figueroa as Homecoming Queen), some of the Hispanic students stepped forward to purchase tickets to the gala. Organizers rebuffed them, declaring that the German Dance was exclusively for white people and that, in any event, the Country Club did not allow Mexicans on their grounds (except as caddies)—or African Americans, for that matter.

The affront prompted parents of the Mexican American graduates to initiate plans for what subsequently came to be called the Mexican American Senior Dance, or Mexican American Senior Prom. The first celebration (in 1959) was held at the Town House Hotel but thereafter moved to the San Angelo Coliseum. It developed into a grand display of consummate achievement, featuring all the pomp and circumstance of a formal ball. For the rest of the century, if not beyond, organizers (the students themselves) produced an extravaganza that included a specially-invited speaker (sometimes an accomplished alumnus), a master of ceremonies who recognized student achievements as the graduates entered the floor accompanied by their parents, and a segment allowing organizations and groups to grant scholarships to worthy recipients. The formal phase of the prom ended with a dance, with music provided by a distinguished band sufficiently versatile to play both Mexican and American music.[83] In later years, students from Lakeview High School would be welcomed into the celebration.

The school experience for Mexican American children at a time of integration only nominally resembled olden days when Mexicans were segregated by intention and design, unwelcome in class, considered as second-class citizens, and thought unworthy of an education beyond the primary grades. As had others before them, several by the 1950s reflected pleasurably on their high school years, some expressing gratitude toward particular teachers who had influenced their lives. Such was the case for Yolanda Esqueda Smith, who along with her siblings attended the Sanderson, Texas, schools and continued into the integrated high school. In her remembrances, she singled out teachers who were fair to their Mexican American students. "One teacher was Mrs. Savage. She was a superb person who brought out the best in her students." Esqueda Smith believed Mrs. Savage to be dedicated to the job and came to increasingly admire her as the years passed. Also remembered fondly was Mr. Norman Rath. "He was a very considerate, compassionate person," both as the principal and the basketball coach, Esqueda Smith noted.[84] At Blackwell Elementary School in Marfa, where students tried to learn under less-than-ideal conditions, students would long remember teachers such as Willie Harper, Mildred Shannon, Evelyn Davis, and others who taught them with devotion and dedication.[85]

At the same time, the potential for attending college no longer seemed improbable. In fact, by the 1950s and most certainly by the 1960s acquiring a university education had become a goal of many determined high school graduates. Excited by their children's accomplishments, parents willingly accepted sacrifices to see their loved ones achieve something that had been well-nigh unthinkable for them. Enhancing prospects for underprivileged Americans by the 1960s was assistance from the federal government in the form of subsidies, among them Pell Grants. The government provided benefits for veterans, helping with tuition expenses and monthly living allowances.

Accessible in West Texas during this period were Sul Ross State College in Alpine and San Angelo Junior College in San Angelo. By the early 1960s and certainly by the latter years of that decade, Mexican Americans had become a small but distinguishable component of the student population on both campuses. A legislative act in 1965 elevated San Angelo Junior College to a four-year institution; two years later, Mexican Americans were among those in San Angelo College's (SAC) first graduating class. From that small corps of Mexican Americans attending SAC, Angelo State University (as the legislature officially named it in 1969) by 2010 had become a Hispanic Serving Institute with more than 25 percent of a 10,000-student population being Latino.

A BICULTURAL GENERATION

At the mid-twentieth century mark, *lo americano* was demonstrable in a Tejano readiness to accept more of the broader society's cultural preferences, offerings, and tastes. By then, the growing tendency among an Americanized generation of Mexican Americans was to have Catholic Mass (or Protestant church services) conducted either in English or celebrated in a bilingual manner. Americanization was equally pronounced during that era in Tejano West Texans' mounting appetite for hearing (and dancing to) rock 'n' roll music. Baby Boomers in particular shared English-language radio listening with time spent tuned to Spanish-language radio stations. The greater exposure to English words caused a trend, as noted earlier, towards code-switching—a language practice in which speakers substituted English words for Spanish terms, or vice versa. Then there was a desire to conform in the realm of fashion, so that West Texas Tejanos embraced the era's modish dress wear and hairstyling. Mexican American girls sought to fit in by wearing their hair in ponytails and donning the poodle skirts of the 1950s and the miniskirts of the following decade. Young men in high school, throughout the state and country, during the 1950s and into the early days of the 1960s sported the ducktail hairdo of the time and attempted the accentuation of their cool look with heavily starched blue jeans.

English-language newspapers supplanted the Spanish-language print medium as a preferred news source. At the state level, fewer Mexicans by the mid-1950s were reading *La Prensa* of San Antonio (founded in 1913), a downtrend the editors attributed to younger people being able to read English.[86] When in April 1961, Juan Rivera Jr. of Presidio (ever a predominantly Spanish-speaking town) announced he would assume management of the newspaper *The International*, he renamed it *The Presidio Voice*. "It would be same paper as *The International* and was to remain apolitical to boost Presidio's climate," he announced, and would "fight vandalism, communism, and general delinquency and carry the motto 'Truth will Prevail.'"[87] Border residents, however, continued to have access to Spanish-language newspapers from Mexico and other parts of the Big Bend.

Mutualistas and fraternal societies no longer maintained their pre–World War II standing. People certainly harbored altruistic outlooks, but the movement by the 1950s was to join mainstream service organizations or fraternal orders. Because established fellowship groups such as the Lions Clubs International and the Rotary International in the postwar era continued to display a reluctance to integrate, Mexican Americans in some towns founded their own service clubs. These parallel units, while segregated, nonetheless functioned to offer services equivalent to those of the local Anglo-dominant Internationals. Leading these emerging Hispanic organizations were usually members of a cohort that some historians identify as the GI Generation: that is, they were veterans of either World War II or the Korean conflict or belonged to a civilian corps imbued with the anti-communist, pro-democratic and pro-capitalist values of the Cold War. In Marfa, one history of Presidio County contains the following information for 1954: "Hector Valdes was chosen to head the Lions Club for the coming year. E. D. Segura of Marfa was awarded the Order of St. Gregory the Great by Pope Pius XII for his many years of outstanding work in both civic and church affairs."[88]

In Midland and San Angelo, those responsible for the establishment of their respective Lions Clubs were men whose feelings about serving humankind were generally shaped by either their war experience or the democratic ideals of the 1940s and 1950s. In Midland, when Mexican Americans founded the East Side Lions Club in 1956—then a separate club existing alongside five or six already active Lions Clubs—they chose Ciro Sánchez, a World War II veteran, as the club's first president.[89] San Angelo Mexican Americans, led by cohorts of the World War II era, organized the Southside Lions Club in 1959 and soon after gained a reputation as a most active group assisting the Lions International to undertake blood drives, support programs for children in need of physical therapy treatments, and fund efforts to help youngsters experiencing poor eyesight.[90]

An Expanding Professional Corps

Revised attitudes about the "place" of Mexicans, better educational opportunities, ongoing acculturation, and Mexican American resourcefulness in exploiting the changes underway in the quarter century after World War II collectively augured well for social, economic, and political improvement within Tejano communities. Scholars point out that by 1970 the proportion of Texas Mexicans working in white-collar occupations was somewhere between 30 percent and 40 percent—a discernible (albeit still unsatisfactory) advancement from the 90 percent listed in 1930 as constituting a proletarian group.[91]

Perhaps this statewide progression did not generally extend to Texas Mexicans of the Edwards Plateau and Trans-Pecos. But it should have, since over the decades there had grown an identifiable middle class comprised of restaurateurs, merchants, and other commercial and business types who earned their livelihood serving poorer members of the community. Further, more men and women after World War II entered professional capacities, indicating that headway into white-collar positions was not a divergence from Tejano upward mobility in the rest of the state. Indeed, privately printed family memoirs and personal family albums as well as county histories that feature family profiles and biographies are replete with stories of Mexican Americans who achieved incredible successes that once upon a time were almost impossible for them. These West Texas accounts list Hispanics as being high-ranking military figures, scientists, physicians, college administrators, corporate leaders, attorneys, accomplished politicians, real estate agents, newspaper editors, influential law enforcement officials, and much more.

The existing literature, furthermore, points up several standout individuals whose successes exemplify the advances West Texas Mexican Americans made in the professional sphere. They are spotlighted here due in part to the singular reputations they established, to their legacy, and—in the considered judgment of writers—to the role they played in the making of their respective communities. Certainly, there are many more notables whose place in history is yet to be recovered.

In 1950 and extending into 1953, Noé Lara Camúñez assumed the duties of principal at Sam Houston Elementary School in San Angelo's south side barrio. Descended from one of the town's Mexican American first families (he was brother to Eva Camúñez), he had—in pursuit of a career as a schoolteacher—first attended San Angelo Junior College (1936), then Sul Ross State Teachers College (1937), and finally Southwest Texas Teachers College in San Marcos where he graduated in 1940. Following service in World War II, Camúñez accepted a teaching post in Del Rio, where he lived from 1946 to 1949. He then enrolled at the University of Texas and within the year returned to his hometown to assume the job of principal at Sam Houston Elementary.

While in San Angelo, Camúñez became well known and respected for his commitment to education, for his proud display of being Mexican American, and for his participation in community affairs. Determined to develop closer ties with his students and the barrio, he recruited two Mexican American teachers (one of them his wife) and reached out to parents through house visits. Such contact allowed him not only to consult with families as to their children's progress but to offer them information with which they could gain access to health care and government assistance. Attentive to his students' bicultural character, he got them involved in *fiestas patrias* celebrations at school and at the wider observances held at Sedeño Plaza. While remaining focused on his school duties, Camúñez did not forego commitments he felt professionals owed to the broader society. In 1952, at the invitation of the membership, he joined San Angelo's Human Relations Committee, whose mission it was to guard against discrimination against Mexican Americans. Also, he undertook work with the Tom Green County Tuberculosis Association.

His success in San Angelo was such that outside opportunities soon beckoned, and in 1953 he left to assume new responsibilities in San Antonio. His accomplishments as an effective administrator won him a promotion in 1960 to J. T. Brackenridge, one of the largest elementary schools in the state, and brought him a plethora of awards and citations of merit during the rest of the decade. In San Angelo, he is remembered as a caring educator and iconic role model. In 1988, the San Angelo Independent School District dedicated the library at Fort Concho Elementary School in honor of Noé Lara Camúñez.[92]

Another educator prominent during the years after World War II was Lucía Rede Madrid, a teacher in Redford, Texas. She was sister to Lucy Rede Franco, mentioned earlier as having been the first Mexican American to have enrolled at Sul Ross State College (1920). A high school graduate from her hometown of Marfa, Lucía Rede Madrid enrolled at Sul Ross Teachers College in 1932, receiving teacher certification in 1937 and acquiring employment at various border settlements before moving to Ballinger to teach in the Mexican school. Upon marriage in 1941, she moved to Redford where her husband oversaw the Madrid family lands and managed their grocery store. At the same time as she raised her family, she continued her education, enrolling during summers at Sul Ross State College in pursuit of a master's degree, which she acquired in 1965. Around 1955, she resumed her career teaching at the local school in Redford.

Conditions during the 1950s at Redford were less than satisfactory as the school owned no books, a problem common in remote areas of West Texas. Matters called for improvisation, prompting Madrid to check out books for students from distant Marfa (eighty miles away), the headquarters for the Independent School District to which Redford belonged. Fortuitous in improving circumstances at Redford was the establishment in 1965 of the national Project Head Start program, in which during the summers Madrid found work. Still disadvantaged by a dearth of teaching resources, she introduced an approach to the local Head Start program that in time came to be likened to the Montessori Method. She led children in free explorations of the local geophysical environment. Outside activity gave students space and freedom to be inventive; the outdoors encouraged them to apply both mind and body to the learning process. Using reed stems gathered at riverbeds, youngsters constructed designs obtained from their own imagination. Rocks with words scribbled on them served to expand vocabulary (both in English and Spanish). Other objects of the outdoors allowed eager learners to craft toys and various playthings. The approach to learning soon attracted interest (and kudos) from elementary school teachers in West Texas and beyond.

More fame (and greater acclaim) would come to Mrs. Madrid after her retirement in 1978. To fill the absence of a library in her hometown, she started in 1979 to assemble, through donations, what would act as a depository to receive, store, and make available books for circulation. People learning of her ongoing acquisition project, originally housed at her husband's grocery store, donated works to the extent that by the late 1980s the Redford library stocked some 12,000 volumes. In recognition of her incredible achievement, Governor Bill Clements in 1990 inducted Madrid into Texas Women's Hall of Fame. That same year President George H. W. Bush bestowed upon her the silver medallion of the President's Volunteer Service Award. Other honors and recognitions followed.[93]

During the 1950s and continuing into the 1970s, educational inequality in Alpine drew Pete Gallego into political activism. His family had long-standing residence in town, having moved there during the 1930s. Pete received his public-school education in Alpine, then entered military service during World War II. Upon war's end, he enrolled at Sul Ross State Teachers College, graduating in 1949 with a BBA degree.

While a successful Alpine businessman in his own right—working in the family's Green Café (now called Gallego's Mexican Restaurant)—he was concerned that the system of education in town during the 1950s did not prepare Mexican American children for achieving social mobility. Specifically, he worried that education at Centennial (the "Mexican school") lagged behind that at Central Ward, the Anglo elementary school. In an effort to address the disparity and improve conditions at Centennial, he ran for the school board and won election in 1959, continuing in his position until 1974. Unsuccessful for the next few years in bringing about appreciable improvement for Mexican American students, he aligned himself with the venture underway throughout the state in the latter 1960s to end the practice of segregation in most elementary schools. In the fall of 1969, he led other Alpine activists in a campaign to desegregate Centennial, seeing it to success in 1969 (this episode is discussed further below). Contemporaneously, he joined legal efforts, which he continued into the early 1970s, to desegregate school systems in other parts of West Texas.[94] His legacy rests on the historical accomplishments he brought about in Alpine and on the work of his children, who continued laboring for the betterment of the Mexican American community. Pete Gallego Jr., who served as state legislator for District 74 from 1991 to 2012 and subsequently as US representative for Texas's 23rd congressional district (2013–2015), won appointment as president of Sul Ross State University in 2020.[95]

Another West Texan well known for his civic activism and advocacy for better Mexican American schooling during the 1950s and 1960s was Pete Terrazas. A native to Fort Stockton, he left home in 1949 for St. Mary's University in San Antonio in pursuit of a degree in business administration. Upon his return to town, he promptly moved to establish himself as an independent business owner, prospering for the next two decades. As of 1954 he ran a successful accounting and tax office; in 1955 he started a drivers' license school for Spanish speakers and in 1956 he founded Terrazas Furniture at 106 North Main, expanding the store to Pecos in 1964. At the same time, he earned a reputation around Fort Stockton as a voice for Mexican Americans demanding news, information, and features to be broadcast in Spanish. Between 1954 and 1970 he served as master of ceremonies and program director of Spanish-language programs at KFST radio station and between 1967 and 1968 was MC and program director of the Spanish variety program at KVKM-TV in Monahans, Texas.

Terrazas's importance in Fort Stockton history rests on his civic, social, and political attainments. During the decades of the 1950s and continuing into the 1960s he held membership in the Lions Club, the Chamber of Commerce, and the Pan American Association; he served as director in the Lions Club and in the Pan American Association as chairman. As to his political involvement, he won distinction in the 1950s for his tenure as president of the local LULAC council and between 1954 and 1955 for being named outstanding LULAC of the National Organization, an honor that recognized his "meritorious" service. In a major achievement, he gained election to the Fort Stockton City Council in 1955, the first Mexican American to win a seat in that body, continuing in that capacity until 1963. Education was a subject of serious concern to him: to that end, he helped the school system in 1965 to develop preschool education courses and in 1968 to improve adult education and GED classes. Also in 1968, Terrazas served as a member of the Advisory Committee of Vocational Educational Program. In 1970, he won election to the Fort Stockton Independent School District and for years following was president of the school board.[96]

POST–WORLD WAR II POLITICS, 1945–1970

Community efforts led by individuals such as Pete Gallego and Pete Terrazas were part of the civic and political activism that engaged Mexican Americans in Texas during the post–World War II era. The wellsprings of this postwar political momentum have been traced to numerous sources, among them the growth from the 1940s through the 1960s of the earlier referenced Mexican American middle class. Spurring the collective commitment of this cohort of professionals and white-collar workers were increased levels of education, the effects of urbanization and consumerism, and, of course, biculturation.[97]

In reality, it need not have taken forces particular to post-1945 to mobilize Mexican Americans politically. Long residence in the state could in and of itself have fostered increased politicization, incentivizing leaders to organize communities and confront issues of injustice. As much occurred in Melvin, Texas, in McCulloch County.

Melvin, despite its isolation and size, had in its *colonia* a group of involved individuals headed by Señor Rafael Riojas, an established merchant in town and president of La Asociación de Padres y Maestros Latino Americana (LAPTA). In 1944, on a trip to San Antonio, Señor Riojas visited with M. C. Gonzales, State Chairman of the Spanish-speaking PTA and the National Executive Secretary of LULAC, to see if he could assist with ending school segregation in Melvin. In October, Mr. Riojas wrote (speaking for the LAPTA) to Mr. Gonzales and to Alonso Perales, the well-known spokespersons then examining cases of discrimination against Tejanos, apprising them of the restrictions on Mexican children at La Escuela Latino-Americana, i.e., the Mexican grammar school, and the dreadful physical condition of the building in which they studied. Gonzales contacted Dr. L. A. Woods, State Superintendent of Public Instruction. In January 1945, Woods directed Dr. Joseph R. Griggs, Director of Supervision, Department of Education, to visit Melvin and investigate affairs there. Griggs indeed found conditions in town to be as dire as described by Riojas and recommended that Melvin school officials take immediate action to address LAPTA's complaints. School trustees swiftly promised to make improvements in the Mexican school and, as a further concession, would permit with the start of the 1945–1946 academic year the enrollment of Mexican American students of the sixth and seventh grades to the main public (Anglo) school.

But Riojas and Latin American PTA rejected such a solution in March 1945, noting that segregation would still exist in the primary school; they wished for the children to be enrolled in the Anglo school starting in the fourth grade (as was done in neighboring Brady) so they could lose their fears of Anglo intimidation and be able to learn English at an earlier age.

Notwithstanding the protests, the school board had its way: it permitted sixth and seventh graders only to enroll at the Anglo school for the 1945–1946 year. Ultimately, it was the court ruling in *Delgado v. Bastrop* (1948) that ended segregation in Melvin—and brought satisfaction to the Mexican American community. For the 1948–1949 year, the MISD allowed fourth and fifth graders to transfer to the main campus. The existence of the Melvin Mexican School ended in the school year of 1949–1950. The first grade was kept there for one year, however, but then moved to the main Anglo campus where a separate room was designated for these children.[98] Overshadowing most drives toward school integration, however, were ones led by LULAC and the American GI Forum, both of which expanded their outreach beyond the cities to address Mexican American grievances in the more rural sections of the state.

Although LULAC in the postwar years continued its statewide commitments to improving the well-being of Tejanos, little has been written about its activities in West Texas. From what can be learned from the scholarship written on San Angelo's LULAC Council 152 (chartered in 1948), however, members undertook investigations of discrimination in public places, such as in restaurants and theaters, as well as in city-maintained facilities like the municipal swimming pool. The organization complained about such unfair practices to the Good Neighbor Commission in Austin and to officials in Mexico. Members also condemned inequalities in the city's public schools, especially at Sam Houston Elementary where the school board continued to neglect the deplorable and unsanitary condition of the school's latrines. School programs generally overlooked Sam Houston students, LULAC disclosed, for they were left out of participation in the Little Olympics. By the early 1950s, however, Council 152's determination to bring improvements to the San Angeleño community passed into a period of quiescence.[99]

More is known of the AGIF's work on behalf of West Texas Tejanos for the era between 1945 and 1970. The forum appeared in South Texas during the late 1940s as a group intended to help veterans, but it soon found itself drawn into the politics of that region. In West Texas, civic activists by the mid-1950s (and in some places even earlier) had founded AGIF chapters in Del Rio, San Angelo, Odessa, Midland, Pecos, and various other towns.[100] The AGIF's involvement in West Texas reached such a point of public notice that during the years of the 1950s and 1960s it distracted from the work led by related organizations such as LULAC.

Local chapters aimed to improve community life through various efforts. They looked into instances of discrimination, segregation, and prejudice. In cities like San Angelo and Odessa during the 1950s, local forum members appealed to city officials for better public utility services and for other necessities basic to decent standards of life. As well, AGIF members undertook poll tax drives and launched barrio campaigns to persuade people to use the vote as an avenue that would end in social, economic, and political betterment. The AGIF in the two cities earned community support for the concern it showed for poverty-stricken families in the barrio. Assisting in the pursuit of these AGIF objectives were a Ladies Auxiliary and the Junior GI Forum. The latter's activities included raising money through raffles, golf tournaments, and dances for the purpose of granting scholarships and aiding neighborhood residents facing financial distress or needing hospital care.[101]

In San Angelo, AGIF activism reached a heyday during the early years of the 1960s. The chapter placed emphasis on the need to purchase the poll tax, approached businesses about discriminatory practices, and reminded officials of the city's neglect of street conditions and poor lighting on the Mexican side of town. AGIF members wrote letters to the local newspaper denouncing racism and acts of discrimination.[102] Statewide, the AGIF took the lead to end the prevailing policy of separate schools for Anglos and Mexicans. Specific to West Texas, the AGIF in 1949 (as indicated above) reported the existence of school segregation in several West Texas towns, among them Del Rio, San Angelo, Pecos, Alpine, Sonora, Ozona, Sanderson, and Marathon.[103]

In early 1949, Cristóbal P. Aldrete, an AGIF member, charged the Del Rio ISD (DRISD) with practicing segregation in the elementary schools. As noted earlier in this chapter, the district assigned Mexican American students to West End Elementary and to Garfield Elementary while Anglos attended North Heights Elementary. To assess Aldrete's accusations, State Superintendent Dr. L. A. Woods dispatched his assistant Terrell M. Trimble to Del Rio. Trimble reported the situation to be as the AGIF described it. Woods acted expeditiously and lifted state accreditation from the DRISD. Predictably, the school system appealed the ruling to the State Board of Education and in its judgment, the State Board decided that segregation was no longer an issue in light of the DRISD's newly implemented policy of "free choice."[104]

Desegregation did not come to Del Rio until August 1971. The moving force there was the federal courts, however, not the AGIF. The catalyst for federal intervention was the perpetual dispute between the DRISD and the San Felipe ISD (SFISD) over which should rightfully collect revenue due them from the presence of Laughlin AFB. The base stood closer to SFISD but the children of military personnel went to DRISD schools; student enrollment proved a boon to DRISD as it benefited from the income Anglo attendance yielded. The question of federal monies (the SFISD felt it had a stronger right to it since the base was closer to it) led William Wayne Justice of the Federal District Court in Tyler to intervene, and in part his solution to the money question desegregated Del Rio.

Judge Justice, as part of the far-reaching *United States v. The State of Texas* (which extended to all Texas school districts), ordered the DRISD and the SFISD to consolidate under a detailed desegregation plan he formulated. The entire community would now be governed by one school district, to be called San Felipe-Del Rio Consolidated Independent School District (SFDRCISD). The judge was precise to ensure that full integration would result at every level: all students would attend some grades in the Mexican part of town and while others would go to schools situated in the Anglo section of Del Rio. He directed:

> Kindergartners were to meet at Houston Elementary; first and second grades at Travis and Austin Elementaries; and third through sixth grades at Garfield Elementary, North Heights Elementary, and Memorial Middle School. The seventh and eighth graders were to meet at the Del Rio Junior High; the ninth graders at the old San Felipe High, and the rest of the high school grades, tenth through twelfth, at Del Rio High.[105]

For the most part, however, the AGIF was behind several West Texas school desegregation campaigns during the 1950s and 1960s. In 1952, it (alongside LULAC) intervened in Pecos ISD's contesting the district's newly implemented zoning plan. The two organizations argued on behalf of local complainants that the proposal (previously discussed) established residential segregation in the junior high schools, making East Pecos Junior High predominantly Mexican and Pecos Junior High mainly Anglo. The AGIF and LULAC also took notice of the segregated elementary schools and thus demanded the school system integrate them so that Mexican American students at Earl Bell and West Pecos Elementary could enjoy the facilities available at the Anglo elementary school. Both organizations assailed the system for its "free choice" option, urging board members to repeal the selection as it permitted Anglos to pick their preferred school. The parents' protest came to no avail, however, as in 1954 Commissioner of Education J. W. Edgar and the State Board of Education accepted the Pecos zoning plan, noting that it had no discriminatory intent.

But then in 1968, a new organization named the Mexican American Legal Defense and Education Fund (MALDEF) took up the case as part of a wider mission to review related instances of school segregation throughout Texas and elsewhere. Representing the Pecos Mexican American community, MALDEF in 1971 reached agreement with school officials on a mutually acceptable plan for desegregation, threatening litigation if the district did not comply with the settlement.[106] The AGIF and LULAC investigated other cases of school segregation in West Texas, although only in Sonora did the AGIF and MALDEF play an advocacy role. In Alpine, local organizers took up their own campaign for educational equality. In Marfa, segregation ended by general consent.

In Sonora, the AGIF partnered with the Mexican American community in addressing allegations of school segregation, although ultimately it was the intervention of the Justice Department and MALDEF that ended the status quo. The Justice Department entered the case in May 1969, making it the "first time," scholars note, "that the Justice Department had filed intervention in behalf of Mexican Americans." But the Justice Department's interest in the matter soon subsided, and in December 1969, Isael Pérez, Victoriano Chávez, Santos Hernández, and Eugenio González, assisted by MALDEF, filed suit on behalf of students at L. W. Elliott Elementary School. In the case of *Perez, et al. v. Sonora Independent School District, the Board of Trustees of the Sonora ISD, et al.* (June 30, 1970), school officials consented to an agreement with MALDEF to end segregation in the Sonora ISD (as indicated above, MALDEF negotiated a similar accord in 1971 with the Pecos school district). With integration achieved, Mexican American students enrolled at the Sonora Elementary School. "La Elliott" gradually fell victim to time, the building sinking into disrepair until just the concrete foundation survived by the early twenty-first century. Its remains sit on private property.[107]

Mexican American leaders in Alpine, among them the aforementioned Pete Gallego, viewed school segregation as a problem best handled by locals (from the onset, they had declined the AGIF's offer of assistance). For decades, Mexican Americans in Alpine had lived with a school policy mandating children attend Centennial grammar (the Mexican school) and Anglo-American children go to Central Ward grammar. Initially, Gallego and fellow activists pursued an avenue of peaceful negotiations in their drive to end the practice, only to be rebuffed by determined opposition from the school board and the Alpine Chamber of Commerce. Organizers thus turned for assistance to Mexican American state legislators. This strategy produced an invitation for citizens of Alpine to meet with a party of legislators in Austin. On July 27, 1969, a delegation of Mexican Americans drove in a caravan of vehicles to Austin and the next day presented their grievances before the representatives.

The legislators now took up the Alpine Mexican American community's cause, asking Alpine Superintendent Clarence L. Winn to meet with them in Austin. At said meeting (August 11, 1969), Winn presented a consolidation plan that the school board had just adopted on July 30. As per terms, all elementary students would attend Central while both the junior high and high school would be fully integrated. Fulfilling its promise to desegregate, the school board officially adopted this arrangement on August 15, 1969. Not leaving consolidation to chance, the majority of Mexican American parents on opening day in 1969 registered their children at Central, leaving Centennial with little attendance to justify continued operation.[108] Over time, the school system in Alpine evolved so that PK–4 students today enroll at Alpine Elementary, grades 5–8 attend Alpine Middle, and 9–12 go to Alpine High School.[109]

In Marfa, racial segregation was most blatant at Blackwell Elementary (in south Marfa). As the designated "Mexican school" since its opening in 1908, Blackwell Elementary (as of post–World War II, a total of six structures occupied the school's site) accommodated all Mexican youngsters in grades one through eight. But then, with the passage of the Civil Rights Act of 1964, the town's Anglo population seems to have conceded to the forces of change. Blackwell closed in January 1965, bringing together Mexican Americans and their Anglo peers from Marfa Elementary at a newly built school.

The transition, however, was not without incident. A story perpetuated over the years (it is unclear whether it is based on fact or legend) maintains that upon desegregation, students at Blackwell Elementary School had to haul their own desks to the newly constructed school; they transported them on a pickup and unloaded the desks at the integrated campus. Another version of this episode supposes that "students were told to pick up their chairs and desks, and they walked the furniture to their new campus, about a mile away."[110]

Present alongside the AGIF and LULAC in the various campaigns of the late 1960s was the "Chicano Movement" (as the undertaking came to be called nationwide), headed by a younger generation of Mexican Americans. Compared to the older organizations' approaches toward improving life for Mexican Americans, however, the latter's challenge to the power structure was more strident and daring. Its organizers and spokespersons belonged to a cohort of Baby Boomers (whereas AGIF and LULAC leaders were, according to scholarship, part of the Mexican American Generation) inspired by the anti-war protests of the era, the Black civil rights crusade, and the many anti-establishment movements of that age, including that underway in California by farm workers. Many of them high schoolers and college age adults, Chicanos expressed anger (as did some of the older generation, who at times advised them) at the treatment of the poor, the neglected, and the marginalized: for the most part, oppressed people of color.

Historians have yet to give deserved attention to this phase of Mexican American politics demonstrated outside the greater urban centers of the state and in the rural areas of South Texas. Militancy—generally associated with the *movimiento* (the Movement)—as it bore upon the region of the Edwards Plateau and the Trans-Pecos borderlands thus remains relatively unstudied. At this point in time, however, historians might infer that it was late-1960s stirrings that encouraged individuals such as Pete Gallego and fellow activists in Alpine, and the several plaintiffs in Sonora, to contest segregation.

In Del Rio, the movement came to light in the latter years of the 1960s as some of the youths in town allied themselves with the Mexican American Youth Organization. MAYO, as the organization was commonly called, had been founded in San Antonio in 1967, its mission to find solutions to problems historically afflicting Mexican Americans, among them segregation, inferior schooling, police harassment, labor exploitation, and more. As a product of its age, MAYO had a militant leaning.

VISTA, the Volunteers in Service to America, arrived in Del Rio in early 1969. This federal program, created in 1965 to assist the downtrodden in dealing with poverty through community projects, set up office in the town's San Felipe district. It hired local personnel to carry out its mission: among their recruits were MAYO activists, three of whom in January engaged in strenuously criticizing what they perceived as an unfair judgment recently rendered by a grand jury against Mexican Americans. MAYO's intrusiveness into general community matters troubled local officials, and in February 1969 Val Verde County commissioners announced the dissolution of VISTA. They argued that VISTA workers—namely those affiliated with MAYO—had become too politically involved and had violated federal guidelines.

To protest the commissioners' decision (which had been endorsed by the governor of Texas), MAYO planned a public demonstration. On March 14, 1969, organizers led a march down the streets of Del Rio, only to have it disrupted by police authorities. Undeterred, the membership prepared for another march, scheduling it for Palm Sunday, March 30. MAYO now appealed to sympathizers from across the state, inviting them to Del Rio to join them in support of their grievance. Thousands responded and amassed at the Del Rio Civic Center into an immense crowd that filed along a three-mile stretch of city streets, exclaiming slogans such as "Chicano Power" and "Viva la Raza" along the way. The procession came to a halt at the Val Verde County Courthouse where leaders, both local and prominent figures from throughout the state, gave passionate speeches condemning the many wrongs Chicanos faced. There also, the marchers issued the Del Rio Manifesto, a pronouncement regarded as a "Mexican American Declaration of Independence and Bill of Rights."

The effort in Del Rio to resurrect VISTA ended unsuccessfully. But the spirit of the Chicano Movement persisted into the next decade, for MAYO remained active in the city for years after.[111]

Expressions of militant discontent in San Angelo surfaced around 1967, manifested in letters sent to the editor of the *Standard-Times*, the city's newspaper. The state of impatience, disillusionment, and desire to advance solutions to social problems led a group of students at Angelo State University in 1969 to coalesce under the name of the Chicano Student Organization (CSO). By the late 1960s, the CSO was pressing the university for classes and services germane to Mexican American culture, doing volunteer work in the city, and engaging in voter registration drives. In the winter of 1970, CSO volunteers traveled to Crystal City in South Texas and there helped teach students boycotting classes in protest of discriminatory school policies.

Urged by the political stirrings across the state, two Mexican Americans campaigned in the 1970 at-large city election for positions in the city commission. Electioneering that year proved more animated than had earlier Mexican American campaigns for local office, as one candidate spoke for the rising mood of discontent and confrontational politics. It seemed, however, that what set the two hopefuls apart was their approach to achieving change, for both hoped to foster better communications among the citizenry and, more urgently, to secure stronger connections between city management and different parts of town, for there remained in the barrios needed attention to the sewer system, unlighted streets, and the upkeep of park areas. In the end, the candidate with the more mainstream platform gained the city commission seat.[112]

ON WEST TEXAS TEJANO HISTORY

World War II may be considered as denoting a tipping point in United States history.[113] While much stayed in place across the nation, visible change was nonetheless conspicuous politically, economically, and socially. Said another way, the postwar era was one in which an older way of life was blunted by the winds of change. The new becoming engulfed the Edwards Plateau and Trans-Pecos borderlands.

The transformation affected the West Texas countryside, boding favorably for those engaged in cattle and sheep raising as well as for farmers counting on irrigated lands. Oil discoveries brought new promises both to industrialists and to ordinary folks, especially in the Midland and Ector County areas. The moving forces of the age did not pass over the cities: postwar growth embraced Del Rio, San Angelo, Midland, and Odessa. The consumerism of the period stoked cultural change across the land, boosted further by the cultural revolution of the 1960s. Dismantled during this time was the old order of race control; by the 1960s pre–Cold War attitudes toward people of color were in a state of dissolution. Segregation, among the most blatant forms of discrimination, withered to an almost complete demise. Society came to accept expressions of ethnic pride. The multiple currents spreading across the country and the Lone Star State from the late 1940s and into the 1970s nudged West Texas closer to the rest of the state and to the contours of its broader narrative.

These developments nationally and regionally acted upon Mexican Americans in West Texas, aligning their history with that of Tejanos living east of the 100th meridian. As in other parts of the state, the Mexican American population in West Texas grew, foretelling a historical instance where the demographic makeup of the region would soon resemble that existing outside it. The Tejano presence in cities such as Del Rio, San Angelo, Midland, and Odessa expanded as it did in San Antonio, Laredo, Brownsville, and Corpus Christi, although by no means did their numbers convert those West Texas towns into grand metropolises. Increasingly into the 1960s, more young West Texas Mexican Americans finished school, equaling the graduation rates of their fellow students in South Texas; many of these West Texas Tejanos went on to pursue college degrees, perhaps at Sul Ross or Angelo State University, if not at the larger state campuses. As was the case statewide, white-collar workers, businesspersons, and professionals augmented the West Texas middle class. West Texas Mexican Americans, like most Tejanos, became increasingly Americanized. But as did their counterparts in South Texas (and across the nation for that matter), they picked and chose from American offerings and kept what was dear to their Mexican heritage. They remained bicultural in identity.

Some turned to politics as a direct path to community improvement: tumble the old order, then climbing the social ladder would be easier. Thus did the citizens of Alpine and Sonora face down school officials and integrate the local schools. Elsewhere in West Texas, Hispanics lent support to the national AGIF and LULAC during the postwar era, and then in the latter years of the 1960s to MALDEF as these organizations worked to root out entrenched practices once intended to control Mexicans. Officeholders at local and county levels implemented strategies that remedied barrio neglect. Public pressure forced white people to acknowledge Mexican Americans as co-equals. As the Chicano Movement spread throughout the state after 1967, many West Texas Tejanos embraced it.

But West Texas is West Texas, so that Mexican American history in the region is not an exact iteration of the history shaped by fellow Mexicanos in other parts of the state. During the 1960s, people in South Texas and the major cities in the state largely joined the several political outbursts of the day. Certainly, as indicated above, Tejano West Texans engaged in the decade's activism, but their involvement overall seems not to have been as intense as it was in South Texas. "Viva Kennedy" clubs, strong in South Texas in 1960, appeared to have attracted only passing interest in West Texas. The Political Association of Spanish-speaking Organizations (PASSO), that middle-class liberal organization so prominent in cities such as San Antonio and Houston in the early 1960s, did not spread widely into West Texas. South Texas walkouts in the late 1960s by high schoolers bound on revising district policies that discriminated against them in elections to student councils or selection as cheerleaders gained small traction in West Texas; some did take place, but not until after 1970. Labor strikes erupted in South Texas (including the much-publicized farm workers strike in the Lower Rio Grande Valley in 1966) and in the larger urban areas of the state during the 1960s, yet the scholarship on West Texas does not (at least for the moment) record similar actions. The Chicano literary renaissance of the 1960s hardly spread to the Edwards Plateau and Trans-Pecos.

Perhaps the overall political, economic, and social lag in West Texas Tejano history was due to the bond between the region and the US West where many of these movements also trailed behind ones elsewhere in Texas. Certainly, those living in the Edwards Plateau and Trans-Pecos borderlands have historically identified themselves with a western heritage, similar to how populations generally associate with the culture of the particular region in which they live. Geographers would expect as much, for they do find people identifying with a specific place and thus relating to a "vernacular region."[114]

CHAPTER 6

INTO THE
TWENTY-FIRST CENTURY

A fter 1970, West Texas built upon advances made during the post–World War II era. The economic sector remained dependent on the tried-and-true industries of oil production, stock (cattle, sheep, and goat) raising, and irrigated farming. While constituting a reliable source of profits, each industry posed problems. Oil exploration damaged the land and the underground, especially with companies turning to fracking, a field method involving the use of pressure by pumping fluids at ground level to force openings in subterranean spots where oil might be deposited.[1] Large-scale livestock raising, despite innovations in range management, still damaged grazing lands, allowing brush, cacti, and wild vegetation to grow uncontrolled. Problems with farm irrigation did not abate. Underground water tables continued to diminish, foreboding a future when irrigation as a method to enhance farm production would be discontinued.[2]

Still, West Texas progress paralleled developments underway across the greater state of Texas. While long distances separated towns and settlements, the region did not lag too far behind that side of the state east of the 100th meridian. Urbanization continued apace, especially among the larger cities of Odessa, Midland, Del Rio, and San Angelo. All four of these urban sites saw their respective universities grow (each had graduate programs) and their health care institutions expand. Remoteness did not stifle connections to the wonders of the electronic revolution. Internet links, cable television, and wireless phone service became commonplace by the late twentieth century. A network of roads and interstate highways kept the Edwards Plateau and Trans-Pecos borderlands bonded to the rest of the country. Despite their uncontested membership in the state, West Texans still identified themselves as being "western."

SUSTAINED POPULATION GROWTH

Tejano communities situated in the several counties surveyed in this book continued growing at a sustained pace during the late twentieth century and into the early decades of the 2000s.[3] The 1980 federal census, which identified (conveniently for researchers) ethnic Mexicans as "Spanish Origin Persons by Type of Spanish Origin and Race," enumerated 128,351 Hispanic or Latino people among a total population of 475,222. As of that census year, Tejanos comprised 27 percent of that overall count. During the subsequent forty years, the Mexican-origin group (i.e., Hispanic or Latino) surged to 351,007, overtaking the Anglo (and other races) population. Tejanos in 2020 constituted 55 percent of the 637,764 denizens in the several West Texas counties under study.

Table 1
Hispanic / Latino Population in West Texas Counties, 1980

County	Total	Mexican and Other Latino	Hispanic or Latino %
Val Verde	35,910	22,001	61.3%
Edwards	2,033	960	47.2%
Kinney	2,279	1,221	53.6%
Sutton	5,130	2,037	39.7%
Real	2,469	531	21.5%
Menard	2,346	649	27.7%
Kimble	4,063	701	17.3%

McCulloch	8,739	1,562	17.9%
Schleicher	2,820	689	24.4%
Concho	2,915	780	26.8%
Tom Green	84,784	16,839	19.9%
Runnels	11,872	2,219	18.7%
Coleman	10,439	922	0.9%
Coke	3,196	363	11.3%
Sterling	1,206	279	23.1%
Irion	1,386	256	18.5%
Reagan	4,135	1,271	30.7%
Terrell	1,595	684	42.9%
Pecos	14,681	6,901	47.0%
Reeves	15,801	9,547	60.4%
Crockett	4,608	2,301	50.0%
Ward	13,796	3,626	26.3%
Crane	4,600	1,099	23.9%
Loving	91	16	17.6%
Winkler	9,944	2,348	23.6%

Ector	115,374	23,790	20.6%
Midland	82,636	11,727	14.2%
Glasscock	1,304	376	28.8%
Upton	4,619	1,218	26.4%
Presidio	5,188	3,905	75.3%
Brewster	7,573	3,143	41.5%
Jeff Davis	1,647	745	45.2%
Culberson	3,315	2,056	62.0%
Hudspeth	2,728	1,589	58.2%
	475,222	128,351	27.0%

1980 Census of Population, vol. I. Characteristics of the Population, Chap. B, General Population Characteristics, pt. 45, Texas, PC80-1-B45 (Washington, DC: Dept. of Commerce, 1982), Table 16: "Total Persons and Spanish Origin Persons by Type of Spanish Origin and Race: 1980," 45-43 to 45-46.

Table 2
Hispanic / Latino Population in West Texas Counties, 2020

County	Estimated Total Pop.	Total Hispanic or Latino Pop.	Hispanic or Latino %	Foreign-born %
Val Verde	47,564	39,478	83.0%	22.2%
Edwards	1,438	794	55.2%	9.1%

Kinney	3,130	1,928	61.6%	12.7%
Sutton	3,319	2,160	65.2%	13.1%
Real	2,826	825	29.2%	1.9%
Menard	1,982	709	35.8%	5.1%
Kimble	4,365	1,065	24.4%	4.7%
McCulloch	7,538	2,472	32.8%	5.6%
Schleicher	2,429	1,348	55.5%	8.0%
Concho	3,341	1,139	34.1%	13.4%
Tom Green	119,411	50,153	42.0%	5.4%
Runnels	9,943	3,569	35.9%	4.5%
Coleman	7,735	1,439	18.6%	6.5%
Coke	3,321	751	22.6%	4.8%
Sterling	1,381	569	41.2%	6.6%
Irion	1,552	408	26.3%	3.6%
Reagan	3,253	2,358	72.5%	14.3%
Terrell	724	390	53.9%	0.8%
Pecos	15,118	10,582	70.0%	13.7%
Reeves	14,487	10,923	75.4%	18.0%

Crockett	3,068	2,070	67.5%	10.8%
Ward	11,194	6,391	57.1%	9.3%
Crane	4,680	3,136	67.0%	24.0%
Loving	57	12	21.1%	1.2%
Winkler	7,415	4,715	63.6%	15.5%
Ector	161,091	104,226	64.7%	15.6%
Midland	167,969	80,961	48.2%	13.8%
Glasscock	1,149	444	38.6%	22.9%
Upton	3,265	1,815	55.6%	9.2%
Presidio	6,140	5,145	83.8%	43.0%
Brewster	9,450	4,281	45.3%	12.7%
Jeff Davis	1,949	602	30.9%	12.7%
Culberson	2,193	1,592	72.6%	14.2%
Hudspeth	3,287	2,557	77.8%	42.6%
	637,764	351,007	55.0%	

Data derived from: https://www.census.gov/quickfacts/fact/table/US/PST045221 population estimates, July 1, 2021, accessed December 17, 2022.

Movement into West Texas between the late twentieth century and 2020 was noticeably Mexican (of native and foreign origins), transforming the Edwards Plateau and Trans-Pecos to become increasingly "brown," although the population persisted as mixed Anglo and Tejano (and a small percentage of other races). Migration into the region from other parts of the state and nation, as well as from natural reproduction, accounted for this turn as immigration from Mexico by this time was a lesser factor in population expansion. According to the 2020 US census, the foreign born, excepting a few counties, constituted less than 15 percent of total population in each county.[4]

As they had in 1980, Mexican Americans in 2020 preferred living in counties having greater possibilities for economic progress and featuring modern amenities. Such attractions were most likely to be found in Ector, Midland, Val Verde, and Tom Green Counties. Not surprisingly, 78 percent of all Mexican Americans living in the Edwards Plateau and Trans-Pecos region resided in those four geographic divisions. As per the 2020 census, 104,226 Mexican-origin inhabitants made their home in Ector County, 80,961 in Midland County, 39,478 in Val Verde County, and 50,153 in Tom Green County. In each, the majority of Mexicans were to be found in the county seat. Odessa (Ector County) had a Hispanic concentration of 68,277, Midland (Midland County) of 61,066, Del Rio (Val Verde County) of 30,088, and San Angelo (Tom Green County) of 43,654.[5] In total, 57.9 percent of the entire Texas-Mexican population in the Edwards Plateau and Trans-Pecos lived in these four cities.

At a macro level, almost all West Texas counties saw the number of Hispanics grow between 1980 and 2020. Of course, such gains were moderate compared to those Ector, Midland, Val Verde, and Tom Green Counties experienced. But the increases were enough that in counties such as Val Verde, Ector, Edwards, Kinney, Sutton, Schleicher, Reagan, Terrell, Presidio, Pecos, Reeves, and Crockett, Mexican Americans demographically outnumbered Anglos (and other races). Only in the ranch counties of Edwards, Jeff Davis, and Culberson, and in the oil and gas counties of Terrell, Crockett, and Upton, did there appear a decline, albeit slight, in the number of Mexican American inhabitants.

POLITICS IN THE AGE OF HISPANICS
El Movimiento Continues
The Chicano Movement in West Texas persisted into the 1970s, although its treatment in the scholarship remains lean. Its presence is fairly well documented for San Angelo, Texas, and here it is used as a case study demonstrating how dissatisfaction with the status quo drew different groups, with their own approaches, to address the problems and issues of the day, among them municipal

neglect of the barrio, lack of representation in local political offices, racist actions, and discrimination.

Motivated in San Angelo by the Chicano Movement were, on the one hand, individuals who came from the ranks of WWII veterans and those who had grown to adulthood during the 1940s. This cohort sought office in 1971 and 1972, vying for positions in the San Angelo School Board, promising to represent Mexican American constituents effectively in what had always been an all-white body. Contrasting to what would be considered the moderation of the GI Generation was the militancy of younger men and women highly influenced by the leftist nature of the movement. Some in this group had been active in the late 1960s, among them students from Angelo State University. In September 1971, they along with counterparts from Central High School formed a chapter of the Mexican American Student Organization (MAYO), an activist group founded by students in San Antonio in 1967 and bent on finding solutions to age-long problems facing Mexican Americans. The San Angelo MAYO membership committed itself to bringing about unity in the community, pressuring the city to direct attention to barrio issues, and overall to helping improve conditions for Mexican Americans. In 1971, San Angelo MAYO allied itself with the Raza Unida Party (RUP), a third-party politically portraying itself as a force representing interests apposite to Mexican Americans.

From 1972 through 1974, San Angeleños had the choice of voting for Mexican American Raza Unida, Democratic, or Republican candidates campaigning for city, county, chief of police, and school board seats. Only one person of Mexican descent during those years won election, a member of the older generation who earned a place in the city commission.[6] West of San Angelo in the Permian Basin, manifestations of Chicanismo surfaced during the mid-1970s when locals in Odessa concerned with long-standing injustices committed by policemen established a chapter of the Brown Berets, a community organization founded in California to safeguard against police brutality.

Dramatizing police brutality in the region during the latter years of the decade were the cases of Tiburcio Griego Santome and Alberto "Larry" Ortega Lozano. Tiburcio Griego Santome (age 37) was arrested in Saint Lawrence (Glasscock County) on November 6, 1977, for disorderly conduct at a church festival. According to law enforcement agents who made the arrest, Santome became unruly in the police car while being driven to jail, and in an ensuing struggle was

INTO THE TWENTY-FIRST CENTURY

shot four times and killed. Despite protests from West Texas LULAC councils, the officers responsible went unpunished.

More immediate for the coming of the Chicano Movement to the Permian Basin, and to Odessa proper, was the death of Alberto "Larry" Ortega Lozano (27 years old) during a police call on January 10, 1978, following a vehicle accident. As per the arresting officers, Lozano had been uncooperative at the scene and had to be subdued by physical force. Lozano disputed the officers' version of the apprehension, claiming he had been beaten up at the time of arrest and afterwards, upon being booked at the jail. Then, Lozano continued, he was repeatedly beaten and emotionally abused while in custody.

On January 22, 1978, according to deputies, Lozano became aggressive and combative in jail and was killed in the attempt to subdue him. Suspicious of the agents' account of Lozano's death, his family called for outside investigations. Three autopsies were conducted in all: they varied as to cause of death, but the pathologists ultimately allowed that Lozano had died due to injury caused by accidental compression to the larynx as the officers wrestled to overpower him. At a press conference held by the Brown Berets on January 24, 1978, the Berets and the Lozano family called for an FBI inquiry into the killing of Lozano. But efforts by community people, the Lozano family, the Brown Berets, LULAC, the GI Forum, and others to have local and state authorities, the Federal Bureau of Investigation, and the Department of Justice investigate the episode came to naught—in the end no one was prosecuted for the killing. However, the case of police brutality against Larry Lozano left its mark on the Odessa Mexican American community; no longer would Chicanos overlook injustices when they took place.[7]

Hispanic Politics

Sometime during the 1970s, *el movimiento* in San Angelo, Odessa, and other places in West Texas began to decline. Texas, like the rest of the country, entered an era of political moderation, leaving behind the intensity that had been generated by the social reform movements of the 1960s and 1970s and the protests against the Vietnam War during that same time period.

Leaders in Texas Mexican communities, whether politicians, businesspeople, or professionals, now accepted the term "Hispanic." The label had been chosen by the federal government in the 1970s in its quest to find an acceptable identifier for racial and ethnic groups (the Office of Management and Budget used the term as an identifier in the census forms of 1980).[8] For the Mexican American leadership of the post–Chicano era, whose politics lay in "work within the system" approaches, this term supplanted "Chicano," which had never been universally acceptable within Tejano communities, as it was considered controversial (identifiable as it was with militancy). "Hispanic" appeared more palatable for use and discourse within political and economic circles.[9]

Compared to the pre-1970 era, remarkable has been the political advancement of West Texas Hispanics. Significant in opening up opportunities on the political front were changes that occurred during the 1960s, due both to the social movements of the era and to federal legislation. The Civil Rights Act of 1964 and the Voting Rights Acts of 1965, in particular, gave minority peoples throughout the nation opportunities for ethnic uplift that had not existed previously. Then, the national parties (especially the Democratic Party) developed policies specific to incorporating women and minorities into party ranks.[10] Last, population increases (noted earlier in this chapter) added to the voting numbers among West Texans.

Equally responsible for political progress after the decade of the 1970s were movements undertaken by both grassroots activists and Mexican American leaders to have politicians allow the Hispanic electorate greater opportunities for engagement in the political system. In pursuing such a cause, they embarked on voter registration drives among an expanding voting-age population and launched campaigns for single-member districts.[11] They further called upon government to lobby universities into assisting college-aged students to finance their higher education and into pursuing affirmative action plans permitting the hiring of Hispanic-descent individuals who would serve as role models.

The accommodating response from educational institutions armed West Texas political leaders (not only those of the post-1970 era, but of the Mexican American generation who had long been involved in political organizing) with individuals qualified and prepared for greater political involvement and office holding.[12] These prospects included middle-class women and men who came from ranks of the business and professional world, many with experience in positions of influence. Pursuing an ethnic agenda, which addressed issues of civil rights, discrimination, jobs, housing, and stereotypes, this cohort practiced moderate mainstream politics.

In San Angelo, LULAC Council 637, organized in May 1973 by individuals reluctant to see any decline in political engagement following the Chicano era, took up the task of finding solutions to issues affecting Mexican Americans locally. Members generally came from the ranks of the educated professional class, most with a moderate political bent opting to pursue change through bureaucratic channels. Aside from the traditional drives to raise scholarship funds, they took aggressive stances during the 1970s and 1980s, challenging hiring practices within the San Angelo Independent School District as well as at Angelo State University (1978). In 1982, LULAC scored, with the support of the AGIF and West Texas Legal Services, a significant victory when it forced an agreement with Tom Green County to redistrict County Precinct 1 so that it would contain a Mexican-Black majority.

An exception to those of the 1970s who came from the ranks of the professional and college-educated corps—i.e., those who espoused moderate politics and followed conventional approaches—was María Cárdenas, whose political ties could be traced to RUP of the early 1970s. Cárdenas lived in the barrio and until receiving her degree in 1982 lacked the professional credentials of her 1970s contemporaries. Using Chicano-era confrontational approaches, she successfully led the campaign in 1976 to bring about a single-member system to the city of San Angelo.

In the first election following redistricting, Cárdenas won the post of representative of City Commission District 3, the predominantly Mexican American barrio in San Angelo. In that capacity, she spoke frankly when championing Mexican American causes. One contemporary described her style: "Dressing simply and talking directly, Cárdenas accomplished most of her goals by a technique that involved shrewdness, brashness, and intimidation of foes with charges of racism." In 1980, Cárdenas was recognized as one of the twenty-five most powerful people in San Angelo. Her political career declined after 1984 when she failed to win as representative of County Commission Precinct 1, a larger area that included Anglo Americans unaccepting of her barrio approach to politics. María Cárdenas passed away in 1993.[13]

CIVIC PROGRESS AND SOCIAL MOBILITY

Political progress in San Angelo continued into the twenty-first century, as it did throughout West Texas. In the region of the Edwards Plateau and Trans-Pecos as of 1970, the number of Mexican American individuals in government posts was sparse. By 2020, Mexican Americans were a staple throughout the region at almost all levels of government service.

Data collected by *Texas Almanac* researchers for the years 1970 and 2020 respectively inform of noteworthy advancement. In the several counties that constitute the Edwards Plateau and Trans-Pecos, the number of Hispanic elected officials jumped from eleven in 1970 to some 109 in 2020. Of this latter number, 47 (figures arrived via a hand count of the *Texas Almanac* data) were women, indicating a healthy gender presence (about 43 percent) throughout the region. The larger share of individuals served in such capacities as county clerk, assessor collector, and district clerk, most conspicuously in counties that as of 2020 had increased to, or achieved, status as a Hispanic majority.

As of 2020, those Hispanic-majority counties had the greatest Hispanic representation in elected posts (both male and female), including sheriffs, county clerks, district clerks, assessor collectors, and county commissioners. The county seats of those counties having a Hispanic population advantage were more likely to have a Hispanic mayor as well as an appointed city manager. Underrepresentation in the region was to be found in the positions of county judge, county attorney, and district attorney.[14]

Matching the stride of those winning at the county level were Mexican Americans elected locally, in city councils, school boards, and chiefs of police. These developments in county and city offices indicated a catching-up of sorts, or at least staying even with, gains made by Tejanos in other parts of the state, including urban areas. Before the 1970s, it had been difficult for West Texas Tejanos to equal the political advances of their South Texas counterparts, for example. That ceased to be the case in the twenty-first century.

Social and economic improvement occurred alongside political achievements. Responsible for such progress was mobilization by organizations such as LULAC, AGIF, and MALDEF, as well as community clubs and associations pressing for quality education for Mexican Americans, both in the public schools and at colleges and universities. As has been noted, government at the same time hastened institutions of higher learning to increase opportunities that would allow minority people better access to college classrooms. One significant outgrowth of these actions was that the "college graduation rate [among Mexican Americans in Texas] more than doubled" between 1990 and 2010.[15] Among graduates were educators (teachers, principals, superintendents, professors, and college administrators), doctors, attorneys, judges, engineers, architects, business managers, and a host of other middle- and upper-class professionals. Education led to occupational promotion and social progress.

As of 2010, concludes a recent study, a good percentage of the total Mexican American population throughout the state of Texas held what may be considered white-collar, lower middle-class, or middle-class jobs, such as in sales/clerical, proprietorship, managerial, and professional. Upward mobility, the study's findings indicate, occurred noticeably among women. In 2010, almost 25 percent of Tejanas statewide were working in managerial and professional fields.[16] There is no significant reason to believe that the pattern of social mobility for Mexican Americans in West Texas differed from that of the greater Mexican American population in the state.

Such statistics, of course, accentuated the persistence of class divisions with the broader Texas Mexican community. As of 2010, about 40 percent of the Mexican American workforce in the state remained concentrated in the service and labor categories.[17] Much was the same in West Texas.

LINGERING RACE ATTITUDES

Notwithstanding the changes in race tolerance evident by the 1960s, West Texas remained a borderlands still amenable to prejudice against Mexicans, as was the rest of the state. Elected officials continued attempts to disfranchise segments of the Mexican population by enacting laws that suppressed voting or diluted voting strength through gerrymandering and redistricting plans. Persistent discussions in West Texas about immigration, the border wall, and White Replacement Theory stigmatized Mexican Americans, lumping them with "undesirable aliens" who could someday displace Anglos politically and otherwise. The Border Patrol and police forces used racial profiling, associating such Mexican American features as dark skin, straight black hair, height, and even body image with malicious intentions.

There remained the thought that Mexicans must be of foreign birth even if they descended from ancestors who had lived in the United States for generations. Stories circulated of hate groups and armed militias harassing Mexican-origin people in West Texas, maintaining that the US was not home for foreigners. Elements within the majority population bullied school boards, commanding that the educational system cease and desist from teaching critical race theory, negating the racist side of Texas history and instead emphasize American patriotism and exceptionalism.

REMEMBRANCES

Mexican-descent people played a central role in shaping West Texas, for it was they who first engaged—in their transnational thrust into the Big Bend area before the arrival of Euro Americans—in a community-building process that continued for centuries. Mexicans advanced the region agriculturally, commercially, and industrially. Generally working at low-paying and back-breaking jobs, they helped develop the various economic sectors of the Edwards Plateau and Trans-Pecos: ranching, conspicuously by their service as cowhands and sheepshearers, and farming by clearing brush land, chopping weeds, planting cotton, and finally picking it. They enhanced regional progress by doing the most hazardous work demanded in the silver and quicksilver mines of the Big Bend. Mexicans bolstered oil field productivity performing no less arduous work than in the mines—using picks and shovels, they dug the necessary ditches, then laid the metal pipelines that transported the raw oil to the refineries. It was Mexican laborers behind the building of the region's infrastructure; as railroad crew members, they put down iron rails from the 100th meridian to El Paso. Those fortunate to have gained middle-class standing partnered with their Anglo counterparts in firming up the West Texas business components as white-collar professionals and managerial personnel.

Mexican Americans further engaged in shaping West Texas by nurturing it into a multicultural borderlands. They established their own ethnic communities, recognizable by the language of Mexico; clubs and self-help organizations; churches (both Catholic and Protestant) that met their needs; the media of Spanish-language radio stations and newspapers; business enterprises that catered to their cultural tastes; leisure activities such as *bailes*; and the persistent observance of Mexican national holidays and other familiar customs and traditions. Mexican Americans fixed upon West Texas society an ethnic way of life, enriching the region in the process, making it multicultural in character and flavor.

The West Texas borderlands, like others elsewhere, dictated adaptation and accommodation to local circumstances, and certainly of Mexican migrants arriving therein during the seventeenth century to find Indigenous people as occupants. Further adjustment became necessary after the 1850s as Anglos pushed westward past the 100th meridian and took control of institutional life. As the years passed, Mexicans seeking a livelihood amidst a white population assumed an American identity, although the degree of acculturation varied. Always impacting identity was contact with mainstream institutional life and interaction with a spectrum of American personnel, including employers, school administrators, clergymen, and politicians. In a syncretizing process, Mexicans accepted and absorbed the ethos of the dominant culture. Hybridity meant being proud citizens and accepting their nation's call in time of war, honoring the political system and striving to participate in it, and joining the social order.

In recent years, groups have sought to remember their ancestors' role as community builders and the manner in which previous generations molded West Texas into a multicultural region. Those participating in such a mission are dedicated people—all of whom identify as Americans—genuinely interested in ensuring that history preserve their Mexican predecessors' involvement (if not their own) in the making of West Texas. Such is the case of Mexican American preservationists in Marfa (Presidio County). At Blackwell Elementary School between 1908 and 1965 (as noted in chapter 5), children had been segregated, neglected by school administrators, and punished for speaking their native language. Despite that experience, some had gone through Blackwell and retained fond remembrances of their school days and harbored "wonderful memories" of being schooled by dedicated Anglo teachers. Thus did alumni of the school, under the name of the Blackwell School Alliance, work for years to keep the building from being razed and to preserve its history. That history, of course, embraced an era stretching back centuries, one in which Mexicans adjusted to historical moments and contributed to West Texas life as both immigrants and citizens.

The efforts of the Blackwell School Alliance reached success in November 2022 when the National Park Service designated the Blackwell School a national historic landmark. Gretel Enck, president of the Blackwell School Alliance, responded with gratification: "We really hope that this [the authorization of Blackwell as a national historic site] opens up doors for other stories of Hispanic, Latino history to be told." One alum noted succinctly: "The preservation of the Blackwell School here allows for a little bit of Hispanic history to be exposed."[18] The reference, plainly, was to a Mexican American experience, for while practices like segregation served as reminders of being Mexican, experiences involving caring teachers (and other assimilating forces of the times) inclined subjects to identify as Americans.

Melvin (McCulloch County), its population today just more than 150 inhabitants, for decades was the scene of a thriving semiautonomous, self-reliant Mexican farming community. It did not survive the drought of the first half of the 1950s, however. Those nostalgically attached to Hispanic Melvin have in recent years undertaken steps to preserve the lengthy Mexican presence there, fully cognizant of how immigrants from Mexico, as well as settlers from different parts of Texas, shaped the town and its surroundings socially and economically, if not politically. Several have passionately researched and documented their families' history, written historical booklets about "la colonia Mexicana de Melvin," audiotaped or video-recorded older folks' remembrances, made public presentations using PowerPoint slideshows, collected newspaper clippings, amassed memorabilia, and assembled photo albums in efforts to perpetuate the imprint Mexican Americans had on Melvin, Texas.

Recently, a group of preservationists working under the name of the Junta Patriótica have pursued an initiative to restore La Plataforma Jiménez, a public hall built in Melvin sometime during the late 1920s and functioning into the 1960s as a setting for family gatherings, patriotic festivals, dances, graduation ceremonies, and much more. The group hopes the preserved historic site will become a monument remindful of a place (Melvin) that shaped identity and produced a remarkable list of overachievers, among them educators, physicians, professors, military figures, and corporate executives.[19]

In San Angelo in 2018, historically minded individuals founded the Hispanic Heritage Committee of San Angelo for the purpose of "educating and providing public awareness of the Hispanic community's impact throughout the past, present, and future." This committee soon morphed into the Hispanic Heritage Museum and Cultural Center (HHMCC). The group today attempts through several means, including art exhibitions, educational programs, library collections, historical writings, and public events, to give recognition to the history and accomplishments of Hispanics in San Angelo and nearby vicinities.

In seeking to preserve the memory of Mexican American community building, the HHMCC assists the local Lions Club stage the annual *fiestas patrias* celebrations (held in town since the 1880s) and, as of 2019, taking the lead in organizing the observation of the Día de los Muertos during Hispanic Heritage Month (September 15 to October 15). More ambitiously, the HHMCC plans to build in San Angelo a permanent museum that would be appropriately named the Hispanic Heritage Museum and Cultural Center. It would serve as a depository for maintaining artifacts, undertaking research projects, sponsoring educational sessions, and perpetuating the record of those who identify themselves as Hispanic Americans. Its members publicize their work through the Facebook page "Hispanic Heritage Museum and Cultural Center," created in 2019.[20]

RECTIFYING TEJANO HISTORY

This borderlands study rectifies that which some historians find amiss in Tejano history scholarship: to wit, the misrepresentation and neglect of the history of Mexican Americans in West Texas.[21] According to this imputation, the existing literature overlooks the geographic expanse from the 100th meridian west to El Paso. It assumes that Mexican American residents of West Texas did not make a notable mark on history; the center of that history making, it appears from the weight of the scholarship, is South Texas and the larger urban metropolises in the state. Even if West Texas Mexicans were history makers, their community life could not have been as dynamic as elsewhere. After all, it is supposed, West Texas was not densely populated, nor as long settled by Mexicans, as were the South Texas homeland and the larger urban enclaves.

This Edwards Plateau and Trans-Pecos Borderlands history counters such interpretations. First, it recognizes that West Texas is a particular sphere with definable geographic boundaries, its setting (a part of the larger US West) shaping Tejano life and differentiating it somewhat from life in South Texas. Then, it shows that there has been an active population of history makers engaged in persistent community building, going back to as early as the 1770s. In the Mexican world of the West Texas *colonia* existed a vibrancy (evident in the lively perpetuation of Mexican-based customs, traditions, religious beliefs, language, leisure activities, and other sociocultural practices) comparable to those present in any other borderlands (including those separated by large distances from the US–Mexico border). In the course of time, as the presence of *"lo americano"* bore upon *"lo mexicano,"* Mexican American communities became even more animated as individuals increasingly engaged in the broader realm of mainstream life, including the world of business, politics, the law, medicine, education, and other significant fields. As an overview, this monograph records the agency of mainly poor people who through time struggled to survive amidst racism, poverty, and back-breaking work, yet left an imprint on West Texas that counters the notion that West Texas Mexicanos were not active historical characters.

NOTES

PREFACE

1. James T. Matthews, "The Edwards Plateau and Permian Basin," in *West Texas: A History of the Giant Side of the State*, eds. Paul H. Carlson and Bruce Glasrud (Norman: University of Oklahoma Press, 2014), 59–60; and Miguel A. Levario, "The Trans-Pecos–Big Bend Country," in ibid., 74–75.

2. Pekka Hämäläinen and Samuel Truett, "On Borderlands," *The Journal of American History* 98, no. 2 (September 2011): 338–61; Samuel Truett and Elliot Young, eds., *Continental Crossroads: Remapping U.S.–Mexico Borderlands History* (Durham, NC: Duke University Press, 2004); Pekka Hämäläinen and Benjamin H. Johnson, eds., *Major Problems in the History of North American Borderlands: Documents and Essays* (Boston, MA: Wadsworth, Cengage Learning, 2012); Benjamin H. Johnson and Andrew R. Graybill, eds., *Bridging National Borders in North America: Transnational and Comparative Histories* (Durham, NC: Duke University Press, 2010); and Miguel Ángel González-Quiroga, *War and Peace on the Rio Grande Frontier, 1830–1880* (Norman: University of Oklahoma Press, 2020).

3. Studies focusing on Texas borderlands communities along the Rio Grande would include, among others, Armando C. Alonzo, *Tejano Legacy: Rancheros and Settlers in South Texas, 1734–1900* (Albuquerque: University of New Mexico Press, 1998); Daniel D. Arreola, *Tejano South Texas: A Mexican American Cultural Province* (Austin: University of Texas Press, 2002); and Omar Valerio-Jiménez, "Borderlands History in the *Southwestern Historical Quarterly*," *Southwestern Historical Quarterly* CXXV, no. 4 (April 2022). An example of homeland making in the

Texas Panhandle, southern Oklahoma, and eastern New Mexico region is Joel Zapata, "The Mexican Southern Plains: The Making of an Ethnic Mexican Homeland" (PhD diss., Southern Methodist University, 2019).

4. Hämäläinen and Truett, "On Borderlands," 346–47.

5. Studies on the histories of communities throughout the US continue to augment borderlands scholarship. Select works on the US Midwest include: Bryan Winston, "Mexican Corridors: Migration and Community Formation in the Central United States, 1900 to 1950" (PhD diss., Saint Louis University, 2019); Ann V. Millard and Jorge Chapa, et al., eds., *Apple Pie and Enchiladas: Latino Newcomers in the Rural Midwest* (Austin: University of Texas Press, 2004); Sujey Vega, *Latino Heartland: Borders and Belonging in the Midwest* (New York: New York University Press, 2015); and Omar Valerio-Jiménez and Santiago Vaquera-Vásquez, et al., eds., *The Latina/o Midwest Reader* (Champaign: University of Illinois Press, 2017). On the US South there are Julie M. Weise, *Corazón de Dixie: Mexicanos in the U.S. South Since 1910* (Chapel Hill: University of North Carolina Press, 2015); Heather A. Smith and Owen J. Furuseth, eds., *Latinos in the New South: Transformations of Place* (Abingdon, Oxfordshire: Routledge, 2016); and Perla M. Guerrero, *Nuevo South: Latinas/os, Asians, and the Remaking of Place* (Austin: University of Texas Press, 2017). Histories of Mexican American communities in the Pacific Northwest include, among others: Erasmo Gamboa and Carolyn M. Buan, *Nosotros: The Hispanic People of Oregon* (Portland: Oregon State University Press, 1995); Erlinda V. Gonzales-Berry and Marcela Mendoza, *Mexicanos in Oregon: Their Stories, Their Lives* (Portland: Oregon State University Press, 2010); Mario Jiménez Sifuentez, *Of Forests and Fields: Mexican Labor in the Pacific Northwest* (New Brunswick, NJ: Rutgers University Press, 2016); and Jerry García, ed., *We Are Aztlán: Chicanx Histories in the Northern Borderlands* (Pullman: Washington State University Press, 2017).

CHAPTER 1

1. Donald E. Chipman, *Spanish Texas, 1519–1821* (Austin: University of Texas Press, 1992), 61–62.

2. Ibid.

3. Ibid., 69–70.

4. Israel Mendoza de Levario, *A Brief Chronicle of Presidio del Norte:*

Homeland of the Jumano (Austin: La Junta Press, 2012), 13.

5. Ibid., 18, 21.

6. Ibid.

7. Ibid., 14, 16.

8. Virginia Madison, *How Come It's Called That? Place Names in the Big Bend Country* (New York: October House Inc., 1968), 102, 108; "Pilares," "Presidio," "Concho River," "Pecos River," "Alamito Creek," "Cibolo Creek," and "Santa Elena Canyon," Handbook of Texas Online.

9. Oakah Jones, "Settlements and Settlers at La Junta de los Ríos, 1759–1822," *Journal of Big Bend Studies* 3 (January 1991): 52.

10. Carlysle Graham Raht, *The Romance of Davis Mountains and Big Bend Country* (El Paso: The Rahtbooks Company, 1919; revised ed. Odessa: The Rahtbooks Company, 1963), 119 and 230–31; Roy L. Swift and Leavitt Corning Jr., *Three Roads to Chihuahua: The Great Wagon Roads That Opened the Southwest, 1823–1883* (Austin: Eakin Press, 1988), 37–38; C. Wayne Applegate and Howard G. Hanselka, *La Junta de los Rios del Norte y Conchos* (El Paso: Texas Western Press, 1974), 36. Also, Cecilia Thompson, *A History of Marfa and Presidio County, 1535–1946*, 2 vols. (Austin: Nortex Press, 1985), I, 107.

11. Thompson, *A History of Marfa and Presidio County*, I, 99; Mendoza de Levario, *A Brief Chronicle of Presidio del Norte*, 17.

12. "Ronquillo Land Grant," Handbook of Texas Online; "Presidio County," ibid; Thompson, *A History of Marfa and Presidio County*, I, 39, 40, 66–67; Leavitt Corning Jr., *Baronial Forts of the Big Bend: Ben Leaton, Milton Faver and Their Private Forts in Presidio County* (San Antonio: Trinity University Press, 1969), 22.

13. Corning Jr., *Baronial Forts of the Big Bend*, 21, Appendix B, 105–12; Arthur R. Gómez, *A Most Singular Country: A History of Occupation in the Big Bend* (Santa Fe: National Park Service; Salt Lake City: Charles Redd Center for Western Studies, Brigham Young University, 1990), 95; "Fort Leaton," Handbook of Texas Online.

14. Glen Sample Ely, *Where the West Begins: Debating Texas Identity* (Lubbock: Texas Tech University Press, 2011), 20.

15. George J. Morgenthaler, *The River Has Never Divided Us: A Border History of La Junta de los Rios* (Austin: University of Texas Press, 2004), 80–81, 97; Corning Jr., *Baronial Forts of the Big Bend*, 22, 77.

16. Corning Jr., *Baronial Forts of the Big Bend*, 45, 58–59, 63–64; "Fort Leaton," Handbook of Texas Online.
17. Thompson, *A History of Marfa and Presidio County*, I, 66.
18. Robert M. Utley, "The Range Cattle Industry in the Big Bend of Texas," *Southwestern Historical Quarterly* LXIX, no. 4 (April 1966): 423–24.
19. Ely, *Where the West Begins*, 44.
20. Gómez, *A Most Singular Country*, 96, 97; Raht, *The Romance of Davis Mountains and Big Bend Country*, 146; Helen Simons and Cathryn A. Hoyt, eds., *Hispanic Texas: A Historical Guide* (Austin: University of Texas Press, 1992), 300; Paul Wright, "Population Patterns in Presidio County in 1880," *Journal of Big Bend Studies* 7 (January 1995): 187, 194.
21. Robert Wooster, *Frontier Crossroads: Fort Davis and the West* (College Station: Texas A&M University Press, 2006), 40–41; Thompson, *A History of Marfa and Presidio County*, I, 61.
22. Thompson, *A History of Marfa and Presidio County*, I, 61–62, 66; Lucy Miller Jacobson and Mildred Bloys Nored, *Jeff Davis County, Texas* (Fort Davis: Fort Davis Historical Society, 1993), 57; Glen Sample Ely, *The Texas Frontier and the Butterfield Overland Mail, 1858–1861* (Norman: University of Oklahoma Press, 2016), 298; "San Antonio-El Paso Mail," Handbook of Texas Online.
23. Ely, *Where the West Begins*, 39, 41, 43–44, 49, 54–55, 72, 73.
24. Raht, *The Romance of Davis Mountains and Big Bend Country*, 152; Jacobson and Nored, *Jeff Davis County, Texas*, 105.
25. Robert A. Calvert, et al., *The History of Texas*, 6th ed. (Hoboken, NJ: Wiley-Blackwell, 2020), 172.
26. Marsha Lea Daggett, *Pecos County History*, 2 vols. (Pecos County Historical Commission, 1973–1983), I, 99–102; Raht, *The Romance of Davis Mountains and Big Bend Country*, 152–57, 161, 194, 203; Clayton W. Williams, *Texas' Last Frontier: Fort Stockton and the Trans-Pecos, 1861–1895*, Ernest Wallace ed. (College Station: Texas A&M University Press, 1982), 102–3, 129, 155–57, 178, 185, 187, 220, 222, 247; Thompson, *A History of Marfa and Presidio County*, I, 106, 118, 135; Jacobson and Nored, *Jeff Davis County, Texas*, 105–6; August Santleben, *A Texas Pioneer: Early Staging and Overland Freighting Days on the Frontier of Texas and Mexico*, I. D. Affleck, ed. (New York: Neale Publishing Company, 1910), 143–44; Whitehead Memorial Museum, *La Hacienda: An Official Bicentennial*

Publication (Del Rio: The Museum, 1976), 5; and Gus Clemens, *The Concho Country* (San Antonio: Mulberry Avenue Books, 1980), 61, 63.

27. Patrick Dearen, *Crossing Rio Pecos* (Fort Worth: Texas Christian University Press, 1996), 17–19; Thompson, *A History of Marfa and Presidio County*, I, 118.

28. Ely, *Where the West Begins*, 49.

29. Arnoldo De León, *San Angeleños: Mexican Americans in San Angelo, Texas* (San Angelo: Fort Concho Museum Press, 1985), 14–15; Raht, *The Romance of Davis Mountains and Big Bend Country*, 127; "San Antonio-El Paso Mail," Handbook of Texas Online.

30. Wooster, *Frontier Crossroads*, ix, 74–75; Wright, "Population Patterns in Presidio County in 1880," 194; Thompson, *A History of Marfa and Presidio County*, I, 107.

31. Daggett, *Pecos County History*, I, 99–100, 102; María Eva Flores, CDP, "The Good Life the Hard Way: The Mexican American Community of Fort Stockton, Texas, 1930–1945" (PhD diss., Arizona State University, 2000), 14.

32. Wright, "Population Patterns in Presidio County in 1880," 196–97.

33. Wooster, *Frontier Crossroads*, 75, 126; Thompson, *A History of Marfa and Presidio County*, I, 107.

34. Flores, "The Good Life the Hard Way," 14–15, 31; Thompson, *A History of Marfa and Presidio County*, I, 107, 119; Daggett, *Pecos County History*, I, 99, 135.

35. Raht, *The Romance of Davis Mountains and Big Bend Country*, 175; Williams, *Texas' Last Frontier*, 120. Daggett, *Pecos County History*, II, 184, relates Garza's connection to the Torres family. Daggett, *Pecos County History*, I, 135, defines preemption as being commonly known as "squatter's rights. It was validated by the state legislature in order to encourage settlement. Under this act, a person could settle on a piece of land and live in it with the prior right of having it surveyed, paying for it, and later, getting title for 160 acres of that land." Clayton Williams, "First Two Irrigation Projects on Pecos River in Texas," *Permian Historical Annual* 15 (December 1975), 6n2 states: "Preemption Act was approved by legislature on August 12, 1870, for a maximum of 160 acres."

36. Daggett, *Pecos County History*, I, 149, 152; Raht, *The Romance of Davis Mountains and Big Bend Country*, 175; Flores, "The Good Life the Hard

Way," 32–33; Williams, "First Two Irrigation Projects on Pecos River in Texas," 2; Clayton Williams, "The Pontoon Bridge on the Pecos, 1869–1880," *Permian Historical Annual* 18 (December 1978): 12, 15; and Dearen, *Crossing Rio Pecos*, 77.

37.   Douglas Braudaway, "The 'Origins' of Del Rio, Texas: Documenting Myths and Mything Documentation," *Journal of South Texas* 23, no. 1 (Spring 2010): 51, 63–64; Steven W. Prewitt, "'We Didn't Ask to Come to This Party': Self Determination Collides with the Federal Government in the Public Schools of Del Rio, Texas, 1890–1971" (PhD diss., University of Houston, 2000), 1, 25, 31, 33, 42; "Del Rio, Texas" and "Paula Losoya Taylor," Handbook of Texas Online.

38.   Allan A. Stovall, *Nueces Headwater Country: A Regional History* (San Antonio: Naylor Press, 1959), 8, 9. Not too many Tejanos have found Edwards County as appealing as had Sánchez and his family: as of the year 2020, the total population in the county was just over 2,000. "Edwards County, Texas," Wikipedia, https://en.wikipedia.org, accessed January 5, 2022. Like neighboring Edwards County, Real County has not attracted a large Mexican American population. As of the year 2000, its total population amounted to 3,047 people, with 22.58 percent of the population being Hispanic or Latino.

39.   Kimble County Historical Survey Committee, *Recorded Landmarks of Kimble County* (Junction, TX: The Committee, 1971), 218–19. "Kimble County, Texas," Wikipedia, https://en.wikipedia.org, accessed January 6, 2022; "Bear Creek," Handbook of Texas Online.

40.   Menard County Historical Society, *Menard County History: An Anthology* (San Angelo: Anchor Publishing Co., 1982), 76.

41.   De León, *San Angeleños*, 14–15.

42.   Earl H. Elam, "Acculturation on the Rio Grande Frontier: The Founding of San José del Polvo and the Family of Lucía Rede Madrid," *Journal of Big Bend Studies* 5 (January 1993): 82–87; Thompson, *A History of Marfa and Presidio County*, I, 119, 133–34; Madison, *How Come It's Called That?*, 114.

43.   Louise S. O'Connor and Cecilia Thompson, *Marfa and Presidio County, Texas: A Social, Economic, and Cultural Study, 1990–2008*, 2 vols. (Bloomington, IN: Xlibris, 2014), II, 422.

44.   Madison, *How Come It's Called That?*, 112–14.

45.   Arnoldo De León and Kenneth L. Stewart, "Tejano Demographic Patterns

and Socio-economic Development," *The Borderlands Journal* VII, no. 1 (Fall 1983): 6.

46.   Colonel Nathaniel Alston Taylor, *The Coming Empire, or, Two Thousand Miles in Texas on Horseback* (New York: A. S. Barnes & Company, 1877), 265.

47.   Marcos E. Kinevan, *Frontier Cavalryman: Lieutenant John Bigelow with the Buffalo Soldiers in Texas* (El Paso: Texas Western Press, 1998), 108.

48.   Waterman Lilly Ormsby, *The Butterfield Overland Mail* (San Marino: The Huntington Library, 1942), Lyle H. Wright and Josephine M. Bynum, eds., 64, 68.

49.   Sam Woolford, ed., "The Burr G. Duval Diary," *Southwestern Historical Quarterly* LXV (April 1962): 490, 493.

50.   Ely, *Where the West Begins*, 20, 76; Daggett, *Pecos County History*, II, 184.

51.   Paul Wright, "Residential Segregation in Two Early West Texas Towns," *Southwestern Historical Quarterly* CII (January 1999): 300, and Wright, "Population Patterns in Presidio County in 1880," 189–90; Ely, *Where the West Begins*, 20, 78.

52.   Virginia Madison, *The Big Bend Country of Texas* (Albuquerque: University of New Mexico Press, 1955), 74; Raht, *The Romance of Davis Mountains and Big Bend Country*, 162; Thompson, *A History of Marfa and Presidio County*, I, 109.

53.   In the early 1890s, I. J. Bush, a medical doctor assigned to Fort Davis, affirmed that overall Mexican women in West Texas were of the lower class. I. J. Bush, *Gringo Doctor* (Caldwell, ID: Caxton Printers, Ltd., 1939), 37.

54.   *San Antonio Herald*, May 25, 1868, 2; Wright, "Residential Segregation in Two Early West Texas Towns," 305; Wright, "Population Patterns in Presidio County in 1880," 190–91; Wooster, *Frontier Crossroads*, 125–28.

55.   Williams, *Texas' Last Frontier*, 261.

56.   De León, *San Angeleños*, 23, 152–53.

57.   Wooster, *Frontier Crossroads*, 126.

58.   Jacobson and Nored, *Jeff Davis County, Texas*, 94, and section titled "The Birth of 'Old' Presidio County," in ibid., 95; Barry Scobee, *Fort Davis, Texas: 1583–1965* (Fort Davis: Barry Scobee, 1963), 98–99. See further, Thompson, *A History of Marfa and Presidio County*, I, 131–32, 140, 143, 151, 176.

59. Raht, *The Romance of Davis Mountains and Big Bend Country*, 15; Joe C. Primera, "Los Hermanos Torres: Early Settlers of Pecos County," *The Permian Historical Annual* XX (1980): 90; Flores, "The Good Life the Hard Way," 32; Alice Evans Downie, *Terrell County, Texas, Its Past, Its People: A Compilation, Pictures of and Writings by or About People, Places, and Events in Terrell County* (Sanderson: Terrell County Heritage Commission, 1978), 37; Daggett, *Pecos County History*, I, 109.

60. Primera, "Los Hermanos Torres," 90; Raht, *The Romance of Davis Mountains and Big Bend Country*, 215.

61. Daggett, *Pecos County History*, I, 121, 152, and ibid., II, 184–85.

62. De León, *San Angeleños*, 140.

63. Grace Bitner, "The History of Tom Green County, Texas" (unpublished MA thesis, University of Texas, 1931), 34–36. Others listed as appointed by the district court (meeting in April 1875) to the grand jury for the month of July 1875 besides Guillermo Alderette were Juan Guardarama, Joaquín Belardo, and Trinidad Jaques. The petit jury of twelve men (again for July 1875) included Raphael Escobedo, Nestor Voel, Félix Subia, and Desidoro López. See further Grace Bitner, "Early History of the Concho Country and Tom Green County," *West Texas Historical Association Yearbook* IX (October 1933): 17–18.

64. Clemens, *The Concho Country*, 92. Unknown is the number of ethnic Mexicans whose service in politics history has overlooked, especially in towns and counties having historically small Tejano populations. One example may be that of Melitón Morales, who served on the first jury following Kimble County's organization in 1876. Kimble County Historical Survey Committee, *Recorded Landmarks of Kimble County*, 218.

65. Madison, *How Come It's Called That?*, 112–14.

66. Raht, *The Romance of Davis Mountains and Big Bend Country*, 194; Wright, "Population Patterns in Presidio County in 1880," 186; Thompson, *A History of Marfa and Presidio County*, I, 120.

67. Daggett, *Pecos County History*, II, 192.

68. Thompson, *A History of Marfa and Presidio County*, I, 138, 351; Wright, "Population Patterns in Presidio County in 1880," 186–87.

69. De León, *San Angeleños*, 140.

70. Gómez, *A Most Singular Country*, 93, 100.

71. Dearen, *Crossing Rio Pecos*, 65; Williams, *Texas' Last Frontier*, 126, 205,

207; Daggett, *Pecos County History*, I, 133, 149, 222, and ibid., II, 184; Williams, "First Two Irrigation Projects on Pecos River in Texas," 2; Raht, *The Romance of Davis Mountains and Big Bend Country*, 175.

72. Williams, "First Two Irrigation Projects on Pecos River in Texas," 2; Williams, "The Pontoon Bridge on the Pecos, 1869–1880," 12, 15; Dearen, *Crossing Rio Pecos*, 77.

73. Primera, "Los Hermanos Torres," 89–90; Flores, "The Good Life the Hard Way," 32; Williams, *Texas' Last Frontier*, 205, 207; Daggett, *Pecos County History*, I, 134 and ibid., II, 184; Dearen, *Crossing River Pecos*, 64, 65–66; Williams, "First Two Irrigation Projects on Pecos River in Texas," 4.

74. Williams, "First Two Irrigation Projects on Pecos River in Texas," 4; Williams, "The Pontoon Bridge on the Pecos, 1869–1886," 15; Dearen, *Crossing Rio Pecos*, 65–66; Daggett, *Pecos County History*, I, 134 (column 2); and Doug Braudaway, "Torres Family, Founders of Langtry," online publication of Val Verde County Historical Commission. Google Search: "Torres Family—Founders of Langtry, Texas" accessed June 10, 2021.

75. Quote is from Dearen, *Crossing Rio Pecos*, 65.

76. Williams, *Texas' Last Frontier*, 207; Daggett, *Pecos County History*, I, 222, and II, 184; Primera, "Los Hermanos Torres," 92–93; Google Search: Doug Braudaway, "Torres Family—Founders of Langtry, Texas."

77. Daggett, *Pecos County History*, I, 222, and II, 184; Google Search: Braudaway, "Torres Family—Founders of Langtry, Texas"; Williams, *Texas' Last Frontier*, 135, 207, 220–21; Dearen, *Crossing Rio Pecos*, 66.

78. Primera, "Los Hermanos Torres," 91–92.

79. Daggett, *Pecos County History*, I, 101–2, 128, 152, 156, 164–65, 168, 170.

80. Wooster, *Frontier Crossroads*, 41, 127; Wright, "Population Patterns in Presidio County in 1880," 192.

81. Thompson, *A History of Marfa and Presidio County*, I, 119, 133–34, 141, 200; Jacobson and Nored, *Jeff Davis County, Texas*, 124; Elam, "Acculturation on the Rio Grande Frontier," 82–87.

82. Braudaway, "The 'Origins' of Del Rio, Texas," 63–64; Prewitt, "'We Didn't Ask to Come to This Party,'" 1, 25, 31, 33–34, 42; *San Antonio Express*, January 24, 1883, 2; "Paula Losoya Taylor," Handbook of Texas Online; Whitehead Memorial Museum, *La Hacienda*, 3, 5, 369.

83. Williams, *Texas' Last Frontier*, 81–82; Gómez, *A Most Singular Country*, 98.

84. Williams, *Texas' Last Frontier*, 81–82, 129, 155, 159, 178, 185, 187; Santleben, *A Texas Pioneer*, 143.

85. Thompson, *A History of Marfa and Presidio County*, I, 109; Raht, *The Romance of Davis Mountains and Big Bend Country*, 164.

86. Kenneth L. Stewart and Arnoldo De León, "Education, Literacy, and Occupational Structure in West Texas, 1860–1900," *West Texas Historical Association Yearbook* LX (1984), in Arnoldo De León, ed., *Tejano West Texas* (College Station: Texas A&M University Press, 2015), 35.

87. Bill Green, *The Dancing Was Lively: Fort Concho, Texas, A Social History, 1867–1882* (San Angelo: Fort Concho Sketches Pub. Co., 1974), 63; Flores, "The Good Life the Hard Way," 14; Wooster, *Frontier Crossroads*, 126; Daggett, *Pecos County History*, I, 135; Jacobson and Nored, *Jeff Davis County*, 63.

88. Flores, "The Good Life the Hard Way," 14; Williams, *Texas' Last Frontier*, 83; Jacobson and Nored, *Jeff Davis County*, 63.

89. Wooster, *Frontier Crossroads*, 126, Table 9.1 titled "Civilian Occupations at Fort Davis, 1880."

90. Daggett, *Pecos County History*, I, 101, 152.

91. Williams, *Texas' Last Frontier*, 309, 370; Raht, *The Romance of Davis Mountains and Big Bend Country*, 163; Arnoldo De León and Kenneth L. Stewart, *Tejanos and the Numbers Game: A Socio-Historical Profile from the Federal Censuses, 1850–1900* (Albuquerque: University of New Mexico Press, 1989), 33; Wright, "Population Patterns in Presidio County in 1880," 193.

92. Clemens, *The Concho Country*, 87.

93. Stewart and De León, "Education, Literacy, and Occupational Structure in West Texas," De León, ed., *Tejano West Texas*, 35.

94. Clemens, *The Concho Country*, 60–61; Green, *The Dancing Was Lively*, 32.

95. Daggett, *Pecos County History*, I, 135.

96. AnneJo P. Wedin, *The Magnificent Marathon Basin: A History of Marathon, Texas, Its People and Events* (Austin: Nortex Press, 1989), 3; Williams, *Texas' Last Frontier*, 309; Clemens, *The Concho Country*, 87.

97. Jacobson and Nored, *Jeff Davis County*, 63; Charles Judson Crane, *The Experiences of a Colonel in the Infantry* (New York: Knickerbocker Press, 1923), 114.

98. Raht, *The Romance of Davis Mountains and Big Bend Country*, 235.

99. Clemens, *The Concho Country*, 84, 85; William D. Green, "Land Settlement in West Texas: Tom Green County, A Case Study, 1874–1903" (PhD diss., Texas Tech University, 1981), 102.

100. Williams, "The First Two Irrigation Projects on the Pecos River in Texas," 2, 4; Glenn Justice, *Little Known History of the Texas Big Bend: Documented Chronicles from Cabeza de Vaca to the Era of Pancho Villa* (Odessa, TX: Rimrock Press, 2001), 79. The Spanish word for these types of "underground holes" is *zapas* (or *sapas*). When people from Mexico first arrived in Del Rio before the Civil War, they improvised by relying on such underground dwellings (*zapas* were commonly used in Mexico, mainly by people having to move often). That section of modern-day Del Rio, which came to be known as San Felipe, was originally called "Las Sapas," for obvious reasons. Diana Sotelo Zertuche, *The Spirit of Val Verde* (Del Rio: Diana Sotelo Zertuche Publisher, 1985), 153–54.

101. Enrique R. Madrid, "The History and Future of Adobe in La Junta de los Ríos: Social Dimensions of Adobe Making," *Journal of Big Bend Studies* 17 (2005): 38; Joe Graham, "Texas-Mexican Vernacular Architecture," Handbook of Texas Online; Joe S. Graham, *The Jacal in the Big Bend: Its Origins and Evolution*, Robert J. Mallouf, ed. (Alpine, TX: Chihuahua: Desert Research Institute, 1988).

102. Madrid, "History and Future of Adobe in La Junta de los Ríos," 39; J. O. Langford, *Big Bend: A Homesteader's Story* (Austin: University of Texas Press, 1952), 63; "Adobe," Handbook of Texas Online; and Joe Graham, "Texas-Mexican Vernacular Architecture," Handbook of Texas Online.

103. Raht, *The Romance of Davis Mountains and Big Bend Country*, 149; "Fort Davis," Handbook of Texas Online.

104. Woolford, "The Burr G. Duval Diary," 497. But another contemporary had a slightly different conclusion, noting that at Fort Stockton "the houses are all adobe, except the quarters of the officers, which are of stone." Taylor, *The Coming Empire*, 333.

105. Raht, *The Romance of Davis Mountains and Big Bend Country*, 130.

106. Taylor, *The Coming Empire*, 333; Jennie Parks Ringgold, *Frontier Days in the Southwest* (San Antonio: Naylor Co., 1952), 8.

107. Raht, *The Romance of Davis Mountains and Big Bend Country*, 217.

108. Mrs. Mattie Belle Anderson, "Reminiscences of Mattie Belle Anderson, Texas, Fort Davis, Texas," Eugene C. Barker Texas History Center,

University of Texas Archives, Austin, Texas, 1929, 1.

109. Raht, *The Romance of Davis Mountains and Big Bend Country*, 256.

110. John Ernest Gregg, "The History of Presidio County" (unpublished MA thesis, UT Austin, 1933), republished in *Voice of the Mexican Border* (Marfa, TX: Centennial Edition, 1936), 35.

111. Williams, "First Two Irrigation Projects on Pecos River in Texas," *Permian Historical Annual* 15 (December 1975): 2, citing the 1870 Fort Davis surgeon's report.

112. Taylor, *The Coming Empire*, 360.

113. Daggett, *Pecos County History*, I, 125–26.

114. Dearen, *Crossing Rio Pecos*, 65; Williams, *Texas' Last Frontier*, 126, 205, 207; Daggett, *Pecos County History*, I, 133, 222, and ibid., II, 184; Williams, "First Two Irrigation Projects on Pecos River in Texas," 2.

115. Williams, "First Two Irrigation Projects on Pecos River in Texas," 2; Williams, "The Pontoon Bridge on the Pecos, 1869–1880," 12, 15; Dearen, *Crossing Rio Pecos*, 77.

116. Williams, "First Two Irrigation Projects on Pecos River in Texas," 4; Williams, "The Pontoon Bridge on the Pecos, 1869–1886," 12; Dearen, *Crossing Rio Pecos*, 65–66; Daggett, *Pecos County History*, I, 134; and Braudaway, "Torres Family, Founders of Langtry."

117. Thompson, *A History of Marfa and Presidio County*, I, 134; Gregg, "The History of Presidio County," in *Voice of the Mexican Border*, 35.

118. Gregg, "The History of Presidio County," in *Voice of the Mexican Border*, 35.

119. Daggett, *Pecos County History*, I, 126, 135–36.

120. Ibid.

121. Braudaway, "The 'Origins' of Del Rio, Texas," 4; Whitehead Memorial Museum, *La Hacienda*, 14–17.

122. Ringgold, *Frontier Days in the Southwest*, 8; Daggett, *Pecos County History*, I, 135.

123. De León, *San Angeleños*, 18–19.

124. Primera, "Los Hermanos Torres," 89; Daggett, *Pecos County History*, I, 152; Flores, "The Good Life the Hard Way," 23, 26, 63, 155–56.

125. Thompson, *A History of Marfa and Presidio County*, I, 108; Wooster, *Frontier Crossroads*, 125–26; Wright, "Population Patterns in Presidio County in 1880," 187; Wright, "Residential Segregation in Two Early

West Texas Towns," 319.

126. According to Clemens, *The Concho Country*, 101, a Catholic church did not exist in San Angelo, for instance, until 1880.

127. Flores, "The Good Life the Hard Way," 190.

128. Wooster, *Frontier Crossroads*, 126; Jacobson and Nored, *Jeff Davis County, Texas*, 186.

129. Zertuche, *The Spirit of Val Verde*, 34.

130. Ibid., 33–34.

131. Green, "Land Settlement in West Texas," 102; Raht, *The Romance of Davis Mountains and Big Bend Country*, 195.

132. Raht, *The Romance of Davis Mountains and Big Bend Country*, 195–96.

CHAPTER 2

1. Arnoldo De León, ed., *Tejano West Texas* (College Station: Texas A&M University Press, 2015), 4–5.

2. Robert A. Calvert, et al., *The History of Texas*, 6th ed. (Hoboken, NJ: Wylie Blackwell, 2020), 169; Clayton W. Williams, *Texas' Last Frontier: Fort Stockton and the Trans-Pecos, 1861–1895*, Ernest Wallace, ed. (College Station: Texas A&M University Press, 1982), 247; Arthur R. Gómez, *A Most Singular Country: A History of Occupation in the Big Bend* (Santa Fe: National Park Service; Salt Lake City: Charles Redd Center for Western Studies, Brigham Young University, 1990), 85; "Victorio," Handbook of Texas Online; De León, ed., *Tejano West Texas*, 4.

3. Gómez, *A Most Singular Country*, 99.

4. De León, ed., *Tejano West Texas*, 20; James T. Matthews, "The Edwards Plateau and Permian Basin," in *West Texas: A History of the Giant Side of the State*, Paul H. Carlson and Bruce A. Glasrud, eds. (Norman: University of Oklahoma Press, 2014), 6.

5. De León, ed., *Tejano West Texas*, 20; Paul H. Carlson, *Texas Woollybacks: The Range Sheep and Goat Industry* (College Station: Texas A&M University Press, 1982), 161.

6. Arnoldo De León and Kenneth L. Stewart, "Tejano Demographic Patterns and Socio-Economic Development," *The Borderlands Journal* VII (Fall 1983).

7. Arnoldo De León and Kenneth L. Stewart, *Tejanos and the Numbers Game: A Socio-Historical Interpretation from the Federal Censuses,*

1850–1900 (Albuquerque: University of New Mexico Press, 1989), 12, Table 1.3; Robert Wooster, *Frontier Crossroads: Fort Davis and the West* (College Station: Texas A&M University Press, 2006), 125; and Marsha Lea Daggett, *Pecos County History*, 2 vols. (Pecos County Historical Commission, 1973–1983), I, 102, 125.

8. Rosie Hatch, et al., *Texas Almanac, 2020–2021* (Austin: Texas State Historical Association, 2020), section titled "Counties of Texas"; and Paul Wright, "The Big Bend Population in 1900: Size, Growth, and Distribution," *Journal of Big Bend Studies* 8 (1996): 135–36. Counties organized in the twentieth century were: Schleicher (1901), Reagan (1903), Terrell (1905), Upton (1910), Culberson (1912), Real (1913), Hudspeth (1917), Crane (1927), and Loving (1931).

9. Matthews, "The Edwards Plateau and Permian Basin," 67.

10. Ibid., 69; Carlson, *Texas Woollybacks*, 157; entries for "Marathon," "Alpine," and "Marfa" from Handbook of Texas Online.

11. Carlson, *Texas Woollybacks*, 112.

12. Williams, *Texas' Last Frontier*, 246.

13. Glen Sample Ely, *Where the West Begins: Debating Texas Identity* (Lubbock: Texas Tech University Press, 2011), 110–11, 113.

14. Stephen Bogener, "The Varied Economy of West Texas," in *West Texas*, Carlson and Glasrud, eds., 182; M. Scott Sosebee, "Agriculture, Ranching, and Rural Life in West Texas," in ibid, 201; "Wool and Mohair Industry," Handbook of Texas Online.

15. Gómez, *A Most Singular Country*, 113; Wright, "The Big Bend Population in 1900," 147–48.

16. Ronnie C. Tyler, *The Big Bend: A History of the Last Texas Frontier* (Washington, DC: US Department of the Interior, National Parks Service, 1975), 136; Cecilia Thompson, *A History of Marfa and Presidio County, 1535–1946*, 2 vols. (Austin: Nortex Press, 1985), I, 173.

17. Kenneth B. Ragsdale, *Quicksilver: Terlingua and the Chisos Mountains Mining Company* (College Station: Texas A&M University Press, 1976), 13.

18. Ibid., 16; Tyler, *The Big Bend*, 138; JoAnn Pospisil, "Mariscal Mine's Contribution to the Quicksilver Industry," *West Texas Historical Association Yearbook* 88 (2012): 98.

19. "Terlingua, Texas," Handbook of Texas Online; Tyler, *The Big Bend*, 139;

Ragsdale, *Quicksilver*, 16.

20. Gómez, *A Most Singular Country*, 101.

21. Pospisil, "Mariscal Mine's Contribution to the Quicksilver Industry," 99–100, 101; Gómez, *A Most Singular Country*, 126–29; Tyler, *The Big Bend*, 144–45.

22. Daggett, *Pecos County History*, I, 102–3; Wooster, *Frontier Crossroads*, 125, 126.

23. Gómez, *A Most Singular Country*, 93, 100; Paul Wright, "Population Patterns in Presidio County in 1880: Evidence from the Census," *Journal of Big Bend Studies* 7 (January 1995), 194.

24. Carlson, *Texas Woollybacks*, 162; Alice Evans Downie, *Terrell County, Texas, Its Past, Its People: A Compilation, Pictures of and Writings by or About People, Places, and Events in Terrell County* (Sanderson: Terrell County Heritage Commission, 1978), 44; Patrick Dearen, *The Devils River: Treacherous Twin to the Pecos, 1535–1900* (Fort Worth: Texas Christian University Press, 2011), 144.

25. Carlson, *Texas Woollybacks*, 162; Downie, *Terrell County, Texas, Its Past, Its People*, 44; Dearen, *The Devils River*, 152–53.

26. Carlson, *Texas Woollybacks*, 162; Downie, *Terrell County, Texas, Its Past, Its People*, 146.

27. Carlson, *Texas Woollybacks*, 162.

28. Ibid.; Downie, *Terrell County, Texas, Its Past, Its People*, 57, 60–61.

29. Downie, *Terrell County, Texas, Its Past, Its People*, 60–62. Also, Tom Green County Historical Preservation League, Inc., *Tom Green County: Chronicles of Our Heritage*, 2 vols. (San Angelo: Tom Green County Historical Preservation League, Inc., 2003), I, 184–85, 222.

30. Daggett, *Pecos County History*, I, 103; Wooster, *Frontier Crossroads*, 125.

31. *San Angelo Standard-Times*, September 21, 1889, reprinted from the *Chattanooga Times*, October 12, 1889, 2.

32. *Coke County Rustler*, Robert Lee, Coke County, December 16, 1898, 1.

33. Ramon F. Adams, *From the Pecos to the Power: A Cowboy's Autobiography* (Norman: University of Oklahoma Press, 1965), 29–30.

34. Mario T. García, "Porfirian Diplomacy and the Administration of Justice in Texas, 1877–1900," *Aztlán: International Journal of Chicano Studies Research* 16 (1985): 5–7.

35. *San Antonio Express*, May 1, 1891, 3.

36. J. Marvin Hunter, *The Trail Drivers of Texas*, 2 vols. (New York: Argosy-Antiquarian, 1963), II, 664.

37. Winifred Kupper, ed., *Texas Sheepman: The Reminiscences of Robert Maudslay* (Austin: University of Texas Press, 1951), 123.

38. *San Antonio Daily Express*, April 18, 1886, 4; *Austin American*, April 20, 1886, 1; *Austin Statesman*, April 20, 1886, 1.

39. *San Antonio Daily Express*, November 5, 1894, 1.

40. *Austin Daily Statesman*, May 8, 1884, 1; May 10, 1884, 1; May 11, 1884, 2; September 6, 1884, 1; November 8, 1986, 1; *Austin Democratic Statesman*, July 26, 1884; García, "Porfirian Diplomacy and the Administration of Justice in Texas," 5–7.

41. *San Antonio Express*, July 26, 1897, 8.

42. *San Antonio Express*, December 7, 1883, 4; December 12, 1883, 4.

43. Thompson, *A History of Marfa and Presidio County*, I, 297; Carlysle Graham Raht, *The Romance of Davis Mountains and Big Bend Country* (El Paso: The Rahtbooks Company, 1919; revised ed. Odessa: The Rahtbooks Company, 1963), 304–5.

44. Mary Jaques, *Texan Ranch Life* (London: Horace Cox, 1894), 360–63. See also *San Angelo Standard*, November 24, 1894, 2.

45. *Austin Statesman*, February 7, 1891, 1; David L. Chapman, "Lynching in Texas" (unpublished MA thesis, Texas Tech University, 1973), 98.

46. On population figures, see De León and Stewart, *Tejanos and the Numbers Game*, 12; De León and Stewart, "Tejano Demographic Patterns and Socio-Economic Development," 6.

47. Paul Wright, "Life on Both Sides of the Tracks in Early Alpine," *West Texas Historical Association Yearbook* LXXIII (1997): 107.

48. Wooster, *Frontier Crossroads*, 125; Thompson, *A History of Marfa and Presidio County*, I, 361.

49. Williams, *Texas' Last Frontier*, 361.

50. *San Angelo Standard*, September 21, 1889, 1; Daggett, *Pecos County History*, I, 158.

51. Glenn Justice, *Little Known History of the Texas Big Bend: Documented Chronicles from Cabeza de Vaca to the Era of Pancho Villa* (Odessa, TX: Rimrock Press, 2001), 36–37.

52. *El Paso Times*, July 22, 1886, 3.

53. Williams, *Texas' Last Frontier*, 272, 343.

54. John Ernest Gregg, "The History of Presidio County" (unpublished MA thesis, UT Austin, 1933), republished in *Voice of the Mexican Border* (Marfa, TX: Centennial Edition, 1936), 55.

55. Thompson, *A History of Marfa and Presidio County*, I, 175–76, 204, 220, 254. On pop. figures, see De León and Stewart, *Tejanos and the Numbers Game*, 12.

56. Wooster, *Frontier Crossroads*, 125.

57. Virginia Madison, *The Big Bend Country of Texas* (Albuquerque: University of New Mexico Press, 1955), 44–45; *San Angelo Standard*, September 13, 1884, 4.

58. Estela Perez Santos, *Texas Came to Me: The Life and Impact of Jesusa Farias on the World* (privately printed, 2021), 25–27, 32, 35, 37–38. Obituary of Gus Noyes may be found in Nestor Pérez, "Colonia Jiménez de Melvin, Texas," unpaginated booklet, section titled "Bits and Pieces," in West Texas Collection, Angelo State University, San Angelo, TX, in file labeled "Melvin, Texas, Collection."

59. Crockett County Historical Society, *History of Crockett County* (San Angelo: Anchor Publishing Co., 1976), 140.

60. Arnoldo De León, *San Angeleños: Mexican Americans in San Angelo, Texas* (San Angelo: Fort Concho Museum Press, 1985), 19–23.

61. Wooster, *Frontier Crossroads*, 126; Justice, *Little Known History of the Texas Big Bend*, 85.

62. Clifford B. Casey, *Alpine, Texas: Then and Now* (Seagraves, TX: Pioneer Book Publishers, 1981), 18, 311; Paul Wright, "Residential Segregation in Two Early West Texas Towns," *Southwestern Historical Quarterly* CII (January 1999): 297.

63. Steven W. Prewitt, "'We Didn't Ask to Come to This Party': Self Determination Collides with the Federal Government in the Public Schools of Del Rio, Texas, 1890–1971" (PhD diss., University of Houston, 2000), 34–35, 42.

64. Thompson, *A History of Marfa and Presidio County*, I, 253–54.

65. Clifford B. Casey, *Mirages, Mysteries and Reality: Brewster County, Texas, The Big Bend of the Rio Grande* (Hereford, TX: Pioneer Book Publishers, 1972), 170, 173.

66. Clifford B. Casey, *Soldiers, Ranchers and Miners in the Big Bend* ([Washington] Division of History, Office of Archeology and Historical

Preservation, 1969), 26–27.

67. Daggett, *Pecos County History*, I, 296; "Brogado, Texas," Handbook of Texas Online; Alton Hughes, *Pecos: A History of the Pioneer West*, 2 vols. (Seagraves, TX: Pioneer Book Publishers, 1978), I, 99–100, 245–46.

68. "Saragosa, Texas," Handbook of Texas Online.

69. Thompson, *A History of Marfa and Presidio County*, I, 214, 347; "Casa Piedra, Texas," Handbook of Texas Online.

70. "Ochoa, Texas," Handbook of Texas Online.

71. Thompson, *A History of Marfa and Presidio County*, I, 173, 301; "Shafter, Texas," Handbook of Texas Online.

72. Wright, "The Big Bend Population in 1900," 142; Albert B. Tucker, "Terlingua Abaja," *Journal of Big Bend Studies* 3 (January 1991): 87–88; Casey, *Mirages, Mysteries and Reality*, 170; Gómez, *A Most Singular Country*, 121.

73. Casey, *Soldiers, Ranchers, and Miners in the Big Bend*, 26–27, 28.

74. Casey, *Mirages, Mysteries and Reality*, 172.

75. Ibid., 125, 172; Gómez, *A Most Singular Country*, 101; Lindsay Baker, *More Ghost Towns of Texas* (Norman: University of Oklahoma Press, 2005), 14.

76. Albert B. Tucker, "The Lost Communities of San Vicente," *West Texas Historical Association Yearbook* LXXII (1996): 108–10; Casey, *Mirages, Mysteries and Reality*, 172; Gómez, *A Most Singular Country*, 160.

77. Joe C. Primera, "Los Hermanos Torres: Early Settlers of Pecos County," *The Permian Historical Annual* XX (1980): 93; Williams, *Texas's Last Frontier*, 275; Daggett, *Pecos County History*, I, 152; Doug Braudaway, "Torres Family, Founders of Langtry," online publication of Val Verde County Historical Commission. Google Search: "Torres Family—Founders of Langtry, Texas," accessed June 10, 2021.

78. J. O. Langford, *Big Bend: A Homesteader's Story* (Austin: University of Texas Press, 1952), 63. Also, Enrique R. Madrid, "The History and Future of Adobe at La Junta de los Rios: Social Dimensions of Adobe Making," *Journal of Big Bend Studies* 17 (2005): 39; "Adobe," Handbook of Texas Online; and Joe Graham, "Texas-Mexican Vernacular Architecture," Handbook of Texas Online.

79. Joe S. Graham, *The Jacal in the Big Bend: Its Origins and Evolution*, Robert J. Mallouf, ed. (Alpine, TX: Chihuahua: Desert Research

Institute, 1988), 22–23; Joe Graham, "Texas-Mexican Vernacular Architecture," Handbook of Texas Online; Graham, "The Jacal in the Big Bend"; Madrid, "History and Future of Adobe in La Junta de los Rios," 38.

80.   Raht, *The Romance of Davis Mountains and Big Bend Country*, 175–76; Williams, *Texas' Last Frontier*, 120, 126, 135, 195, 205, 220–21, 260, 262; Braudaway, "Torres Family Founders of Langtry," online publication for Val Verde County Historical Commission, accessed June 10, 2021; Primera, "Los Hermanos Torres," 89, 91–94; Daggett, *Pecos County History*, I, 128, 132, 222; Patrick Dearen, *Crossing Rio Pecos* (Fort Worth: Texas Christian University Press, 1996), 64–66.

81.   Gómez, *A Most Singular Country*, 101, 106.

82.   Ibid., 101, 103.

83.   Thompson, *A History of Marfa and Presidio County*, I, 195.

84.   Wright, "Residential Segregation in Two Early West Texas Towns," 303, 304–5; Barry Scobee, *Fort Davis, Texas: 1583–1965* (Fort Davis: Barry Scobee, 1963), 157.

85.   Wooster, *Frontier Crossroads*, 127.

86.   Daggett, *Pecos County History*, I, 165, 164, 168.

87.   *San Antonio Express*, January 24, 1883, 2; "Paula Losoya Taylor," Handbook of Texas Online; Whitehead Memorial Museum, *La Hacienda: An Official Bicentennial Publication* (Del Rio: The Museum, 1976), 3, 5, 369; Prewitt, "'We Didn't Ask to Come to This Party,'" 31, 33–34.

88.   Thompson, *A History of Marfa and Presidio County*, I, 264–65.

89.   Alice Jack Dolan Shipman, *Taming the Big Bend: A History of the Extreme Western Portion of Texas from Fort Clark to El Paso* (Austin: Von Boeckmann-Jones Co., 1926)], 125.

90.   *Austin Statesman*, December 31, 1891, 1; *San Angelo Standard-Times*, January 9, 1892, 3; *San Antonio Express*, January 16, 1892, 2, January 17, 1892, 2; Elliott Young, *Catarino Garza's Revolution on the Texas-Mexico Border* (Durham, NC: Duke University Press, 2004), 122, 205. The meaning of *Chinaco*, denoting a "brave, frontier guerrilla soldier," is provided in Pedro Angel Palou Pérez, *5th de Mayo: 1862* (Puebla: Gobierno del Estado de Puebla, Primera Edición Bilingüe, 2000), 12–13, 140–41.

91.   De León, *San Angeleños*, 16, 23–25, 28.

92.   Thompson, *A History of Marfa and Presidio County*, I, 254.

93. María Eva Flores, "The Good Life the Hard Way: The Mexican American Community of Fort Stockton, Texas, 1930–1945" (PhD diss., Arizona State University, 2000), 45–46.

94. Gus Clemens, *The Concho Country* (San Antonio: Mulberry Avenue Books, 1980), 101.

95. Gregg, "The History of Presidio County," in *Voice of the Mexican Border*, 49.

96. Wright, "Life on Both Sides of the Tracks in Early Alpine," 103.

97. Williams, *Texas' Last Frontier*, 318, citing Alvin Wilde, *St. Joseph Catholic Church of Fort Stockton* (privately printed, ca. 1972).

98. Kinney County Historical Society, *Kinney County, 125 Years of Growth, 1852–1977* (Brackettville: Kinney County Historical Society, 1977), 29, 137.

99. Madison, *How Come It's Called That?*, 112–14.

100. Thompson, *A History of Marfa and Presidio County*, I, 315.

101. Arnoldo De León, *The Tejano Community, 1836–1900* (Albuquerque: University of New Mexico Press, 1.

102. Madison, *The Big Bend Country of Texas*, 28–29.

103. Ibid., 30–31.

104. Mody C. Boatright, "The Devil's Grotto," in *Texas and Southwestern Lore*, J. Frank Dobie, ed. (Dallas: Southern Methodist University Press, 1967 [1927]), 102–6. Other works telling the story of "The Devil's Grotto" include Mody C. Boatright, et al., eds., *Mesquite and Willow* (Dallas: Southern Methodist University Press, 1957), 171–74; Elton R. Miles, "The Devil in the Big Bend," in *Tales of the Big Bend*, Elton Miles, ed. (College Station: Texas A&M University Press, 1976), 17–26; and Mody C. Boatright, et al., eds., *Folk Travelers: Ballads, Tales, and Talk* (Austin: Texas Folklore Society, 1953), 205–16.

105. Barry Scobee, *Old Fort Davis* (San Antonio: Naylor Co., 1947), 79–84.

106. Raht, *The Romance of Davis Mountains and Big Bend Country*, 77–81; "Santiago Peak," Handbook of Texas Online.

107. Boatright, "The Devil's Grotto," in *Texas and Southwestern Lore*, Frank J. Dobie, ed., 102–6; Boatright et al., eds., *Mesquite and Willow*, 171–74.

108. De León, *San Angeleños*, 25, 30, 148.

109. Nicholas Villanueva Jr., *The Lynching of Mexicans in the Texas Borderlands* (Albuquerque: University of New Mexico Press, 2017), 28–29; De León,

San Angeleños, 24–25; Arnoldo De León, *Las Fiestas Patrias: Biographic Notes on the Hispanic Presence in San Angelo, Texas* (San Antonio: Caravel Press, 1978), 7.

110. De León, *San Angeleños*, 25, 30, 148.

111. Villanueva, *The Lynching of Mexicans in the Texas Borderlands*, 29; De León, *San Angeleños*, 24–25.

112. Villanueva, *The Lynching of Mexicans in the Texas Borderlands*, 29–30; De León, *San Angeleños*, 25–26.

113. Lucy Miller Jacobson and Mildred Bloys Nored, *Jeff Davis County, Texas* (Fort Davis: Fort Davis Historical Society, 1993), 303.

114. "Reminiscences of Mrs. Mattie Belle Anderson, Teacher, Fort Davis, Texas," Eugene C. Barkers Texas History Center, University of Texas Archives, Austin, Texas, 1929, 2.

115. Jacobson and Nored, *Jeff Davis County, Texas*, 304, 308–9.

116. Gregg, "The History of Presidio County," in *Voice of the Mexican Border*, 50.

117. Prewitt, "'We Didn't Ask to Come to This Party,'" 40.

118. Ibid., 40, 44, 45.

119. De León, *San Angeleños*, 30–31.

120. Villanueva, *The Lynching of Mexicans in the Texas Borderlands*, 31.

121. *San Angelo Standard-Times*, October 20, 1894, 1; October 27, 1894, 1.

122. For a general discussion of the state of "danger and disorder" during the 1880s and 1890s, see De León, *Tejano West Texas*, 4–5.

123. The politics of South Texas are discussed in Arnoldo De León, *Mexican Americans in Texas: A Brief History*, 3rd ed. (Wheeling, IL: Harlan Davidson, 2009), 61–63.

CHAPTER 3

1. Glen Sample Ely, *Where the West Begins: Debating Texas Identity* (Lubbock: Texas Tech University Press, 2011), 110.

2. Arthur R. Gómez, *A Most Singular Country: A History of Occupation in the Big Bend* (Santa Fe: National Park Service; Salt Lake City: Charles Redd Center for Western Studies, Brigham Young University, 1990), 103.

3. Ely, *Where the West Begins*, 110, 113.

4. Paul H. Carlson, *Texas Woollybacks: The Range Sheep and Goat Industry* (College Station: Texas A&M University Press, 1982), 189, 190–91,

196–98; and Google Search: Doug Braudaway, "Texas Sheep and Goat Raisers Association-PDF free," accessed March 19, 2020.

5.   Mario T. García, *Desert Immigrants: The Mexicans of El Paso* (New Haven: Yale University Press, 1981), 18; Gómez, *A Most Singular Country*, 103; Carlson, *Texas Woollybacks*, 192–93.

6.   Arnoldo De León and Kenneth L. Stewart, "Tejano Demographic Patterns and Socio-Economic Development," *The Borderlands Journal* VII (Fall 1983): 6; Arnoldo De León, "Mexican Americans in the Edwards Plateau and Trans-Pecos Region, 1900–2000: A Demographic Study," *Southwestern Historical Quarterly* CXII (October 2008): 158, 159.

7.   De León and Stewart, "Tejano Demographic Patterns and Socio-Economic Development," 6; De León, "Mexican Americans in the Edwards Plateau and Trans-Pecos Region, 1900–2000," 158, 159; John Eusebio Klingemann, "The Population Is Overwhelmingly Mexican; Most of It Is in Sympathy with the Revolution: Mexico's Revolution of 1910 and the Tejano Community in the Big Bend," in *War Along the Border: The Mexican Revolution and Tejano Communities*, Arnoldo De León, ed. (College Station: Texas A&M University Press, 2012), 264, 266, 268; Paul Wright, "Characteristics of Big Bend Mining Towns, 1885–1920," *Journal of Big Bend Studies* 9 (1997): 107–9; Paul Wright, "A Tumultuous Decade: Changes in the Mexican-Origin Population of the Big Bend, 1910–1920," *Journal of Big Bend Studies* 10 (1998): 166, 175–78, 184.

8.   Wright, "Characteristics of Big Bend Mining Towns, 1885–1920," 89.

9.   Monica Perales, *Smeltertown: Making and Remembering a Southwest Border Community* (Chapel Hill: University of North Carolina Press, 2010), 101; Paul Wright, "Work Among Anglos and Hispanics in the Big Bend, 1910," *West Texas Historical Association Yearbook* LXXI (1995): 23.

10.   Gómez, *A Most Singular Country*, 101, 103, 107.

11.   Wright, "A Tumultuous Decade," 169.

12.   Monica Muñoz Martinez, *The Injustice Never Leaves You: Anti-Mexican Violence in Texas* (Cambridge: Harvard University Press, 2018), 122, 127.

13.   Roberto Aguero, *A Legacy of Pride: Shearing Sheep and Angora Goats the Texas Way*, unpublished ms.; Roberto Aguero, *100 Years of Aguero's: 1915–2015, The Manuel and Francisca Aguero Family Story* (privately printed, 2015), n.p., section titled "Preface"; "Barksdale, Texas," Handbook of Texas Online.

14. Estela Perez Santos, *Texas Came to Me: The Life and Impact of Jesusa Farias on the World* (privately printed, 2021), 64.

15. Clifford B. Casey, *Alpine, Texas: Then and Now* (Seagraves, TX: Pioneer Book Publishers, 1981), 330.

16. Alice Evans Downie, *Terrell County, Texas, Its Past, Its People: A Compilation, Pictures of and Writings by or About People, Places, and Events in Terrell County* (Sanderson: Terrell County Heritage Commission, 1978), 55–58, 146.

17. Downie, *Terrell County, Texas, Its Past, Its People*, 61–62; Leta Crawford, *A History of Irion County* (Waco: Texian Press, 1966), 51.

18. Aguero, *100 Years of Aguero's, 1915–2015*, 111; Downie, *Terrell County, Texas, Its Past, Its People*, 60–61; Diana Sotelo Zertuche, *The Spirit of Val Verde* (Del Rio: Diana Sotelo Zertuche Publisher, 1985), 127; Pauline R. Kibbe, *Latin Americans in Texas* (Albuquerque: University of New Mexico Press, 1946), 204.

19. Marsha Lea Daggett, *Pecos County History*, 2 vols. (Pecos County Historical Commission, 1973–1983), II, 164, 253, I, 327.

20. "Hispanic Culture Contributed to Midland's Early Days," *The Thorny Trail* XXV, no. 2, (Spring 1997), n.p.

21. Floyd Leslie Marshall, "History and Present Status of Latin American Education in Melvin, Texas" (MA thesis, Hardin-Simmons University, 1950), 10, 68. This thesis is included in Estela Perez Santos, "A Snapshot of Melvin, Texas, 1905–1955," in West Texas Collection, Angelo State University, San Angelo, Texas, in file labeled "Melvin, Texas, Collection." Also, Nestor Pérez, "Colonia Jiménez de Melvin, Texas," unpaginated booklet, section titled "Cotton Farming," in West Texas Collection, Angelo State University, San Angelo, Texas, in file labeled "Melvin, Texas, Collection." Menard County Historical Society, *Menard County History: An Anthology* (San Angelo: Anchor Publishing Co., 1982), 500.

22. Gómez, *A Most Singular Country*, 158, 161, 163, 165; Susan L. Tanner, "From Castolón to Santa Elena: The People Behind the Ruins," *Journal of Big Bend Studies* 5 (January 1993): 99, 101.

23. Ronnie C. Tyler, *The Big Bend: A History of the Last Texas Frontier* (Washington, DC: US Department of the Interior, National Parks Service, 1975), 147–48; Gómez, *A Most Singular Country*, 135; Clifford B. Casey, *Mirages, Mysteries and Reality: Brewster County, Texas, The Big Bend of the*

Rio Grande (Hereford, TX: Pioneer Book Publishers, 1972), 126; JoAnn Pospisil, "Women and Wax: Female Participation in the Candelilla Wax Industry," *Journal of Big Bend Studies* 8 (1996): 154–55.

24. Casey, *Mirages, Mysteries and Reality*, 126; Pospisil, "Women and Wax," 154; Virginia Madison, *The Big Bend Country of Texas* (Albuquerque: University of New Mexico Press, 1955), 225.

25. Gómez, *A Most Singular Country*, 135; Casey, *Mirages, Mysteries and Reality*, 126.

26. Casey, *Mirages, Mysteries and Reality*, 126; Tyler, *The Big Bend*, 148; Pospisil, "Women and Wax," 156; Madison, *The Big Bend Country of Texas*, 225; AnneJo P. Wedin, *The Magnificent Marathon Basin: A History of Marathon, Texas, Its People and Events* (Austin: Nortex Press, 1989), 109, 166.

27. Casey, *Mirages, Mysteries and Reality*, 126.

28. Tyler, *The Big Bend*, 147; Casey, *Mirages, Mysteries and Reality*, 174–76; Madison, *The Big Bend Country of Texas*, 234.

29. T. Lindsay Baker, *More Ghost Towns of Texas* (Norman: University of Oklahoma Press, 2005), 13, 14; Gómez, *A Most Singular Country*, 115–17.

30. Madison, *The Big Bend Country of Texas*, 170–72; Tyler, *The Big Bend*, 136–37; Glenn Justice, *Little Known History of the Texas Big Bend: Documented Chronicles from Cabeza de Vaca to the Era of Pancho Villa* (Odessa, TX: Rimrock Press, 2001), 48–49.

31. Gómez, *A Most Singular Country*, 117, 119.

32. Tyler, *The Big Bend*, 139, 143.

33. JoAnn Pospisil, "Mariscal Mine's Contribution to the Quicksilver Industry," *West Texas Historical Association Yearbook* 88 (2012): 99, 101, 105.

34. Kenneth B. Ragsdale, *Quicksilver: Terlingua and the Chisos Mountains Mining Company* (College Station: Texas A&M University Press, 1976), 28–29, 36; Tyler, *The Big Bend*, 142; "Chisos Mining Company," Handbook of Texas Online.

35. Cecilia Thompson, *A History of Marfa and Presidio County, 1535–1946*, 2 vols. (Austin: Nortex Press, 1985), II, 4; Charles A. Hawley, "Life Along the Border," in *Publications of the West Texas Historical and Scientific Society*, vol. 20 (Alpine, TX: Sul Ross State University, 1964), 25; Tyler, *The Big Bend*, 139. On Chihuahua as the miners' state of origin, see

Wright, "Characteristics of Big Bend Mining Towns, 1885–1920," 107.

36. Gómez, *A Most Singular Country*, 121, 123; Ragsdale, *Quicksilver*, 40.

37. Tyler, *The Big Bend*, 137, 139, 142.

38. Justice, *Little Known History of the Texas Big Bend*, 48–50; Tyler, *The Big Bend*, 137.

39. Tyler, *The Big Bend*, 139, 142; Art Gómez, "If the Walls Could Speak: Mariscal Mine and the West Texas Quicksilver Industry, 1896–1946," Mining History Association (1998): 31, 33.

40. Justice, *Little Known History of the Texas Big Bend*, 50.

41. Pospisil, "Mariscal Mine's Contribution to the Quicksilver Industry," 103–4.

42. Tyler, *The Big Bend*, 142; Ragsdale, *Quicksilver*, 84; Gómez, *A Most Singular Country*, 123; Thompson, *A History of Marfa and Presidio County*, II, 4; Hawley, "Life Along the Border," 25; Justice, *Little Known History of the Texas Big Bend*, 50.

43. Justice, *Little Known History of the Texas Big Bend*, 50; Tyler, *The Big Bend*, 142; Thompson, *A History of Marfa and Presidio County*, II, 4; Hawley, "Life Along the Border," 25; Gómez, *A Most Singular Country*, 123; Ragsdale, *Quicksilver*, 40; Wright, "Characteristics of Big Bend Mining Towns," 94–95.

44. Tyler, *The Big Bend*, 139; Ragsdale, *Quicksilver*, 160–61.

45. Tyler, *The Big Bend*, 139; Gómez, *A Most Singular Country*, 122; Ragsdale, *Quicksilver*, 80; Thompson, *A History of Marfa and Presidio County*, II, 2–3; Wright, "Characteristics of Big Bend Mining Towns," 109.

46. Tyler, *The Big Bend*, 139; Barry Scobee, *Fort Davis, Texas: 1583–1965* (Fort Davis: Barry Scobee, 1963), 147; Gómez, *A Most Singular Country*, 115–17.

47. Gómez, *A Most Singular Country*, 117, 119.

48. Tyler, *The Big Bend*, 139; Gómez, *A Most Singular Country*, 125; Ragsdale, *Quicksilver*, 49; Wedin, *The Magnificent Marathon Basin*, 106. Hawley in "Life Along the Border" describes a flask of mercury as follows: "Quicksilver flasks are made of wrought iron and will hold 76 pounds of quicksilver. A flask is about the size of a two-quart glass jar. The opening at the top is about one inch in diameter and is threaded and fitted with an iron plug or cork. This cork is screwed in by placing the flask in a strong vise and using a wrench having a handle two or three feet in length. This is necessary in order to prevent loss from leakage, but even so it was unusual

for a shipment to reach St. Louis without some loss being reported" (119).

49. Tyler, *The Big Bend*, 139; Thompson, *A History of Marfa and Presidio County*, II, 4; Hawley, "Life Along the Border," 27; Wright, "Characteristics of Big Bend Mining Towns, 1885–1920," 89; Gómez, *A Most Singular Country*, 125; Lonn Taylor, "Ninety-Six Miles in Ninety-Six Hours: The Marfa-Terlingua Freight Road, 1899–1960," *Journal of Big Bend Studies* 23 (2011): 12–13.

50. Gómez, *A Most Singular Country*, 125; Ragsdale, *Quicksilver*, 47–48.

51. Ragsdale, *Quicksilver*, 47–48; Casey, *Mirages, Mysteries and Reality*, 161.

52. Downie, *Terrell County, Texas, Its Past, Its People*, 150–51.

53. Gómez, *A Most Singular Country*, 125; Ragsdale, *Quicksilver*, 54–55; Tanner, "From Castolón to Santa Elena," 99, 101.

54. Aguero, *A Legacy of Pride*; "Real County" and "Edwards County," Handbook of Texas Online.

55. María Eva Flores, "The Good Life the Hard Way: The Mexican American Community of Fort Stockton, Texas, 1930–1945" (PhD diss., Arizona State University, 2000), 48, 52–55; Downie, *Terrell County, Texas, Its Past, Its People*, 270; Martinez, *The Injustice Never Leaves You*, 126–27.

56. Hawley, "Life Along the Border," 141.

57. Taylor, "Ninety-Six Miles in Ninety-Six Hours," 11.

58. Hawley, "Life Along the Border," 20–21.

59. Ibid., 35–36.

60. Ragsdale, *Quicksilver*, 108.

61. Madison, *The Big Bend Country of Texas*, 51. On early expressions of this lore, see Arnoldo De León, *They Called Them Greasers: Anglo Attitudes Toward Mexicans in Texas* (Austin: University of Texas Press, 1983), 67–68.

62. Hawley, "Life Along the Border," 13.

63. Flores, "The Good Life the Hard Way," 23, 26, 63, 155–56.

64. Nicholas Villanueva Jr., *The Lynching of Mexicans in the Texas Borderlands* (Albuquerque: University of New Mexico Press, 2017), 115; Martinez, *The Injustice Never Leaves You*, 130.

65. Paul Wright, "Residential Segregation in Two Early West Texas Towns," *Southwestern Historical Quarterly* CII (January 1999): 297, 301.

66. Wright, "Residential Segregation in Two Early West Texas Towns," 303–5.

67. Paul Wright, "Four Different Communities: Presidio in 1910, 1920, 1930,

and 1940," *Journal of Big Bend Studies* 25 (2013): 206, 213.

68. Flores, "The Good Life the Hard Way," 155–56.

69. Lucy Miller Jacobson and Mildred Bloys Nored, *Jeff Davis County, Texas* (Fort Davis: Fort Davis Historical Society, 1993), 308–9.

70. Maggie Rivas-Rodríguez, "Integration a Mordidas in Alpine Schools [1969]," *Texas Mexican Americans and Postwar Civil Rights* (Austin: University of Texas Press, 2015), 16.

71. Jacobson and Nored, *Jeff Davis County*, 308–9; Thompson, *A History of Marfa and Presidio County*, II, 61, 74.

72. Steven W. Prewitt, "'We Didn't Ask to Come to This Party': Self Determination Collides with the Federal Government in the Public Schools of Del Rio, Texas, 1890–1971" (PhD diss., University of Houston, 2000), 1–2, 25, 40, 45–46.

73. Arnoldo De León, *San Angeleños: Mexican Americans in San Angelo, Texas* (San Angelo: Fort Concho Museum Press, 1985), 31, 38.

74. Flores, "The Good Life the Hard Way," 210–16.

75. Wedin, *The Magnificent Marathon Basin*, 241, 556; "Marathon," Handbook of Texas Online.

76. Quoted in Ragsdale, *Quicksilver*, 90.

77. Dorothy Person Kerig, *Luther T. Ellsworth: U.S. Consul on the Border during the Mexican Revolution* (El Paso: Texas Western Press, University of Texas at El Paso, 1975), 14–15; and Juan Gómez-Quiñones, *Sembradores, Ricardo Flores Magón y El Partido Liberal Mexicano: A Eulogy and Critique* (Los Angeles: Aztlán Publications, 1973), 29.

78. Klingemann, "The Population Is Overwhelmingly Mexican," 260–63, 267–68; Madison, *The Big Bend Country of Texas*, 50.

79. Madison, *The Big Bend Country of Texas*, 50; Martinez, *The Injustice Never Leaves You*, 121, 130.

80. Klingemann, "The Population Is Overwhelmingly Mexican," 259; Ragsdale, *Quicksilver*, 98–100. Also, Martinez, *The Injustice Never Leaves You*, 130.

81. Glenn Justice, *Revolution on the Rio Grande* (El Paso: Texas Western Press, 1992), 10; George J. Morgenthaler, *The River Has Never Divided Us: A Border History of La Junta de los Rios* (Austin: University of Texas Press, 2004), 187, 191.

82. Gómez, *A Most Singular Country*, 133, 139, 141–42; Justice, *Revolution on*

the Rio Grande, 11; Morgenthaler, *The River Has Never Divided Us*, 187–88; Villanueva, *The Lynching of Mexicans in the Texas Borderlands*, 115–16.

83. Justice, *Revolution on the Rio Grande*, 11; Morgenthaler, *The River Has Never Divided Us*, 187–88; Villanueva, *Lynching of Mexicans in the Texas Borderlands*, 115–16; Casey, *Mirages, Mysteries and Reality*, 131–32; Virginia Madison, *How Come It's Called That? Place Names in the Big Bend Country* (New York: October House Inc., 1968), 42–43; Martinez, *The Injustice Never Leaves You*, 130.

84. Villanueva, *The Lynching of Mexicans in the Texas Borderlands*, 115–17; Thompson, *A History of Marfa and Presidio County*, II, 128.

85. Justice, *Revolution on the Rio Grande*, 22, 26, 28, 29; Villanueva, *The Lynching of Mexicans in the Texas Borderlands*, 124–25.

86. Justice, *Revolution on the Rio Grande*, 31, 36, 41.

87. Ibid., 32.

88. Villanueva, *The Lynching of Mexicans in the Texas Borderlands*, 109, 126–30; Martinez, *The Injustice Never Leaves You*, 126.

89. The story of the massacre is recounted in numerous sources, among them Justice, *Revolution on the Rio Grande*, 36–41, 47; Villanueva, *The Lynching of Mexicans in the Texas Borderlands*, 109, 126–30; Sonia Hernández and John Morán González, *Reverberations of Racial Violence: Critical Reflections on the History of the Border* (Austin: University of Texas Press, 2021), 17, 42–44; Robert Keil, *Bosque Bonito: Violent Times Along the Borderland During the Mexican Revolution*, Elizabeth McBride, ed. (Alpine, TX: Center for Big Bend Studies, Sul Ross University, 2002), chap. 8. *San Angelo Standard-Times*, January 29, 2018, 1A.

90. Justice, *Revolution on the Rio Grande*, 40.

91. Justice, *Revolution on the Rio Grande*, 36–41, 47; Villanueva, *The Lynching of Mexicans in the Texas Borderlands*, 109, 126–30; https://www.texas-observer.org/who-writes-history-the-fight-to-commemorate-a-massacre-by-the-texas-rangers/; Glenn Justice, Welcome to Glenn's Texas History Blog, Rimrock Press, http://www.rimrockpress.com/blog/index.php?entry=entry070202–111903; and http://los-tejanos.com/index.html, all accessed March 31, 2020.

92. Justice, *Revolution on the Rio Grande*, 49–54; Villanueva, *The Lynching of Mexicans in the Texas Borderlands*, 130–32; Keil, *Bosque Bonito*, chap. 9.

93. Justice, *Revolution on the Rio Grande*, 49–54; Villanueva, *The Lynching of*

Mexicans in the Texas Borderlands, 130–32; Keil, *Bosque Bonito*, chap. 9.

94. Gómez, *A Most Singular Country*, 146, 148–49, 153; Morgenthaler, *The River Has Never Divided Us*, 189–91; Justice, *Little Known History of the Texas Big Bend*, chaps. 5–9.

95. Complete coverage of the episode and its aftermath is given in Martinez, *The Injustice Never Leaves You*, chap. 1, "Divine Retribution." Also see Villanueva, *The Lynching of Mexicans in the Texas Borderlands*, 55–62; "Antonio Rodríguez," Handbook of Texas Online. Also, Allan A. Stovall, *Nueces Headwater Country: A Regional History* (San Antonio: Naylor Press, 1959), 254–55. The scholarship offers little elaboration as to local Mexican reaction to the lynching, although newspapers of the era do indicate them present as the mob seized Rodríguez. Perhaps the discrepancy lies in that the Hispanic population in Edwards County as late as 1930 was only 509 (the 1910 federal census did not enumerate ethnicity or race), and in 1910 probably constituted only a small percentage of the 1,000 total residents in town. The tornado that struck Rocksprings on April 12, 1927, killed fourteen individuals of Spanish surname, again a small number compared to the seventy-two deaths it inflicted upon Anglos. According to oral history accounts told by Mexican Americans, the powerful storm, which left some 900 people homeless, was an act of retribution for the lynching of Rodríguez. Martinez, *The Injustice Never Leaves You*, 67–69. *Victoria Weekly Advocate* (Victoria, Texas), November 19, 1910, 1; November 26, 1910, 7. The casualty count is from Stovall, *Nueces Headwater Country*, 341–43. Size of the population in 1930 from De León, "Mexican Americans in the Edwards Plateau and Trans-Pecos Region, 1900–2000," Table 4.

96. Villanueva, *The Lynching of Mexicans in the Texas Borderlands*, 100–101, 80–81.

97. Ibid., 81–83.

98. Ibid., 82–84, 86.

99. Ibid., 85.

100. Ibid., 85–86, 93, 95, 100. See further, Alton Hughes, *Pecos: A History of the Pioneer West*, 2 vols. (Seagraves, TX: Pioneer Book Publishers, 1978), I, 193–96.

101. Casey, *Mirages, Mysteries and Reality*, 135–37; Thompson, *A History of Marfa and Presidio County*, II, 33, 28.

102. Casey, *Mirages, Mysteries and Reality*, 136–37, 139.

103. J. O. Langford, *Big Bend: A Homesteader's Story* (Austin: University of Texas Press, 1952), 107, 114, 116–18, 141.

104. Ibid., 133–35.

105. Ibid., 62–65.

106. Ibid., 141, 143–44.

107. Villanueva, *The Lynching of Mexicans in the Texas Borderlands*, 116.

108. Ibid., 125.

109. Martinez, *The Injustice Never Leaves You*, 128.

110. De León, *San Angeleños*, 21–23, 33–34, 37, 44.

111. Prewitt, "'We Didn't Ask to Come to This Party,'" 1, 25, 44, 46.

112. Wright, "Life on Both Sides of the Tracks in Early Alpine," 97; Wright, "Residential Segregation in Two Early West Texas Towns," 301.

113. Alexander Soto Cano, "The Mexican American Community of Knickerbocker," *West Texas Historical Association Yearbook* LXXIX (October 2003): 24, 28–29, 33.

114. Wright, "Four Different Communities," 197.

115. Earl H. Elam, "Aspects of Acculturation in the Lower Big Bend Region of Texas, 1848–1943," *Journal of Big Bend Studies* 12 (2000): 83; "Redford, Texas," Handbook of Texas Online.

116. Thompson, *A History of Marfa and Presidio County*, I, 347; Louise S. O'Connor and Cecilia Thompson, *Marfa and Presidio County, Texas: A Social, Economic, and Cultural Study 1990–2008*, 2 vols. (Bloomington, IN: Xlibris, 2014), II, 424; "Casa Piedra, Texas," Handbook of Texas Online.

117. O'Connor and Thompson, *Marfa and Presidio County, Texas*, II, 422.

118. "Ruidosa, Texas," Handbook of Texas Online.

119. Martinez, *The Injustice Never Leaves You*, 126–27. From goat milk, common folks made *asadero*, a soft white cheese popular in Mexico. Ethnic Mexicans continued making the treat in Texas.

120. Madison, *The Big Bend Country of Texas*, 170–72; Tyler, *The Big Bend*, 136–37; Justice, *Little Known History of the Texas Big Bend*, 48–49; "Shafter, Texas," Handbook of Texas Online.

121. Baker, *More Ghost Towns of Texas*, 13–14.

122. Gómez, *A Most Singular Country*, 156–57, 213n4; Casey, *Mirages, Mysteries and Reality*, 170; Elam, "Aspects of Acculturation in the Lower Big Bend Region of Texas," 72; Tanner, "From Castolón to Santa Elena,"

99, 101; Albert B. Tucker, "Terlingua Abaja," *Journal of Big Bend Studies* 3 (January 1991): 99, 101; Clifford B. Casey, *Soldiers, Ranchers and Miners in the Big Bend* ([Washington] Division of History, Office of Archeology and Historical Preservation, 1969), 71.

123. Gómez, *A Most Singular Country*, 101; Casey, *Mirages, Mysteries and Reality*, 115, 125; Baker, *More Ghost Towns of Texas*, 14.

124. Gómez, *A Most Singular Country*, 101, 103.

125. Casey, *Mirages, Mysteries and Reality*, 170; Tucker, "Terlingua Abaja," 89, 91, 94.

126. Casey, *Mirages, Mysteries and Reality*, 135, 136, 139; Elam, "Aspects of Acculturation in the Lower Big Bend Region of Texas," 84–85.

127. "Candelaria, Texas," Handbook of Texas Online.

128. Gómez, *A Most Singular Country*, 156–57, 213n3; Casey, *Mirages, Mysteries and Reality*, 170–71; Casey, *Soldiers, Ranchers and Miners in the Big Bend*, 74–75, 97; Casey, *Alpine, Texas*, 329–30.

129. Wright, "Characteristics of Big Bend Mining Towns," 107–9; Casey, *Mirages, Mysteries and Reality*, 143.

130. Gómez, *A Most Singular Country*, 121, 123; Tucker, "Terlingua Abaja," 81, 87; "Terlingua," Handbook of Texas Online.

131. Karen Green, "The Influenza Epidemic of 1918 in Far West Texas," *Journal of Big Bend Studies* 5 (January 1993): 125–26, 129, 131–34. See also Ragsdale, *Quicksilver*, 105–7, 108n85; Wright, "A Tumultuous Decade," 169–73.

132. Langford, *Big Bend: A Homesteader's Story*, 63.

133. Flores, "The Good Life the Hard Way," 56.

134. Langford, *Big Bend: A Homesteader's Story*, 34.

135. Madison, *The Big Bend Country of Texas*, 219, 221; W. D. Smithers, *Chronicles of the Big Bend: A Photographic Memoir of Life on the Border* (Austin: Texas State Historical Association, 1999), 101; Langford, *Big Bend: A Homesteader's Story*, 62.

136. Madison, *The Big Bend Country of Texas*, 218–19; Smithers, *Chronicles of the Big Bend*, 104.

137. Glenn Willeford, "Presidios to Trading Posts: Money, Agriculture, Rare Earth Extraction, and General Business in the Lower Big Bend of Texas, 1759–1961," *Journal of Big Bend Studies* 26 (2014): 162; Martinez, *The Injustice Never Leaves You*, 126–27.

138. Martinez, *The Injustice Never Leaves You*, 127.

139. Ibid.

140. Langford, *Big Bend: A Homesteader's Story*, 48; Smithers, *Chronicles of the Big Bend*, 111.

141. Flores, "The Good Life the Hard Way," 66–67.

142. Casey, *Mirages, Mysteries and Reality*, 202; Thompson, *A History of Marfa and Presidio County*, II, 7, 42, 52, 61, 86; Wright, "Characteristics of Big Bend Mining Towns, 1885–1920," 106.

143. Thompson, *A History of Marfa and Presidio County*, II, 25–26; O'Connor and Thompson, *Marfa and Presidio County, Texas*, II, 384.

144. Daggett, *Pecos County History*, II, 253.

145. Thompson, *A History of Marfa and Presidio County*, II, 61. De León, *San Angeleños*, 31, lists Señora Ella Balencia as teaching in San Angelo, 1902–1904. In Sonora, remembered Eufemia Virgen, "Andrés and I had Lillie Moreno for a school teacher. Our classes were held in a store owned by Mrs. Moreno." Sutton County Historical Society, *Sutton County, 1887–1977* (Sonora: Sutton County Historical Society, 1979), 246.

146. Thompson, *A History of Marfa and Presidio County*, II, 52, 67, 83; Wright, "Characteristics of Big Bend Mining Towns, 1885–1920," 106.

147. Baker, *More Ghost Towns of Texas*, 15; Casey, *Mirages, Mysteries and Reality*, 116–17.

148. Thompson, *A History of Marfa and Presidio County*, II, 52, 143.

149. Ibid., II, 91.

150. Wedin, *The Magnificent Marathon Basin*, 56.

151. Flores, "The Good Life the Hard Way," 56.

152. De León, *San Angeleños*, 44.

153. Tyler, *The Big Bend*, 139; Paul Wright, "Starting Over: Impact of Mexican Revolution Refugees on Big Bend Society," *Journal of Big Bend Studies* 13 (2001): 202.

154. Gómez, *A Most Singular Country*, 116–17, 125; Ragsdale, *Quicksilver*, 47.

155. Tyler, *The Big Bend*, 139; Casey, *Mirages, Mysteries and Reality*, 161; Thompson, *A History of Marfa and Presidio County*, II, 4; Hawley, "Life Along the Border," 27.

156. Gómez, *A Most Singular Country*, 117.

157. Madison, *The Big Bend Country of Texas*, 170; Thompson, *A History of Marfa and Presidio County*, II, 34, 76; and John Ernest Gregg, "The

History of Presidio County" (unpublished MA thesis, UT Austin, 1933), republished in *Voice of the Mexican Border* (Marfa, TX: Centennial Edition, 1936), 38.

158. Gómez, *A Most Singular Country*, 125; Ragsdale, *Quicksilver*, 47; Taylor, "Ninety-Six Miles in Ninety-Six Hours," 12–13.

159. Daggett, *Pecos County History*, II, 474–75.

160. Whitehead Memorial Museum, *La Hacienda: An Official Bicentennial Publication* (Del Rio: The Museum, 1976), 540.

161. Downie, *Terrell County, Texas, Its Past, Its People*, 241.

162. Zertuche, *The Spirit of Val Verde*, 46.

163. Gregg, "The History of Presidio County," in *Voice of the Mexican Border*, 36; "Ochoa, Texas," Handbook of Texas Online.

164. Martinez, *The Injustice Never Leaves You*, 126, 128.

165. Zertuche, *The Spirit of Val Verde*, 124.

166. Hawley, "Life Along the Border," 115–17; Thompson, *A History of Marfa and Presidio County*, II, 52, 124.

167. Thompson, *A History of Marfa and Presidio County*, II, 34, 53, 82.

168. Rosa Lee Wylie, *History of Van Horn and Culberson County, Texas* (Hereford: Pioneer Book Publishers, 1973), 162, 164.

169. Daggett, *Pecos County History*, II, 164.

170. Edwards County History, *History of Edwards County* (Rocksprings Woman's Club; San Angelo: Anchor Publishing Co., 1984), 51.

171. Thompson, *A History of Marfa and Presidio County*, II, 192; O'Connor and Thompson, *Marfa and Presidio County, Texas*, II, 432.

172. Thompson, *A History of Marfa and Presidio County*, II, 13; Wedin, *The Magnificent Marathon Basin*, 58; Tanner, "From Castolón to Santa Elena," 101; Wright, "Characteristics of Big Bend Mining Towns, 1885–1920," 106.

173. Thompson, *A History of Marfa and Presidio County*, II, 82.

174. Hawley, "Life Along the Border," 38.

175. Tom Green County Historical Preservation League, Inc., *Tom Green County: Chronicles of Our Heritage*, 2 vols. (San Angelo: Tom Green County Historical Preservation League, Inc., 2003), I, 150.

176. Thompson, *A History of Marfa and Presidio County*, II, 61.

177. Casey, *Alpine, Texas*, 287.

178. Rivas-Rodríguez, "Integration a Mordidas in Alpine Schools [1969]," 16.

179. Zertuche, *The Spirit of Val Verde*, 34.

180. De León, *San Angeleños*, 26, 37.

181. Tom Green County Historical Preservation League, Inc., *Tom Green County*, I, 150.

182. Pérez, "Colonia Jiménez de Melvin, Texas," section titled "Church History."

183. Crockett County Historical Society, *History of Crockett County* (San Angelo: Anchor Publishing Co., 1976), 140.

184. Jacobson and Nored, *Jeff Davis County, Texas*, 187.

185. Wylie, *History of Van Horn and Culberson County, Texas*, 55.

186. Thompson, *A History of Marfa and Presidio County*, II, 91.

187. Wedin, *The Magnificent Marathon Basin*, 149–50; Casey, *Mirages, Mysteries and Reality*, 104.

188. Flores, "The Good Life the Hard Way," 208–9.

189. B. A. Hodges, *A History of the Mexican Mission Work Conducted by the Presbyterian Church in the United States of America in the Synod of Texas* (Waxahachie: The Woman's Synodical of Texas, 1931), reprinted in Carlos Cortes, et al., *Church Views of the Mexican American* (New York: Arno Press, 1974), 8–10.

190. Downie, *Terrell County, Texas, Its Past, Its People*, 690.

191. Thompson, *A History of Marfa and Presidio County*, II, 110, 121.

192. Wright, "Residential Segregation in Two Early West Texas Towns," 315, 318; Wright, "Starting Over," 97, 211.

193. Martinez, *The Injustice Never Leaves You*, 127.

194. De León, *San Angeleños*, 31, 33, 39.

195. Prewitt, "'We Didn't Ask to Come to This Party,'" 44–48.

196. At Fort Davis, residents recalled years later, two Hispanic ladies during the early 1900s taught school out of their own home. Jacobson and Nored, *Jeff Davis County*, 308. In Del Rio, Tomacita Narvaez Alcina started her own small school during this time and continued her instruction for years after. Zertuche, *The Spirit of Val Verde*, 47.

197. Pérez, "Colonia Jiménez de Melvin, Texas," section titled "Education."

198. Wedin, *The Magnificent Marathon Basin*, 196; Casey, *Mirages, Mysteries and Reality*, 201.

199. Hallie Crawford Stillwell, *I'll Gather My Geese* (College Station: Texas A&M University Press, 1991), 10.

200. Thompson, *A History of Marfa and Presidio County*, II, 61, 190.

201. De León, *San Angeleños*, 26, 33, 39.

202. Ibid., 38–39.

203. Flores, "The Good Life the Hard Way," 208–9.

204. De León, *San Angeleños*, 25, 30.

205. Downie, *Terrell County, Texas, Its Past, Its People*, 200.

206. Ragsdale, *Quicksilver*, 112.

207. Hawley, "Life Along the Border," 37.

208. Thompson, *A History of Marfa and Presidio County*, II, 191; Casey, *Alpine, Texas*, 287–88.

209. Downie, *Terrell County, Texas, Its Past, Its People*, 200.

210. Thompson, *A History of Marfa and Presidio County*, II, 85.

211. De León, *San Angeleños*, 26.

212. Hawley, "Life Along the Border," 118–19.

213. Ibid., 38.

214. Interview in Flores, "The Good Life the Hard Way," 60.

215. See, for example, Daggett, *Pecos County History*, I, 418–19, 422–23; Hughes, *Pecos: A History of the Pioneer West*, 199; Ragsdale, *Quicksilver*, 118–19.

216. De León, *San Angeleños*, 42–43.

217. W. D. Smithers, *Nature's Pharmacy and the Curanderos and the Border Trading Posts* (Alpine: Sul Ross State College, 1961), 16–17, 23; Downie, *Terrell County, Texas, Its Past, Its People*, 131. For an instructive elucidation of curanderismo, see Eliseo Torres, *The Folk Healer: The Mexican American Tradition of Curanderismo* (Kingsville, TX: Nieves Press, [1987]).

218. Pérez, "Colonia Jiménez de Melvin, Texas," section titled "Death and Funerals."

219. Flores, "The Good Life the Hard Way," 67–69.

220. De León, *San Angeleños*, 27–28.

221. Jacobson and Nored, *Jeff Davis County*, 243–44.

222. Casey, *Alpine, Texas*, 287–88.

223. Langford, *Big Bend: A Homesteader's Story*, 54–55.

224. Downie, *Terrell County, Texas, Its Past, Its People*, 200; Jacobson and Nored, *Jeff Davis County*, 243–44; Casey, *Alpine, Texas*, 287–88.

225. Langford, *Big Bend: A Homesteader's Story*, 54.

226. Flores, "The Good Life the Hard Way," 208.

227. Pérez, "Colonia Jiménez de Melvin, Texas," citing the *Brady Standard* of

September 5, 1911, 1, in section titled "Bits and Pieces."

228. De León, *San Angeleños*, 41; Ragsdale, *Quicksilver*, 85–86, 112; Flores, "The Good Life the Hard Way," 57; Downie, *Terrell County, Texas, Its Past, Its People*, 199; Jacobson and Nored, *Jeff Davis County*, 234. Quote is from Hawley, "Life Along the Border," 126–27.

229. Ragsdale, *Quicksilver*, 85–86, 112; Flores, "The Good Life the Hard Way," 57; Downie, *Terrell County, Texas, Its Past, Its People*, 199; Jacobson and Nored, *Jeff Davis County*, 234.

230. Downie, *Terrell County, Texas, Its Past, Its People*, 200.

231. Ibid., 199.

232. Wayne Spiller, compiler, et al., *Handbook of McCulloch County History*, 3 vols. (Seagraves, TX: Pioneer Book Publishers, sponsored by Heart of Texas Historical Museum, 1976), I, 93.

233. Elton Miles, *More Tales of the Big Bend* (College Station: Texas A&M University Press, 1988), 54–56.

234. Ibid., 56–57.

235. Wright, "Residential Segregation in Two Early West Texas Towns," 312–19; Wright, "Starting Over," 197–98, 211.

236. Emilio Zamora, *The World War I Diary of José de la Luz Sáenz* (College Station: Texas A&M University Press, 2014); José A. Ramírez, *To the Line of Fire: Mexican Texans and World War I* (College Station: Texas A&M University Press, 2009); Roberto R. Treviño, "Salt of the Earth: The Immigrant Experience of Gerónimo Treviño," in *War Along the Border: The Mexican Revolution and Tejano Communities*, Arnoldo De León, ed. (College Station: Texas A&M University Press, 2012), 217.

237. Wright, "Life on Both Sides of the Tracks in Early Alpine," 109; and Wright, "Residential Segregation in Two Early West Texas Towns," 317.

238. The existing scholarship is lean in its coverage of Tejano World War I participation. Among the few publications that do cite their involvement are Downie, *Terrell County, Texas, Its Past, Its People*, 202; Wylie, *History of Van Horn and Culberson County, Texas*, 169; and Casey, *Alpine, Texas*, 397.

239. Hawley, "Life Along the Border," 127.

240. Wright, "Life on Both Sides of the Tracks in Early Alpine," 106.

241. Madison, *The Big Bend Country of Texas*, 75.

242. Flores, "The Good Life the Hard Way," 70–71.

243. Arnoldo De León, "Blowout 1910 Style: A Chicano School Boycott in

West Texas," *Texana* XII (1974); Villanueva, *The Lynching of Mexicans in the Texas Borderlands*, 36–40.

244. Emilio Zamora, *The World of the Mexican Worker in Texas* (College Station: Texas A&M University Press, 1993); Arnoldo De León, *Mexican Americans in Texas: A Brief History*, 3rd ed. (Wheeling, IL: Harlan Davidson, 2009), 95–96.

245. Ragsdale, *Quicksilver*, 77–78.

246. Madison, *The Big Bend Country of Texas*, 190–91; Ragsdale, *Quicksilver*, 76–77.

247. "South Texas Plains," Handbook of Texas Online.

248. Ely, *Where the West Begins*, 7–8, 11, 15–16, 102–10, 124, 128; Ty Cashion, "What's the Matter with Texas? The Great Enigma of the Lone Star State in the American West," *Montana: The Magazine of Western History* 55, no. 4 (Winter 2005): 8.

249. Ely, *Where the West Begins*, 21–22, 89.

250. Ibid., 85–86.

251. The several essays in Hernández and González, eds., *Reverberations of Racial Violence*, seem to concur that almost all the atrocities committed against Mexicans—by law officials, Texas Rangers, and citizens acting outside the law—occurred in South Texas. On page 2, the editors write: "Some of the worst racial violence in US history took place along the US–Mexican borderlands and particularly in South Texas from 1910 to 1919."

252. Arnoldo De León, "Region and Ethnicity: Topographical Identities in Texas," in *Many Wests: Place, Culture, and Regional Identity*, David M. Wrobel and Michael C. Steiner, eds. (Lawrence: University Press of Kansas, 1997), 259–74; Daniel D. Arreola, *Tejano South Texas: A Mexican American Cultural Province* (Austin: University of Texas Press, 2002), 62, 194–200.

CHAPTER 4

1. Clifford B. Casey, *Mirages, Mysteries and Reality: Brewster County, Texas, The Big Bend of the Rio Grande* (Hereford, TX: Pioneer Book Publishers, 1972), 167, 168–69; A. E. Skinner, *The Rowena Country: A Short History* (Wichita Falls, TX: Nortex Offset Publications Inc., 1973), 71; Marsha

Lea Daggett, *Pecos County History*, 2 vols. (Pecos County Historical Commission, 1973–1983), I, 146; Cecilia Thompson, *A History of Marfa and Presidio County, 1535–1946*, 2 vols. (Austin: Nortex Press, 1985), II, 280–81; Paul Wright, "Factors Associated with Income: The Big Bend in 1930," *Journal of Big Bend Studies* 19 (2007): 133; Monica Muñoz Martinez, *The Injustice Never Leaves You: Anti-Mexican Violence in Texas* (Cambridge: Harvard University Press, 2018), 126–27.

2. Schleicher County Historical Society, *A History of Schleicher County* (San Angelo: Anchor Publishing Co., 1979), 38, 43; Paul H. Carlson, *Texas Woollybacks: The Range Sheep and Goat Industry* (College Station: Texas A&M University Press, 1982), 191.

3. Glen Sample Ely, *Where the West Begins: Debating Texas Identity* (Lubbock: Texas Tech University Press, 2011), 113; Crockett County Historical Society, *History of Crockett County* (San Angelo: Anchor Publishing Co., 1976), 58; Schleicher County Historical Society, *A History of Schleicher County*, 44, 39.

4. Carlson, *Texas Woollybacks*, 192–93, 197–99.

5. Robert L. Martin, *The City Moves West: Economic and Industrial Growth in Central West Texas* (Austin: University of Texas Press, 1969), 104–5; Richard R. Moore, *West Texas After the Discovery of Oil: A Modern Frontier* (Austin: Pemberton Press, 1971), 8–11, 14–16.

6. James T. Matthews, "The Edwards Plateau and Permian Basin," in *West Texas: A History of the Giant Side of the State*, Paul H. Carlson and Bruce Glasrud, eds. (Norman: University of Oklahoma Press, 2014), 69–70; Gus Clemens, *The Concho Country* (San Antonio: Mulberry Avenue Books, 1980), 136–39; Martin, *The City Moves West*, 109–12.

7. Paul Wright, "Four Different Communities: Presidio in 1910, 1920, 1930, and 1940," *Journal of Big Bend Studies* 25 (2013): 198.

8. For a detailed quantification of both Mexican American and Anglo-American population as it existed in West Texas as of 1930, see Arnoldo De León, "Mexican Americans in the Edwards Plateau and Trans-Pecos Region, 1900–2000: A Demographic Study," *Southwestern Historical Quarterly* CXII (October 2008): 157, 158–59 (Tables 3 and 4): 160–61.

9. B. Youngblood and A. B. Cox, *An Economic Study of a Typical Ranch Area on the Edwards Plateau of Texas*, Texas Agricultural Experiment

Station Bulletin, no. 297 (College Station: Texas A&M College, 1922), 53, 308, 312.

10. Diana Sotelo Zertuche, *The Spirit of Val Verde* (Del Rio: Diana Sotelo Zertuche Publisher, 1985), 41.

11. Hallie Crawford Stillwell, *I'll Gather My Geese* (College Station: Texas A&M University Press, 1991), 79–81; Virginia Madison, *The Big Bend Country of Texas* (Albuquerque: University of New Mexico Press, 1955), 219–20; Glenn Willeford, "Presidios to Trading Posts: Money, Agriculture, Rare Earth Extraction, and General Business in the Lower Big Bend of Texas, 1759–1961," *Journal of Big Bend Studies* 26 (2014): 157.

12. Stillwell, *I'll Gather My Geese*, 81, 97–101.

13. Carlson, *Texas Woollybacks*, 201, 206.

14. Alice Evans Downie, *Terrell County, Texas, Its Past, Its People: A Compilation, Pictures of and Writings by or About People, Places, and Events in Terrell County* (Sanderson: Terrell County Heritage Commission, 1978), 55–58.

15. Nestor Pérez, "Colonia Jiménez de Melvin, Texas," unpaginated booklet, section titled "Sheep Shearing," West Texas Collection, Angelo State University, San Angelo, TX, in file labeled "Melvin, Texas, Collection."

16. Youngblood and Cox, *An Economic Study of a Typical Ranch Area on the Edwards Plateau of Texas*, 312; Downie, *Terrell County, Texas, Its Past, Its People*, 57, 60–61, 597.

17. Downie, *Terrell County, Texas, Its Past, Its People*, 61; Mario Juárez Cruz, "Tasinques," *San Angelo Standard-Times*, February 23, 2020, 1B.

18. T. J. Cauley, "Cotton Moves West: An Account of Some of the Agricultural Changes Which Have Created a New Cotton Empire," *Texas Monthly* 3 (1929): 344–45, 347; Ely, *Where the West Begins*, 15.

19. Pérez, "Colonia Jiménez de Melvin, Texas," section titled "Cotton Farming." Also, Daggett, *Pecos County History*, I, 327.

20. Paul Wright, "Starting Over: Impact of Mexican Revolution Refugees on Big Bend Society," *Journal of Big Bend Studies* 13 (2001): 201, says: "even when schools were available in the Big Bend, attendance was sporadic." Also, Wright, "Four Different Communities," 208–9, and Tom Green County Historical Preservation League, Inc., *Tom Green County: Chronicles of Our Heritage*, 2 vols. (San Angelo: Tom Green County Historical Preservation League, Inc., 2003), I, 148.

21. Skinner, *The Rowena Country*, 73, 75, 84; María Eva Flores, "The Good Life the Hard Way: The Mexican American Community of Fort Stockton, Texas, 1930–1945" (PhD diss., Arizona State University, 2000), 98, 271; Arnoldo De León, *San Angeleños: Mexican Americans in San Angelo, Texas* (San Angelo: Fort Concho Museum Press, 1985), 35; Paul Wright, "Build It and They Will Come: Boom and Bust in Presidio," *Journal of Big Bend Studies* 20 (2008): 44; Wright, "Four Different Communities," 208–9; Wright, "Factors Associated with Income," 133–37; Thompson, *A History of Marfa and Presidio County*, II, 291; John Ernest Gregg, "The History of Presidio County" (unpublished MA thesis, University of Texas, Austin, 1933), republished in *Voice of the Mexican Border* (Marfa, TX: Centennial Edition, 1936), 37, 46; Susan L. Tanner, "From Castolón to Santa Elena: The People Behind the Ruins," *Journal of Big Bend Studies* 5 (January 1993): 99, 101; Albert B. Tucker, "Terlingua Abaja," *Journal of Big Bend Studies* 3 (January 1991): 89, 95; Tom Green County Historical Preservation League, Inc., *Tom Green County: Chronicles of Our Heritage*, I, 148; Abelardo Baeza, "La Escuela de Don Clemente: History of the Madero Ward Elementary School in Alpine, Texas, 1919–1936," *Journal of Big Bend Studies* 7 (January 1995): 43; Schleicher County Historical Society, *A History of Schleicher County*, 186, 187; Roger M. Olien and Diana Davids Olien, *Oil Booms: Social Change in Five Texas Towns* (Lincoln: University of Nebraska Press, 1982), 114; Pérez, "Colonia Jiménez de Melvin, Texas," section titled "Cotton Farming."

22. "Castolón," Handbook of Texas Online.

23. Olien and Olien, *Oil Booms*, 25, 110, 112.

24. JoAnn Pospisil, "Mariscal Mine's Contribution to the Quicksilver Industry," *West Texas Historical Association Yearbook* LXXXVII (2012): 101, 105.

25. Kenneth B. Ragsdale, *Quicksilver: Terlingua and the Chisos Mountains Mining Company* (College Station: Texas A&M University Press, 1976), 215, 234, 159–60, 165–66, 169, 178, 234, 262–65.

26. Arthur R. Gómez, *A Most Singular Country: A History of Occupation in the Big Bend* (Santa Fe: National Park Service; Salt Lake City: Charles Redd Center for Western Studies, Brigham Young University, 1990), 126–29; Ronnie C. Tyler, *The Big Bend: A History of the Last Texas Frontier* (Washington, DC: US Dept of the Interior, National Parks Service,

1975), 144–45.

27. Pospisil, "Mariscal Mine's Contribution to the Quicksilver Industry," 107.

28. Gómez, *A Most Singular Country*, 126–29; Tyler, *The Big Bend*, 144–45.

29. Pospisil, "Mariscal Mine's Contribution to the Quicksilver Industry," 101, 105, 106, 107, and Art Gómez, "If the Walls Could Speak: Mariscal Mine and the West Texas Quicksilver Industry, 1896–1946," Mining History Association (1998): 31, 33.

30. Tyler, *The Big Bend*, 142; Pospisil, "Mariscal Mine's Contribution to the Quicksilver Industry," 98, 105–6.

31. Pospisil, "Mariscal Mine's Contribution to the Quicksilver Industry," 105, 106.

32. Gómez, *A Most Singular Country*, 126–29; Tyler, *The Big Bend*, 144–45; Pospisil, "Mariscal Mine's Contribution to the Quicksilver Industry," 101, 105, 106, 108.

33. Casey, *Mirages, Mysteries and Reality*, 182.

34. Downie, *Terrell County, Texas, Its Past, Its People*, 599.

35. Casey, *Mirages, Mysteries and Reality*, 177; AnneJo P. Wedin, *The Magnificent Marathon Basin: A History of Marathon, Texas, Its People and Events* (Austin: Nortex Press, 1989), 114.

36. Clifford B. Casey, *Alpine, Texas: Then and Now* (Seagraves, TX: Pioneer Book Publishers, 1981), 353, 378, 352, 342.

37. "Hispanic Culture Contributed to Midland's Early Days," *The Thorny Trail* XXV, no. 2, (Spring 1997): n.p.

38. Thompson, *A History of Marfa and Presidio County*, II, 227, 260; Olien and Olien, *Oil Booms*, 110, 118; Downie, *Terrell County, Texas, Its Past, Its People*, 358.

39. Ragsdale, *Quicksilver*, 113.

40. Downie, *Terrell County, Texas, Its Past, Its People*, 55–58, 60–61.

41. Skinner, *The Rowena Country*, 73.

42. Arnoldo De León, "Los Tasinques and the Sheep Shearers' Union of North America: A Strike in West Texas," in *Tejano West Texas*, Arnoldo De León, ed. (College Station: Texas A&M University Press, 2015), chap. 8.

43. Ragsdale, *Quicksilver*, 127–30.

44. Flores, "The Good Life the Hard Way," 135.

45. Wright, "Four Different Communities," 206–8.

46. Ely, *Where the West Begins*, 88–90, 92; De León, *San Angeleños*, 40, 53–54;

Flores, "The Good Life the Hard Way," 250; Ragsdale, *Quicksilver*, 112; Thompson, *A History of Marfa and Presidio County*, II, 385, 406; Downie, *Terrell County, Texas, Its Past, Its People*, 358; Roberto Aguero, *100 Years of Aguero's: 1915–2015, The Manuel and Francisca Aguero Family Story* (privately printed, 2015), n.p., section titled "Prologue."

47. Madison, *The Big Bend Country of Texas*, 101; Wright, "When They Were Equal," 110, 113; Ely, *Where the West Begins*, 88; Flores, "The Good Life the Hard Way," 84–85; De León, *San Angeleños*, 53–54.

48. Flores, "The Good Life the Hard Way," 87–99; Thompson, *A History of Marfa and Presidio County*, II, 385, 405–6.

49. Thompson, *A History of Marfa and Presidio County*, II, 258–59; Schleicher County Historical Society, *A History of Schleicher County*, 71, 208; Daggett, *Pecos County History*, I, 332; Crockett County Historical Society, *History of Crockett County*, 118; Tom Green County Historical Preservation League, Inc., *Tom Green County: Chronicles of Our Heritage*, I, 150; Kimble County Historical Commission, *Families of Kimble County* (Junction, TX: Kimble County Historical Commission; Shelton Press, 1985), 119, 345.

50. Casey, *Alpine, Texas*, 375.

51. Steven W. Prewitt, "'We Didn't Ask to Come to This Party': Self Determination Collides with the Federal Government in the Public Schools of Del Rio, Texas, 1890–1971" (PhD diss., University of Houston, 2000), 4, 20.

52. Ragsdale, *Quicksilver*, 138; Flores, "The Good Life the Hard Way," 172.

53. Downie, *Terrell County, Texas, Its Past, Its People*, 359.

54. Floyd Leslie Marshall, "History and Present Status of Latin American Education in Melvin, Texas" (MA thesis, Hardin-Simmons University, 1950), 11. This thesis is included in Estela Perez Santos, "A Snapshot of Melvin, Texas, 1905–1955," in West Texas Collection, Angelo State University, San Angelo, Texas, in file labeled "Melvin, Texas, Collection."

55. Prewitt, "'We Didn't Ask to Come to This Party,'" 2–4, 40, 59; Daggett, *Pecos County History*, I, 309–12, 423; Lucy Miller Jacobson and Mildred Bloys Nored, *Jeff Davis County, Texas* (Fort Davis: Fort Davis Historical Society, 1993), 331; Kinney County Historical Society, *Kinney County, 125 Years of Growth, 1852–1977* (Brackettville: Kinney County Historical Society, 1977), 115; Kenneth B. Ragsdale, *Big Bend Country: Land of*

the Unexpected (College Station: Texas A&M University Press, 1998), 31–32; R. D. Holt, ed., *Schleicher County: Or Eighty Years of Development in Southwest Texas* (Eldorado, TX: The Eldorado Success, 1930), 55, 57; Schleicher County Historical Society, *A History of Schleicher County*, 186–87; Tom Green County Historical Preservation League, Inc., *Tom Green County: Chronicles of Our Heritage*, I, 148, 307; Flores, "The Good Life the Hard Way," 158–59, 161; Baeza, "La Escuela de Don Clemente," 41, 43; De León, *San Angeleños*, 38–40, 54.

56. Olien and Olien, *Oil Booms*, 123.

57. Flores, "The Good Life the Hard Way," 155–59, 166–77.

58. Olien and Olien, *Oil Booms*, 123.

59. Prewitt, "'We Didn't Ask to Come to This Party,'" 58–59.

60. De León, *San Angeleños*, 37, 50.

61. Prewitt, "'We Didn't Ask to Come to This Party,'" 44, 46, 70.

62. Baeza, "La Escuela de Don Clemente," 44–45.

63. Paul Wright, "Residential Segregation in Two Early West Texas Towns," *Southwestern Historical Quarterly* CII (January 1999): 312, 315–17, 319.

64. Manuel H. Peña, *The Texas-Mexican Conjunto: History of a Working-Class Music* (Austin: University of Texas Press, 1985), 126.

65. Douglas Braudaway, "Santos Garza: The Father of San Felipe Schools," *Journal of South Texas* 19 (Fall 2006): 212.

66. Teresa Palomo Acosta and Ruthe Winegarten, *Las Tejanas: 300 Years of History* (Austin: University of Texas Press, 2003), 97; Casey, *Mirages, Mysteries and Reality*, 116–17; W. D. Smithers, *Chronicles of the Big Bend: A Photographic Memoir of Life on the Border* (Austin: Texas State Historical Association, 1999), 119; "María G. Sada," Handbook of Texas Online.

67. Casey, *Alpine, Texas*, 319.

68. Wayne Spiller, compiler, et al., *Handbook of McCulloch County History*, 3 vols. (Seagraves, TX: Pioneer Book Publishers, sponsored by Heart of Texas Historical Museum, 1976), I, 91, citing the *Melvin Enterprise*, September 20, 1938; Pérez, "Colonia Jiménez de Melvin, Texas," section titled "Education."

69. Braudaway, "Santos Garza," 212.

70. Flores, "The Good Life the Hard Way," 72, 76, 110–14, 133–34; Gregg, "The History of Presidio County," 38; Ragsdale, *Quicksilver*, 123–27; Wedin, *The Magnificent Marathon Basin*, 55–58, 68; Thompson,

A History of Marfa and Presidio County, II, 237, 476, 520; Louise S. O'Connor and Cecilia Thompson, *Marfa and Presidio County, Texas: A Social, Economic, and Cultural Study, 1990–2008*, 2 vols. (Bloomington, IN: Xlibris, 2014), II, 219–20; Downie, *Terrell County, Texas, Its Past, Its People*, 284; Casey, *Alpine, Texas*, 317, 339; Wright, "Factors Associated with Income," 144, Table 3.

71.   Prewitt, "'We Didn't Ask to Come to This Party,'" 21–22; Flores, "The Good Life the Hard Way," 132, 169; Thompson, *A History of Marfa and Presidio County*, II, 392; De León, *San Angeleños*, 50–51; Daggett, *Pecos County History*, II, 164; Wright, "Four Different Communities," 217, 219; Wright, "Factors Associated with Income," 153.

72.   Wedin, *The Magnificent Marathon Basin*, 104, 246; Thompson, *A History of Marfa and Presidio County*, II, 348, 396, 406; O'Connor and Thompson, *Marfa and Presidio County, Texas*, II, 383; Spiller, compiler, et al., *Handbook of McCulloch County History*, I, 93, citing the *Melvin Enterprise*, September 20, 1938; Pérez, "Colonia Jiménez de Melvin, Texas," sections titled "Bits and Pieces" and "Education."

73.   Daggett, *Pecos County History*, II, 164; Daggett, *Pecos County History*, I, 309.

74.   De León, *San Angeleños*, 44; Flores, "The Good Life the Hard Way," 77–78; Prewitt, "'We Didn't Ask to Come to This Party,'" 53–54; Braudaway, "Santos Garza," 212–13.

75.   Zertuche, *The Spirit of Val Verde*, 159.

76.   "Centennial Monument Erected in McCulloch County," *Brady Standard-Herald*, July 6, 2016, Section B, 1; Menard County Historical Society, *Menard County History: An Anthology* (San Angelo: Anchor Publishing Co., 1982), 172, 500; Marshall, "History and Present Status of Latin American Education in Melvin, Texas," 68.

77.   Downie, *Terrell County, Texas, Its Past, Its People*, 596.

78.   Tucker, "Terlingua Abaja," 89, 94–95; Tanner, "From Castolón to Santa Elena," 99–101; Gregg, "The History of Presidio County," 37; Wright, "Factors Associated with Income," 133–34.

79.   De León, *San Angeleños*, 37–38, 56–57; Flores, "The Good Life the Hard Way," 194–97, 200–205, 216–18; Crockett County Historical Society, *History of Crockett County*, 118; Irion County Historical Society, *A History of Irion County*, 68; Schleicher County Historical Society, *A History of Schleicher County*, 208; Tom Green County Historical Preservation League

Inc., *Tom Green County: Chronicles of Our Heritage*, I, 269; Zertuche, *The Spirit of Val Verde*, 35.

80. Casey, *Mirages, Mysteries and Reality*, 233; Irion County Historical Society, *A History of Irion County*, 68; Schleicher County Historical Society, *A History of Schleicher County*, 207, 208; Daggett, *Pecos County History*, II, 332; Sutton County Historical Society, *Sutton County, 1887–1977*, 318; Kinney County Historical Society, *Kinney County, 125 Years of Growth*, 137.

81. B. A. Hodges, *A History of the Mexican Mission Work Conducted by the Presbyterian Church in the United States of America in the Synod of Texas* (Waxahachie: The Woman's Synodical of Texas, 1931), reprinted in Carlos Cortes, et al., *Church Views of the Mexican American* (New York: Arno Press, 1974), 10.

82. De León, *San Angeleños*, 38.

83. Tom Green County Historical Preservation League, Inc., *Tom Green County: Chronicles of Our Heritage*, I, 262–63.

84. De León, *San Angeleños*, 57.

85. Casey, *Mirages, Mysteries and Reality*, 247; Maggie Rivas-Rodríguez, "Integration a Mordidas in Alpine Schools [1969]," *Texas Mexican Americans and Postwar Civil Rights* (Austin: University of Texas Press, 2017), 16.

86. Downie, *Terrell County, Texas, Its Past, Its People*, 597, 358.

87. Allan A. Stovall, *Nueces Headwater Country: A Regional History* (San Antonio: Naylor Press, 1959), 369; Edwards County History, *History of Edwards County* (Rocksprings Woman's Club; San Angelo: Anchor Publishing, Co., 1984), 113–14.

88. Spiller, compiler, et al., *Handbook of McCulloch County History*, I, 591.

89. Thompson, *A History of Marfa and Presidio County*, II, 258–59; Schleicher County Historical Society, *A History of Schleicher County*, 208; Daggett, *Pecos County History*, I, 332; Crockett County Historical Society, *History of Crockett County*, 118; De León, *San Angeleños*, 39, 56–57.

90. De León, *San Angeleños*, 56; Irion County Historical Society, *A History of Irion County*, 68; Crockett County Historical Society, *History of Crockett County*, 118; Flores, "The Good Life the Hard Way," 217–18; Downie, *Terrell County, Texas, Its Past, Its People*, 600.

91. De León, *San Angeleños*, 38, 56; Schleicher County Historical Society, *A*

History of Schleicher County, 208.

92. Flores, "The Good Life the Hard Way," 195–97, 218.

93. Ibid., 201–5.

94. Irion County Historical Society, *A History of Irion County,* 68; Daggett, *Pecos County History,* I, 332.

95. Crockett County Historical Society, *History of Crockett County,* 118.

96. Prewitt, "'We Didn't Ask to Come to This Party,'" 58–59; Flores, "The Good Life the Hard Way," 158–59, 161, 178; Wright, "When They Were Equal," 115.

97. Prewitt, "'We Didn't Ask to Come to This Party,'" 27–28.

98. Ragsdale, *Quicksilver,* 133, 135; H. W. "Pat" Patterson, "Crisis at the Molinar School," *Journal of Big Bend Studies* 2 (January 1990); Ragsdale, *Big Bend Country,* 30.

99. Olien and Olien, *Oil Booms,* 112, 123; "Hispanic Culture Contributed to Midland's Early Days," *The Thorny Trail* XXV, no. 2, (Spring 1997), n.p.

100. Wedin, *The Magnificent Marathon Basin,* 196.

101. Jacobson and Nored, *Jeff Davis County, Texas,* 311–13. Officials named the school after Mattie B. Anderson, who arrived to teach at Fort Davis in 1883.

102. Schleicher County Historical Society, *A History of Schleicher County,* 186.

103. Guadalupe Salinas, "Mexican-Americans and the Desegregation of Schools in the Southwest," in *Voices: Readings from El Grito: A Journal of Contemporary Mexican American Thought, 1967–1973,* Octavio Ignacio Romano-V, ed. (Berkeley, CA: Quinto Sol Publications, 1973), 377; Tim Archuleta, "School, End of Segregation Remembered," in archive.gosangelo.com/news, posted October 16, 2010; accessed August 31, 2021.

104. De León, *San Angeleños,* 39–40; Tom Green County Historical Preservation League, Inc., *Tom Green County: Chronicles of Our Heritage,* I, 307–8; Flores, "The Good Life the Hard Way," 156–57, 170.

105. Prewitt, "'We Didn't Ask to Come to This Party,'" 3–4, 73, 96–98.

106. De León, *San Angeleños,* 55–56; Thompson, *A History of Marfa and Presidio County,* II, 393; Flores, "The Good Life the Hard Way," 170, 177–81.

107. De León, *San Angeleños,* 55; Flores, "The Good Life the Hard Way," 176–77; Baeza, "La Escuela de Don Clemente," 45–46, 47–49; Rivas-Rodriguez, *Texas Mexican Americans & Post-War Civil Rights,* 22–23.

108. Thompson, *A History of Marfa and Presidio County*, II, 430.

109. Prewitt, "'We Didn't Ask to Come to This Party,'" 1–2, 21–22, 43, 51–54, 93–98, 100.

110. De León, *San Angeleños*, 55, 78; Thompson, *A History of Marfa and Presidio County*, II, 211, 468, 469; O'Connor and Thompson, *Marfa and Presidio County, Texas*, I, 383–84; Wright, "Four Different Communities," 208.

111. Marshall, "History and Present Status of Latin American Education in Melvin, Texas," 14, 17, 31–32; Spiller, compiler, et al., *Handbook of McCulloch County History*, I, 89; Pérez, "Colonia Jiménez de Melvin, Texas," section titled "Education"; *Brady Standard*, April 18, 1944, 1; August 22, 1944, 1; September 4, 1945, 1; and April 23, 1946, 1.

112. Prewitt, "'We Didn't Ask to Come to This Party,'" 1–2, 21–22, 43, 51–54, 93–98, 100.

113. Marshall, "History and Present Status of Latin American Education in Melvin, Texas," 8–9, 11, 27–28; Pérez, "Colonia Jiménez de Melvin, Texas," section titled "Education."

114. Flores, "The Good Life the Hard Way," 166.

115. Baeza, "La Escuela de Don Clemente," 49.

116. Thompson, *A History of Marfa and Presidio County*, II, 386, 393.

117. Prewitt, "'We Didn't Ask to Come to This Party,'" 65. See also De León, *San Angeleños*, 53; Pérez, "Colonia Jiménez de Melvin, Texas," section titled "Education."

118. De León, *San Angeleños*, 39; Flores, "The Good Life the Hard Way," 151–55.

119. Downie, *Terrell County, Texas, Its Past, Its People*, 666.

120. Miles, *More Tales of the Big Bend*, 58–62.

121. Ibid., 62–66.

122. Thompson, *A History of Marfa and Presidio County*, II, 237, 316, 372.

123. De León, *San Angeleños*, 51.

124. Pérez, "Colonia Jiménez de Melvin, Texas," section titled "Business."

125. Downie, *Terrell County, Texas, Its Past, Its People*, 200.

126. Thompson, *A History of Marfa and Presidio County*, II, 237, 316, 372.

127. De León, *San Angeleños*, 57.

128. Pérez, "Colonia Jiménez de Melvin, Texas," section titled "Junta Patriótica."

129. Downie, *Terrell County, Texas, Its Past, Its People*, 200; Salvador Guerrero, *Memorias: A West Texas Life* (Lubbock: Texas Tech University Press,

1991), 51.

130. De León, *San Angeleños*, 57.

131. De León, *San Angeleños*, 41, 57. Juntas patrióticas during the 1920s and 1930s were similarly active in communities such as Alpine and Melvin. Casey, *Alpine, Texas*, 378; Pérez, "Colonia Jiménez de Melvin, Texas," section titled "Junta Patriótica."

132. Thompson, *A History of Marfa and Presidio County*, II, 431.

133. Spiller, compiler, et al., *Handbook of McCulloch County History*, I, 93, citing the *Melvin Enterprise*, September 20, 1938, 1.

134. Flores, "The Good Life the Hard Way," 217–18, 130–32.

135. Zertuche, The Spirit of Val Verde, 193; "Carrera de Cintas," Wikipedia, https://en.wikipedia.org, accessed December 19, 2021; and "Carrera de Cintas," https://www.youtube.com/watch?v=A8JV_yN80t0, accessed December 19, 2021.

136. Downie, *Terrell County, Texas, Its Past, Its People*, 200; Betty L. Dillard and Karen L. Green, "Beeves and Baseball: The Story of the Alpine Cowboys," *Journal of Big Bend Studies* 11 (1999): 172; Flores, "The Good Life the Hard Way," 80–85; Casey, *Alpine, Texas*, 401.

137. De León, *San Angeleños*, 57–58; Guerrero, *Memorias: A West Texas Life*, 52–54.

138. Zertuche, *The Spirit of Val Verde*, 124.

139. Thompson, *A History of Marfa and Presidio County*, II, 267, 308.

140. De León, *San Angeleños*, 38.

141. W. D. Smithers, *Nature's Pharmacy and the Curanderos and the Border Trading Posts* (Alpine: Sul Ross State College, 1961), 16–17, 23 passim; Joe S. Graham, "The Role of the Curandero in the Mexican American Folk Medicine System in West Texas," in *American Folk Medicine: A Symposium*, Wayland D. Hand, ed. (Los Angeles: University of California Press, 1976); Grover H. (Dean) Smith, "Curanderismo: Mexican Folk Healing," *Journal of Big Bend Studies* 7 (January 1995).

142. Ragsdale, *Big Bend Country*, 33–35.

143. Ragsdale, *Quicksilver*, 174–75, 178.

144. Madison, *The Big Bend Country of Texas*, 78.

145. Ragsdale, *Quicksilver*, 120–22; Smithers, *Chronicles of the Big Bend*, 56.

146. Madison, *The Big Bend Country of Texas*, 77.

147. Ragsdale, *Quicksilver*, 121–23; Thompson, *A History of Marfa and*

Presidio County, II, 334, 349; Madison, *The Big Bend Country of Texas*, 75; Smithers, *Chronicles of the Big Bend*, 6, 57, 60.

148. Madison, *The Big Bend Country of Texas*, 75; Ragsdale, *Quicksilver*, 122–23; Flores, "The Good Life the Hard Way," 115.

149. Thompson, *A History of Marfa and Presidio County*, II, 349; Smithers, *Chronicles of the Big Bend*, 61–62.

150. Charles H. Harris III and Louis R. Sadler, *The Texas Rangers in Transition: From Gunfighters to Criminal Investigators, 1921–1935* (Norman: University of Oklahoma Press, 2019), chap. 5.

151. Ragsdale, *Quicksilver*, 123–27.

152. Thompson, *A History of Marfa and Presidio County*, II, 291, 385; Flores, "The Good Life the Hard Way," 120–22; De León, *San Angeleños*, 42.

153. Wright, "Residential Segregation," 312, 315–17, 319.

154. According to Wright in "When They Were Equal," Americanization was by then noticeable in that: "The 1930 census indicated that 60 and 56 percent in Alpine and Marfa respectively who were age 10+ could speak English" (116).

155. Thompson, *A History of Marfa and Presidio County*, II, 549.

156. Flores, "The Good Life the Hard Way," 226–27.

157. De León, *San Angeleños*, 46–47.

158. Ragsdale, *Quicksilver*, 232, 234–36, 241, 247–49.

159. De León, *San Angeleños*, 46–47. For the torment and distress of US-born Mexican Americans living in Melvin, some of whom repatriated to Mexico, see Estela Perez Santos, *Texas Came to Me: The Life and Impact of Jesusa Farias on the World* (privately printed, 2021), 92, 99, 101.

160. De León, *San Angeleños*, 46, 47, 49.

161. Flores, "The Good Life the Hard Way," 112–13.

162. Ibid., 108–10.

163. Ragsdale, *Quicksilver*, 249.

164. Ibid.

165. De León, *San Angeleños*, 49; Flores, "The Good Life the Hard Way," 137–38; Jacobson and Nored, *Jeff Davis County*, 274–75, 277; Wright, "Four Different Communities," 219.

166. De León, San Angeleños, 49; Flores, "The Good Life the Hard Way," 76, 139–40.

167. Flores, "The Good Life the Hard Way," 76, 135–37.

168. Wright, "When They Were Equal," 129.

169. Wright, "Starting Over," 209–10; Paul Wright, "Life on Both Sides of the Tracks in Early Alpine," *West Texas Historical Association Yearbook* LXXIII (1997): 106.

170. Ragsdale, *Quicksilver*, 154–55.

171. Flores, "The Good Life the Hard Way," 77–79.

172. De León, *San Angeleños*, 54; Mario T. García, *Mexican Americans: Leadership, Ideology & Identity, 1930–1960* (New Haven: Yale University Press, 1989), 47.

173. "*Del Rio ISD v. Salvatierra*," Handbook of Texas Online; De León, *San Angeleños*, 51; Flores, "The Good Life the Hard Way," 86; Thompson, *A History of Marfa and Presidio County*, II, 356.

174. Prewitt, "'We Didn't Ask to Come to This Party,'" 21, 95.

175. Ibid., 4; "*Del Rio ISD v. Salvatierra*," Handbook of Texas Online.

176. Prewitt, "'We Didn't Ask to Come to This Party,'" 60–61, 64–65; *Del Rio ISD v. Salvatierra*, Handbook of Texas Online. Similar collaboration between the local LULAC chapter and the state organization occurred in 1934 when Mexican sheepshearers went on strike. Arnoldo De León, "Los Tasinques and the Sheep Shearers' Union of North America: A Strike in West Texas, 1934," *Tejano West Texas* (College Station: Texas A&M University Press, 2015), 117, 125n9.

177. Prewitt, "'We Didn't Ask to Come to This Party,'" 66–67; "*Del Rio ISD v. Salvatierra*," Handbook of Texas Online.

178. "*Del Rio ISD v. Salvatierra*," Handbook of Texas Online.

179. Ibid.; Prewitt, "'We Didn't Ask to Come to This Party,'" 68.

180. Guadalupe San Miguel Jr., *"Let All of Them Take Heed": Mexican Americans and the Campaign for Educational Equality in Texas, 1910–1981* (Austin: University of Texas Press, 1987), 89n78; and Prewitt, "'We Didn't Ask to Come to this Party,'" 68.

181. San Miguel, *"Let All of Them Take Heed,"* 78–79; Prewitt, "'We Didn't Ask to Come to This Party,'" 3–4, 68.

182. De León, *San Angeleños*, 52.

183. Ibid.; Mario T. García, "Mexican Americans and Politics of Citizenship," *New Mexico Historical Review* 59 (April 1984): 188, 198–201; Mark Overmyer-Velásquez, "Good Neighbors and White Mexicans: Constructing Race and Nation on the Mexico-U.S. Border," *Journal of*

American Ethnic History 33 (Fall 2013): 23–24.

184. De León, *San Angeleños*, 53–54.
185. Thompson, *A History of Marfa and Presidio County*, II, 356, 439.
186. Flores, "The Good Life the Hard Way," 172–77.
187. Ibid., 87–93.
188. Arnoldo De León, "Wartime USA: West Texas Tejanos in WWII and Korea," in *Tejano West Texas* (College Station: Texas A&M University Press, 2015), 127–45. While this work is broad in coverage, it remains to be augmented by further studies.
189. Such compilations may be found in Estela Perez Santos, *The Perez Journey* (privately printed, n.d.), unpaginated booklet, section titled "Those Who Served," in West Texas Collection, Angelo State University, San Angelo, TX, in file labeled "Melvin, Texas, Collection." Also, Pérez, "Colonia Jiménez de Melvin, Texas," section titled "Veterans."
190. N. H. Pierce, *The Free State of Menard: A History of the County* (Menard: Menard News Press, 1946), 203–13 (the book features photos of all killed in action, including those Mexican Americans who lost their lives in battle); Spiller, compiler, et al., *Handbook of McCulloch County History*, II, 337. On Del Rio and Val Verde County, see Zertuche, *The Spirit of Val Verde*, 263.
191. Documents (in the form of letters, official correspondence, memoranda, and miscellaneous records) in the personal possession of the author, provided in March 2022, courtesy of Mr. David Díaz, who as executive director of the Midland Hispanic Chamber of Commerce oversaw the park's construction.
192. Arnoldo De León, *Mexican Americans in Texas: A Brief History*, 3rd ed. (Wheeling, IL: Harlan Davidson, 2009), 115–16; Flores, "The Good Life the Hard Way," 147.
193. Ely, *Where the West Begins*, 21–22, 84.

CHAPTER 5

1. "Introduction: West Texas, An Overview," in *West Texas: A History of the Giant Side of the State*, Paul H. Carlson and Bruce A. Glasrud, eds. (Norman: University of Oklahoma Press, 2007), 4; quote is from Schleicher County Historical Society, *A History of Schleicher County* (San Angelo: Anchor Publishing Co., 1979), 78.

2. Crockett County Historical Society, *History of Crockett County* (San Angelo: Anchor Publishing Co., 1976), 58, 60.

3. Paul H. Carlson, *Texas Woollybacks: The Range Sheep and Goat Industry* (College Station: Texas A&M University Press, 1982), 212–13.

4. Schleicher County Historical Society, *History of Schleicher County*, 79–80.

5. Ibid.; Crockett County Historical Society, *History of Crocket County*, 58, 60.

6. Carlson, *Texas Woollybacks*, 205.

7. Monte L. Monroe, "The West Texas Environment," in *West Texas*, Carlson and Glasrud, eds., 21; James T. Matthews, "The Edwards Plateau and Permian Basin," in *West Texas*, Carlson and Glasrud, eds., 71; Keith J. Volanto, "A New Texas Emerges: The Long-Term Impact of World War II, 1945–1960," in *Texas and Texans in World War II, 1941–1945*, Christopher B. Bean, ed. (College Station: Texas A&M University Press, 2022), 317–20.

8. Matthews, "The Edwards Plateau and Permian Basin," 71; Glen Sample Ely, *Where the West Begins: Debating Texas Identity* (Lubbock: Texas Tech University Press, 2011), 113, 115.

9. Carlson, *Texas Woollybacks*, 205, 207, 210, 213; Crockett County Historical Society, *History of Crockett County*, 59.

10. Ely, *Where the West Begins*, 15, 103; Marsha Lea Daggett, *Pecos County History*, 2 vols. (Pecos County Historical Commission, 1973–1983), I, 145–46.

11. Roger M. Olien and Diana Davids Hinton, *Wildcatters: Texas Independent Oilmen*, 2nd ed. (College Station: Texas A&M University Press, 2007), 82–85; Samuel D. Myers, *The Permian Basin: Petroleum Empire of the Southwest*, 2 vols. (El Paso: Permian Press, 1977), II, 20–22.

12. Arnoldo De León, "Mexican Americans in the Edwards Plateau and Trans-Pecos Region, 1900–2000: A Demographic Study," *Southwestern Historical Quarterly* CXII (October 2008): 163; Roger M. Olien and Diana Davids Olien, *Oil Booms: Social Change in Five Texas Towns* (Lincoln: University of Nebraska Press, 1982), 167–69.

13. Myres, *The Permian Basin*, II, 340–41; Matthews, "The Edwards Plateau and Permian Basin," 71.

14. Robert L. Martin, *The City Moves West: Economic and Industrial Growth in Central West Texas* (Austin: University of Texas Press, 1969), 112; Olien and Olien, *Oil Booms*, 167–69.

15. Arnoldo De León, "What's Amiss in Tejano History? The Misrepresentation and Neglect of West Texas," *Southwestern Historical Quarterly* CXX, no. 3 (January 2017): 328.

16. Ibid., 329.

17. For convenience, I relied on the 1980 census as it categorized the Mexican-descent population as "Spanish-Origin Persons by Type of Spanish Origin and Race" (see Table 1). Also, De León, "Mexican Americans in the Edwards Plateau and Trans-Pecos Region," 158–59.

18. Arnoldo De León, *San Angeleños: Mexican Americans in San Angelo, Texas* (San Angelo: Fort Concho Museum Press, 1985), chaps. 5 and 6; http://www.sanangelosheep.info, accessed October 11, 2021.

19. De León, "Mexican Americans in the Edwards Plateau and Trans-Pecos Region," 165–67.

20. "Del Rio, Texas," Wikipedia, https://en.wikipedia.org, accessed January 10, 2022; Steven W. Prewitt, "'We Didn't Ask to Come to This Party': Self Determination Collides with the Federal Government in the Public Schools of Del Rio, Texas, 1890–1971" (PhD diss., University of Houston, 2000), 127–28.

21. De León, "Mexican Americans in the Edwards Plateau and Trans-Pecos Region," 159, Table 4, and p. 151.

22. Ibid., Table 4.

23. Ibid., Table 5, 164, 166.

24. Manuel Peña, *The Texas Mexican Conjunto: History of a Working-Class Music* (Austin: University of Texas Press, 1985), 126, 131.

25. Mario Juárez Cruz, "Tasinques," *San Angelo Standard-Times*, February 23, 2020, 1B; Roberto Aguero, *A Legacy of Pride: Shearing Sheep and Angora Goats the Texas Way*, unpublished manuscript; Diana Sotelo Zertuche, *The Spirit of Val Verde* (Del Rio: Diana Sotelo Zertuche Publisher, 1985), 127, 207; Kimble County Historical Commission, *Families of Kimble County* (Junction, TX: Kimble County Historical Commission; Shelton Press, 1985), 119; Menard County Historical Society, *Menard County History: An Anthology* (San Angelo: Anchor Publishing Co., 1982), 172; Edwards County History, *History of Edwards County* (Rocksprings Woman's Club; San Angelo: Anchor Publishing Co., 1984), 53–54.

26. Alice Evans Downie, *Terrell County, Texas, Its Past, Its People: A Compilation, Pictures of and Writings by or About People, Places, and Events*

in Terrell County (Sanderson: Terrell County Heritage Commission, 1978), 600.

27. Schleicher County Historical Society, *A History of Schleicher County* (San Angelo: Anchor Publishing Co., 1979), 81.

28. Sutton County Historical Society, *Sutton County, 1887–1977* (Sonora: Sutton County Historical Society, 1979), 110–11, 127.

29. De León, "Mexican Americans in the Edwards Plateau and Trans-Pecos Region," 161, 163, 165.

30. Olien and Olien, *Oil Booms*, 116, 118–19.

31. Downie, *Terrell County, Texas, Its Past, Its People*, 599.

32. Olien and Olien, *Oil Booms*, 116.

33. David Montejano, *Anglos and Mexicans in the Making of Texas, 1836–1986* (Austin: University of Texas Press, 1987), chap. 12 titled "The Demise of Jim Crow for Texas Mexicans."

34. Montejano, *Anglos and Mexicans in the Making of Texas*, 270.

35. Letter of Raymond Wheat, May 12, 1948, Dr. Hector P. García Papers, Special Collections and Archives, Mary and Jeff Bell Library, Texas A&M University–Corpus Christi.

36. Alonso Perales, *Are We Good Neighbors?* (New York: Arno Press, 1974), 79, 80, 213, 218–220; De León, *San Angeleños*, 76; Olien and Olien, *Oil Booms*, 121.

37. Perales, *Are We Good Neighbors?*: 79, 214–15, 218. David Montejano, "The Beating of Private Aguirre: A Story About West Texas during World War II," in *Mexican Americans & World War II*, Maggie Rivas-Rodríguez (Austin: University of Texas Press, 2005), 51.

38. Ely, *Where the West Begins*, 85.

39. Perales, *Are We Good Neighbors?*, 81; Montejano, "The Beating of Private Aguirre," op cit., 52–53, 55–58.

40. Perales, *Are We Good Neighbors?*, 230–31.

41. *San Angelo Standard-Times*, March 2, 1953, 1. Also, interviews with residents of Sonora (preferring anonymity) who lived at that time.

42. De León, *San Angeleños*, 53; Perales, *Are We Good Neighbors?*: 213, 219, 265, 218–19; Louise S. O'Connor and Cecilia Thompson, *Marfa and Presidio County, Texas: A Social, Economic, and Cultural Study, 1990–2008*, 2 vols. (Bloomington, IN: Xlibris LLC, 2014), I, 325; Sterry Butcher, "Marfa's Blackwell School Has Painful Past. That's Why the Town Wants

to Save It," *Texas Monthly*, January 2019, online post, accessed August 31, 2021.

43. Perales, *Are We Good Neighbors?*, 214–15 ; Olien and Olien, *Oil Booms*, 121.

44. References for this period may be found in Kimble County Historical Commission, *Families of Kimble County* (Junction, TX: Kimble County Historical Commission; Shelton Press, 1985), 119; Roberto Aguero, *100 Years of Aguero's: 1915–2015, The Manuel and Francisca Aguero Family Story* (privately printed, 2015), n.p., section titled "Prologue."

45. Olien and Olien, *Oil Booms*, 119, 112–13; Butcher, "Marfa's Blackwell School Has Painful Past."

46. Carl Allsup, *The American G.I. Forum: Origins and Evolution* (Austin: Center for Mexican American Studies and the University of Texas Press, 1982), 85; Carlos M. Alcala and Jorge C. Rangel, "De Jure Segregation of Chicanos in Texas Schools," *Harvard Civil Rights-Civil Liberties Law Review* 7, no. 2 (March 1972): 360–61.

47. Alcala and Rangel, "De Jure Segregation of Chicanos in Texas Schools," 327–28.

48. Allsup, *The American G.I. Forum*, 87.

49. Allsup, *The American G.I. Forum*, 85–86; Prewitt, "'We Didn't Ask to Come to This Party,'" 3–4, 73, 81; Guadalupe San Miguel Jr., *"Let All of Them Take Heed": Mexican Americans and the Campaign for Educational Equality in Texas, 1910–1981* (Austin: University of Texas Press, 1987), 128–29.

50. De León, *San Angeleños*, 40, 78.

51. Olien and Olien, *Oil Booms*, 117, 123.

52. Allsup, *The American G.I. Forum*, 90–91; Alcala and Rangel, "De Jure Segregation of Chicanos in Texas Schools," 341.

53. Maggie Rivas-Rodríguez, "Integration a Mordidas in Alpine Schools [1969]," *Texas Mexican Americans and Postwar Civil Rights* (Austin: University of Texas Press, 2015), 17; *Texas Observer*, August 15, 1969, 11.

54. Perales, *Are We Good Neighbors?*, 214, 218–19; Alcala and Rangel, "De Jure Segregation of Chicanos in Texas Schools," 328, 367–68; San Miguel, *"Let All of Them Take Heed,"* 176.

55. O'Connor and Thompson, *Marfa and Presidio County, Texas*, I, 298, 324, 325; ibid., II, 254–56, 259, 270; Butcher, "Marfa's Blackwell School Has Painful Past"; Lonn Taylor, *Marfa for the Perplexed* (Marfa: Marfa Book

Company, 2018), 113.

56. Allsup, *The American G.I. Forum*, 91.

57. Paul Wright, "Four Different Communities: Presidio in 1910, 1920, 1930, and 1940," *Journal of Big Bend Studies* 25 (2013): 206–8.

58. Tim Archuleta, "School, End of Segregation Remembered," in archive. gosangelo.com/news, posted October 16, 2010, accessed August 31, 2021.

59. Gretel Enck, "The Complicated History at One of America's Segregated Schools," National Parks Conservation Association, blog post August 31, 2020, accessed August 31, 2021.

60. Montejano, *Anglos and Mexicans in the Making of Texas*, 262–87.

61. De León, *San Angeleños*, 94–95.

62. Spanish speakers referred to these mom-and-pop operations as *tienditas*; one West Texas writer recalled that barrio dwellers during the pre-1940s era called them *"tiendas de no hay"* as they stocked bare essentials and staff usually answered "We do not have that" when asked about any given item. Salvador Guerrero, *Memorias: A West Texas Life* (Lubbock: Texas Tech University Press, 1991), 21.

63. Olien and Olien, *Oil Booms*, 117.

64. Crockett County Historical Society, *A History of Crockett County*, 118.

65. "Hispanic Culture Contributed to Midland's Early Days," *The Thorny Trail* XXV, no. 2, (Spring 1997), n.p.

66. Kinney County Historical Society, *Kinney County, 125 Years of Growth, 1852–1977* (Brackettville: Kinney County Historical Society, 1977), 137.

67. "Hispanic Culture Contributed to Midland's Early Days," *The Thorny Trail* XXV, no. 2, (Spring 1997), n.p.

68. De León, *San Angeleños*, 80.

69. Zertuche, *The Spirit of Val Verde*, 33–34.

70. Schleicher County Historical Society, *A History of Schleicher County*, 227–28.

71. Downie, *Terrell County, Texas, Its Past, Its People*, 239.

72. *Brady Standard*, July 18, 1947, 1; July 13, 1948, 1; Wayne Spiller, compiler, et al., *Handbook of McCulloch County History*, 3 vols. (Seagraves, TX: Pioneer Book Publishers, sponsored by Heart of Texas Historical Museum, 1976), I, 591.

73. Manuel Peña, *The Mexican American Orquesta* (Austin: University of Texas Press, 1999), 139–41.

74. O'Connor and Thompson, *Marfa and Presidio County, Texas*, I, 180.

75. Arnoldo De León, *Las Fiestas Patrias: Biographic Notes on the Hispanic Presence in San Angelo, Texas* (San Antonio: Caravel Press, 1978).

76. A remembrance of movie attendance in the 1960s is provided in Aguero, *100 Years of Aguero's*, n.p., section titled "Vamos a Las Vistas."

77. For specific references to dance halls, see Guerrero, *Memorias*, 107; De León, *San Angeleños*, 85. See further Aguero, *100 Years of Aguero's*, for a personal account of such dances (specifically in Camp Wood).

78. Cordelia Chávez Candelaria, "Pachucos," *Encyclopedia of Latino Popular Culture* (Greenwood Press, 2004), II, 610–11.

79. US Census of Population: 1960. Final Report PC (2)—1B, "Persons of Spanish Surname," Table 1, p. 2, https://www.census.gov/library/publications/1965/dec/population-pc-2-1b.html.

80. Tom Green County Historical Preservation League, Inc., *Tom Green County: Chronicles of Our Heritage*, 2 vols. (San Angelo: Tom Green County Historical Preservation League, Inc., 2003), I, 300.

81. Thomas H. Kreneck, *Mexican American Odyssey: Felix Tijerina, Entrepreneur and Civic Leader, 1905–1965* (College Station: Texas A&M University Press, 2001), 12–13, 218, 225, 233, 235–36, 244, 246, 253.

82. De León, *San Angeleños*, 79.

83. Ibid., 92–93.

84. Downie, *Terrell County, Texas, Its Past, Its People*, 359.

85. Enck, "The Complicated History at One of America's Segregated Schools"; Butcher, "Marfa's Blackwell School Has Painful Past."

86. Cited in Arnoldo De León, *Mexican Americans in Texas: A Brief History*, 3rd ed. (Wheeling, IL: Harlan Davidson, 2009), 84, 124.

87. O'Connor and Thompson, *Marfa and Presidio County, Texas*, I, 244.

88. Ibid., I, 192.

89. "Hispanic Culture Contributed to Midland's Early Days," *The Thorny Trail* XXV, no. 2, (Spring 1997), n.p.

90. De León, *San Angeleños*, 91–92.

91. Peña, *The Texas Mexican Conjunto*, 126, 131; Montejano, *Anglos and Mexicans in the Making of Texas*, Table 17, 298.

92. Ed Tinney, "'I'll Keep My Children': The Life of Pioneer Educator Noé Lara Camúñez," *West Texas Historical Association Yearbook* LXXV (1999): 23–31.

93. Kenneth B. Ragsdale, *Big Bend Country: Land of the Unexpected* (College Station: Texas A&M University Press, 1998), 58–64, 67; O'Connor and Thompson, *Marfa and Presidio County, Texas*, I, 383–84.

94. Alcala and Rangel, "De Jure Segregation of Chicanos in Texas Schools," 328, 368.

95. Mary Beard, "The Right to Learn: Desegregation in a West Texas Town," *Texas Historian: Publication of the Junior Historians of Texas* LII, no. 5 (May 1992): 9–12; "Pete Gallego," Wikipedia, https://en.wikipedia.org, accessed March 21, 2022.

96. Daggett, *Pecos County History*, II, 477.

97. Montejano, *Anglos and Mexicans in the Making of Texas*, 299.

98. Melvin, Texas, Collection, West Texas Collection, Angelo State University, San Angelo, Texas. Also, Floyd Leslie Marshall, "History of Present Status of Latin American Education in Melvin, Texas (MA thesis, Hardin-Simmons University, 1950), 14–17. This thesis is included in Estela Perez Santos, "A Snapshot of Melvin, Texas, 1905–1955" (privately printed, n.d.), West Texas Collection, Angelo State University, San Angelo, Texas, in file labeled "Melvin, Texas, Collection."

99. De León, *San Angeleños*, 73–75.

100. De León, *San Angeleños*, 74–75; Guerrero, *Memorias*, 107–9; Allsup, *The American G.I. Forum*, 90.

101. De León, *San Angeleños*, 74–76; Guerrero, *Memorias*, 107–9.

102. De León, *San Angeleños*, 89.

103. Allsup, *The American G.I. Forum*, 87.

104. Allsup, *The American G.I. Forum*, 85; Prewitt, "'We Didn't Ask to Come to This Party,'" 81–84.

105. Douglas Braudaway, "Desegregation in Del Rio," *Journal of South Texas* 13 (2000): 245–55, quote is from p. 255.

106. Allsup, *The American G.I. Forum*, 90–91; Guadalupe San Miguel Jr., *"Let All of Them Take Heed,"* 176–77; Alcala and Rangel, "De Jure Segregation of Chicanos in Texas Schools," 368.

107. San Miguel, *"Let All of Them Take Heed,"* 176; Alcala and Rangel, "De Jure Segregation of Chicanos in Texas Schools," 367–68; Guadalupe Salinas, "Mexican-Americans and the Desegregation of Schools in the Southwest," in *Voices: Readings from El Grito: A Journal of Contemporary Mexican American Thought, 1967–1973*, Octavio Ignacio Romano-V., ed. (Berkeley,

CA: Quinto Sol Publications, 1973), 377; and Archuleta, "School, End of Segregation Remembered."

108. Rivas-Rodríguez, "Integration a Mordidas in Alpine Schools [1969]," 17, 37–42; Beard, "The Right to Learn," 10.

109. https://alpine.esc18.net/, accessed September 20, 2021.

110. Butcher, "Marfa's Blackwell School Has Painful Past"; Enck, "The Complicated History at One of America's Segregated Schools"; Taylor, *Marfa for the Perplexed*, 113–14; O'Connor and Thompson, *Marfa and Presidio County, Texas*, I, 298; ibid., II, 254–56, 270.

111. Armando Navarro, *Mexican American Youth Organization: Avant-Garde of the Chicano Movement in Texas* (Austin: University of Texas Press, 1995), 160–68; David Montejano, *Quixote's Soldiers: A Local History of the Chicano Movement, 1966–1981* (Austin: University of Texas Press, 2010), 72, 74–75, 88–80.

112. De León, *San Angeleños*, 97–102, 105.

113. On "tipping points," see Walter L. Buenger, "Making Sense of Texas and Its History," *Southwestern Historical Quarterly* CXII, no. 1 (July 2017): 1–26.

114. Terry Jordan, "The Concept and Method," in *Regional Studies: The Interplay of Land and People*, Glen E. Lich, ed. (College Station: Texas A&M University Press, 1992), 19.

CHAPTER 6

1. Paul H. Carlson and Bruce A. Glasrud, eds., *West Texas: A History of the Giant Side of the State* (Norman: University of Oklahoma Press, 2007), 71.

2. Glen Sample Ely, *Where the West Begins: Debating Texas Identity* (Lubbock: Texas Tech University Press, 2011), 113, 115, 108–9, 126.

3. Unless otherwise indicated, the discussion on population growth draws on findings contained in Table 1 and Table 2.

4. We might assume that the larger percentage of the foreign born were from Mexico, with the rest from Europe.

5. Data are derived by taking the total population estimates, July 1, 2021, of each city and multiplying by percent of Hispanic or Latino. https://www.census.gov/quickfacts/fact/table/US/PST045221, accessed December 17, 2022.

6. Arnoldo De León, *San Angeleños: Mexican Americans in San Angelo, Texas*

(San Angelo: Fort Concho Museum Press, 1985), 104–9.

7. Joel Zapata, "The South-by-Southwest Borderlands' Chicana/o Uprising: The Brown Berets, Black and Brown Alliances, and the Fight against Police Brutality in West Texas," in *Civil Rights in Black and Brown: Histories of Resistance and Struggle in Texas*, Max Krochmal and J. Todd Moye, eds. (Austin: University of Texas Press, 2021), 103–4, 105–11, 113–14.

8. Neil Foley, *Mexicans in the Making of America* (Cambridge: Harvard University Press, 2014), 180.

9. Arnoldo De León, *Mexican Americans in Texas: A Brief History*, 3rd ed. (Wheeling, IL: Harlan Davidson, 2009), 155.

10. Benjamin Márquez, *Democratizing Texas Politics: Race, Identity, and Mexican American Empowerment, 1945–2002* (Austin: University of Texas Press, 2014), 2.

11. Ibid.

12. Ibid.

13. Above discussion on San Angelo, Texas, politics from De León, *San Angeleños*, 111–18. See also Arnoldo De León, "María Cárdenas: San Angelo Chicano Era Activist," in *Tejano West Texas*, Arnoldo De León (College Station: Texas A&M University Press, 2015), 156–68.

14. *Texas Almanac and State Industrial Guide, 1970–1971* (Dallas: A. H. Belo Corporation, 1969), 595–614; *Texas Almanac, 2020–2021* (Austin: Texas State Historical Association, 2020), 478–88, 497–508. Other secondary sources document women serving elsewhere in positions of public trust during the years between 1970 and 2020. They note Joanne Lara holding office as justice of the peace in Fort Davis and Precilla Rodríguez in Balmorhea (Reeves County) during the 1980s. Also, indicated as being mayor of Presidio in 1997 is Alcee Tavarez and Dora Alcala as mayor of Del Rio in 2003. Teresa Palomo Acosta and Ruthe Winegarten, *Las Tejanas: 300 Years of History* (Austin: University of Texas Press, 2003), 260; and Sonia A. García, et al., *Políticas: Latina Public Officials in Texas* (Austin: University of Texas Press, 2008, 138–39.

15. Martha Menchaca, *The Mexican American Experience in Texas: Citizenship, Segregation, and the Struggle for Equality* (Austin: University of Texas Press, 2022), 249.

16. Ibid.

17. Ibid.

18. *San Angelo Standard-Times*, November 6, 2022, 6B and 8B; Sterry Butcher, "Marfa's Blackwell School Has Painful Past. That's Why the Town Wants to Save It," *Texas Monthly*, January 2019, online, accessed August 31, 2021.

19. George Carmack, "Melvin: A Tale of Three Cities," *San Antonio Express-News*, September 22, 1979, 1B; *Brady Standard-Herald*, October 19, 2022, 1A; *San Angelo Standard-Times*, October 24, 2022, 1A and 5A.

20. SanAngeloHispanicHeritage.org; *Conexión San Angelo*, San Angelo, Texas, September 3, 2020; *San Angelo Standard-Times*, July 23, 2021; October 4, 2021.

21. Arnoldo, De León, "What's Amiss in Tejano History?: The Misrepresentation and Neglect of West Texas," *Southwestern Historical Quarterly* CXX, no. 3 (January 2017).

BIBLIOGRAPHY

BOOKS

Acosta, Teresa Palomo, and Ruthe Winegarten. *Las Tejanas: 300 Years of History*. Austin: University of Texas Press, 2003.

Adams, Ramon F. *From the Pecos to the Power: A Cowboy's Autobiography*. Norman: University of Oklahoma Press, 1965.

Aguero, Roberto. *A Legacy of Pride: Shearing Sheep and Angora Goats the Texas Way*. Unpublished work.

———. *100 Years of Aguero's, 1915–2015: The Manuel and Francisca Aguero Family Story*. Privately printed, 2015.

Allsup, Carl. *The American G.I. Forum: Origins and Evolution*. Austin: Center for Mexican American Studies and the University of Texas Press, 1982.

Applegate, C. Wayne, and Howard G. Hanselka. *La Junta de los Rios del Norte y Conchos*. El Paso: Texas Western Press, 1974.

Baker, Lindsay. *More Ghost Towns of Texas*. Norman: University of Oklahoma Press, 2005.

Boatright, Mody C., et al., eds. *Mesquite and Willow*. Dallas: Southern Methodist University Press, 1957.

Bush, I. J. *Gringo Doctor*. Caldwell, ID: The Caxton Printers, Ltd., 1939.

Calvert, Robert A., et al. *The History of Texas*, 6th ed.; Hoboken, NJ.: Wiley-Blackwell, 2020.

Carlson, Paul H. *Texas Woollybacks: The Range Sheep and Goat Industry*. College Station: Texas A&M University Press, 1982.

Carlson, Paul H., and Bruce Glasrud, eds. *West Texas: A History of the Giant Side of the State*. Norman: University of Oklahoma Press, 2014.

Casey, Clifford B. *Alpine, Texas: Then and Now*. Seagraves, TX: Pioneer Book Publishers, 1981.

————.*Mirages, Mysteries and Reality: Brewster County, Texas, The Big Bend of the Rio Grande*. Hereford, TX: Pioneer Book Publishers, 1972.

————.*Soldiers, Ranchers and Miners in the Big Bend*. Washington Division of History, Office of Archeology and Historical Preservation, 1969.

Chipman, Donald E. *Spanish Texas, 1519–1821*. Austin: University of Texas Press, 1992.

Clemens, Gus. *The Concho Country*. San Antonio: Mulberry Avenue Books, 1980.

Corning, Leavitt, Jr. *Baronial Forts of the Big Bend: Ben Leaton, Milton Faver and Their Private Forts in Presidio County*. San Antonio: Trinity University Press, 1969.

Crane, Charles Judson. *The Experiences of a Colonel in the Infantry*. New York: Knickerbocker Press, 1923.

Crawford, Leta. *A History of Irion County*. Waco: Texian Press, 1966.

Crockett County Historical Society. *History of Crockett County*. San Angelo: Anchor Publishing Co., 1976.

Daggett, Marsha Lea. *Pecos County History*, 2 vols. Pecos County Historical Commission, 1973–1983.

Dearen, Patrick. *Crossing Rio Pecos*. Fort Worth: Texas Christian University Press, 1996.

————. *The Devils River: Treacherous Twin to the Pecos, 1535–1900*. Fort Worth: Texas Christian University Press, 2011.

De León, Arnoldo. *Las Fiestas Patrias: Biographic Notes on the Hispanic Presence in San Angelo, Texas*. San Antonio: Caravel Press, 1978.

————.*Mexican Americans in Texas: A Brief History*, 3rd ed. Wheeling, IL: Harlan Davidson, 2009.

————.*San Angeleños: Mexican Americans in San Angelo, Texas*. San Angelo: Fort Concho Museum Press, 1985.

————. *The Tejano Community, 1836–1900*. Albuquerque: University of New Mexico Press, 1982.

————, ed. *Tejano West Texas*. College Station: Texas A&M University Press, 2015.

————, ed. *War Along the Border: The Mexican Revolution and Tejano Communities*. College Station: Texas A&M University Press, 2012.

De León, Arnoldo, and Kenneth L. Stewart. *Tejanos and the Numbers Game: A Socio-Historical Profile from the Federal Censuses, 1850–1900*. Albuquerque: University of New Mexico Press, 1989.

Dobie, J. Frank, ed. *Texas and Southwestern Lore*. Dallas: Southern Methodist University Press, 1967. Originally published in 1927.

Downie, Alice Evans. *Terrell County, Texas, Its Past, Its People: A Compilation, Pictures of and Writings by or About People, Places, and Events in Terrell County*. Sanderson: Terrell County Heritage Commission, 1978.

Edwards County History. *History of Edwards County*. Rocksprings Woman's Club. San Angelo: Anchor Publishing Co., 1984.

Ely, Glen Sample. *Where the West Begins: Debating Texas Identity*. Lubbock: Texas Tech University Press, 2011.

Foley, Neil. *Mexicans in the Making of America*. Cambridge: Harvard University Press, 2014.

García, Mario T. *Desert Immigrants: The Mexicans of El Paso*. New Haven: Yale University Press, 1981.

——.*Mexican Americans: Leadership, Ideology & Identity, 1930–1960*. New Haven: Yale University Press, 1989.

García, Sonia, et al. *Políticas: Latina Public Officials in Texas*. Austin: University of Texas Press, 2008.

Goetz, Philis M. Barragán. *Reading, Writing, and Revolution: Escuelitas and the Emergence of a Mexican American Identity in Texas*. Austin: University of Texas Press, 2020.

Gómez, Arthur R. *A Most Singular Country: A History of Occupation in the Big Bend*. Santa Fe, NM: National Park Service. Salt Lake City: Charles Redd Center for Western Studies, Brigham Young University, 1990.

Gómez-Quiñones, Juan. *Sembradores, Ricardo Flores Magón y El Partido Liberal Mexicano: A Eulogy and Critique*. Los Angeles: Aztlán Publications, 1973.

Graham, Joe S. *The Jacal in the Big Bend: Its Origins and Evolution*. Edited by Robert J. Mallouf. Alpine, TX: Chihuahua: Desert Research Institute, 1988.

Green, Bill. *The Dancing Was Lively: Fort Concho, Texas, A Social History, 1867–1882*. San Angelo: Fort Concho Sketches Pub. Co., 1974.

Guerrero, Salvador. *Memorias: A West Texas Life*. Lubbock: Texas Tech University Press, 1991.

Harris, Charles H., III, and Louis R. Sadler. *The Texas Rangers in Transition: From Gunfighters to Criminal Investigators, 1921–1935*. Norman: University of Oklahoma Press, 2019.

Hawley, Charles A. "Life Along the Border." In *Publications of the West Texas Historical and Scientific Society*, vol. 20. Alpine, TX: Sul Ross State

University, 1964.

Hodges, B. A. *A History of the Mexican Mission Work Conducted by the Presbyterian Church in the United States of America in the Synod of Texas.* Waxahachie: The Woman's Synodical of Texas, 1931. Reprinted in Carlos Cortes, et al. *Church Views of the Mexican American.* New York: Arno Press, 1974.

Holt, R. D., ed. *Schleicher County: Or Eighty Years of Development in Southwest Texas.* Eldorado, TX: The Eldorado Success, 1930.

Hughes, Alton. *Pecos: A History of the Pioneer West,* 2 vols; Seagraves, TX: Pioneer Book Publishers, 1978.

Irion County Historical Society. *A History of Irion County.* San Angelo: Anchor Publishing Co., 1978.

Jacobson, Lucy Miller, and Mildred Bloys Nored. *Jeff Davis County, Texas.* Fort Davis: Fort Davis Historical Society, 1993.

Jaques, Mary. *Texan Ranch Life.* London: Horace Cox, 1894.

Justice, Glenn. *Little Known History of the Texas Big Bend: Documented Chronicles from Cabeza de Vaca to the Era of Pancho Villa.* Odessa, TX: Rimrock Press, 2001.

———. *Revolution on the Rio Grande.* El Paso: Texas Western Press, 1992.

Keil, Robert. *Bosque Bonito: Violent Times Along the Borderland During the Mexican Revolution.* Edited by Elizabeth McBride. Alpine, TX: Center for Big Bend Studies, Sul Ross University, 2002.

Kerig, Dorothy Person. *Luther T. Ellsworth: U.S. Consul on the Border during the Mexican Revolution.* El Paso: Texas Western Press, University of Texas at El Paso, 1975.

Kibbe, Pauline R. *Latin Americans in Texas.* Albuquerque: University of New Mexico Press, 1946.

Kimble County Historical Commission. *Families of Kimble County.* Junction, TX: Kimble County Historical Commission; Shelton Press, 1985.

Kimble County Historical Survey Committee. *Recorded Landmarks of Kimble County.* Junction, TX: The Committee, 1971.

Kinevan, Marcos E. *Frontier Cavalryman: Lieutenant John Bigelow with the Buffalo Soldiers in Texas.* El Paso: Texas Western Press, 1998.

Kinney County Historical Society. *Kinney County, 125 Years of Growth, 1852–1977.* Brackettville: Kinney County Historical Society, 1977.

Kreneck, Thomas H. *Mexican American Odyssey: Felix Tijerina, Entrepreneur and Civic Leader, 1905–1965.* College Station: Texas A&M University Press, 2001.

Kupper, Winifred, ed. *Texas Sheepman: The Reminiscences of Robert Maudslay.* Austin: University of Texas Press, 1951.

Langford, J. O. *Big Bend: A Homesteader's Story.* Austin: University of Texas Press, 1952.

Madison, Virginia. *The Big Bend Country of Texas.* Albuquerque: University of New Mexico Press, 1955.

———.*How Come It's Called That? Place Names in the Big Bend Country.* New York: October House Inc., 1968.

Márquez, Benjamin. *Democratizing Texas Politics: Race, Identity, and Mexican American Empowerment, 1945–2002.* Austin: University of Texas Press, 2014.

Martin, Robert L. *The City Moves West: Economic and Industrial Growth in Central West Texas.* Austin: University of Texas Press, 1969.

Martinez, Monica Muñoz. *The Injustice Never Leaves You: Anti-Mexican Violence in Texas.* Cambridge: Harvard University Press, 2018.

Menard County Historical Society. *Menard County History: An Anthology.* San Angelo: Anchor Publishing Co., 1982.

Menchaca, Martha. *The Mexican American Experience in Texas: Citizenship, Segregation, and the Struggle for Equality.* Austin: University of Texas Press, 2022.

Mendoza de Levario, Israel. *A Brief Chronicle of Presidio del Norte: Homeland of the Jumano.* Austin: La Junta Press, 2012.

Miles, Elton. *Tales of the Big Bend.* College Station: Texas A&M University Press, 1976.

Montejano, David. *Anglos and Mexicans in the Making of Texas, 1836–1986.* Austin: University of Texas Press, 1987.

———.*Quixote's Soldiers: A Local History of the Chicano Movement, 1966–1981.* Austin: University of Texas Press, 2010.

Moore, Richard R. *West Texas After the Discovery of Oil: A Modern Frontier.* Austin: Pemberton Press, 1971.

Morgenthaler, George J. *La Junta de los Rios: The Life, Death, and Resurrection of an Ancient Desert Community in the Big Bend Region of Texas.* Bourne, TX: Mockingbird Books, 2006.

———.*The River Has Never Divided Us: A Border History of La Junta de los Rios.* Austin: University of Texas Press, 2004.

Myers, Samuel. *The Permian Basin: Petroleum Empire of the Southwest*. El Paso: Permian Press, 1977.

Navarro, Armando. *Mexican American Youth Organization: Avant-Garde of the Chicano Movement in Texas*. Austin: University of Texas Press, 1995.

O'Connor, Louise S., and Cecilia Thompson. *Marfa and Presidio County, Texas: A Social, Economic, and Cultural Study, 1990–2008*, 2 vols.; Bloomington, IN: Xlibris LLC, 2014.

Olien, Roger M., and Diana Davids Hinton. *Wildcatters: Texas Independent Oilmen*, 2nd ed. College Station: Texas A&M University Press, 2007.

Olien, Roger M., and Diana Davids Olien. *Oil Booms: Social Change in Five Texas Towns*. Lincoln: University of Nebraska Press, 1982.

Ormsby, Waterman Lilly. *The Butterfield Overland Mail*. Edited by Lyle H. Wright and Josephine M. Bynum. San Marino: The Huntington Library, 1942.

Peña, Manuel H. *The Mexican American Orquesta*. Austin: University of Texas Press, 1999.

———. *The Texas-Mexican Conjunto: History of a Working-Class Music*. Austin: University of Texas Press, 1985.

Perales, Alonso. *Are We Good Neighbors?* New York: Arno Press, 1974.

Pierce, N. H. *The Free State of Menard: A History of the County*. Menard: Menard News Press, 1946.

Ragsdale, Kenneth B. *Big Bend Country: Land of the Unexpected*. College Station: Texas A&M University Press, 1998.

———. *Quicksilver: Terlingua and the Chisos Mountains Mining Company*. College Station: Texas A&M University Press, 1976.

Raht, Carlysle Graham. *The Romance of Davis Mountains and Big Bend Country*. El Paso: The Rahtbooks Company, 1919. Revised ed. Odessa: The Rahtbooks Company, 1963.

Ramírez, José A. *To the Line of Fire: Mexican Texans and World War I*. College Station: Texas A&M University Press, 2009.

Ringgold, Jennie Parks. *Frontier Days in the Southwest*. San Antonio: Naylor Co., 1952.

Rivas-Rodríguez, Maggie. *Mexican Americans & World War II*. Austin: University of Texas Press, 2005.

San Miguel, Guadalupe, Jr. *"Let All of Them Take Heed": Mexican Americans and the Campaign for Educational Equality in Texas, 1910–1981*. Austin:

University of Texas Press, 1987.

Santleben, August. *A Texas Pioneer: Early Staging and Overland Freighting Days on the Frontier of Texas and Mexico.* Edited by I. D. Affleck. New York: Neale Publishing Co., 1910.

Santos, Estela Perez. *Texas Came to Me: The Life and Impact of Jesusa Farias on the World.* Privately printed, 2021.

Schleicher County Historical Society. *A History of Schleicher County.* San Angelo: Anchor Publishing Co., 1979.

Scobee, Barry. *Fort Davis, Texas: 1583–1965.* Fort Davis, TX: Barry Scobee, 1963.

———. *Old Fort Davis.* San Antonio: Naylor Co., 1947.

Shipman, Alice Jack Dolan. *Taming the Big Bend: A History of the Extreme Western Portion of Texas from Fort Clark to El Paso.* Austin: Von Boeckmann-Jones Co., 1926.

Simons, Helen, and Cathryn A. Hoyt. *Hispanic Texas: A Historical Guide.* Austin: University of Texas Press, 1992.

Skinner, A. E. *The Rowena Country: A Short History.* Wichita Falls: Nortex Offset Publications Inc., 1973.

Smithers, W. D. *Chronicles of the Big Bend: A Photographic Memoir of Life on the Border.* Austin: Texas State Historical Association, 1999.

———. *Nature's Pharmacy and the Curanderos and the Border Trading Posts.* Alpine, TX: Sul Ross State College, 1961.

Spiller, Wayne, compiler, et al. *Handbook of McCulloch County History,* 3 vols. Seagraves, TX: Pioneer Book Publishers, sponsored by Heart of Texas Historical Museum, 1976.

Stillwell, Hallie Crawford. *I'll Gather My Geese.* College Station: Texas A&M University Press, 1991.

Stovall, Allan A. *Nueces Headwater Country: A Regional History.* San Antonio: Naylor Press, 1959.

Sutton County Historical Society. *Sutton County, 1887–1977.* Sonora, TX: Sutton County Historical Society, 1979.

Swift, Roy L., and Leavitt Corning Jr. *Three Roads to Chihuahua: The Great Wagon Roads That Opened the Southwest, 1823–1883.* Austin: Eakin Press, 1988.

Taylor, Colonel Nathaniel Alston. *The Coming Empire, or, Two Thousand Miles in Texas on Horseback.* New York: A. S. Barnes & Company, 1877.

Texas Almanac and State Industrial Guide, 1970–1971. Dallas: A. H. Belo

Corporation, 1969.

Texas Almanac, 2020–2021. Austin: Texas State Historical Association, 2020.

Thompson, Cecilia. *A History of Marfa and Presidio County, 1535–1946*, 2 vols. Austin: Nortex Press, 1985.

Tom Green County Historical Preservation League, Inc. *Tom Green County: Chronicles of Our Heritage*, 2 vols. San Angelo: Tom Green County Historical Preservation League, Inc., 2003.

Tyler, Ronnie C. *The Big Bend: A History of the Last Texas Frontier*. Washington, DC: US Dept of the Interior, National Parks Service, 1975.

Villanueva, Nicholas, Jr. *The Lynching of Mexicans in the Texas Borderlands*. Albuquerque: University of New Mexico Press, 2017.

Wedin, AnneJo P. *The Magnificent Marathon Basin: A History of Marathon, Texas, Its People and Events*. Austin: Nortex Press, 1989.

Whitehead Memorial Museum. *La Hacienda: An Official Bicentennial Publication*. Del Rio: The Museum, 1976.

Williams, Clayton W. *Texas' Last Frontier: Fort Stockton and the Trans-Pecos, 1861–1895*. Ernest Wallace, ed. College Station: Texas A&M University Press, 1982.

Wooster, Robert. *Frontier Crossroads: Fort Davis and the West*. College Station: Texas A&M University Press, 2006.

Wylie, Rosa Lee. *History of Van Horn and Culberson County, Texas*. Hereford: Pioneer Book Publishers, 1973.

Youngblood, B., and A. B. Cox. *An Economic Study of a Typical Ranch Area on the Edwards Plateau of Texas*. Texas Agricultural Experiment Station Bulletin, no. 297. College Station: Texas A&M College, 1922.

Zamora, Emilio. *The World of the Mexican Worker in Texas*. College Station: Texas A&M University Press, 1993.

———. *The World War I Diary of José de la Luz Sáenz*. College Station: Texas A&M University Press, 2014.

Zertuche, Diana Sotelo. *The Spirit of Val Verde*. Del Rio, TX: Diana Sotelo Zertuche Publisher, 1985.

ARTICLES AND BOOK CHAPTERS

Alcala, Carlos M., and Jorge C. Rangel. "De Jure Segregation of Chicanos in Texas Schools." *Harvard Civil Right-Civil Liberties Law Review* 7, no. 2 (March 1972).

Baeza, Abelardo. "La Escuela de Don Clemente: History of the Madero Ward Elementary School in Alpine, Texas, 1919–1936." *Journal of Big Bend Studies* 7 (January 1995).

Beard, Mary. "The Right to Learn: Desegregation in a West Texas Town." *Texas Historian: Publication of the Junior Historians of Texas* LII, no. 5 (May 1992).

Bitner, Grace. "Early History of the Concho Country and Tom Green County." *West Texas Historical Association Yearbook* IX (October 1933).

Bogener, Stephen. "The Varied Economy of West Texas." In *West Texas: A History of the Giant Side of the State*, edited by Paul H. Carlson and Bruce A. Glasrud. Norman: University of Oklahoma Press, 2014.

Braudaway, Douglas. "Bracketing Bean: The Other Two Leaders in Langtry, Texas." *Journal of Big Bend Studies* 20 (2008).

———. "Desegregation in Del Rio." *Journal of South Texas* 13 (2000).

———. "Santos Garza: The Father of San Felipe Schools." *Journal of South Texas* 19 (Fall 2006).

———. "The 'Origins' of Del Rio, Texas: Documenting Myths and Mything Documentation." *Journal of South Texas* 23, no. 1 (Spring 2010).

Buenger, Walter L. "Making Sense of Texas and Its History." *Southwestern Historical Quarterly* CXXI, no. 1 (July 2017).

Candelaria, Cordelia Chávez. "Pachucos." *Encyclopedia of Latino Popular Culture*, 2 vols. Westport, CT: Greenwood Press, 2004.

Cano, Alexander Soto. "The Mexican American Community of Knickerbocker." *West Texas Historical Association Yearbook* LXXIX (October 2003).

Cashion, Ty. "What's the Matter with Texas?: The Great Enigma of the Lone Star State in the American West." *Montana: The Magazine of Western History* 55, no. 4 (Winter 2005).

Cauley, T. J. "Cotton Moves West: An Account of Some of the Agricultural Changes Which Have Created a New Cotton Empire." *Texas Monthly* 3 (1929).

Cruz, Mario Juárez. "Tasinques," *San Angelo Standard-Times*, February 23, 2020, 1B.

De León, Arnoldo. "Blowout 1910 Style: A Chicano School Boycott in West Texas." *Texana* XII (1974).

———. "Eva Camúñez Tucker: Hispanic Philanthropist in the Concho Country." *Journal of Big Bend Studies* 15 (2003).

———. "María Cárdenas: San Angelo Chicano Era Activist." In *Tejano West Texas*, edited by Arnoldo De León. College Station: Texas A&M University

Press, 2015.

———. "Mexican Americans in the Edwards Plateau and Trans-Pecos Region, 1900–2000: A Demographic Study." *Southwestern Historical Quarterly* CXII, no. 2 (October 2008).

———. "Post–World War II Tejano Farm Labor: A Remembrance." *Southwestern Historical Quarterly* CXXIV, no. 2 (October 2020).

———. "Region and Ethnicity: Topographical Identities in Texas." In *Many Wests: Place, Culture, and Regional Identity*, edited by David M. Wrobel and Michael C. Steiner. Lawrence: University Press of Kansas, 1997.

———. "Los Tasinques and the Sheep Shearers' Union of North America: A Strike in West Texas, 1934." *West Texas Historical Association Yearbook* LV (1979).

———. "Wartime USA: West Texas Tejanos and WWII and Korea." In *Tejano West Texas*, edited by Arnoldo De León. College Station: Texas A&M University Press, 2015.

———. "What's Amiss in Tejano History?: The Misrepresentation and Neglect of West Texas." *Southwestern Historical Quarterly* CXX, no. 3 (January 2017).

De León, Arnoldo, and Kenneth L. Stewart. "Tejano Demographic Patterns and Socio-Economic Development." *The Borderlands Journal* VII (Fall 1983).

Dillard, Betty L., and Karen L. Green. "Beeves and Baseball: The Story of the Alpine Cowboys." *Journal of Big Bend Studies* 11 (1999).

Elam, Earl H. "Acculturation on the Rio Grande Frontier: The Founding of San José del Polvo and the Family of Lucía Rede Madrid." *Journal of Big Bend Studies* 5 (January 1993).

———. "Aspects of Acculturation in the Lower Big Bend Region of Texas, 1848–1943." *Journal of Big Bend Studies* 12 (2000).

García, Mario T. "Mexican Americans and the Politics of Citizenship." *New Mexico Historical Review* 59 (April 1984).

———. "Porfirian Diplomacy and the Administration of Justice in Texas, 1877–1900." *Aztlán* XVI (1985).

Gómez, Art. "If the Walls Could Speak: Mariscal Mine and the West Texas Quicksilver Industry, 1896–1946." Mining History Association (1998).

Graham, Joe A. "The Role of the Curandero in the Mexican American Folk Medicine System in West Texas." In *American Folk Medicine: A Symposium*, edited by Wayland D. Hand. Los Angeles: University of California Press, 1976.

Green, Karen. "The Influenza Epidemic of 1918 in Far West Texas." *Journal of*

Big Bend Studies 5 (January 1993).

"Hispanic Culture Contributed to Midland's Early Days." *The Thorny Trail* XXV, no. 2 (Spring 1997).

Jones, Oakah. "Settlements and Settlers at La Junta de los Ríos, 1759–1822." *Journal of Big Bend Studies* 3 (January 1991).

Jordan, Terry. "The Concept and Method." In *Regional Studies: The Interplay of Land and People*, edited by Glen E. Lich. College Station: Texas A&M University Press, 1992.

Klingemann, John Eusebio. "The Population Is Overwhelmingly Mexican, Most of It Is in Sympathy with the Revolution: Mexico's Revolution of 1910 and the Tejano Community in the Big Bend." In *War Along the Border: The Mexican Revolution and Tejano Communities*, edited by Arnoldo De León. College Station: Texas A&M University Press, 2012.

Levario, Miguel A. "The Trans-Pecos-Big Bend Country." In *West Texas: A History of the Giant Side of the State*, edited by Paul H. Carlson and Bruce Glasrud. Norman: University of Oklahoma Press, 2014.

Madrid, Enrique R. "The History and Future of Adobe at La Junta de los Rios: Social Dimensions of Adobe Making." *Journal of Big Bend Studies* 17 (2005).

Matthews, James T. "The Edwards Plateau and Permian Basin." In *West Texas: A History of the Giant Side of the State*, edited by Paul H. Carlson and Bruce A. Glasrud. Norman: University of Oklahoma Press, 2014.

Monroe, Monte L. "The West Texas Environment." In *West Texas: A History of the Giant Side of the State*, edited by Paul H. Carlson and Bruce A. Glasrud. Norman: University of Oklahoma Press, 2014.

Montejano, David. "The Beating of Private Aguirre: A Story About West Texas during World War II." In *Mexican Americans & World War II*, edited by Maggie Rivas-Rodríguez. Austin: University of Texas Press, 2005.

Overmyer-Velásquez, Mark. "Good Neighbors and White Mexicans: Constructing Race and Nation on the Mexico Border." *Journal of American Ethnic History* 33 (Fall 2013).

Patterson, H. W. "Crisis at the Molinar School." *Journal of Big Bend Studies* 2 (January 1990).

Pospisil, JoAnn. "Mariscal Mine's Contribution to the Quicksilver Industry." *West Texas Historical Association Yearbook* LXXXVII (2012).

———. "Women and Wax: Female Participation in the Candelilla Wax Industry." *Journal of Big Bend Studies* 8 (1996).

Primera, Joe C. "Los Hermanos Torres: Early Settlers of Pecos County." *Permian Historical Annual* XX (1980).

Rivas-Rodríguez, Maggie. "Integration a Mordidas in Alpine, Schools [1969]." *Texas Mexican Americans and Postwar Civil Rights*. Austin: University of Texas Press, 2015.

Salinas, Guadalupe. "Mexican-Americans and the Desegregation of Schools in the Southwest." In *Voices: Readings from El Grito: A Journal of Contemporary Mexican American Thought, 1967–1973*, edited by Octavio Ignacio Romano-V. Berkeley, CA: Quinto Sol Publications, 1973.

Smith, Grover H. (Dean). "Curanderismo: Mexican Folk Healing." *Journal of Big Bend Studies* 7 (January 1995).

Stewart, Kenneth L., and Arnoldo De León. "Education is the Gateway: Comparative Patterns of School Attendance and Literacy Between Anglos and Tejanos in Three Texas Regions, 1850–1900." *Aztlán* XVI (1985).

Tanner, Susan L. "From Castolón to Santa Elena: The People Behind the Ruins." *Journal of Big Bend Studies* 5 (January 1993).

Taylor, Lonn. Ninety-Six Miles in Ninety-Six Hours: The Marfa-Terlingua Freight Road, 1899–1960." *Journal of Big Bend Studies* 23 (2011).

Tinney, Ed. "'I'll Keep My Children': The Life of Pioneer Educator Noé Lara Camúñez." *West Texas Historical Association Yearbook* LXXV (1999).

Tucker, Albert B. "The Lost Communities of San Vicente." *West Texas Historical Association Yearbook* LXXII (1996).

———. "Terlingua Abaja." *Journal of Big Bend Studies* 3 (January 1991).

Utley, Robert M. "The Range Cattle Industry in the Big Bend of Texas." *Southwestern Historical Quarterly* LXIX, no. 4 (April 1966).

Volanto, Keith J. "A New Texas Emerges: The Long-Term Impact of World War II, 1945–1960." In *Texas and Texans in World War II, 1941–1945*, edited by Christopher B. Bean. College Station: Texas A&M University Press, 2022.

Willeford, Glenn. "Presidios to Trading Posts: Money, Agriculture, Rare Earth Extraction, and General Business in the Lower Big Bend of Texas, 1759–1961." *Journal of Big Bend Studies* 26 (2014).

Williams, Clayton. "First Two Irrigation Projects on Pecos River." *Permian Historical Annual* 15 (December 1975).

———. "The Pontoon Bridge on the Pecos, 1869–1880." *Permian Historical Annual* 18 (December 1978).

Woolford, Sam, ed. "The Burr G. Duval Diary." *Southwestern Historical Quarterly*

LXV (April 1962).

Wright, Paul. "The Big Bend Population in 1900: Size, Growth, and Distribution." *Journal of Big Bend Studies* 8 (1996).

———. "Build It and They Will Come: Boom and Bust in Presidio." *Journal of Big Bend Studies* 20 (2008).

———. "Characteristics of Big Bend Mining Towns, 1885–1920." *Journal of Big Bend Studies* 9 (1997).

———. "Factors Associated with Income: The Big Bend in 1930." *Journal of Big Bend Studies* 19 (2007).

———. "Four Different Communities: Presidio in 1910, 1920, 1930, and 1940." *Journal of Big Bend Studies* 25 (2013).

———. "Life on Both Sides of the Tracks in Early Alpine." *West Texas Historical Association Yearbook* LXXIII (1997).

———. "Population Patterns in Presidio County in 1880: Evidence from the Census." *Journal of Big Bend Studies* 7 (January 1995).

———. "Property Ownership in the Early Big Bend." *West Texas Historical Association Yearbook* LXXVI (2000).

———. "Residential Segregation in Two Early West Texas Towns." *Southwestern Historical Quarterly* CII (January 1999).

———. "Starting Over: Impact of Mexican Revolution Refugees on Big Bend Society." *Journal of Big Bend Studies* 13 (2001).

———. "A Tumultuous Decade: Changes in the Mexican-Origin Population of the Big Bend, 1910–1920." *Journal of Big Bend Studies* 10 (1998).

———. "When They Were Equal: Alpine and Marfa in 1940." *Journal of Big Bend Studies* 26 (2014).

———. "Work Among Anglos and Hispanics in the Big Bend, 1910." *West Texas Historical Association Yearbook* LXXI (1995).

Wright, Robert E. "Transient Clergy on the Trans-Pecos Area, 1848–1892." *Journal of Big Bend Studies* 18 (2006).

Zapata, Joel. "The South-by-Southwest Borderlands' Chicana/o Uprising: The Brown Berets, Black and Brown Alliances, and the Fight against Police Brutality in West Texas." In *Civil Rights in Black and Brown: Histories of Resistance and Struggle in Texas*, edited by Max Krochmal and J. Todd Moye. Austin: University of Texas Press, 2021.

U.S. Bureau of the Census. 1980 Census of Population, vol. I Characteristics of the Population, Chap. B, General Population Characteristics, pt. 45,

Texas, PC80-1-B45 (Washington, DC: Dept. of Commerce, 1982), Table 16: "Total Persons and Spanish Origin Persons by Type of Spanish Origin and Race: 1980."

"United States Census Bureau. "Texas: 2020 Census," United States Census Bureau, United States Government, accessed October 25, 2022, https://www.census.gov/library/stories/state-by-state/texas-population-change-betwee n-census-decade.html."

NEWSPAPERS
Austin American, April 1886.

Austin Statesman, May 1884, April 1886, November 1886, February 1891, December 1891.

Austin Daily Statesman, May 1884.

Austin Democratic Statesman, July 1884.

Brady Standard Herald, July 6, 2016, October 19, 2022.

El Paso Times, July 1886.

San Antonio Herald, May 1868.

San Antonio Daily Express, January 1883, June 1883, December 1883, April 1886, May 1891, January 1892, November 1894, July 1897.

San Angelo Standard-Times, September 1884, October 1884, October 1886, January 1892, October 1894, November 1984, June 1895, September 1889, October 1889, March 1953, January 2018, September 2021, October 2021, October 2022, November 2022.

THESES AND DISSERTATIONS
Bitner, Grace. "The History of Tom Green County, Texas." MA thesis, University of Texas, 1931.

Chapman, David L. "Lynching in Texas." MA thesis, Texas Tech University, 1973.

Flores, María Eva, CDP. "The Good Life the Hard Way: The Mexican American Community of Fort Stockton, Texas, 1930–1945." PhD diss., Arizona State University, 2000.

Green, William D. "Land Settlement in West Texas: Tom Green County, A Case Study, 1874–1903." PhD diss., Texas Tech University, 1981.

Gregg, John Ernest. "The History of Presidio County." MA thesis, University of Texas, Austin, 1933. Reprinted in *Voice of the Mexican Border*. Marfa, TX: Centennial Edition, 1936.

Marshall, Floyd Leslie. "History and Present Status of Latin American Education in Melvin, Texas." MA thesis, Hardin-Simmons University, 1950.

Prewitt, Steven W. "'We Didn't Ask to Come to This Party': Self Determination Collides with the Federal Government in the Public Schools of Del Rio, Texas, 1890–1971." PhD diss., University of Houston, 2000.

MISCELLANEOUS

Anderson, Mrs. Mattie Belle. "Reminiscences of Mattie Belle Anderson, Texas, Fort Davis, Texas." Eugene C. Barker Texas History Center, University of Texas Archives, Austin, Texas, 1929.

ONLINE SOURCES

Archuleta, Tim. "School, End of Segregation Remembered." Archive.gosangelo. com/news, October 16, 2010, accessed August 31, 2021.

Braudaway, Doug. "Texas Sheep and Goat Raisers Association-PDF free." Google Search.

Braudaway, Doug. "Torres Family, Founders of Langtry." Online publication of Val Verde County Historical Commission. Google Search "Torres Family— Founders of Langtry, Texas."

Butcher, Sterry. "Marfa's Blackwell School Has Painful Past. That's Why the Town Wants to Save It." *Texas Monthly*, January 2019, accessed August 31, 2021.

Enck, Gretel. "The Complicated History at One of America's Segregated Schools." National Parks Conservation Association Blog Post, August 31, 2020, accessed August 31, 2021.

Handbook of Texas Online: "Adobe"; "Alamito Creek"; "Alpine, Texas"; "Antonio Rodríguez"; "Barksdale, Texas"; "Bear Creek"; "Brogado, Texas"; "Candelaria, Texas"; "Casa Piedra, Texas"; "Castolón, Texas"; "Chisos Mining Company"; "Cibolo Creek"; "Concho River"; *Del Rio ISD v. Salvatierra*; "Edwards County"; "Fort Davis"; "Fort Leaton"; "Marathon, Texas"; "Marfa, Texas"; "Mariscal Mountain"; "Mercury Mining Company"; "Ochoa, Texas"; "Pecos River"; "Pilares, Texas"; "Presidio, Texas"; "Presidio County"; "Real County"; "Redford, Texas"; "Ronquillo Land Grant"; "Ruidosa, Texas"; "Maria G. Sada"; "San Antonio-El Paso Mail"; "Santa Elena Canyon"; "Santiago Peak"; "Saragosa, Texas"; "Shafter, Texas"; "South Texas Plains"; "Paula Losoya Taylor"; "Terlingua, Texas"; "Texas-Mexican Vernacular

Architecture"; "Victorio"; "Wool and Mohair Industry."
Justice, Glenn. Welcome to Glenn's Texas History Blog, Rimrock Press, http://www.rimrockpress.com/blog/index.php?entry=entry070202–111903; and http://los-tejanos.com/index.html.
SanAngeloHispanicHeritage.org

ARCHIVES
Melvin, Texas, Collection, West Texas Collection, Angelo State University, San Angelo, Texas.
Pérez, Nestor. "Colonia Jiménez de Melvin, Texas." In Melvin, Texas, Collection, West Texas Collection, Angelo State University, San Angelo, Texas.
Santos, Estela Perez. *The Perez Journey*. In Melvin, Texas, Collection, West Texas Collection, Angelo State University, San Angelo, Texas.

INDEX

Arnoldo De León served as a member of the Angelo State University Department of History from 1973 to 2015. Upon his retirement, the Board of Regents of the Texas Tech University System bestowed upon him the title of Distinguished Professor of History Emeritus, and the history department now bears his name. He has published many books on American history, Texas history, Mexican American history, and Latin American history.

(Photo courtesy of Angelo State University)

www.ingramcontent.com/pod-product-compliance
Lightning Source LLC
Chambersburg PA
CBHW020445100426
42812CB00036B/3459/J